Japanese War Crimes

The Search for Justice

Japanese War Crimes

Peter Li
editor

Transaction Publishers
New Brunswick (U.S.A.) and London (U.K.)

Library of Congress Catalog Number: 2002073100
ISBN: 0-7658-0890-0
Printed in the United States of America

Library of Congress Cataloging-in-Publication Data

Japanese war crimes : the search for justice / Peter Li, editor.
     p. cm.
    Portions of book originally published in East Asia: An International Quarterly, fall 2000, vol. 18, no. 3 and winter 2001, vol. 19, no. 4; and includes sample of presentations at International Citizens' Forum on War Crimes and Redress, held December 10-12, 1999, in Tokyo.
    Includes bibliographical references and index.
    ISBN 0-7658-0890-0 (pbk. : alk. paper)
    1. World War, 1939-1945—Atrocities—Congresses. 2. Sino-Japanese Conflict, 1937-1945—Atrocities—Congresses. 3. War criminals—Japan—Congresses. I. Li, Peter, 1935- II. International Citizens' Forum on War Crimes and Redress (1999 : Tokyo, Japan)

D804.J3 J37 2002
940.54'05'952—dc21

                         2002073100

Contents

Preface

There comes a point in time when it is no longer necessary to try to understand why Japan cannot apologize, why the Japanese soldiers committed their acts of barbarism and brutality, or why the emperor of Japan was exonerated from all war crimes culpability. Nor does it matter any more to count more accurately how many innocent victims were killed during the Nanjing Massacre, how many Americans and allied POWs were senselessly tortured and killed, or how many times the Japanese "field tested" biochemical weapons in China, killing hundreds of thousands. Now is the time for the Japanese government to acknowledge its war crimes responsibility if Japan wants to maintain a rightful place in the international family of nations and play a meaningful role in the United Nations. And if Japan wants to gain the trust of other Asian nations, it must first settle its moral and legal obligations.

This book expresses in the simplest and clearest terms possible the reasons why Japan should take up the responsibility for its war crimes, apologize to the victims of its wartime atrocities, and pay appropriate reparations to the victims. This book is a call to action. There is no need for complicated arguments and sophisticated analysis. The world has waited long enough for Japan to come to the realization that it must acknowledge its own wrongdoing during World War II. To the aged victims of these atrocities, time is of the essence: justice delayed is justice denied.

It may seem unimportant to those who ask, "What good does an apology do after so many years?" For those who suffered gross injustices, an official, unequivocal apology means the healing of wounds. It means the restoration of human dignity; it means lifting the burden of half a century of suffering and shame. "An apology is a decisive moment in a complex restorative project arising from an unaccountable infraction and culminating in remorse and reconciliation."[1]

As the Nobel Prize laureate for literature, Oe Kenzaboru has written, "[Japan's] unwillingness to come to terms with its past is not just morally offensive, it prevents Japan from playing its proper role in Asia."[2] Without rehabilitation, without reintegration into Asian society, Japan's status will remain ambiguous in the minds of its Asian neighbors. Japan will never be fully trusted, even though it has become an economic superpower; its moral stature will always be small in the eyes of its Asian neighbors. Unlike those in the West who have come to see Japan as a reformed nation, a new civil society, many East Asians still view Japan with suspicion and see the revival of militarism in Japan as a real possibility.

The arguments in this book are straightforward. There are five main themes defined in the five sections of this collection. In "It's Never Too Late to Seek Justice" the issues of reconciliation, accountability, the Tokyo War Crimes Trial, and Emperor Hirohito's war crimes responsibility are explored. "The American POW Experience Remembered" includes the shocking account of the Bataan Death March by an American soldier and American POW's slave-labor experience in a Japanese coalmine. "Psychological Reponses" to war atrocities discusses the socio-psychological effects of the Nanjing Massacre and a Japanese doctor's reflections on performing vivisection in China. The way in which Japanese war crimes have been dealt with in the theater and cinema is the focus of "Artistic Responses." And central to "History Will not Forget" are the questions of memory, political amnesia, trauma, biochemical warfare, the atomic bomb, and redress. The complexity of the issues and the massive scale of the number of people affected dictate this multitude of perspectives.

In spite of Japan's historical amnesia and its culture of denial, history will not let them forget. Through memory and public monuments, we honor the wishes of the victims to never be forgotten. As Vera Schwartz has pointed out, "to recall and relive" is the only way one can, and one must, approach catastrophe. It is never too late to seek justice, as long as men remain connected with the past through cultural and personal memory.[3]

We must take our common humanity as the basis on which to settle these unresolved issues of war. As Mencius (372-289 B.C.) had stated so forcefully: "Anyone without the heart of sympathy and compassion is not human; anyone with a heart of shame and dislike is not human; anyone without a heart of modesty and courtesy is not human; and anyone with a heart of right and wrong is not human."

There are many individuals who have given me inspiration and encouragement when I started this project several years ago. Beginning as a topic for a senior seminar on East Asian Societies at Rutgers University, this project has become an intellectual as well as an emotional challenge. Many students in my classes have contributed to this book without knowing it. There are too many names to mention; I thank them all for their participation.

My personal history also had a small role to play in this project. It was a wartime incident that my mother used to tell us, my sister and myself, when we were young. It was late in August of 1937, a few months before the attack on Nanjing, when our family had to flee from Nanjing and go to Shanghai on our way to America. But even then, the Japanese had already started their aerial bombardment of the Nanjing-Shanghai region. The train had to stop along the way whenever Japanese airplanes flew overhead and began their bombing and machine gunning; the passengers would flee from the train to seek cover in the nearby bushes and fields until the planes passed. My mother would clutch me, two years old at the time, under her arm and run for cover. If we were lucky we would make it back to the train. If not, then our bodies would be found in the fields along the train tracks. Fortunately, we did make it safely to Shanghai.

Many members of the Global Alliance for Preserving the History of the Sino-Japanese War (GA) and the Alliance for Preserving the Truth of the Sino-Japanese War have been most helpful and supportive. In particular I would like to acknowledge the help of Ignatius Ding and Eugene Wei, who have gone out of their way show me their current work on biochemical warfare. Eugene's selfless dedication in establishing the American Museum of Asian Holocaust of World War II in Falls Creek, Pennsylvania is a model for us all. Ivy Lee, president of the Global Alliance, has contributed her article on the San Francisco Peace Treaty to this volume. Linda Goetz Holmes and Lester H. Tenney, whose works are included here, are two individuals whose humanity and courage have been an inspiration. Many Japanese friends and acquaintances that I have met in the past several years have also moved me with their unflinching determination to set the record straight. Among them, the most memorable was my meeting with the playwright and actor couple Yoshiji Watanabe and his wife Kazuko Yokoi. They have devoted their lives wholly to performing their powerful play *Reunion*, with their company Imagine 21, throughout many parts of Japan, China, and recently in the

United States. Their personal commitment to telling the truth about Japanese aggression and atrocities has moved many and gained them much praise and gratefulness—and threats from the Japanese rightwing extremists. Excerpts from their play are included in this volume.

This play was had a cathartic effect on many who watched it. One person wrote to the playwright after the performance: "My parents were killed by the Japanese army. I have always hated the Japanese. I even hated meeting them. But after seeing your play, everything changed. I really changed. Thank you very much." My thanks also to Dr. Kevin Chiang, one of the translators of the play and a member of the Alliance in Memory of the Victims of the Nanjing Massacre, New York for making contact with the Watanabes in my hour of need. Thanks also to my colleague Paul Schalow, who was the guest editor of the first special issue of *East Asia*, "Japanese War Atrocities and Redress."

Finally, I wish express my grateful thanks to my colleague and friend Irving Louis Horowitz, the Hannah Arendt Distinguished Professor Emeritus of Sociology and Political Science at Rutgers University, and Mary Curtis, president of Transaction Publishers. If it had not been for their constant encouragement, cajoling, and reprimanding, who knows when this volume would have ever come to fruition. When I turned in the manuscript after many extensions of the deadline, Mary wrote me: "If you don't turn in your manuscript now, it would not be a war crime, but it would be a crime against humanity." In order to avoid another crime against humanity in this world, I humbly submit this book. For any shortcomings therein, I am solely responsible. Lastly, thanks to my family for their encouragement and putting up with my many hours of brooding over a morbid topic and the messy attic.

Peter Li
Highland Park, NJ

Notes

1.   N. Tavuchis, *Mea Culpa: A Sociology of Apology and Reconciliation*. Stanford: Stanford Univ. Press, 1991.
2.   Oe Kenzaburo, "Denying History Disables Japan," The *New York Times Magazine*, July 2, 1995.
3.   Vera Schwartz, *Bridge Across Broken Time: Chinese and Jewish Cultural Memory*. Yale University Press, 1998.

1

An Overview: Japan's War Responsibility and the Pan-Asian Movement for Redress and Compensation

Paul Schalow

The genesis for this volume, *Japanese War Crimes: The Search for Justice*, began with the International Citizens' Forum on War Crimes and Redress conference held in Tokyo on December 10-12, 1999. The Forum was co-sponsored by the Global Alliance for Preservation of the History of World War II in Asia, from the United States, and the Japanese Organizing Committee, in Japan. This conference was historic in that the three-day conference was attended by over three thousand people, and the participants were international in nature and included many Japanese scholars, historians, former veterans, and lawyers who were representing Asian victims in the Japanese courts. Participants came from China, Taiwan, Korea, the Philippines, Hong Kong, the United States, and Canada. Lester I. Tenney represented the American POWs of the Japanese, and Mark Weintraub represented the Canadian Jewish Congress. Some of the articles included in this volume originated at that conference; others originated at a later date.

Judging from the number of works that has appeared and conferences held in the past ten years, it should be noted that the pursuit of justice for the victims of Japanese war crimes in World War II has grown more vigorous rather than weakening. There is a greater sense of urgency as more and more of the victims are suffering from ill health, old age, and death—justice delayed becomes justice denied.

The Nanjing Massacre and the sexual slavery of "Comfort Women" (*ianfu*) have received extensive coverage in both the academic and popular press in recent years, but the actual scope of the movement for redress and compensation is growing bigger and more complex with every passing year. Besides the Nanjing Massacre and sexual slavery, Asian victims are suing for justice for: the forced relocation to Japan of Chinese and Korean slave laborers who toiled under brutal conditions in civil engineering, mining, and heavy industry; indiscriminate machine-gunning, incendiary shelling, and bombing of civilian targets in China; the extermination of villages in Manchuria by murder, pillage, and burning; the illegal use of biological and chemical weapons in warfare and of human subjects for biological and chemical weapons research; the vivisection and murder of human subjects for purposes of medical education and experimentation; ongoing and often fatal environmental degradation caused by poison gas and bombs abandoned by the Japanese military after the defeat; the systematic looting of hundreds of thousands of irreplaceable books from Chinese libraries; and the plundering of Asia's wealth, including gold, cash, and art objects that were removed to Japan.

At issue is Japan's "war responsibility" (*senso sekinin*), broadly defined as the criminal acts of war for which Japan should be held legally and morally accountable. The daunting complexity of the issue was made clear in the many writings that have appeared in recent years. Our purpose is to familiarize readers with the bitter legacy shadowing Japan's relationship with its Asian neighbors at the dawn of a new century and new millennium.

One of the central themes of the Forum was "justice." Speaker after speaker testified, however, that true justice was impossible for either the dead or the survivors who suffered at the hands of the Japanese during the Pacific War. Given Japan's brutal wartime actions in Asia and the impossibility of true justice, what sort of "redress and compensation" were Asian victims seeking from the Japanese government? Was it money they wanted? It became clear in the course of the Forum that monetary compensation was not the primary issue. First and foremost, victims and their families wished for symbolic justice in the form of an official statement of apology by the Japanese government and sincere efforts to compensate them for their suffering. Unfortunately, the Japanese government has been very reluctant to take responsibility in any concrete way for the suffering of fellow Asians at the hands of the Japanese imperial armies during the Pacific War. Historians have proved that this state of affairs is a result of post-war American policies that, by emphasizing Japan's economic recovery and American political interests over the interests of justice in Asia, left the pre-war Japanese ruling elite virtually intact.

In the course of the Forum, it became clear that the Japanese government's decades-long refusal to accept responsibility and apologize for war crimes in Asia has infuriated and insulted not just survivors but many Asian people and their governments as well. This anger now serves to fuel the flames of the redress and compensation movement against Japan.

Very much on the minds of the audience and speakers at the Forum was the example of Nazi Germany. Here was a state that between 1939-45 slaughtered approximately 11 million or more people belonging to groups deemed "inferior" according to Nazi ideology: Jews, Poles, Gypsies, homosexuals, the physically handicapped, and the mentally ill. Immediately after the war Germany's new government had been held accountable by the world for Nazi crimes against humanity, for which there was a genuine sense of revulsion among Germans and non-Germans alike. Nazi leaders were tried and imprisoned or executed, a system of compensation for survivors was implemented, government leaders made sincere public apologies, and by the 1980s justice was felt to have been served. The question was raised repeatedly at the Forum, "Why cannot Japan respond to Asia similarly?" For the Asian victims of Japanese war crimes, Germany represented the "model" of what a state ought to do in compensating its victims in war. Although it could be argued that this is an idealized view of Germany's response to its Nazi past, the existence of the German model seems to serve, in its own way, as a catalyst for the Asian movement that now demands redress and compensation from Japan.

The sad fact is that the majority of Japanese born after the war are incapable of comprehending the issue of "war responsibility" in all of its ramifications. This is because the postwar generation has not been educated accurately about Japan's wartime role and has come to perceive Japan primarily as a victim of the Pacific War, not a perpetrator. Those who experienced the war firsthand knew the truth about Japan's aggression and destruction outside Japan, but the history they have passed on is one-dimensional. The war undeniably brought death and suffering to Japanese soldiers and citizens on a scale never seen before or since, but the destruction, death, and suffering endured by other Asians at the hands of the Japanese during the war years has been conveniently forgotten. The younger generation is thus largely ignorant of the facts and perceives Japan only as a victim of war, not as a perpetrator or aggressor. It is fair to say that few are capable of assessing adequately whether Asian victims' demands for redress and compensation are reasonable or unreasonable.

Unfortunately, Japanese ignorance about Japan's role in the war is more a product of deliberate miseducation than of oversight. School textbooks, which in Japan must pass the scrutiny of the government's Ministry of Education (Monbusho), convey to Japan's children a carefully controlled image of wartime Japan. Until lawsuits in the 1980s challenged the Ministry of Education's whitewashing policies, textbooks were not allowed to say that Japan had invaded China, only that Japan "entered" China; the Nanjing massacre (when acknowledged at all) was nothing more than a small-scale military "incident" resulting from an unfortunate breakdown in military discipline; the annexation and occupation of Korea and the increasingly draconian policies towards Koreans were barely touched upon. In short, any actions that might place the emperor, the state, or the ruling elite in a bad light were excised from the history books. When the truth about Japan's wartime aggression started to appear in children's textbooks, belatedly and in small increments, in the 1990s, it led to a conservative political backlash that included calls by prominent educators to "teach our children a history of Japan that they can be proud of." According to this way of thinking, a shameful past is not something to be acknowledged, reflected upon, and overcome, but to be ignored or whitewashed, and forgotten.

In a sense, the American atomic bombings of Hiroshima and Nagasaki in the closing days of the war have provided the Japanese with justification for devising a cultural discourse in which Japan is the innocent victim, rather than the guilty perpetrator, of the Pacific War. Americans, to be sure, have had their own difficulties acknowledging their feelings of guilt about the production and deployment of the atomic bomb, but for Japan the atomic bombings serve as undeniable proof of Japan's victimhood. The post-war literature of Hiroshima and Nagasaki appears to provide convincing testimony that no one was made to suffer more terribly in the war than the Japanese themselves. Next to the horrors of the atomic bombings, some would argue, what do the sufferings of Nanjing, the comfort women, and the slave laborers amount to? Because the annual August ritual of "remembering Hiroshima" and "remembering

Nagasaki" is divorced from any other contexts, such as "remembering Nanjing" or "remembering Pearl Harbor," the atomic bombings have sometimes functioned to absolve Japan of blame in the war and have relieved its citizens from the necessity of reflecting upon their wartime role. Memory is an integral part of social and cultural cohesiveness, but incomplete or selective memory is a dangerous thing.

Japan's propensity to position itself as a victim, coupled with the post-war generation's lack of education about the facts of Japan's wartime atrocities in Asia, means that many Japanese people find it psychologically disorienting to be asked to recognize the victimhood of others, especially when it involves admitting the unfamiliar possibility of Japan as victimizer and perpetrator. The former mayor of Nagasaki, Motoshima Hitoshi, was one of several speakers at the Forum who addressed the Japanese reluctance to admit that Japan had committed evil acts in the Pacific War. He described denial as a cultural mechanism whose purpose was to preserve the sanctity of Japan's imperial system. Motoshima publicly stated on the occasion of the anniversary of the Nagasaki atomic bombing in 1988 that the Showa Emperor, Hirohito, bore some responsibility for the war but had been exonerated by General MacArthur's Occupation policies in order to ensure the well-being of the Japanese people. To political conservatives, this statement was tantamount to treason. On January 18, 1990, one year after Hirohito's death, Motoshima was shot in an assassination attempt by a right-wing extremist. The bullet struck just above the heart, and he was fortunate to survive.

If Asian demands for justice continue to grow in ferocity, fueled by frustration in the face of Japanese denial, the Japanese government may find itself increasingly isolated from its Asian neighbors. More than once at the Forum speakers and members of the audience raised the disturbing possibility that Japan will respond to that sense of isolation by renouncing its peace constitution and trying to reassert itself militarily in East Asia. In fact, a proposal to delete Article 9 (renouncing war as a method of resolving international conflict) from the Occupation-era Japanese constitution was under consideration in the Japanese Diet during its 145th ordinary session in 1999, shortly before the Forum met. The argument used in the Diet debates was that Japan ought to have the right to be a "normal" (*futsu*) nation, legally capable—like any other nation—of waging war. To Asian ears, especially in the light of Japan's intransigence regarding redress of Pacific War atrocities, the prospect of a Japan with military capabilities sounds nightmarish.

More than one speaker at the Forum suggested that Japan has already begun to reassert itself as a military power, partially in response to United States military policy encouraging Japan to play a larger role in its national defense. As Nishikawa Shigenori expressed it, "We are on the brink of a new era of war. Even though we haven't accepted our postwar responsibilities, we are again already in the midst of a new pre-war era." It would be the ultimate irony if Asian demands for justice from Japan were to produce the opposite result, bringing about Japan's isolation and remilitarization instead of apology and redress.

Japanese speakers and members of the audience at the Forum showed that there are numerous individual Japanese who are willing to face Japan's unpleasant wartime record and enter into a dialogue with their Asian compatriots about Japan's war responsibility. Some are academicians and activists who have struggled with the issue of war responsibility as an educational or political issue. Some are lawyers who have recognized the validity of Asian calls for justice and attempted, often at great personal risk, to bring their cases for judgment before the Japanese court system. Others are everyday people whose first-hand knowledge of the truth, as imperial soldiers or the children of soldiers, has led them to come forward and acknowledge publicly Japan's, and their own, war responsibility.

The mood at the end of the Forum was hopeful but realistic, showing that participants understood well the nature of the obstacles that stand in the way of the movement for redress and compensation. The possibility of a broad-ranging reassessment by the Japanese people regarding Japan's wartime atrocities may seem less likely with each passing year, but, even so, individuals of conscience must continue to confront Japan's wartime legacy in the classrooms and courtrooms of Japan. If the Forum accomplished anything, it was to illustrate that justice is not governed by a statute of limitations. It is not too late for the Japanese government to respond with compassion and justice and set the record straight.

It is our hope that this book will help clarify for our readers the moral grounds of Asian demands for redress and compensation from Japan. Our purpose is to encourage constructive dialogue among Asians, non-Asians, and Japanese concerning the problem of Japan's war responsibility. In that sense, our book echoes the "Tokyo Appeal" adopted by the Forum on December 12, 1999, which concluded with this statement: "We solemnly declare that by boldly confronting the historical truth of the 20th century, we will seek and ensure reconciliation and peace in the 21st century."

Part I

It's Never Too Late to Seek Justice

2

Japan's War Crimes:
Has Justice Been Served?

Michael M. Honda

I am here today to address the issue of Japan's war crimes. I was invited to speak primarily because I authored an Assembly Joint Resolution in the 1999 session of the California State Legislature calling on Japan to formally apologize for war crimes and to pay reparations to the victims of those war crimes. I am a teacher by training, but want to be clear that I am not an expert on the issue of war and the atrocities that inevitably appear to accompany war.

What I want to share with you is my point of view on this issue and why I think it is important to pay attention to an issue that took place more than 50 years ago. It is a view that is personal, stemming from something uniquely American. It is a view that reflects the "new" Asian Pacific American or APA community. Finally, it is a view that is based on and supported by established legal and moral precedent.

Why Me, a Japanese-American?

The foundation for my work on this issue began long before I introduced the resolution. Though the war crimes of Japan were largely unknown to me at the time, my involvement in the Redress issue begins with the internment of my family and relatives in 1942. Let me briefly touch on how the Japanese American Redress Movement influenced my involvement in Assembly Joint Resolution 27, or what my staff and I call "AJR 27."

As I became involved in the Civil Rights movement in the 1960s it was clear to me and to many other activists that the Japanese-American community was wounded. One would only have to talk to a fellow Japanese-American from Hawaii to see the difference. Japanese-Americans from Hawaii saw mainland Japanese-Ameri-

11

cans as different from them—they considered us bitter, maladjusted, and dysfunctional—because we never recovered from the impact of the internment. The Japanese-Americans in Hawaii avoided the mass relocation that took place on the mainland and the calamity that came with it. Of course, as a community we on the mainland lost millions in assets, families were torn apart, and communities were forever lost. However, the greatest damage that was done was to our dignity as human beings and as Americans—we lost self-respect as a community; a loss that was not suffered by fellow Japanese-Americans in Hawaii.

I became a leader in a movement to call for an apology and reparations. It was not a call for money—though the payment of reparations retains symbolic significance. It was not a call to embarrass the government or punish those that conspired to rob us of our dignity. It was a request to acknowledge the truth and to allow us to begin the process of healing our communal wounds.

The impact of the apology and reparations is far reaching. As a community, Japanese-Americans still harbor bitterness and many remain forever scarred. However, the apology and reparations have allowed many of us to put aside our bitterness and constructively look back at our responses to the internment. Since the passage of the Civil Liberties Act of 1988, our community has delved deeper into the issues that divided our community during our internment.

One of the issues now being unearthed is the victimization of those interned in the camps that refused to be drafted until their civil rights were restored. There is much pain surrounding this issue and many are critical of the role of the Japanese-Americans Citizens League. As many in our community are—like myself—approaching the qualifying age for the senior discount, it is important to deal with these issues while folks are still alive.

The apology by the U.S. Government to the Japanese American community did not "make us whole" and it did not please everyone. However, it did succeed in bringing closure in two infinitely critical ways: (1) It stipulated the truth—establishing once and for all that our community was innocent and the internment was not justified; and (2) It recognized that our community suffered immeasurably. By paying reparations, the U.S. Government accepted symbolic responsibility for the detrimental effects on us. Those of us who love this country very deeply, now had grounds to defend it.

There are significant parallels between the Japanese American Redress Movement and the international call for reparations for Japanese war atrocities.

A writer in a 1987 *Harvard Civil Rights Review* article identified several prerequisites for meritorious redress claims: (1) a human injustice must have been committed; (2) it must be well documented; (3) the victims must be identifiable as a distinct group; (4) the current members of the group must continue to suffer harm; and (5) such harm must be causally connected to the past injustice.[1] Victims of both the Japanese-American Internment and Japan's war atrocities meet these criteria.

When we started our redress movement, few Americans knew of the experience of Japanese-Americans during WW II. I must confess that until a few years ago, I was only vaguely familiar with Japan's WW II war crimes. I understood that there were war crimes trials and members of the Japanese military were executed. However, it was apparent that I knew a great deal more about WW II war crimes in Europe than in Asia.

For this reason AJR 27 serves an important purpose—to educate people about what happened in Asia during WW II. The fact that the atrocities were committed by a military operating under the Japanese flag is in many ways irrelevant. The fact that it happened 50 years ago is also irrelevant. The people that died as a result of the atrocities cannot be brought back—however, it is very important that people today know that the victims lived and how they died. What is important is that we restore some honor to the lives of those who died in very undignified ways. Some "one"—or some "thing"— is accountable, and justice demands accountability.

Why Now? Why After so Long?

Part of the answer is generational. Time is not on our side—many of the perpetrators and the victims are old and near death. In order to accomplish something in their lifetime, we must act now.

Another part of the answer relates to the growth in the APA community. AJR 27 represents an issue important to what can only be called the "new" APA community. The APA community is 40 percent larger than it was 10 years ago. Some regions have experienced exponential growth in the APA population. For example, since 1980, Santa Clara County's Asian population has increased 405 percent.

One in three residents in Santa Clara County is foreign born and over half of the APAs are immigrants.

With the increase in numbers the profile of the APA community has changed dramatically in the same period. When I was growing up, Asians were mostly Japanese, Chinese, and Filipinos. However, the last decade has seen new faces with the influx of immigrants from Cambodia, Korea, India, Laos, Taiwan, Thailand, and Vietnam.

As the newer members of the APA community assimilate and speak out, new issues emerge. Since many members of the new APA community are immigrants, it is not surprising that the issues important to them are international in nature. AJR 27 may be one of the first of these issues.

Though the "new" APA community appears as a homogenous group, on closer examination it is obvious that the APA community is very diverse. Languages and cultures are very distinct, and nationalism runs very deep. Past historic conflicts, such as WW II, impact very strongly the relationships within the larger APA community today.

I have learned that there are Filipino-American families in America that will not patronize Japanese-American businesses and will not buy Japanese cars. There are Chinese-American parents that will not permit their children to date Americans of Japanese descent. While there is always friction between ethnic groups, it is not uncommon to find that the pain caused by WW II still defines relationships within the APA community today.

As a call for recognition of basic human rights, AJR 27 reaches across historic barriers in the APA community. AJR 27 represents, in my mind, an important step in finding common ground among APAs. As Americans, representatives of the Chinese, Filipino, Japanese, Korean, and Indo-American communities have joined with veteran groups and organizations representing civilian survivors in support of AJR 27. Though many in the APA community are foreign born there is something uniquely American about AJR 27.

While in our minds it is an American characteristic to seek justice, it is equally an American characteristic to tolerate dissent. So it is not surprising that not everyone in the APA community believes that AJR 27 is a good idea. When the Japanese-American reparations movement began, we faced the identical source of dissent. Many believed that too much time had passed, that it was water under the bridge, and that it would re-ignite racist sentiment against Japanese-Americans.

I value the views of my more conservative and protective friends. However, I disagreed then and disagree now. I do not believe that it is ever too late to fight for the dignity of human life—to see justice done. Nor do I believe that the pursuit of justice should be deterred or postponed because we fear backlash from those who adhere to the tenets of racism and hate.

While Americans do not have a monopoly on the matter, many patriots like myself believe that at the essence of being American is liberty and justice. As Americans we are guaranteed the freedom to seek justice—to redress wrongs. Supporters of AJR 27 are united not as individuals, but as Americans.

I believe this to be a historic moment in the history of the Asian Pacific American community, one that may have far-reaching consequences in the new millennium—not just for APAs but for all Americans. It has been my privilege to participate in an issue where barriers of language, culture, and historic conflict are being set aside to further a greater humanitarian objective.

Can Violations of International Law be Barred by Treaty?

I am not an expert on international law, but it appears well settled that treaties cannot extinguish individual claims. A 1994 *Hastings College Law Review* article[2] examined this issue in depth. The authors, Karen Parker and Jennifer Chew, found that to the degree that such treaties, including the San Francisco Peace Treaty of 1951, contained provisions extinguishing individual claims such provisions are void.

In 1907, Laza Oppenheim, in his text *International Law: A Treatise*, wrote:

> It is a unanimously recognized customary rule of International Law that obligations which are at variance with universally recognized principles of International Law cannot be the object of a treaty. If for instance a State entered into a convention with another State not to interfere in the case the latter should appropriate a certain part of the Open Sea, or should command its vessels to commit piratical acts on the Open Sea, such a treaty would be null and void, because it is a principle of International Law that no part of the Open Sea may be appropriated, and it is the duty of every State to interdict to its vessels the commission of piracy on the High Seas.

Let me put it another way. A crime in California is not an issue to be negotiated between the perpetrator and the victim. How could we maintain order if we allowed murderers and rapist to go free, because the perpetrator reached an agreement with the family of the victim? Under our laws the crime is a crime against society and it is not an issue for individuals to negotiate.

In the same way, a violation of human rights is a crime against all of humanity and is not subject to treaties between countries. Neither individuals nor countries can conspire to avoid the applicable laws. To do otherwise undermines the very purpose of laws.

Has Japan Apologized? Have Reparations been Paid?

Without delving into an area that for many is intentionally clouded and confusing, the best answer to both these questions is "yes" and "no."

Several officials of the Japanese Government have apologized. Yet, other high ranking officials continue to deny that atrocities took place. Yes, some form of reparations have been paid or made available. Yes, treaties have been signed resolving issues between governments. Yet, there are many individual claims, including the claims of those forced into sexual slavery, that are not precluded by treaties and are actionable under international law.

Some argue that since some apologies have been made and some reparations paid, the issues are settled. I disagree. The issue is not whether Japan can on technical grounds elude responsibility. The question is whether justice has been done.

In the case of the Japanese-American pursuit of redress, our government claimed that under the exigencies of wartime, it was legitimate to suspend the constitution and deprive a group of citizens of their rights. Many seek to apply the same "excuse" to the case of Japan's war atrocities. They say war is a horrible thing and therefore all that occurs during war is inherently excusable.

Obviously, I disagree. The Hague Convention of 1907, to which Japan was a signatory, also disagrees. The Hague Convention recognizes that even in war international law applies. The Hague Convention prohibited rape, torture, and forced labor including prostitution against both combatants and civilians. The Hague Convention also supports the mechanism of redress for violations of international law. It states in Article III:

> A belligerent party which violates the provisions of said Regulations shall, if the case demands, be liable to pay compensation. It shall be responsible for *all* acts committed by persons forming part of its armed forces.

At best, Japan's acceptance of responsibility is a mixed bag. At worst, it has been described as institutionalized national amnesia. The "yes/no" nature of Japan's acceptance of responsibility could be resolved with a clear and unambiguous apology approved by the Diet. The "yes/no" nature of reparations could be settled with an offer of settlement of individual claims by the Japanese Government.

Though I am hesitant to draw any comparisons between Japan's war crimes and Germany's war crimes, I believe that Germany provides a clear example for Japan to follow. Though Germany has been criticized, it is my belief that Germany has made a good faith effort to accept responsibility. And though administering a reparations program is an enormously complex undertaking, Germany has demonstrated that it is possible.

How far should Japan go in further apologies and reparations? I believe that there are others more qualified than I to make that determination. However, as I knew that my government had not done enough until the 1988 Civil Liberties Act became law, I know that what Japan has done up to now is not enough. I am proud to be an American of Japanese ancestry. However, I cannot defend Japan's response to its conduct during WW II.

Conclusion

I did not introduce AJR 27 with the purpose of embarrassing the Japanese government. I leave the punishment of war criminals who are in hiding to the lawyers. I do not wish to compare the inhumane acts of the past with those of the present. I do not desire to open a debate on the validity of foreign policy decisions made at the end of WW II. Circumstances from that time have changed significantly. I know only of a community that has been wounded. I do not deny that there may be others.

I ask that the burden of the injustice be lifted from the lives of the survivors and the families of the dead. Only the government of Japan can lift the burden and only the lifting of the burden can set them free.

I have watched my community suffer as a result of the internment. I have seen the value of an apology and symbolic reparations. I want very much today to convey to you that my community was damaged by the internment, but more importantly we were burdened by the injustice.

The apology and reparations contained in the 1988 Civil Liberties Act lifted the burden of the injustice—it made my community free. Contained in the apology was the truth—our truth—and, indeed, it was the truth that lifted the burden and that set us free.

I ask for no more for the victims of Japan's war atrocities than I asked for my own community: To bring closure—(1) Stipulation of the truth—establishing once and for all that the victims were innocent and their suffering was not justified; and (2) Symbolic recognition that they have suffered immeasurably by paying reparations, thereby showing that the Japanese Government assumes full responsibility for their suffering.

Let me close with one final comment. Pearl Buck once said, "None who have always been free can understand the terrible fascinating power of the hope of freedom to those who are not free." I fought our battle for redress fueled by the hope of freedom for my community. I have joined this struggle for redress fueled by the hope of others who wish for nothing more than to be free . . . and deserve nothing less.

Notes

1.   Mari J. Matsuda, "Looking to the Bottom: Critical Legal Studies and Reparations," *Harvard Civil Liberties—Civil Rights Law Review* 22 (1987): 323, 362-97.
2.   *Hastings International and Comparative Law Review* 497 (1994), 17.

3

Probing the Issues of Reconciliation More than Fifty Years after the Asia-Pacific War

Ivy Lee

Japan began its invasion of China and war with Asia long before WW II started in Europe. By the end of the Asia-Pacific War, 1931-1945, it was estimated that the Japanese Imperial Military killed over 10 million people in China alone. But the numbers convey only part of the story. In the wake of its invasion, the military committed unspeakable atrocities on a grand scale, incurring war responsibility not only from damages it inflicted on invaded countries, but also from the crimes against humanity it perpetrated against individual victims.

Subsequent to its surrender in 1945, Japan signed a treaty with the U.S. and over forty other Allied Powers in 1951 that came to be known as the San Francisco Peace Treaty, or SFPT. The Treaty, engineered by the U.S. to eliminate the possibility of war reparations from Japan, *presumably* settled Japan's war responsibilities and other war-related issues. The terms of the Treaty were so favorable that Oe Kenzaburo (1997), the Nobel Laureate, concluded that the Japanese, as a result, "have not reflected on the meaning of defeat seriously." (p. 292) Instead, using the Treaty as a shield, Japan subsequently refused to address fully and shoulder squarely its moral and remaining legal war responsibilities.

As expected, Asian countries that suffered most from Japan's invasion put up intense resistance to the terms of the treaty. However, even before the process for negotiating the treaty began, as Dower (1999) puts it in his *Embracing Defeat*, "One of the most pernicious aspects of the occupation [of Japan] was that the Asian peoples who had suffered most from imperial Japan's depredations—the Chinese,

19

Koreans, Indonesians and Filipinos, had no serious role, no influential presence at all in the defeated land. They became invisible." (p. 27) Then, when confronted with Asian resistance to the treaty and against the backdrop of rising communism in the East and its determination to project its power in the Pacific, the U.S. moved to exclude such countries as China and Korea from the peace conference in San Francisco.

In the end, few of the victimized Asian countries became signatories to the Peace Treaty. According to Price (2001), "As a result for Japan, the peace treaty represented a second '*datsu-A-ron*' or Japan 'leaving Asia' in the wake of which was left a legacy of unresolved disputes related to territory and reparations." Although the Treaty may have cemented Japan's alliance with the U.S. and expedited its economic recovery, it also enabled Japan to foster a policy of historical amnesia with regard to the war. (Clemons, 2001) Thus, rather than being an instrument that has secured peace and justice, in the eyes of Japan's neighbors and victims of atrocities the treaty remains an obstacle to genuine reconciliation.

Half a century of alliance between Japan and the U.S. saw the Bush Administration urging Japan to play a larger role in the regional security of Asia within the framework of the bilateral security treaty the U.S. signed with Japan a few hours after the signing of the Peace Treaty. Formal revision of the "Peace Constitution," with the abolition of Article 9, a measure that was inconceivable previously, is now a likely prospect. (Jameson, 2001) More recently, Prime Minister Koizumi pledged logistic and other support for the United States after the September 11 terrorist attacks. (Kyodo News on the Web, 2001) Understandably, Asian countries view these recent moves with deep distrust, as piecemeal changes appear to put Japan on the road to fully remilitarizing.

Thus, on one level the war has ended for more than half a century. On another, it continues with a raging debate over Japan's unresolved war responsibility to the extent that it is entirely reasonable to ask whether the Asia-Pacific War has really ended. Orville Schell, of the University of California, Berkeley, chair of the conference organized by the Japan Society of Northern California in honor of the fiftieth anniversary of the Peace Treaty, explicitly recognized this debate by calling for an accounting of the "issue of war guilt, which hovers over every occasion that Japan attends like Banquo's ghost." (Burress, 2001)

Reconciliation Defined

Clearly, this is a situation that calls for reconciliation. After massive human rights violations, reconciliation is part and parcel of a peace-building process. It is an effort to establish a new and constructive relationship between the perpetrators and the victims based on shared principles of justice, equity, and mutual respect. Without reconciliation, conflicting parties may come to some sort of accommodation, perhaps an uneasy truce, but seldom an enduring peace. In reconciliation, the parties involved take steps to ensure that justice be served. They then work to remove the residues of mistrust which, if unaddressed, would linger as latent sources for future conflicts. (Jeong, 1999) If the Peace Treaty represents a second *"datsu-A-ron"* or Japan "leaving Asia," reconciliation is ultimately a process of reintegrating Japan into Asia as an Asian nation.

Parties who have a Stake in Reconciliation

It may be unclear from the above discussion that another party, other than the perpetrators and the victims, has an interest in reconciliation. The third party takes shape more distinctly when we analyze the September 11 events. Sorting through the implications of that day, we realize how much our global village is affected. For lack of a better word, humanity, or the international community, has a stake in the Sept 11 attacks as well. For, after the attacks, not only has our value of the dignity of individual lives been outraged, but our concept of behavior that is due from civilized individuals has also been violated. We consider it incumbent on us, who may or may not be directly affected, to bring the criminals who committed these atrocities to justice.

The Dawn of International Humanitarian Law

Thus it can be seen that humanity is implicated in the "crimes against humanity," a central tenet in the development of international humanitarian law. Further, the concept of crimes against humanity may be traced to principles of war that were recognized as far back as the fifth century B.C. by the Greeks and the Persians. In an essentially inhumane endeavor such as war, nations were judged according to two basic principles, whether these were explicitly formulated and ratified or not. They were the principles of necessity and humanity. (Neier, 1998) Under the first, that which was necessary militarily to vanquish the enemy might be done, while under the second, a defining idea of a civilized society, that which caused unnecessary suffering was prohibited. The first principle was constrained by the second so as to delimit war and to set the parameters for acceptable conduct with due respect for humanity.

In the seventeenth century, Hugo Grotius, a Dutch scholar who came to be regarded as the father of international law, extolled the protection of the lives of innocent persons, of women and children and of non-combatants or prisoners of war as "rules of moderation that we would call humanitarian rules of war." (del Russo, 1971, p. 8) Further, Grotius expounded on the notion that individuals were not merely citizens of particular states but of the world community.

Beginning in the nineteenth century, formal international agreements that embodied these principles were ratified by governments. The first international agreement was signed by European governments in Geneva in 1864. Thirty-five years later, in 1899, a "Convention with Respect to the Laws and Customs of War on Land" was adopted at The Hague. By the outbreak of WW II, additional international agreements on the laws of war had been adopted at conferences that met at The Hague and Geneva.

It is important to note that the international community recognizes that there are crimes so fundamental, so widely accepted that they have the force of "customary international law" although they may not be explicitly codified in any international agreements. For example, The Hague Convention of 1899 states in its preamble: "Until a more complete code of laws is used, the High Contracting Parties think it is right to declare that in cases not included in the Regulations adopted by them, populations and belligerents remain under the protection and empire of the principles of international law as they result from the usages established between civilized nations, from the laws of humanity and the requirements of public conscience." (Neier, 1998, p. 16)

Further, from this preamble the notion grew that these customary international laws should bind a state regardless of whether it has formally ratified a treaty to accept its obligations or not. Thus, those who fail to uphold these obligations are termed by the community of nations to be the "enemies of humanity." Unless a state claims it is neither a member of the international community nor subscribes to the ancient principle of humanity, it is bound by such customary laws.

What Each Party Must Do to Bring about Reconciliation

As shown, the values for justice and humanity from which the more recent international humanitarian laws emerged have ancient roots. Ideally, these principles and/or customary international laws function in such a way as to prevent crimes against humanity from occurring. However, when massive human rights violations occur, as in the Asia-Pacific War, what must each party do?

The perpetrators must acknowledge and accept responsibility and atone for their abuses. They must assure the victims and the international community alike that they have assimilated the lessons of humanity. Furthermore, they must demonstrate a desire to be reintegrated into the international community to live in peace, harmony, and mutual respect with the rest of humanity. In turn, the victims must believe their injustices are being redressed in order for them to feel that they have regained some measure of their dignity and move beyond their sense of being violated. They, too, must be committed to building a new relationship and a future in which erstwhile enemies are able to live together in peace, harmony, and mutual respect. Thus, reconciliation is a complex, multi-step, interactive process between the perpetrators and victims. (Jeong, 1999)

In addition, there must be a mutuality of desires, i.e., the victims cannot unilaterally bring about reconciliation, nor should they be the only ones to seek it. Recurrence of crimes against humanity becomes less likely when both perpetrators and victims develop a commitment to share a common future in which mutual trust and harmony reign. Since reconciliation aims to reintegrate the perpetrators and the victims into the same community of humanity, it presupposes a shared universe of discourse between the two. In the case of the Asia-Pacific War, this means an open dialogue between Japan and its neighbors to result in an understanding of Japan's expansionist wars in the first half of the twentieth century, its violations of human rights, and their severity and implications.

Finally, humanity must ensure that the damage done to the fabric of a civilized society is repaired and similar atrocities will not recur in the future. This means the international community must aggressively pursue the truth regarding human rights violations and demand accountability from the perpetrators and justice for the victims. For only then would our faith in humanity be restored, our sense of justice reaffirmed, and the broken social bonds mended.

Thus, the international community not only has a stake in seeing the aggressor and victimized states achieve peace in the region after the Asia-Pacific War, but in providing the appropriate conditions for reconciliation to take place.

The Struggle for Truth and Accountability in Reconciliation

More than fifty years after the end of the war, a review of the Japanese government's actions suggests a nation unwilling to acknowledge and accept responsibility for its past atrocities. On the other hand, neither did the international community provide conditions favorable to holding Japan accountable.

As a result, a sizeable percentage of Japanese appear to feel no sense of collective guilt or responsibility for the devastation Japan inflicted on the Asia-Pacific region through its expansionist wars. Instead, these Japanese see themselves more as victims than victimizers. To them, Hiroshima, not Nanjing, is the prime symbol of the war's cruelty in Asia, and the firebombing of Tokyo by America a mark of indiscriminate slaughter of civilians.

For geopolitical and other reasons, the U.S. is the main culprit in corrupting the process of holding Japan accountable. Prior to its co-opting the peace process in negotiating the SFPT, the U.S. subverted the Tokyo War Crimes Tribunal. The chief defendant, Emperor Hirohito, was never put on trial, despite cries in America, Britain, China, and elsewhere. According to Bix (2000), by absolving the emperor, General MacArthur hoped to exempt the Japanese people themselves from any shared sense of responsibility, thus making it easier to rebuild and pacify a shattered but hostile country. Hirohito died in 1989, his image so completely sanitized that political leaders from all over the world came to pay tribute at his funeral. Many loyal Japanese did conclude that if the emperor was blameless, so were they.

The United States further undermined the pursuit of truth when occupational authorities exchanged immunity from prosecution for leaders of Unit 731 in return for the information they gathered of the gruesome human experimentation on Chinese civilians and Allied prisoners of war. (Harris, 1999) Initially, researchers after the war thought the scope of Japan's biochemical warfare efforts and its related human experimentation was limited. However, as more evidence came to light, the estimate of those who died and the extent of areas affected continually rise.

Harris (2001), author of *Factories of Death*, revised his estimate upward in a recent letter to the *LA Times* as follows: "...the Japanese slaughtered between 10,000 and 12,000 prisoners while conducting biowarfare experiments in their death factories in China and other occupied territories. They killed at least 250,000 men, women and children in field tests during the war. The plague germs they unleashed at the time still haunt China today. Periodic epidemics of plague erupt in those parts of China once subjected to plague field tests." Yin (2001), in his recently published *The Rape of Biological Warfare: Japanese Carnage in Asia During WW II*, submitted evidence that the biological warfare conducted by Japan was better developed and more widely used in China, Burma, and Thailand than was initially thought. According to Yin, in 1944 among the seventy Divisions of the Japanese Imperial Army, sixty were equipped with the special units for biological warfare while in 1941 only eighteen divisions had these special units.

The pursuit of truth and accountability for Japan's crimes against humanity, partial at best during the Tokyo War Crimes Tribunal, provided fertile grounds for Japan's subsequent denial of responsibility. After the Tokyo Tribunal, with the Cold War structure firmly in place, Japan escaped further questioning. It took full advantage of this environment to hide one of the ugliest practices during the war: the coercion of hundreds of thousand of women, euphemistically called "Comfort Women," into sexual slavery to service Japanese troops. After repeated denials, on August 4, 1993, the Japanese government finally acknowledged publicly its complicity when confronted with incontrovertible evidence.

Apology and Reconciliation

According to social scientists who postulate a sequence of events leading to eventual reconciliation (Fisher, 1999), perpetrators must offer an apology along with or after acknowledging responsibility for the atrocities. Tavuchis (1991), commenting on its importance, said, "An apology is a decisive moment in a complex restorative project arising from an unaccountable infraction and culminating in remorse and reconciliation." (p. 45)

Whether Japan has rendered an unequivocal apology is one of the most hotly contested topics between the Japanese government and the victims that frequently confound observers. The media carried reports of Japan's most recent apology extended by Prime Minister Koizumi while he was in China, and again in Korea, to try to ease strains before the October 2001 Asia Pacific Economic Cooperation summit in Shanghai. (*Asahi Shimbun*, 2001) So to most observers, Japan has apologized, while critics of Japan appear unreasonable with their continual demands for apologies.

However, in the struggle for accountability, when the perpetrators have trouble acknowledging their crimes, it is critical that the apology be perceived as genuine and involving true remorse and contrition. The previously cited apologies are given against the background of Japan's constant refusal to confront its wartime past. (Gedda, 2001) As can be seen from the *Asahi Shimbun* article cited above, the immediate context of textbook revisionism and Yasukuni Shrine visit further contribute to doubts of Japan's sincerity.

For despite strong protests both within Japan and in China and Korea, revisionist junior high school history textbooks were published for use in 2002 after having passed the Japanese Education Ministry's textbook screening process. Carrying the nation's imprimatur on historical truth, these texts either gloss over or are silent on the widely known atrocities committed by Japan during WW II. Over and above these protests, Japanese right-wingers are heard to insist that each nation has the right to interpret and teach its own history and that these protests amounted to interference in Japan's internal affairs. (Struck, 2001)

Further straining the already fragile relations between Japan and its neighbors is the Yasukuni Shrine visit by Koizumi in August of 2001. Created by the government in the late nineteenth century, the. shrine was part of an explicit effort to use the state-sponsored religion to build nationalistic loyalty. Today it stands as a symbol of Japan's militaristic past. Enshrined in it are Class A war criminals and lesser war criminals along with others who died in the wars; a shrine visit would be equivalent to a German chancellor visiting a memorial dedicated to Hitler and his Nazi henchmen. Understandably, a visit to the shrine is anathema to victims of Japan's aggressive wars. (The Associated Press, 2001; Herskovitz, 2001)

The Struggle for Justice and Compensation in Reconciliation

Japan adamantly refuses to compensate the victims of its atrocities. In lawsuits filed against Japan, the Japanese government repeatedly claims it has already fulfilled its war obligations specified under the SFPT and other subsequent bilateral treaties and agreements. Additionally, both the U.S. and Japan maintain that Article 14 (b) of the SFPT provides an impenetrable shield for claims not only against the Japanese government but against Japanese corporations as well. Judge Walker, in dismissing the POW slave labor lawsuits, relied heavily on an *amicus curiae* brief filed by the Justice Department in consultation with the State Department in which the U.S. government sided with Japan against its own veterans to assert that Article 14 (b) barred individual claims stemming from signatory states.

Victims and many in Congress note the position taken by the U.S. government in litigation against Japan and Japanese corporations represents a 180-degree turn from the position it took in the Holocaust cases. (Tokudome, 2001) Japan's insistence on having fulfilled its legal obligations to the oblivion of the moral dimensions of its atrocities has not gone unnoticed either.

Legal opinions vary as to whether Article 14 (b) actually extinguished the rights of individuals to claim for crimes against humanity. A typical argument advanced by legal scholars asserts that states, as signatories of the Treaty, cannot extinguish individual rights which do not belong to them. (Maier, 2000)

However, none of the arguments touch on the central point that treaties are meant to settle questions between/among states; they are not documents designed to protect individual rights. In the case of a state foregoing its right to diplomatic protection of its citizens or abandoning its claims for political reasons, the individuals are left unprotected unless they can make claims for themselves outside of treaty provisions.

Fortunately, the individual right to claim compensation was recognized under international law dating back to Article 3 of the Hague Convention of 1907. Victims have the right, which no treaty made between or among nations can waive or abrogate, to claim for crimes against humanity. This is the right that the Japanese and U.S. governments have totally ignored, or maintain was taken care of through the San Francisco Peace Treaty.

Consequently, the victims reject the previously mentioned apologies as being "personal" and insufficient. They are not true expressions of Japan's national conscience. Neither has Japan acknowledged unconditionally the devastation it caused during the first half of the twentieth century.

From the victims' perspective, had Japan wished to show genuine remorse, it would have enacted legislation in the Diet, similar in spirit to the Civil Liberties Act of 1988 in which the U.S. government apologized and made compensation for the internment of Japanese Americans during WW II. Had Japan truly learned its lessons from the war, it would not have recurrent struggles with other Asian countries over its war history; instead, it would have wanted those lessons preserved and passed on to future generations. As President Kim of Korea said, he appreciated Koizumi's statement of remorse, but wanted "...to stress that the Prime Minister's expression of his recognition of history must be implemented concretely and publicly." (as reported by Kitano, 2001)

Progress or Regression in Reconciliation?

Thus, if reconciliation is conceived of as a process, this process could be characterized as stalled at best, and regressive at worst. Any move by the victims to reconcile would be ineffective against Japan's refusal to confront and address the aforementioned problems of accountability. Any progress would be unlikely given the victims' perception of Japan's insincerity in apologizing and its unwillingness to provide restitution to individual victims.

And yet the international community has little choice but to work for conditions that would lead to eventual reconciliation. Besides, the pursuit of justice is one of the most powerful of human forces. We cannot very well say "let's forgive and forget," for it would constitute our rejection of the rule of law. Nor can we do nothing, for we would be sending a message that we would tolerate a future where war crimes and crimes against humanity may be committed with impunity. Then not only would past war criminals be exonerated, but new war criminals would be encouraged.

Germany's Reconciliation

In may be instructive at this point to look to Germany for a more or less successful model of reconciliation with the Jewish people. Germany started on the right foot by recognizing it has a moral as well as a legal responsibility for the Holocaust. Chancellor Konrad Adenauer (Germany Compensation for National Socialist Crimes, 1996) addressed the legislature in 1951 as follows: "...unspeakable crimes have been committed in the name of the German people, calling for moral and material indemnity..."

Germany has also been at the forefront of an elaborate system of Holocaust restitution for the Jewish State, the survivors, and heirs of the victims. It has prosecuted Nazi war criminals that had escaped punishment, banished any manifestations of its Nazi past, criminalized the denial of the Holocaust, instituted days of remembrance, and constructed museums and memorials as constant reminders of the past.

Based on the German model, and in an effort to unify the global redress movement, The Global Alliance for Preserving the History of WW II in Asia, Global Alliance or GA for short, has set forth explicit organizational goals with specific demands derived from these goals. The goals are: that Japan shall offer an official and unequivocal apology with equitable compensations for its war victims and that it shall rectify its distortion and whitewashing of its war history. The list of specific demands includes, among others: authorizing full disclosure and preservation of documents relating to this dark chapter of history, mandating inclusion and teaching lessons of humanity garnered from Japan's wars of aggression, and establishing a national day of remembrance. (More detailed information pertaining to the mission, goals, and demands of GA can be obtained at the website: www.GAinfo.org.)

The Global Alliance's list may appear long and involved. As Germany has carried out restitution on all these fronts, the question is whether the international community could demand less from Japan, the other aggressor of the war who committed similar atrocities.

Americans, the Global Redress Movement, and Reconciliation

Organizations like GA emerged in the 90s with the growth of a global redress movement. The latter, in turn, evolved from the maturation of the international human rights movement. The message of this redress movement is loud and clear. The world will not stand idly by while Japanese war crimes have gone unpunished for more than fifty years after the end of the war; neither will enduring peace in the region be attained without reconciliation between the aggressor and the victimized nations.

The redress movement encompasses the Japanese who are urging their government to confront its past; it also includes Asians and Asian Americans in the U.S. and worldwide POWs and victims of the Japanese Imperial Military. The challenge for this movement is to unify these disparate groups to speak with a single voice while molding them into a global force with which the Japanese government must contend. Participants of this redress movement seek to encourage, demand, and failing these efforts, pressure the Japanese government to accept responsibility for its past.

Japan has shown itself to be responsive to international pressure, especially pressure from the U.S. Therefore, as Americans, we have a duty to call on our government to stop siding with the Japanese government against our POWs in courts, especially when we are sending troops onto foreign soil once again to fight a war. Otherwise we forfeit our claim to be the staunchest defender of human rights. We have a duty to demand that our government challenge the claim that textbook revisionism is a domestic affair and protest against visits to the Yasukuni Shrine. (Lincoln, 2001) Without this, other Asian nations would remain deeply suspicious of our indulgence for Japan's questionable attitudes and controversial actions.

More generally, we should urge our government to speak up about the need for Japan to come to terms with its past if we are to be a true friend to Japan. We must help Japan reintegrate into Asia if Japan is to be our effective ally in the region. We must ensure accountability does not die with the last victim by educating the public and by seeking to incorporate this dark chapter of history into our school curriculum. We must encourage future generations to internalize the lessons for which humanity paid the heavy price of the Asia-Pacific War. We must make it clear to Japan that the past and the present constantly intersect, and that there is no looking forward without casting a backward glance first.

As a member of the community of nations who have a stake in peace in Asia, we must do all of the above and more to nurture the seeds of reconciliation. If looking away was the hallmark of the twentieth century, let us take with us into the new millennium the knowledge of our past mistakes and the immeasurable suffering of the victims. Let us help Japan recover its wartime past and disavow our role in its historical amnesia. Only when we have done our part will the day for reconciliation be close at hand.

References

Bix, Herbert. 2000. *Hirohito and the Making of Modern Japan*. New York: Harper Collins.
Burress, Charles. 2001, September 22. Cracks in the Japan-U.S. Partnership. *Japan Times Online*.

Clemons, Steven C. 2001, September 4. Recovering Japan's Wartime Past—and Ours. *New York Times.*

del Russo, Alessandra Luini. 1971. *International Protection of Human Rights.* Washington D.C.: Lerner Law Book Co., Inc.

Dower, John. 1999. *Embracing Defeat: Japan in the Wake of WW II.* New York/London: W.W. Norton/The New Press.

Fisher, Ronald. 1999. Social Psychological Processes in Interactive Conflict Analysis and Reconciliation. In Ho-Won Jeong (ed.), *Conflict Resolution: Dynamics, Process and Structure* (pp. 81-104). Aldershot: Ashgate.

Gedda, George. 2001, August 15. Japan Has Trouble Acknowledging Past. Associated Press writer. *Dailynews.yahoo.com.*

Germany Compensation for National Socialist Crimes. 1996, March 6. Foreign Claims Settlement Commission of the U.S. Department of Justice.

Harris, Sheldon Harris. 1999. *Factories of Death: Japanese Biological Warfare, 1932-45, and the American Coverup.* New York: Routledge.

Harris, Sheldon Harris. 2001, October 1. Letter to the editor. *LA Times.*

Herskovitz, Jon. 2001, August 15. Academic Criticizes Koizumi Over Shrine Visit. *Reuters.*

Jameson, Sam. 2001, August 23. Japan Not Innately Militaristic. *The Japan Times Online.*

Japanese Premier Visits War Shrine. 2001, August 13. *Associated Press.*

Jeong, Ho-Won. 1999. Research on Conflict Resolution. *Conflict Resolution: Dynamics, Process and Structure* (pp. 3-34). Aldershot: Ashgate.

Kenzaburo, Oe and Kim Chi-ha. 1997. An Autonomous Subject's Long Waiting Coexistence. *The Comfort Women Colonialism, War, and Sex* (a special issue of *Positions: East Asia Cultures Critique*, Vol. 5, No. 1, Spring 1997).

Kitano, Masayuki. 2001, October, 15. Japan PM Voices Remorse, S. Korea Wants Action. *Reuters.*

Koizumi pledges to send SDF to assist U.S. military. 2001, September 19. *Kyodo News on the Web.*

Lincoln, Edward J. 2001, August 15. The Sounds of Silence. *The New Republic online.*

Maier, Harold. 2000, June 8. Statement of Professor Harold G. Maier. Senate Judiciary Committee Hearing.

Neier, Aryeh. 1998. *War Crimes: Brutality, Genocide, Terror and the Struggle for Justice.* New York: Times Books.

Price, John. 2001, June. A Just Peace? The 1951 San Francisco Peace Treaty in Historical Perspective. Working Paper No. 78. Japan Policy Research Institute.

Struck, Doug. 2001, April 18. New Text Reopening Old Wounds: Revisionist History in Japan Minimizes Atrocities Before, During WWII. *The Washington Post.*

Tavuchis, N. 1991. *Mea Culpa: A Sociology of Apology and Reconciliation.* Stanford: Stanford Univ. Press.

Tokudome, Kinue. 2001, September 5. The 50th Anniversary of the San Francisco Peace Treaty Unresolved Issues Revisited in the United States. *Ronza.* Japan.

Yin, James. 2001. *The Rape of Biological Warfare: Japanese Carnage in Asia During WW II.* San Francisco, Northpole Light.

Zhu. Resolving textbook, shrine issues key to better ties. 2001, October 12. *The Asahi Shimbun.*

4

Victor's Justice and Japan's Amnesia: The Tokyo War Crimes Trial Reconsidered

Maria Hsia Chang and Robert P. Barker

The Problem

Among Japan's many considerable achievements must be its swift recovery from the devastation of the Second World War. More than recovery, in a matter of decades, postwar Japan became an economic superpower. But material prosperity seemed to have an amnesiac effect on the Japanese people's historical memory, acting, in the words of Ian Buruma, like "a blanket of snow...hiding all traces, muffling all sound." Japanese novelist Oe Kenzaburo and literary critic Matsumoto Kenichi maintain that, as a consequence, the Japanese people had neither "faced up to their crimes," nor atoned for their wartime "atrocities."[1]

For much of the postwar period, the Japanese government repeatedly rewrote school textbooks to conceal and minimize Imperial Japan's World War II deeds.[2] As late as 1990, for example, Tokyo's top officials still insisted that accounts of the Nanjing massacre had been fabricated.[3] Only after Emperor Hirohito's death on January 10, 1989, did the government begin to confront its wartime past. In May 1990, eighty years after Japan annexed (and subsequently colonized) Korea, Emperor Akihito, eldest son of Hirohito, apologized for his country's colonial abuses with a bow to the visiting South Korean President Roh Tae Woo.[4] In 1992, during his visit to China, Akihito spoke of his "profound regret" at the "many and great sufferings" caused by Japan to China.[5] In 1993, the Liberal Democratic Party (LDP) was dislodged from its long-held position as Japan's ruling party when it lost an election to the national legislature (Diet). Only then did the newly elected prime minister, Hosokawa Morihiro of the Japan New Party, admit that his country had been "aggressive" and "colonial" during the war.[6] This was followed, in 1995, by a resolution of the lower house of the Diet expressing *hansei* (which can mean reflection, self-examination, or remorse) for the wartime suffering endured by "people abroad, particularly in Asian countries."[7] Although only 230 of the lower house's 511 members voted in favor of the resolution (with the rest either boycotting or voting no), and although the resolution pointedly eschewed using the word "apology," the resolution nevertheless constituted considerable progress in Japan's coming to terms with its past, albeit half a century after the war had ended. That progress, however, may be short-lived.

In recent years, Japanese scholars and professionals have detected among their co-nationals increasing attempts to revise history, together with an effort to revive the Shinto religion that had played a crucial role in wartime propaganda.[8] LDP legislators publicly endorsed a film that glorified war criminals as honorable *samurai* and represented the invasion of China as a just campaign, while Tokyo governor and former cabinet minister Ishihara Shintaro maintained that the massacre of innocent men, women, and children in Nanjing was "a story made up by the Chinese."[9] LDP government officials have visited the Yasukuni (Shinto) Shrine to pay homage to war criminals; Japan's courts upheld the right of its military (Self-Defense Force) to enshrine war dead as Shinto deities,[10] in contravention of the Constitution's separation of church and state. (Article 20 of the 1947 Constitution specifies that "The state and its organs shall refrain from...any...religious activity.")[11] In 1999, despite opposition from human rights groups, the Diet made official the Hinomaru rising sun emblem as Japan's national flag, and "Kimigayo,"[12] a hymn to the emperor, its national anthem.[13]

All this was exacerbated by Prime Minister Mori Yoshiro, who recently made a series of intemperate remarks that were reminiscent of the wartime period. Then, Imperial Japan had legitimated its aggression and colonization of Asia with an ultra-nationalist ideology of its emperor as a god wielding absolute power over the putatively superior Yamato race. On May 15, 2000, speaking before a political-religious group, the Association of Shinto Shrines,[14] Mori urged his people to "firmly embrace" the idea of Japan as a "divine nation with the emperor at its core."[15] Several weeks later, he resurrected another prewar idea—that of *kokutai* (national polity)[16]—which was used to describe a political system of state supremacy and absolute obedience to a divine emperor. In so doing, Mori seemed to have forgotten that Japan's Constitution implicitly rejects the emperor's divinity,[17] not to mention Hirohito's explicit renunciation of "the false conception that the Emperor is divine" in his Imperial Rescript of January 1, 1946.[18]

Given the attitude of its government leaders, it is not surprising that the Japanese people, with the exception of certain intellectuals[19] and war veterans,[20] remain at once ignorant and in denial of their country's war atrocities.[21] As an example, notwithstanding the Imperial Japanese Army's brutalities against the Allied POWs and the inhumane medical experiments of Unit 731, Tokyo University professor Fujioka Nobukatsu argued that Japan was fundamentally different from Nazi Germany in that although Japan might have fought "a slightly high-handed patriotic war," it did not commit "crimes against humanity."[22] In 1999, Fujioka and a colleague published a book declaiming Iris Chang's *The Rape of Nanking* for its "untruths" and "disinformation."[23] That October, a Japanese civic group canceled its plan to show a film about the massacre after receiving dozens of phone calls warning of possible interference.[24] On January 23, 2000, a seminar claiming the Nanjing massacre never happened was held in a "peace museum" in Osaka. The fact that the museum was founded by the Osaka prefectural and municipal governments seemed to confer official imprimatur and approval on the seminar.[25] According to Shizuoka University lecturer Koike Yoshiyuki, many Japanese simply refuse "to accept that the Massacre ever took place."[26]

Worse than denial is the disposition on the part of some Japanese to discredit and malign their critics. It is said that there is an international Jewish conspiracy to attack and humiliate Japan. That conspiracy is allegedly spearheaded by organizations like the Simon Wiesenthal Center which, having exhausted their search for Nazi war criminals, have turned to Japan as a new target to justify their continued existence.[27] Other Japanese are convinced that the overseas Chinese community has made a "cottage industry" out of their insistence on Japan's accountability for its wartime deeds. Like the Jews, those overseas Chinese are motivated by venal and careerist considerations, having "made a profession" out of their pursuit.[28]

Views such as these, if they were expressed in Germany or France, would be proscribed under legislation forbidding Holocaust denial.[29]

It is true that there are Germans who are afflicted with moral anesthesia, especially authors of radical right-wing publications such as
Gerhard Frey's *Deutsche National-Zeitung*. The difference is that,
unlike their German counterparts, the "Dr. Feelgoods"[30] of Japanese history are not confined to an extremist fringe and thus cannot
easily be dismissed as crackpots. Not only are they supported by
powerful politicians in the once-again ruling LDP,[31] the revisionists
have a large audience in the popular media, especially among the
youth who are described as being "sick of having to answer for the
sins of their elders." Some of Japan's "henchmen intellectuals"
(*yojinboteki chishikijen*) count book sales in the hundreds of thousands.[32] In effect, in Japan today atrocity denial can be the path to
fame and adulation.

In its attitude and behavior concerning its past, postwar Japan
cannot be more different than Germany. To begin with, West
Germany's political leaders were drawn from those who had served
in the pre-Nazi Weimar Republic; Japan's postwar government, in
contrast, enjoyed a high measure of continuity with its wartime predecessor. As early as 1951, despite domestic popular opposition,
West German Chancellor Konrad Adenauer admitted that the German people were responsible for the Holocaust and that it was their
"moral obligation" to make reparations.[33] In contrast, it took the
Japanese government forty-eight years after the war had ended, in
1993, to offer its first apology. Nor has a Japanese politician ever
gone down on his knees, as Chancellor Willy Brandt did in 1970 in
the former Warsaw ghetto, to apologize for his country's historical
crimes. Instead, government officials including Prime Ministers
Nakasone Yasuhiro and Hashimoto Ryutaro have visited the Yasukuni
Shrine to pay homage to 1,000 WWII criminals among the enshrined
war dead.[34]

There are other differences still. The Japanese government continues to refuse to pay compensations to those it had brutalized in
the war,[35] despite public opinion polls that showed a majority of the
Japanese people to be in favor of compensations.[36] Germany, in
contrast, will have paid almost $60 billion by 2005 to its wartime
victims and their families.[37] Whereas Germany opened all its wartime archives to researchers and investigators, Tokyo not only refuses to open its archives, but denies the existence of certain files
altogether, specifically those concerning military sexual slavery (the
"comfort women") and biochemical warfare experiments (the infa-

mous Unit 731). The German government has been cooperative in identifying and bringing Nazi war criminals to justice, and has responded to requests by the U.S. Department of Justice to verify the names of more than 60,000 war criminals. Tokyo, in contrast, has refused to cooperate with such investigations and has stonewalled Washington's repeated requests to verify the names of suspect individuals.[38] Whereas righteous Germans regularly turn out in tens of thousands to protest against neo-Nazi beliefs and actions, the Japanese people eschew such populist expressions of disapproval for their "henchmen intellectuals." All of which led Buruma to observe that, compared with the West Germans, the Japanese "have paid less attention to the suffering they inflicted on others, and shown a greater inclination to shift the blame."[39]

These differences between postwar Japan and Germany are all the more confounding because Japan's war atrocities were arguably no less than those of Nazi Germany. As Japan scholar Gavan McCormack explained,[40]

> [W]hile genocidal intent was unique to the Nazis, overall the casualties and destruction in the Asian war matched, and even exceeded, those on the European front.... In some respects, Japan was guilty of crimes which even the Nazis did not commit—trading in opium to finance the activities of its puppet governments, bacteriological and gas warfare, and (in China) the scorched-earth policies to force the evacuation of vast areas.

The reluctance on the part of some in Japan, especially the LDP party and government, to undertake an honest look at the wartime behavior of Imperial Japan has been attributed to, among other reasons, the alleged unfairness of the Tokyo war crimes trial, formally known as the International Military Tribunal (IMT) for the Far East. For its critics, the tribunal was really an occasion for revenge because "the victors judged the vanquished."[41] That perception "left a legacy of resentment"[42] among the Japanese and has contributed to their conviction that Japan was a victim, instead of an aggressor, in World War II that culminated in America's atom bombing of Hiroshima and Nagasaki. Whether Japan was judged fairly in the IMT remains, therefore, a question of some import and significance.

The Tokyo War Crimes Trial

The International Military Tribunal in Tokyo lasted two and half years, from May 3, 1946 to November 4, 1948. There were eleven judges: one each from Australia, Canada, China, France, Great Britain, India, the Netherlands, New Zealand, the Philippines, the Soviet Union, and the United States. The twenty-eight defendants were comprised of four former prime ministers, eleven former ministers, two former ambassadors, and eight high-ranking military generals. They were accused of being members of a "criminal, militaristic clique" in the Japanese government which pursued policies of "aggressive wars" that caused "great damage to the interests of peace-loving peoples, as well as to the interests of the Japanese people themselves."[43] Individually, or as members of organizations, the defendants were charged with a total of fifty-five crimes, categorized as crimes against peace, war crimes, and crimes against humanity.

What distinguishes "crimes against peace" from "war crimes" and "crimes against humanity" has to do with how morality *of* war differs from morality *in* war. Crimes against peace pertain to the morality of war as their perpetrators are accused of having started wars for the wrong reasons. War crimes, in contrast, refer to violations of morality in war; crimes against humanity can occur in times of peace as well as in war.[44]

After hearing testimony from more than 400 persons and receiving some 4,000 items of documentary evidence, the tribunal delivered its majority judgment, in some cases with a narrow margin of six-to-five. All the defendants were found guilty of one or more of the following crimes: for being "part of a conspiracy to carry out wars of aggression" (i.e., crimes against peace) in East Asia and the Indian and Pacific Ocean areas, and for "ordering, authorizing, permitting, or not taking adequate measures to prevent the occurrence of conventional war crimes."[45] *In effect, the only crimes for which the defendants were not found culpable were crimes against humanity.* Seven of the defendants were sentenced to death by hanging, sixteen to life in prison, one to twenty years imprisonment, and one to seven years imprisonment. The criminal cases of three defendants were dismissed: two had died during the trial; a third was found to be mentally incompetent.

A number of criteria are generally used to evaluate the legitimacy of war crimes trials. Those criteria include:[46]

- the legal basis of the tribunal;
- the body of applicable laws used in the trial; and
- the fairness of the conduct of the proceedings, including the primacy accorded to principles of due process.

Legal Basis of the Tribunal

Although wars have been fought since the beginning of human history, war crimes trials were rare prior to 1944.[47] At the end of World War I, the victorious Allies gathered together to determine the fate of those most responsible for the war. Towards that purpose, the Treaty of Versailles (articles 227-230) provided for the trials of those Germans thought to be guilty of war crimes. Germany managed to convince the Allied powers that Germans should prosecute their war criminals. The Supreme Court of Germany at Leipzig concluded its trial of accused war criminals by convicting only six individuals, with initial sentences of imprisonment ranging from a mere six months to four years. In effect, the prosecution of WWI criminals was a failure. As one writer observed, "Leipzig convincingly demonstrated that the international community could not trust the domestic courts of defeated nations to render impartial justice."[48]

Mindful of the Leipzig precedent, the Allies in World War II were determined to conduct their own war crimes trials. But for those trials to be legitimate rather than "mere indiscriminate revenge,"[49] they had to have standing in law. In that regard, much hinged on the Potsdam Declaration of July 26, 1945, which provided the mandate for the Nuremberg and Tokyo Tribunals. Concerning Japan, article 10 of the Potsdam Declaration stated that, although "We do not intend that the Japanese shall be enslaved as a race or destroyed as a nation, *but stern justice shall be meted out to all war criminals,* including those who have visited cruelties upon our prisoners."[50] In effect, the Declaration provided whatever standing in law that could be claimed by the Tokyo Tribunal.

The problem was with the authors of the Potsdam Declaration. Critics of the IMT emphasize the fact that the Declaration was written by the United States, Great Britain, China, and the Soviet Union—all victorious powers in World War II. Those critics question whether the victorious were entitled to try the defeated. More than that, some maintain that the partisan nature of the Declaration had tainted both the Declaration as well as the Tokyo Tribunal that it mandated. In effect, instead of being an instrument of impartial justice, the Tokyo Tribunal from its beginning was a "creature of political decision-making."[51]

The integrity of the tribunal was further compromised by the dominance of the United States, which gave the tribunal the appearance of being "an American court."[52] That dominance began with the charter that defined the constitution, jurisdiction, and functions of the trial. Not only was the Tokyo Charter (modeled upon Nuremberg's) drafted entirely by the United States with no participation from neutral countries, it was approved by U.S. General Douglas MacArthur on behalf of the Allied Powers in the Far East.[53] Furthermore, unlike the Nuremberg Tribunal, the Tokyo trial had only one chief prosecutor, who was an American. The United States' high profile led one of the dissenting judges, the Netherlands' B.V.A. Röling, to suggest that the tribunal might be perceived as an act of revenge for the national humiliation inflicted by the Japanese attack on Pearl Harbor. By publicly demonstrating Japan's savagery and barbarity, the trial could also be used to justify the American use of atomic weapons at Hiroshima and Nagasaki. [54]

All of which led one observer to conclude that the Tokyo Tribunal appears in retrospect almost to have been designed to render it vulnerable to the charge of "victor's justice." Its legitimacy, as a consequence, was "damagingly diminished."[55] As Senator Howard Taft put it, "The trial of the vanquished by the victors cannot be impartial, no matter how it is hedged about with the forms of justice.... About this whole judgment there is the spirit of vengeance, and vengeance is seldom justice."[56] The questionable legal basis of the Tokyo Tribunal contributed to the decision of Indian judge Radhabinod Pal to acquit each and every one of the accused of all the charges.[57]

Applicable Laws

A second criterion for evaluating the legitimacy of war crimes trials has to do with the laws that are invoked and utilized in the trial. In the case of the Tokyo Tribunal, the laws were those governing crimes against peace, war crimes, and crimes against humanity.

Crimes against peace. The first category, that of "crimes against peace," was characterized by the Nuremberg Tribunal as "essentially an evil thing" and "the supreme international crime."[58] In the Tokyo Charter, those crimes were defined as "the planning, preparation, initiation, or waging of a declared or undeclared *war of aggression*, or *a war in violation of international law*...or participation in a common plan or *conspiracy* for the accomplishment of any of the foregoing."[59] Despite the IMT's majority ruling that the defendants committed "crimes against peace," critics remain skeptical about whether Japan indeed undertook a "war of aggression" or "a war in violation of international law" or had a "conspiracy" to accomplish either.

To begin with, at the time of the Second World War, it is argued, there was no absolute prohibition of war nor was there a total ban on the first use of violence. Such a prohibition could be found neither in the Covenant of the League of Nations nor in the 1928 Kellogg-Briand Pact of Paris.[60]

As for the charge of "war of aggression," the problem is that before Nuremberg and Tokyo, there was no definition of aggression derived from general practice and accepted as law by all states. Nor was "conspiracy" to commit aggression a crime in international law at the time; that crime was created *ex post facto* by the Tokyo Tribunal.[61] It was only since December 14, 1974 that an effort was made to address what constituted "wars of aggression." According to article 5 of a United Nations General Assembly resolution, "No consideration of whatever nature, whether political, economic, military or otherwise, may serve as a justification for aggression."[62] That first effort was evidently a failure as the meaning of "war of aggression" remains unclear today because the term "crime of aggression" is left undefined in the Rome Statute of the 1999 international criminal court.[63]

Compounding the problem of a lack of definition for "wars of aggression" are the ambiguities surrounding how those wars might be distinguished from legitimate wars of self-defense. Critics of the Tokyo Tribunal maintain that, until 1944, the United States, Great Britain, and France had agreed that aggression was not a crime in international law because they believed that war in self-defense could not be prohibited. Justice Röling, for example, argued that not only was violence in self-defense, including military action against non-military threats, still condoned, the Pact of Paris reserved for each state "the prerogative of judging for itself what action that right of self-defense covered and when it came to play."[64]

A standard contention made by ardent Japanese nationalists is that Japan's surprise attack on Pearl Harbor was provoked by the U.S. oil embargo that forced Japan to go to war to defend itself. There is also the question of whether Japan's fear of communism from the Soviet Union, coupled with anxiety about dependence on raw materials, had played a decisive role. Other Japanese, however, eschew the self-defense argument by taking a broader and longer historical perspective. Professor Takano Yuichi, as an example, maintained that the Pacific war, for which the argument of self-defense plausibly might be made, was really "an extension" of a pattern of "wars of aggression" undertaken by Japan in China and elsewhere, a pattern that began as early as 1910-15 when Japan annexed Korea and issued its Twenty-One Demands to China. Given that pattern, Takano argued, "the legal judgment that Japan launched aggressive wars can be made."[65]

In order to defend its jurisdiction amidst these legal uncertainties, the Tokyo Tribunal took recourse to the argument that Japan had initiated a war in violation of international law—specifically, the Kellogg-Briand Pact. In article I of the Pact, the contracting parties had solemnly condemned recourse to war for the solution of international controversies, and renounced it as an instrument of national policy in their relations with one another.[66] Japan, being a signatory to this treaty, was subject to every one of its provisions, rules, and principles. Thus, the Tokyo Tribunal argued, any country (such as Japan) that resorted to war as an instrument of national policy violated the Pact and committed "a crime in so doing."[67]

Even assuming that the Pact of Paris did outlaw wars, aggressive or defensive, it is unclear whether individuals could be held accountable for acts of state.[68] Professor Knut Ipsen of Rohr University maintained that although he believed that Japan's resort to war was illegal at the time, the obligation to renounce war was for states, not individuals. As a consequence, the jurisdiction of the tribunal with regard to crimes against peace "remains doubtful."[69] Ipsen's skepticism as to the culpability of individual defendants is shared by many Japanese,[70] which could explain the immense popularity of *Pride*, the top-earning domestic film in Japan in 1998. In the movie, wartime (1941-44) prime minister General Tojo Hideki, who authorized the surprise attack on Pearl Harbor, is portrayed as a national hero, instead of a convicted and executed war criminal.[71]

War crimes. Article 5 of the Tokyo Charter defined "war crimes" as "violations of the laws or *customs of law.*"[72] Unlike the case with "crimes against peace," the Tokyo Tribunal seems to be on firm ground with respect to war crimes.

"Customs of law" refer to generally accepted codes of conduct between states. According to Ipsen, long before World War II, it had been a general practice of states that conventional war crimes could be tried and punished by the power(s) that captured and detained the offenders. More than that, this practice was also in conformity with international law, specifically the 1929 Geneva Convention Relating to the Treatment of Prisoners of War (POWs), of which Japan and the Allied powers were signatories and to which they were bound. Article 45 of the Convention prescribed that the Japanese defendants at Tokyo, as POWs of the Allied powers, "shall be subject to the laws, regulations, and orders in force in the armies of the detaining Power."[73] *In effect, according to both international law and the customs of law, it was entirely legitimate for the Allied powers to try their captive Japanese defendants for war crimes.*

The particular war crimes with which the Tokyo defendants were charged were also specified in the Geneva Convention. As examples, article 2 stated that POWs "must at all times be humanely treated and protected, particularly against acts of violence"; article 3 specified that POWs "have the right to have their person and their honor respected"; article 4 prescribed that Japan, like other states, "is bound to provide for" the maintenance of POWs. Furthermore, POWs "captured in unhealthful regions or where the climate is injurious for persons coming from temperate regions, shall be transported, as soon as possible, to a more favorable climate" (art. 9); POWs "shall be lodged in buildings or in barracks affording all possible guarantees of hygiene and healthfulness" (art. 10); and the food ration of prisoners of war "shall be equal in quantity and quality to that of troops at base camps" (art. 11). And while Japan "may utilize the labor of able prisoners of war," officers and persons of equivalent status are excepted (art. 27). More than that, not only must POWs who are used as laborers be properly maintained, cared for, treated, and paid wages (art. 28), none "may be employed at labors for which he is physically unfit" (art. 29), nor can their labor have "direct relation with war operations" (art. 31) or be "unhealthful or dangerous" (art. 32).[74] All of which was grossly violated by Japan in its treatment of Allied POWs—as in the Bataan Death March, the three Sandakan Death Marches, the construction of the Burma-Thailand Railroad, the 80Kilo Camp, and the Banaka Island Massacre. That could explain the much higher death rate (27 percent) of POWs held by the Japanese, as compared with the death rate of 4 percent of POWs held by Germany.[75] Arguably, the Japanese subjected Chinese POWs to even worse treatment: many were summarily executed; others (along with some Allied POWs) were used as subjects for biochemical warfare experiments, deliberately infected with anthrax and bubonic plague.

Although Japan never ratified the 1929 Geneva Convention, being a signatory did confer a moral obligation to abide by the convention's provisions, in accordance with an accepted principle of international law that simply by signing a treaty, a government immediately is obliged not to violate the spirit of that treaty. Regardless, the Hague Convention (IV) of 18 October 1907 Respecting the Laws and Customs of War on Land, which *was* ratified by Japan, contained prescriptions almost identical to those of the Geneva Convention.

As examples, according to the Annex to the Hague Convention, "Prisoners of war...must be humanely treated" (art. 4); "The State may utilize the labour of prisoners of war according to their rank and aptitude, officers excepted. The tasks shall not be excessive and shall have no connection with the operations of the war.... Work done for the State is paid for" (art. 6); "The Government into whose hands prisoners of war have fallen is charged with their maintenance...[who] shall be treated as regards board, lodging, and clothing on the same footing as the troops of the Government who captured them" (art. 7); "The obligations of the belligerents with regard to the sick and wounded are governed by the Geneva Convention" (art. 21); "[I]t is especially forbidden—(a) To employ poison or poisoned weapons; (b) To kill or wound treacherously individuals belonging to the hostile nation or army; (c) To kill or wound an enemy who, having laid down his arms, or having no longer means of defence, has surrendered at discretion; (d) To declare that no quarter will be given...; (g) To destroy or seize the enemy's property" (art. 23); "The attack or bombardment...of towns, villages, dwellings, or buildings which are undefended is prohibited" (art. 25); and "The pillage of a town or place, even when taken by assault, is prohibited" (art. 28).[76]

Japan had contravened every one of the above articles. Not only were the Allied POWs not "humanely treated" by the Japanese military, they were summarily executed,[77] forced to march great distances in arduous circumstances (as in the Bataan Death March), and to labor on war-related projects (such as the construction of the Burma-Thailand Railroad) without compensation. In their biochemical warfare experiments in Manchuria and other parts of China, the Japanese military employed "poison or poisoned weapons." The dissection of more than 3,000 live humans (mainly Chinese) without anesthesia must count as "treacherous killing and wounding."

In their *sanko-sakusen* (burn, murder, plunder) campaign in Northern China, the Japanese military most certainly "pillaged" and "destroyed the enemy's property." And in their seven weeks of rape and
mayhem in Nanjing in 1937-38, the Japanese committed nothing
less than "crimes against humanity" itself. As recounted by Iris
Chang,[78]

> Tens of thousands of young men were...mowed down by machine guns, used for
> bayonet practice...and in decapitation contests...or soaked with gasoline and burned
> alive.... An estimated 20,000-80,000 Chinese women were raped. Many soldiers went
> beyond rape to disembowel women, slice off their breasts, nail them alive to walls.
> Fathers were forced to rape their daughters, and sons their mothers.... Not only did live
> burials, castration, the carving of organs, and the roasting of people become routine, but
> more diabolical tortures were practiced, such as hanging people by their tongues on iron
> hooks or burying people to their waists and watching them get torn apart by German
> shepherds.

The framers of the Hague Convention IV were motivated not just
to protect combatants in war, but also the wellbeing of civilians. It
was stated in the Preamble that the convention was "animated by the
desire to serve, even in this extreme case [of war], the interests of
humanity." To that effect, the convention was "intended to serve as
a general rule of conduct for the belligerents in their mutual relations *and in their relations with the inhabitants.*" It was for that reason that article 3 of the Annex to the Hague Convention IV specified
that "In the case of capture by the enemy," both combatants and
non-combatants "have a right to be treated as prisoners of war."[79]

In contravention of the above article, the Japanese army made no
distinctions between combatants and civilians, meting out severe
punishment to non-combatants whom they suspected of participating in people's resistance movements and guerrilla activities in China
and elsewhere, on the grounds that these constituted acts of hostility
toward Japan. In many cases, those who were arrested, whether combatants or noncombatants, were not treated as POWs under the laws
of war, but executed on the spot. The crews of American warplanes
taken prisoner by the Japanese army during the Pacific War were
frequently summarily executed[80]—all in violation of article 23(c) of
the Hague Convention.

Article 3 of the Hague Convention IV also stipulated that "A bel-
ligerent party which violates the provisions of the said Regulations
shall, if the case demands, be liable to pay compensation."[81] Despite that injunction, the Japanese government, to this day, refuses
to compensate either governments or individuals (such as former

Allied POWs and "comfort women") who had been victimized in the war.

In effect, in its war conduct, Imperial Japan had contravened two international laws: the 1929 Geneva Convention as well as the 1907 Hague Convention IV. More than international laws, Japan also violated its own customs of law. The Preamble to the Hague Convention IV had acknowledged the impossibility of formulating "regulations covering all the circumstances which arise in practice." Recognizing that, "in cases not included in the Regulations adopted...the inhabitants and the belligerents remain under the protection and the rule of the principles of the law of nations, *as they result from the usages established among civilized peoples*, from the laws of humanity, and the dictates of the public conscience."[82] The Japanese have complained that the Tokyo Tribunal was Eurocentric "in its legal ideas, its personnel, and its historical thinking."[83] But the fact of the matter is that, concerning the treatment of POWs and civilians, Japan's own customs of war are remarkably similar to those of Europe.

To begin with, Japan's traditional warrior code—the samurai's *bushido*—called for compassion for the weak, including wounded enemies, and allowed for honorable surrender. Miyamoto Musashi, a famous samurai swordsman, taught that a warrior had more responsibility than merely the defeat of his enemies. He must know the difference between right and wrong in the affairs of men, and must strive for inner understanding and judgment.[84] The "Regulations" for samurai warriors written by a famous general in 1412 forebade "the wanton taking of a life" and instead instructed samurai to be "humane, courteous, and kind." Failure to follow these precepts brought dishonor and "an unbearable sensation of shame."[85]

When the samurai class was abolished and replaced with a modern conscript army in the early years of Meiji Japan, the code of *bushido* did not die with them. Instead, the way of the samurai was infused into the new army and served as its standard of conduct for the Japanese soldier. Throughout Japan's wars with China and Russia at the turn of the century, its armed forces behaved with admirable restraint. In the Sino-Japanese War of 1894-95, although the Chinese mutilated Japanese POWs, the Japanese refrained from reciprocal behavior (except at Port Arthur). Japanese restraint was even more notable in the Russo-Japanese War of 1904-05, given the provocations from the Russians who made no effort to disguise their racist contempt for the Japanese, calling them "yellow monkeys" that would be "smashed" by Russians "like mosquitoes." Despite Russian racism and the appalling physical conditions in which the war was fought, the Japanese did not behave brutally. Instead, they treated the bodies of dead Russians with respect and showed exceptional kindness to their wounded enemy, inspiring a British newsman to marvel at the "chivalry displayed by the Japanese soldier to a fallen foe" and "the considerate treatment accorded to Russian prisoners which could not be excelled in point of consideration by any army in the world."[86]

All that began to change in the 1930s. As the Japanese government disseminated its propaganda on the racial superiority of the Yamato race and their mission to colonize the Asian peoples into a Greater East Asia Co-Prosperity Sphere, Japan's military became increasingly brutal.[87] What eventually resulted were actions in China and elsewhere which were nothing less than crimes against humanity.

Crimes against humanity. The countless acts of unspeakable brutality inflicted by the soldiers and officers of Imperial Japan against POWs and unarmed civilians must certainly qualify as "crimes against humanity." Those crimes were defined in the IMT Charter as "murder, extermination, enslavement, deportation, and other inhumane acts committed before or during the war, or persecutions on political or racial grounds."[88]

Despite clear instances of "crimes against humanity" committed by the Japanese military, this was the one category of war crimes on which the defendants at the Tokyo Tribunal were acquitted. There are divergent opinions on whether crimes against humanity even existed in international law at the time, as well as whether the Tokyo Tribunal had valid jurisdiction over such crimes.

As an example, Tokyo University professor Onuma Yasuaki maintained that "crimes against humanity," like crimes against peace, were unknown in international law at the time of the outbreak of World War II. "Therefore, to treat them as crimes was a violation of the principle of *nullum crimen sine lege, nulla poena sine lege* [unless there is a law, there can be no crime; unless there is a law, there can be no punishment]."[89] Similarly, Justice Pal thought that the Tokyo Tribunal had no right to try the defendants for crimes against peace and against humanity because "the victors could not establish new crimes and new definitions and punish prisoners according to them." To do otherwise might itself violate international law.[90]

There are others, however, who took the opposite view. Ipsen, for one, believed that the condemnation of murder and other inhumane acts was a general principle of law at the time, recognized by every civilized nation. "Therefore, within these limits, crimes against humanity may be derived from a recognizable source of international law." And, although at the time of the Tokyo trial there was no precedent in international law for jurisdiction over such crimes to be conferred on an international tribunal, "article 43 of the Hague Regulations made it a lawful act to establish such jurisdiction."[91] All of which led Ipsen to conclude that, "with regard to crimes against humanity, the IMT had an assured basis in the international law then in force."[92]

Conduct of Trial (Due Process)

Of the three criteria for evaluating the legitimacy of war crimes trials, the Tokyo Tribunal seems particularly vulnerable with regards to its procedural shortcomings. Justice Pal, for one, noted that "from the beginning," the tribunal had "a casualness toward legal niceties," which made the result a "foregone" conclusion.[93]

To begin with, the official languages of the tribunal were English and Japanese, neither of which was spoken by the French and Soviet judges who, nevertheless, "continued to function as a judge self-confidently."[94] Among the eleven judges, only Pal had any background in international law. More than their professional training and competence, the impartiality of the judges is also questioned. As Richard Minear, a professor of international law at the University of Massachusetts, pointed out,[95]

> All eleven justices shared the disability of being citizens of the victor nations. Five justices were vulnerable to more specific challenge: that they had prior involvement in the issues to come before the tribunal; that they lacked the necessary languages; that they were not judges. All five supported the majority judgment, if not all of the sentences....

Furthermore, critics maintain that the judges' impartiality was compromised because eight of the eleven judges represented countries that were direct victims of Japanese militarism, with one judge a victim of the Bataan Death March in the Philippines.[96] Others, however, had the opposite complaint: that Japan's victims had *not* been adequately represented in the tribunal. Although Asians suffered the greatest damage in the war, only three of the eleven judges at the trial represented Asian countries[97] (China, the Philippines, India);

more egregious still was the lack of representation for Korea that had been "brutally" colonized by Japan for thirty-five years.[98]

Another procedural problem was the partisanship of the leading Americans in the tribunal. For instance, Justice William O. Douglas admitted that the Tokyo trial was never intended "as a free and independent tribunal to adjudge the rights of petitioners under international law." Instead, it was an instrument of the military and of the executive branches of government as "[i]t took its law from its creator." For his part, Justice Robert Jackson, the American chief prosecutor and reportedly the main author of the IMT Charter, was reported to have said that "One of the reasons this was a military tribunal, instead of an ordinary court of law, was in order to avoid precedent-creating effect of what is done here on our own law."[99]

Yet another procedural shortcoming of the Tokyo Tribunal was its one-sidedness: Japan, the loser, was tried, but "victors are not held accountable, even though their crimes may be known."[100] Japan was not even allowed to raise as issues the actions of the Allied powers, such as the Soviet Union's possible violation of its 1941 Neutrality Pact with Japan, and the United States' atomic bombing of Hiroshima and Nagasaki and the firebombing of Japanese cities which, in Tokyo alone, took the lives of 100,000 civilians. Such "atrocious and inhumane acts"[101] were designed to kill or wound great numbers of ordinary people in order to bring the war to a quick end. (Japan, of course, had engaged in its own bombing of cities, those of Shanghai and Chongqing.)[102]

Those acts by the Allied powers, Justice Pal argued, should have been brought within the purview of the Tokyo Tribunal as subversions of the Geneva Conventions because "[i]f the accused were guilty, the plaintiffs were guilty too."[103] Not to do so was to violate "the fundamental condition that makes a law a law"—its universal applicability. For its critics, the one-sided nature of the trial proved the maxim that "might makes right" and was one of the major factors leading to cynicism about the Tokyo Tribunal.[104] These various procedural shortcomings led Henri Bernard of France to dissent from the IMT's majority ruling. As he put it, "A verdict reached by a tribunal after a defective procedure cannot be a valid one."[105]

Other Criticisms

The Tokyo Tribunal has also been criticized for its sins of omission, beginning with the decision not to indict the individual whom

Sir William Webb (the Australian judge and president of the Tokyo tribunal) called "the leader in the crime." Under Japan's Meiji Constitution, the emperor bore ultimate responsibility for the war, being the supreme leader of the country, commander of the armed forces, and vested with absolute executive power.[106] Despite that, not only was Hirohito not indicted, he was not even summoned as a witness[107]—which was what the tribunal's prosecution and defense both wanted, albeit for different reasons. The defense team desired, above all, to protect and preserve their emperor; the prosecutor, for his part, thought that putting Hirohito on trial would so alienate the Japanese as to make more daunting the Allied postwar occupation and reform of Japan.

Thus it was that the tribunal, motivated by political considerations, indicted and convicted Hirohito's subordinates instead. Its failure to bring the emperor to justice was what mainly distinguished the Tokyo Tribunal from its Nuremberg counterpart. As one critic wrote, although the Nuremberg tribunal was similarly flawed because the victors judged the vanquished, it nevertheless had great moral force because it focused on the most culpable individuals and judged them fairly. The Tokyo trial, in contrast, failed by not prosecuting the emperor but indicted the military commanders instead and, in so doing, "making them heroes for sacrificing themselves."[108]

There were even more serious sins of omission, especially the tribunal's neglect of crimes against humanity—the countless victims of torture, murder, extermination, enslavement, deportation, and other inhumane acts that the Japanese government and military committed in China, Manchuria, Korea, the Philippines, and other parts of Asia. Unlike at Nuremberg, where great emphasis was accorded crimes against humanity, the Tokyo Tribunal not only failed to recognize their importance, but deliberately suppressed evidence of the most heinous cases. Among them was the sexual enslavement of some 200,000 women and girls, mostly Korean. Euphemistically called the "comfort women," they were forced to serve as prostitutes in Japanese military brothels during the war. More egregiously still was the failure on the part of the Tokyo Tribunal to try the Japanese scientists and doctors who conducted biochemical warfare experiments on POWs and civilians in Manchuria and elsewhere.[109] Nor did the tribunal or the United States government pursue the forced POW labor issue, notwithstanding some 20,000 American POWs who were sent to Japan to perform heavy labor for Japanese companies.[110] As a result, "crimes against humanity" was the one criminal category on which all the defendants were acquitted.

Seoul National University professor Paik Choong-Hyun believes that racism probably accounted for why the victorious Allied powers paid very little attention to crimes against humanity—because the victims were Asians. That neglect, in his judgment, must count as "one of the most serious defects of the Tokyo trial."[111] Justice Röling concurs with Paik's censure. For him, the prestige of the tribunal was "severely damaged" by the subsequent revelation of Unit 731[112]—a Japanese research laboratory in Manchuria that conducted bacteriological experiments on POWs and civilians, costing thousands of lives. Unit 731 would have provided a case, rare at the Tokyo trial, of centrally organized war criminality. But the American military authorities wanted to avail themselves of the results of those experiments as well as prevent them from falling into the hands of the Soviet Union. As a result, the judges at the Tokyo Tribunal were kept ignorant, while the Japanese involved in these crimes were promised immunity from prosecution in exchange for divulging the information obtained from the experiments. In this manner, "this, the worst of Japanese crimes, was kept from the tribunal."[113]

Conclusion

More than half a century after the Tokyo war crimes tribunal, it is justly criticized for its many flaws—of victor's justice, procedural defects, and *ex post facto* laws. As professor of law Peter Murphy wrote:[114]

> While displaying some of the trappings of independent judicial bodies, the [Tokyo and Nuremberg] tribunals were in fact dedicated to the administration of "victor's justice." The victorious powers declared what offenses committed by the defeated powers were to be punished and set up *ad hoc* tribunals consisting of judges and prosecutors from their own countries, using their own notions of criminal justice, to ensure that perpetrators would be punished.

But if the Tokyo Tribunal deserves censure for being a "creature of political decision-making," Japan benefited as much as it was victimized. For it was political considerations that sheltered the Japanese emperor from judgment, and it was the politics of the Cold War that led the prosecution to suppress evidence concerning Unit 731 which would certainly have convicted the defendants and others for "crimes against humanity." If justice in the Tokyo Tribunal had been contaminated by politics, Japan profited as much as, if not more than, it suffered because of it.

Article 6 of the Potsdam Declaration had stressed that "There must be eliminated for all time the authority and influence of those who have deceived and misled the people of Japan into embarking on world conquest...."[115] But by 1948, international political considerations became more urgent than the administration of justice. When China fell to the Communists, it seemed that all of Asia was about to go the way of half of Europe. Suddenly, turning Japan into a bastion against the Red Peril took priority; the United States and Great Britain quickly lost their zeal for justice. This process reached breakneck speed with the start of the Korean War in 1950. By then, the American Occupation authorities secretly urged Japan to go against its postwar Constitution (which was written by the Americans to begin with) and remilitarize. To stabilize Japan, the Occupation not only did not stand in the way, but accelerated the return of many suspected as well as convicted war criminals to the reins of power,[116] resulting in a continuity of Japan's pre and postwar political leadership. That continuity goes a long way toward explaining the LDP party and government's ongoing denial, obfuscation, and revision of Japan's wartime deeds.[117]

As for the Tokyo Tribunal's resort to *ex post facto* legislation, lamentable though that was, it did fundamentally change the international law of the time by making individuals liable for criminal acts committed in time of war. No longer could they hide behind their superiors and plead innocence, employing "I was only following orders" as a legal defense. The cause of humanity can only be better served. As Justice Röling allowed, "the Tokyo trial gave real life to ideas that the world needed: the accountability of those responsible for the outbreak of war, and the answerability of military and political leaders for their failure to prevent war crimes."[118]

Despite its flaws, the Tokyo Tribunal (along with its counterpart in Nuremberg) played an important historical role toward the construction of a more just world, for it was at Tokyo and Nuremberg that the modern quest for international criminal justice began.[119] The precedents established at Tokyo ultimately made possible the creation, in the summer of 1999, of the world's first permanent international criminal court, as well as the two *ad hoc* International Criminal Tribunals for Rwanda and the former Yugoslavia.[120]

Those, such as Justice Pal, who exonerated the Tokyo defendants because of concerns with fairness and procedural improprieties risked aiding and abetting the unregenerate individuals who have "personal interest in avoiding justice" so as "to commit further crimes."[121] Pal's dissenting judgment was seized by Japanese nationalists as a vindication of the wartime behavior of their army and the first step toward the restoration of the dignity of the war dead.[122]

In the last analysis, what is *legal* in international law is not necessarily what is *right*. With great probity and sagacity, Professor Onuma concluded that although the Tokyo Tribunal was flawed, it was still legitimate. For Onuma, what was committed in Nanjing and elsewhere were "atrocities" that automatically elicit feelings of shock and revulsion in ordinary people. Those feelings should be heeded, as they reflect "an extremely simple...and universal sense of justice...that is the ultimate *raison d'être* of law." Even critics of the Tokyo Tribunal would probably not go so far as to say that Japan did nothing wrong, nor could they. Japanese may quibble about the number of people killed in Nanjing, but they cannot deny the fact that innocent Chinese citizens were slaughtered by the troops of Imperial Japan. Ideally, the United States should answer for its killing of innocents in Hiroshima and Nagasaki; but to argue that "you too have done wrong, so I should be forgiven my sins" reveals "only a bleak poverty of spirit."[123]

Perhaps Murakami Hatsuichi, curator of Japan's Okunojima Toxic Gas Museum, should have the last word. According to Murakami,[124]

To simply look at the past from the point of view of the victim is to encourage hatred.... At the Hiroshima museum it is easy to feel victimized... But we must realize that we were aggressors too.

Notes

1.   Ian Buruma, *The Wages of Guilt: Memories of War in Germany and Japan* (New York: Farrar Straus Giroux, 1994), pp. 27, 12, 38.
2.   Coco Kubota, "Debate on Nanking Massacre Continues in Japan," *Deutsche Presses-Agentur*, December 11, 1999.
3.   "Japan Unrepentant," http://www.bergen.org/AAST/ Projects/Chinahistory/unrepent.htm.
4 .   "Redemption's Reward," *The Economist*, August 24, 1991, p. 16.
5.   John Breen, "Between God and Man," *History Today*, 48:5 (May 1998), p. 2.
6.   Gavan McCormack, "Japan's Uncomfortable Past," *History Today*, 48:5 (May 1998), p. 5.
7.   Nicholas D. Kristof, "A Big Exception for a Nation of Apologizers," *New York Times*, June 12, 1995, pp. A1, A4. The Diet resolution undoubtedly was made

possible because Japan's prime minister at that time, Murayama Tomiichi, was another non-LDP member, being a member of the Social Democratic Party of Japan.

8.   Gabriel Yiu, "Japan Has a Responsibility to Recognize its War Atrocities," *The Vancouver Sun*, December 28, 1999, p. A15.

9.   Buruma, *Wages of Guilt,* 122; and Kubota, "Debate on Nanking Massacre Continues."

10 .   "The Symbols of Japan Past," *The Economist*, June 3, 1995, p. 31.

11.   "The Constitution of Japan (1947)," http://history.hanover.edu/texts/1947con. html.

12 .   Translated into English, the lyrics to "Kimigayo" are "May the reign of the Emperor continue for a thousand, nay, eight thousand generations and for the eternity that its takes for small pebbles to grow into a great rock and become covered with moss."

13.   Although the Hinomaru (literally, disk of the sun) has been Japan's national flag since 1870, and "Kimigayo" (the Emperor's reign) became the national anthem in 1888, neither was legally recognized as such until the Diet's decision in 1999. Behind the recent legitimization was a long-time split in public opinion in Japan that had prevented legal authorization due to the flag and anthem's links to negative memories of World War II. As a result of the Diet's vote, it is now mandatory for all public schools to fly the flag on national holidays and sing the anthem during ceremonies, despite objections from Japanese pacifists.

14 .   The Association seeks to restore imperial Shinto rituals as state events, as well as state recognition and funding for Japan's many Shinto shrines which were discontinued when the 1947 constitution ended the identification of emperor and state with religion. Only with restoration, the Association believes, will Japan be perceived as the sacred nation that it is, and its domestic and international fortunes revive. Breen, "Between God and Man," pp. 3, 5.

15.   Minoru Tada, "Mori's Remarks: No Time for Anachronisms," *Japan Times Online* (*JTO*), May 26, 2000.

16.   Jon Herskovitz, "Japanese Head to Polls, Mori's Miscues in Mind," *San Francisco Chronicle*, June 24, 2000, p. A1.

17 .   The emperor's humanity is implicit in the Constitution's stipulation, in Article 1, that the emperor derives "his position from the will of the people with whom resides sovereign power." See "The Constitution of Japan (1947)."

18 .   Noah Berlin, "Constitutional Conflict with the Japanese Imperial Role: Accession, Yasukuni Shrine, and Obligatory Reformation," *Journal of Constitutional Law*, I:2 (Fall 1998), pp. 2, 7.

19.   An example is former Tokyo University of Education history professor Saburo Ienaga, who brought three successive lawsuits against the Japanese government's censorship of history textbooks. See "The Secrete Behind the Screen," *The Economist*, September 6, 1997, p. 40.

20.   An example is veteran Hakudo Nagatomi, as recounted by Joanna Pitman, "Repentance: Tokyo-Postcard," *The New Republic*, February 10, 1992, pp. 14-15.

21.   "Ever since the war, younger generations have grown up in the belief that Japan was simply a victim of Allied aggression that culminated in the atom bombing of Nagasaki and Hiroshima, bringing the brave Japanese to their knees." Pitman, "Repentance: Tokyo-Postcard."

22.   McCormack, "Japan's Uncomfortable Past," p. 6.

23.   See Nobukatsu Fujioka and Shudo Higashinakano, *"Za reipu obu Nankin" non kenkyu (Research of "The Rape of Nanking")* (Tokyo: Shodensha, Heisei 11, 1999).

24.   Kubota, "Debate on Nanking Massacre Continues."

25.   Howard W. French, "Internet Raiders in Japan Denounce Rape of Nanjing," *New York Times*, January 31, 2000, p. A8.

26.   Kubota, "Debate on Nanking Massacre Continues in Japan."

27.   Alfred Balitzer and Abraham Cooper, "Japan Ill-Served by its Whitewash of War-time Crimes," *JTO*, February 10, 2000.

28.   An example is an email posting to a discussion forum on Japan, which asserted that "bashers" of Japan, including "the overseas Chinese," have made a "cottage industry out of pursuing the Japanese on the minutest details about this or that atrocity, especially the so-called 'Nanjing Incident.'" The author of this posting maintained that for these "bashers" to discontinue their pursuit of Japan would mean they would "lose their jobs and *raison d'etre*." See Cecil H. Uyehara's posting of January 6, 2001 to japanforum@lists.nbr.org.

29.   McCormack, "Japan's Uncomfortable Past," p. 6.

30.   Kingston, "Blindness Tips the Scales."

31.   Buruma, *Wages of Guilt*, p. 122.

32.   Jeff Kingston, "Lessons of the Nanjing Debate," *JTO*, April 18, 2000. An example is Kobayashi Yoshinori's 400-page *Sensoron: Theory about the War*.

33.   Michael Wolffsohn, *Eternal Guilt? Forty Years of German-Jewish-Israeli Relations* (New York: Columbia University Press, 1993), p. 13; Nana Sagi, *German Reparations* (St. Martin's Press, 1986), p. 3.

34.   In 1985 and 1996, respectively. "Miyazawa Prayed at Yasukuni," *JTO*, May 28, 2000.

35.   In December 2000, the Tokyo High Court upheld a lower-court ruling that the Japanese government has no obligation to pay damages to eighty former "comfort women" and their relatives. "Japan Rejects Sex Slaves Compensation Demand," *San Francisco Chronicle*, December 7, 2000, p. C10.

36.   72 percent of respondents to an Asahi poll of July 20, 1994 said that they thought Japan had "not given enough compensation" to formerly occupied countries; 17 percent said that Japan had given enough. 58 percent of respondents to an Asahi poll of June 28, 1995 thought that the government should compensate "comfort women;" 29 percent said no. From the Roper Center for Public Opinion Research's Japanese Public Opinion Database.

37.   Yiu, "Japan Has a Responsibility."

38.   "Japan vs. Germany," http://www.sjwar.org/japan-vs-germany.htm.

39.   Kingston, "Lessons of the Nanjing Debate."

40.   McCormack, "Japan's Uncomfortable Past," p. 6.

41.   Hosoya Chihiro, "The Tokyo Trial From the Perspective of International Law," in C. Hosoya, N. Ando, Y. Onuma, and R. Minear (eds.), *The Tokyo War Crimes Trial: An International Symposium* (henceforth *TWCT*) (Tokyo, Japan: Kodansha Ltd., 1986), p. 29.

42.   Michael Boxall, "The Full Read on Tojo Nostalgia," *The Vancouver Sun*, August 14, 1999.

43.   "Preface," *TWCT*, p. 8.

44.   Manuel M. Davenport, "War Crimes Trials: The Ethical Issues," *Ethics and Justice*, 2:2 (April 1999), p. 1.

45 .   "Preface," *TWCT*, p. 9.

46.   Jeremy Colwill, "From Nuremberg to Bosnia and Beyond: War Crimes Trials in the Modern Era," *Social Justice*, 22:3 (Fall 1995), pp. 111, 124.

47.   Davenport, "War Crimes Trials," p. 1.

48.   Mary Margaret Penrose, "Lest We Fail: The Importance of Enforcement in International Criminal Law," *American University International Law Review*, 15:2 (2000), p. 328.

49.   Ashis Nandy, "The Other Within: The Strange Case of Radhabinod Pal's Judgment on Culpability," *New Literary History*, 23:1 (Winter 1992), p. 63.

50.   Annex II of "The Potsdam Declaration," *A Decade of American Foreign Policy: Basic Documents, 1941-49* (Washington, D.C.: Government Printing Office, 1950). See http://www.yale.edu/lawweb/avalon/decade/decade17.htm.
51.   Colwill, "From Nuremberg to Bosnia," p. 115.
52.   Awaya Kentaro, "In the Shadows of the Tokyo Tribunal," *TWCT,* p. 84.
53.   Onuma Yasuaki, "The Tokyo Trial: Betweeen Law and Politics," *TWCT,* p. 46.
54.   Colwill, "From Nuremberg to Bosnia," p. 115.
55.   Ibid.
56.   William Safire, *Lend Me Your Ears: Great Speeches in History* (New York: Norton, 1992), p. 597.
57.   Nandy, "The Other Within," p. 47.
58.   Grant M. Dawson, "Defining Substantive Crimes within the Subject Matter Jurisdiction of the International Criminal Court: What is the Crime of Aggression?" *New York Law Journal of International and Comparative Law,* 19 (2000), p. 413.
59.   Knut Ipsen, "A Review of the Main Legal Aspects of the Tokyo Trial and Their Influence on the Development of International Law," *TWCT,* p. 40. Emphasis supplied.
60.   B.V.A. Röling, "Introduction," *TWCT,* p. 21.
61.   Nandy, "The Other Within," p. 50.
62.   Röling, "Introduction," p. 23.
63 .   The delegates were divided between two competing definitions. The first based liability for the crime of aggression on individuals, whereas the second definition placed responsibility with the states themselves. See Lawson, "Defining Substantive Crimes...."
64.   Nandy, "The Other Within," p. 50.
65 .   "Question and Answer Period," *TWCT,* p. 63.
66 .   "Kellogg-Briand Pact of 1928," wysiwyg://97/http://www.yale.edu/lawweb/avalon/kbpact/kbpact.htm.
67.   Ipsen, "A Review of the Main Legal Aspects," pp. 38, 40.
68.   Hosoya, "The Tokyo Trial from the Perspective of International Law," p. 29.
69.   Ipsen, "A Review of the Main Legal Aspects," pp. 40-41.
70.   Röling, "Introduction," p. 18.
71 .   "Controversial Film Tops in Japan," *New York Times,* June 8, 1998.
72.   Ipsen, "A Review of the Main Legal Aspects," p. 41. Emphasis supplied.
73.   Ibid.
74.   "Convention between the United States of America and Other Powers, Relating to Prisoners of War, July 27, 1929," wysiwyg://106/http://www.yale.edu/lawweb/avalon/lawofwar/geneva02.htm.
75.   See, for example, Gavan Daws, *Prisoners of the Japanese: POWs of World War II in the Pacific* (New York: William Morrow and Co., 1994), and Yuki Tanaka, *Hidden Horrors: Japanese War Crimes in World War II* (Boulder, CO: Westview, 1996).
76.   "Convention (IV) Respecting the Laws and Customs of War on Land."
77.   An example are the nine U.S. Marines who were left behind in a commando raid on Makin atoll in the Gilbert Islands in the summer of 1942. They were captured by the Japanese, taken to Kwajalein Island, and beheaded. Carl Nolte, "Honorable Burial at Last for Makin Atoll Heroes," *San Francisco Chronicle*, December 26, 2000, p. A1.
78.   Iris Chang, *The Rape of Nanking: The Forgotten Holocaust of World War II* (New York: BasicBooks, 1998), pp. 4, 6.
79.   "Convention (IV) Respecting the Laws and Customs of War on Land." Emphasis supplied.

80. Awaya, "In the Shadows of the Tokyo Tribunal," p. 80.
81. "Convention (IV) Respecting the Laws and Customs of War on Land."
82. Ibid. Emphasis supplied.
83 . "Preface," *TWCT,* p. 10.
84. Steve Kaufman, et al., *The Martial Artist's Book of Five Rings: The Definitive Interpretation of Miyamoto Musashi's Classic Book of Strategy* (Tokyo, Japan: Charles E. Tuttle, 1994), p. 21.
85. Robert B. Edgerton, *Warriors of the Rising Sun: A History of the Japanese Military* (Boulder, CO: Westview, 1997), pp. 322-323.
86. Ibid., pp. 318-320.
87. Ibid., pp. 323-324.
88. Ipsen, "A Review of the Main Legal Aspect," p. 42.
89. Onuma, "The Tokyo Trial," p. 47.
90. Nandy, "The Other Within," pp. 48, 50.
91. The article stated that, "The authority of the legitimate power having in fact passed into the hands of the occupant, the latter shall take all the measures in his power to restore, and ensure, as far as possible, public order and safety...." See "Convention (IV) of 18 October 1907 Respecting the Laws and Customs of War on Land," http://www.tufts.edu/departments/fletcher/multi/texts/BH036.txt.
92. Ipsen, "A Review of the Main Legal Aspect," p. 43.
93. Nandy, "The Other Within," p. 52.
94. Ibid., pp. 52-53.
95. Richard Minear, "War Crimes Trial," *Kodansha Encyclopedia of Japan* (Tokyo, 1983), pp. 85-86.
96. Nandy, "The Other Within," pp. 52-53.
97. Onuma, "The Tokyo Trial," p. 46.
98. Boxall, "The Full Read on Tojo Nostalgia."
99. Nandy, "The Other Within," p. 52.
100. Röling, "Introduction," p. 26.
101. Awaya, "In the Shadows of the Tokyo Tribunal," pp. 80-81.
102. Gregory Clark, "The Nanjing Number Game," *The Japan Times,* February 7, 2000.
103. Nandy, "The Other Within," pp. 50-51, 65.
104. Onuma, "The Tokyo Trial," p. 45.
105. "Preface," *TWCT,* p. 10.
106. In fact, Tojo had testified in his defense that it was inconceivable that he would have done anything contrary to the emperor's wishes. A day later, he retracted his testimony. Boxall, "The Full Read on Tojo Nostalgia." See also Herbert P. Bix's account of Emperor Hirohito's intimate involvement in the war effort, from the beginning till the end, in *Hirohito and the Making of Modern Japan* (New York: HarperCollins, 2000).
107. "Preface," p. 10; Onuma, "The Tokyo Trial," pp. 45-46.
108. Aryeh Neier, "Watching Rights," *The Nation,* July 31, 1995, p. 119.
109. Ibid.
110. "Ex-POWs Step Up Reparation Campaign," *JTO,* June 30, 2000.
111. "Comments by Paik Choong-Hyun," *TWCT,* pp. 53-54.
112. See, for example, Hal Gold, *Unit 731 Testimony* (Tokyo, Japan: YenBooks, 1996), and Sheldon H. Harris, *Factories of Death: Japanese Biological Warfare, 1932-45, and the American Cover-up* (London: Routledge, 1994).
113. Röling, "Introduction," p. 18.
114. Peter W. Murphy, "Book Review: Judging War Criminals," *Texas International Law Journal,* 335:2 (Spring 2000), p. 325.
115. Annex II, "The Potsdam Declaration."

116.   On December 24, 1948, the day after seven defendants who had been sentenced to death were executed, the Occupation authorities released all the remaining seventeen suspected Class A war criminals, including Kishi Nobusuke and Kodama Yoshio, and announced that there would be no more trials of Class A war criminals. Kishi returned to political life and, in 1957, became prime minister. Kodama became one of the "shadow shoguns" of Japanese politics. Boxall, "The Full Read on Tojo Nostalgia."

117.   This is the thesis of Yoshibumi Wakamiya, *The Postwar Conservative View of Asia: How the Political Right has Delayed Japan's Coming to Terms with its History of Aggression in Asia* (Tokyo, Japan: LTCB International Library Foundation, 1999).

118.   Röling, "Introduction," p. 18.

119.   Murphy, "Book Review."

120.   Penrose, "Lest We Fail," p. 323.

121.   Murphy, "Book Review."

122.   Nandy, "The Other Within," p. 47.

123.   Onuma, "The Tokyo Trial," pp. 48-49, 50-51.

124.   Buruma, *Wages of Guilt*, p. 111. During the war, the island of Okunojima was the site of the largest toxic gas factory in the Japanese Empire. Official Chinese sources claim that more than 80,000 Chinese fell victim to gases produced at the factory.

5

Hirohito's War Crimes Responsibility:
The Unrepentant Emperor

Peter Li

There are few historical figures who have been so controversial as the Showa Emperor, Hirohito, who reigned for sixty-four years, through the tumultuous war period and into the era of peace afterwards. His reign included "economic depression, unconditional defeat, foreign occupation, democratic reform, stable peace, unprecedented prosperity, and the rise to world power."[1] What is more remarkable is the fact that, having escaped all responsibility for the war during the Tokyo War Crimes Trial, he was able to reign for forty-four more years after the war. That he remained on the throne for such a long period of time is a testimony to his astonishing survival skills. But as to how he was able to never admit to any moral, political and/or legal responsibility for the war is a great mystery and paradox.

Of course, judgments about Hirohito vary greatly. He was not by any means a simple man. The fact that no personal writing of his has ever come to light heightens the mystery. It is alleged that he kept a personal diary all his life, but which has never been disclosed. Therefore, to this day the controversy rages on. The image of Hirohito as "a gentle introvert, scholarly and civilized man of peace who found himself emperor of a nation bent on war and conquest" is a popular conception, but obviously an oversimplification. It is believed that he was a lover of peace who may have opposed war but did not know how to or have the power to stop it.[2]

Some have even claimed Hirohito to be Japan's compassionate emperor, a bodhisattva, who lived a quiet and austere life, and had shown great compassion for the suffering of his people.[3] On the other hand, more recent studies based on the latest released docu-

59

ments show Hirohito to have been a well-informed, decisive, and clear-headed emperor, who knew how to use his power and show his displeasure when needed. He often conferred with his advisors and officials, called numerous imperial conferences, and held behind-the-scene liaison conferences. He was not a person ignorant of his power and influence. Evidence indicates that Emperor Hirohito's wartime responsibility is irrefutable.[4] As the supreme commander of the armed forces, he made the ultimate decision to execute the war plans. Without his approval, the plans could not have been carried out.

The most recent study of Hirohito is the monumental volume by Herbert P. Bix, based on the most complete available data. His judgment is a harsh one. Bix states that "he [Hirohito] was actually much smarter and shrewder than most people give him credit for, and more energetic too.... During the first twenty-two years of his reign [1924-1945], he exerted a high degree of influence and was seldom powerless to act whenever he chose to" and "there is much to be learned from what he *does not* say and do as what he does."[5] Hirohito learned his lessons in emperorship well. As the chosen leader of his people and the nation, it was his number one priority to preserve the throne and its authority. In that sense it must be said that Hirohito was a success.

The case of Hirohito is complicated by several factors: 1) his physical appearance and personal temperament, and 2) the system of "irresponsibility" within the hierarchical structure in Japanese society and the emperor system. There is no doubt that in appearance and temperament, Hirohito bears little resemblance to the evil genius of Adolf Hitler. In contrast to Hitler's strident air, outer exuberance, and showmanship, Hirohito was shy, awkward, and withdrawn, rarely making public appearances and/or giving speeches. He lacked the majestic appearance of a monarch, like his grandfather the Meiji Emperor, whom he admired. As many have noted, Hirohito was slight of build, he had a squeaky voice, and was not endowed with great intelligence or imagination. He was slightly hunched and wore thick classes. When he was about to embark on his international tour in 1921, those close to him "were concerned about his health, and because he exhibited a level of personal insecurity ('nervousness') and social awkwardness that they found worrisome in a monarch..."[6]

In his early years, Hirohito was heavily influenced by General Nogi, hero of the Russo-Japanese war, who took young Hirohito under his wing and taught him the importance of "frugality, diligence, patience, manliness, and the ability to exercise strong self-control under difficult conditions. Devotion to duty and love of the military stood equally high in Nogi's vision of the ideal monarch. Under Nogi's tutelage, Hirohito came to an early recognition of his physical weakness, and the need to overcome it by dint of hard work."[7] Although Hirohito was far from Nogi's ideal image of a monarch, he treated Hirohito with great earnestness. It is said that on hearing of the Meiji Emperor's death, General Nogi met with Hirohito, spoke to him for three hours, asking about all the things that he had learned while at the school of which Nogi was principal. During the long interview, Hirohito sat motionless afraid that he might disappoint his master if he fidgeted. After the session was over, General Nogi and his wife both committed *seppuku* (ritual suicide). When Hirohito heard the news, it is said that he alone of his three brothers was overcome with emotion: tears welled up in his eyes and he could hardly speak.[8] He could not hold back his emotions in spite of the fact that he had been disciplined not to display his emotions.

Hirohito's educational schedule was highly regimented under General Nogi's charge. There were four hours of morning instruction each day, followed by lunch. Hirohito usually dined alone, apart from his classmates, on Western food, which was capped off by a glass of milk. In the afternoon there was another hour of formal instruction, followed by physical exercise and military instruction. Hirohito was also given a heavy dose of Confucian teachings, which emphasized that the ruler should "show benevolence to the people, the people show loyalty to those above them, and everyone knows his place in the scheme of things." During this formative period of his life, the young introverted Hirohito developed a love for insects and marine biology, which became his lifelong hobby.[9]

Hirohito's appearance, especially in old age, inspired Kanaji Isamu, a professor at Shitennoji International Buddhist University, to call Hirohito "Japan's Compassionate Emperor."[10] Having seen Hirohito only once at the age of eighty when he was received at the imperial palace to be given an award, Kanaji was overwhelmed by his admiration for the diminutive and modest emperor. In Kanaji's loving portrayal he wrote, "In Buddhist terms, it might be said that the Emperor gave the appearance of *sunyata*, or emptiness. I keenly felt that this simple directness was the key to the Emperor's personality."[11] Upon further reflection, Kanaji concluded, "how then should we refer to the Showa Emperor—the emperor who so moved men with his pure innocence, this unselfish emperor, whose humbleness was infused with deep sympathy for others? ....I believe the most appropriate term for referring to that sovereign is bodhisattva."[12] Hirohito a bodhisattva? It's hard to believe. Obviously, Professor Kanaji completely overlooked the Asia Pacific war and the blood of millions shed in Hirohito's name.

Hirohito was able to score another resounding success in 1975, on his famous Disneyland visit with Mickey Mouse by his side. The aged, smiling Hirohito projected an image of a harmless, peace-loving emperor who was, undoubtedly, helpless in the midst of his wartime militarist officers and advisors.

Many believe that Hirohito was basically a benevolent man, a man who wanted peace, but was swept along by the winds of war. On the other hand, he was raised since birth to believe that he was the center of the Japanese government and of the universe. Although a constitutional monarch in name, he was a divine emperor—a direct descendent of the Sun Goddess Amaterasu Omikami, and he was declared "sacred and inviolable" by the Meiji Constitution. In order to preserve and protect his throne against its enemies, the emperor had to be able to show that he had committed no wrongs and could commit no wrongs. To ensure his own survival, Emperor Hirohito had to be "restrained from expressing his views in a forthright fashion by his advisors, so even though he held strong opinions on many question, he seldom if ever revealed them to anyone outside his small circle of advisors."[13]

This task of "molding the emperor" was the most important influence on Hirohito during his youth and early-manhood. Holding back his emotions and saying as little as possible, and always playing the part of the supreme leader, enabled him to hide behind a "mask" as it were. It made Hirohito's involvement in war decisions vague and ambiguous. For example, at the decisive imperial conference to implement war plans to attack Pearl Harbor, Hirohito quoted a famous haiku of his grandfather, the Meiji Emperor, and stormed out: "Though I consider the surrounding seas as my brothers. Why is it that the waves should rise so high?" He left it to his officials and advisors to puzzle out his true feelings. His statements are often like the pronouncements of the Delphic Oracle. They are ambiguous and can be interpreted in various ways. Therefore, his trusted officials, like Tojo and others, had to learn to observe his manners and expressions and bodily movements to discern his true intentions. On the other hand, he also exhibited a strong sense of duty as emperor by standing in the rain to review students and soldiers. Often he neglected physical activities and pleasures for the sake of understanding the issues concerning the government and the nation.[14]

To portray Hirohito in the most favorable light—as a man of peace—Honjo, Hirohito's chief-aid-de-camp, recorded Hirohito's reflections regarding Japan's military adventurism in China: "I believe that international justice and good faith are important, and I'm striving to preserve world peace.... But the forces overseas [the Kwangdong army] do not heed my commands and are recklessly expanding the incident; they seem bent upon overpowering China by military force. This causes me no end of anguish. This could result in intervention by the major powers and the destruction of our nation and people.... When I think of all these problems, I cannot sleep at night."[15] The truth of the matter was, of course, Hirohito could have severely punished or admonished the officers that disobeyed him. But he did not.

In contrast to this view of Hirohito as a benevolent but powerless man of peace is the view that he had great power and authority granted him by the Constitution. According to the emperor system at the time, the emperor occupied the highest position of authority. He was not a mere figurehead and puppet of the military as some claim. He was granted definitive powers by the Constitution of 1889. "The constitution asserted that the emperor was the successor in an unbroken, sacred blood lineage, based on male descendants, and that the government was subordinated to the monarchy on that basis. It defined him as 'sacred and inviolable,' 'head of the empire,' and 'supreme commander of the armed forces.'"[16] Article XI of the Constitution states that "The emperor has the supreme command of the army and navy." Article XII states that "The emperor determines the organization and the peace standing of the army and navy," and Article XIII states "The emperor makes war, makes peace, and concludes treaties." He also has the power to convoke and dissolve the imperial Diet, issue imperial ordinances in place of law, and appoint and dismiss ministers of state, and other officials. Furthermore, government officials are sworn to be loyal and must defer to and respect the wishes of the emperor.

Even with these seemingly unlimited powers, in the context of Japanese society and culture and consensual decision-making, the emperor still must not expose himself unnecessarily by deliberate action. He must exercise caution in his actions and deliberations. His inviolability does not permit him to make any blatant errors so as to lose the respect of his officials. And he must learn to exercise his powers in subtle ways rather than being direct, such as to advise, cajole, admonish, question, or by using meaningful silences. In fact, he could ask his entire cabinet to resign by simply asking, "How would it be if you, prime minister, resigned?" at which point his prime minister and cabinet would consider themselves dismissed.

Herbert P. Bix and Irokawa Daikichi have shown in their works over and over again that Hirohito was informed of all the war plans and strategies by his military advisors. Between January 1938 to December 1941 eight imperial conferences were called by Hirohito to discuss war plans. This did not take into account the many behind-the-scenes conferences and liaison meetings that preceded the imperial conferences held in the emperor's presence. He was in on all the crucial decisions that were made. There was no way in which Hirohito could be ignorant of what was happening. Furthermore, he was quite exuberant when Japan had its first taste of victory. In the Lord of the Privy Seal Kido's diary was this revealing description of the Hirohito's joy in learning about the Japanese victories in the Pacific:

> The Emperor was beaming like a child. "The fruits of war," he said, "are tumbling into our mouth almost too quickly. The enemy at Bandung on the Java front announced their surrender, and now our army is negotiating for the surrender of forces in the Netherland East Indies. The enemy has surrendered at Surabaja and also on the Burma front has given up Rangoon." He was so pleased.[17]

Perhaps a little reluctant at first, Hirohito was soon drawn into the war fever and became a proactive emperor as the Japanese military continued its victorious march into Southeast Asia. Even if Hirohito were not responsible for starting the Pacific war, certainly his delay in ending it cost Japan and its Asian victims millions of lives. For almost a year, in the face of growing defeat, he urged his generals and admirals to gain one last victory in order to secure better peace terms. During that period of time an additional 1.5 million Japanese were killed. Even Hirohito's most trusted official, the former Prime Minister Tojo Hideki, in a momentary lapse during the Tokyo War Crimes Trial, revealed the truth when he said, "none of us [Japa-

nese] would dare act against the emperor's will."[18] This remark sent
shock waves through the court, for this meant that the emperor would
be ultimately implicated for war responsibility—if this statement were
to stand. However, because MacArthur was determined that the
emperor not be involved in the trials under any circumstances, Tojo
was led by the American chief prosecutor, Keenan, to modify his
statement. Therefore, to this day, the question of war responsibility
remains undecided and the emperor's "nonresponsibility" also remains an unresolved issue.

However, the emperor's nonresponsibility can be a double-edged
sword. On one hand, it allowed Hirohito to remain on the throne for
another forty-four years and rebuild Japan as a world economic
power; on the other, it thwarted Japan's moral growth. The question
of moral responsibility and historical injustice brought on by Japan's
aggression has come back to haunt present-day Japan in spite of its
continued denials. The past wrongs have not gone away. It is regrettable that in Emperor Hirohito's Imperial Rescript, delivered on the
occasion of Japan's surrender, he never mentioned remorse, guilt,
or responsibility for the war. He denied any aggression on the part
of Japan, stating that war was declared on the United States and
Britain "to assure Japan's self-preservation and the stabilization of
East Asia," nor did Japan intend "to infringe upon the sovereignty
of other nations or embark upon territorial aggrandizement." Therefore, he admitted to no wrongdoing nor committed any war crimes.

However, recent world developments, such as the continued de-
mocratization of Asian countries, economic development, and globalization, have highlighted the need for "nations at act morally and
acknowledge their own gross historical injustices" and "questions
of morality and justice are receiving growing attention as political
questions."[19] Many Japanese citizens have realized their need to
address the issues of Japan's past aggressions in Asia. One of the
outstanding representatives of this school of thought is the Nobel
Prize laureate Oe Kenzaburo, who states: "Japan and the Japanese
must work for rehabilitation in Asia. In the history of our modernization in general, but, in particular, in the war of aggression that
was its peak, we lost our right to be a part of Asia and have continued to live without recovering that right. Without that rehabilitation
we shall never be able to eradicate the ambivalence in our attitude
toward our neighbors, the feeling that our relationships aren't real."
Continuing in stronger language, Oe writes, "[Japan's] unwilling-

ness to come to terms with its past is not just morally offensive, it prevents Japan from playing its proper role in Asia."[20]

In his conclusion, Bix indicts both Japan and the United States for their efforts to sweep the question of war responsibility under the rug in the service of other purposes, and thus making it difficult for the Japanese nation as a whole to come to terms with its recent history. To the very end, Emperor Hirohito refused to acknowledge any responsibility for his role in the death of millions as well as brutalities inflicted by his forces under his name in China, Korea, the Philippines, Indonesia, and other Pacific Rim nations. His ability to face his own people and the world indicates his level of shrewdness and insincerity even after he renounced his sacredness and inviolability as the divine emperor. Hirohito met with General MacArthur eleven times after the surrender to work out his defense and to fend off attempts to implicate the emperor by the other Allied nations.

Emperor Hirohito lived his whole life surrounded and protected by his own advisors and officials, and later by the United States, who needed him and his nation as an ally in the Cold War against the Soviet Union and China. As a result, as late as 1975 on his popular visit to the United States, he gave this ominous answer to a reporter's question in regard to how values have changed in Japan since the war. The emperor replied, "I realize that various people have advanced any number of opinions about this since the termination of the war. From the broadest point of view, however, I do not think there has been any change between the prewar and postwar periods."[21] This seems to imply that the emperor and his people have not learned anything from the war experience. This is indeed a sad commentary.

More recently, in December 1990, after Akihito's imperial transition was over following the death of Hirohito, the new emperor granted a press interview. When he was asked about the war he replied, "My generation has lived for a long time without war, and so I have had no time to reflect on the war."[22] Again the imperial household has conveniently sidestepped the issue. As Hirohito became the symbol of the Japanese people's repression of their wartime past, so it seems that his son, Emperor Akihito, is continuing his father's role of denying the past and justifying Japan's historical amnesia. Thus, the conspiracy to shield the emperor from any war time responsibilities at the end of the war has led to the lack of any consciousness of guilt on the part of the imperial family for the millions of lives lost in the war. The central role of the imperial family in the war must be pursued. Thanks to the work of the Women's International War Crimes Tribunal, in December 2000, the "inviolable" Emperor Hirohito was posthumously brought to justice when the presiding Judge Gabrielle Kirk McDonald proclaimed that Hirohito was guilty of the responsibility for the Japanese military enslavement of women during World War II.[23] This is a historic first step.

Notes

1.   Carol Gluck, "Foreword," in Daikichi Irokawa, *The Age of Hirohito* (New York: Free Press, 1995), p. vii.
2.   Leonard Mosely, *Emperor of Japan* (Englewood Cliffs: Prentice-Hall, 1966), p. vii.
3.   Isamu Kanaji, *Hirohito, Japan's Compassionate Emperor*, translated by John Carroll and Iwase Takao (Kao Corporation, 1989).
4.   Daikichi Irokawa, *The Age of Hirohito: In Search of Modern Japan* (New York: Free Press, 1995).
5.   Herbert P. Bix, *Hirohito and the Making of Modern Japan* (New York: Harper Collins, 2000), p. 12.
6.   Bix, p. 15.
7.   Bix, p. 37.
8.   Bix, p. 43.
9.   Bix, p. 48.
10. See Kanaji, *Hirohito, Japan's Compassionate Emperor*.
11. Kanaji, p. 21.
12. Kanaji, p. 34.
13. Honjo Shigeru, *Emperor Hirohito and His Chief-Aid-de-Camp: The Honjo Diaries, 1933-1936*. Translated by Mikiso Hane. (Tokyo: University of Tokyo Press, 1982), p. 46.
14. *Honjo Diaries*, p. 47.
15. *Honjo Diaries*, p. 135.
16. Bix, pp. 7-8.
17. Paul Manning, *Hirohito: The War Years* (New York: Dodd, Mead, 1986).
18. Arnold Brackman, *The Other Nuremberg, The Untold Story of the Tokyo War Crimes Trials* (New York: William Morrow, 1987), p. 353.
19. Elazar Barkan, *The Guilt of Nations* (New York: W.W. Norton, 2000), p. 4.
20. Oe Kenzaburo, "Denying History Disables Japan," *The New York Times Magazine*, July 2, 1995.
21. John Dower, *Japan in War and Peace* (New York: The New Press, 1993), p. 340.
22. Bix, p. 687.
23. See Yayori Matsui, "Women's International War Crimes Tribunal on Japan's Sexual Slavery: Memory, Identity and Society," in this volume.

6

Accountability, Justice, and the Importance of Memory in the "Era of War"

Manuel Prutschi and Mark Weintraub

Today we come together to begin sharing a deeply painful part of Asian history; but we are also ourselves making history today in more ways than one. We at Canadian Jewish Congress are indeed honored by the invitation to address such a committed and esteemed group of world citizens in this great city of Tokyo.

The writer Iris Chang, in the subtitle to her book *The Rape of Nanking*, referred to this massacre as "forgotten." But she, in the very act of writing her book, and so many of you here, through your tireless work, have ensured that what happened at Nanking no longer is forgotten.

"Zachor!" "Remember!" *Zachor* is the Hebrew word for remembrance. It is one of the central commandments that a Jew is required to live by. "To recall and relive," in the words of Vera Schwarcz, author of a work on Chinese and Jewish cultural memory, is the only way one can, one must, approach catastrophe.

Through memory, we honor the wishes of the victims that they never be forgotten. Through memory we ensure that those who were slaughtered in innocence will never be forgotten, each as a complex human individual who lived with achievements, great and small, possessing untold potential. Memory connects us with the victims and thereby engages us in the sacred act of revival, returning them to a form of life so at least their torment and murder will never be lost in oblivion.

The act of remembering also joins us with the survivors in a collective acknowledgement of their suffering. Those of us who are of the second and even third generations removed from these events, by rekindling memory, link ourselves to our survivor parents and grandparents, broadening our understanding and strengthening our love for them.

Memory, however, must not only be internalized. It must also be externalized. The victims and the survivors must be given a voice and that voice, though It may start as a whisper, must end up as a lion's roar. That is how memory can lead to history. Rekindling memory and the writing of history, coupled with advocacy, are the only possible paths that can lead the successor governments of perpetrator states to acknowledge the past and to confront it honestly. Only as a result of such accountability can there come sincere remorse so that the past may be redeemed from absolute evil.

Memory however must not be limited to the extremes of victims and criminal perpetrators. It also must include the righteous: the German John Rabe, for example, who, as the "good man of Nanking," defied the Japanese Imperial Army and saved thousands of the city's Chinese inhabitants. Or the Japanese Senpo Sugihara who, as Consul in Kovno, Lithuania in 1940, also in defiance of his government, issued thousands of visas saving more than 31,000 Jewish refugees. Or the Chinese Consul in Vienna, Dr. Feng Shan Ho, who between 1937 and 1940, once again without permission from his government, issued thousands of lifesaving transit visas to Jews desperate to flee from Austrian and Nazi persecution.

Just recently at the Holocaust Centre in Vancouver, Canada, Dr. Ho's efforts were honoured with an exhibit and memorialization of his simple yet majestic words:

"I thought it only natural to feel compassion and to want to help. From the standpoint of humanity, that is the way it should be."

Ladies and gentlemen, as we gather here in remembrance and advocacy, let us be inspired by the Rabes and the Sugiharas, the Wallenbergs and the Dr. Ho's of this world. Let us, as members of the indivisible human family, enter into a partnership on a mission of *tikkun olam*, the Hebrew words for "repairing the world." And how badly indeed does this world of ours need repair!

The organizers of this Forum have referred to the twentieth century as the "Era of War." This is indeed true, though, with respect, it actually does not go far enough in capturing the monumentally tragic human experience of these past 100 years, a record of inhumanity perhaps unmatched in the history of our species.

The mid-nineteenth century began with the seizure of the African continent by European imperial powers. In one recently documented example of genocide, European fortune hunters, as part of Belgium's colonial policy, devastated the fertile Congo River lands, and as many as 10 million Africans may have perished in the resulting slaughter.

In the Ottoman Empire's Turkey, the so-called ethnic cleansing resulted in the effective murder of up to 1.5 million Armenians between 1915 and 1923. Hitler's remark, "Who today remembers the destruction of the Armenians?" demonstrates with full clarity that the lack of response by the world community to one set of crimes against humanity only encourages mass murderers into believing, quite correctly, that they can get away with other such crimes.

This century has witnessed the suppression of cultural and religious infrastructures and the deaths of millions in Stalin's Soviet Union and Mao's Communist China through various governmental policies. The world watched the ethnic killings in Nigeria-Biafra and the mass murders of the Cambodian middle class by the Pol Pot regime in the countryside killing fields. We have seen the murders of countless Tutsis in the massacres in Rwanda and most recently the destruction of large parts of East Timor's population. As we speak, the massive persecution of Christians continues unchecked in the Sudan and an entire city once again, this time in Chechyna, is targeted for complete destruction by bombing while the sick and elderly are trapped.

As Canadians, we have the responsibility of raising the issue of the horrendous mistreatment endured by members of the Canadian Armed Forces at the hands of the Japanese military, after the fall of Hong Kong on Christmas Day, 1941. They were confined in brutal prison camps, where they were summarily executed or subjected to starvation or beatings, with many dying as a result of their captivity.

As Canadians speaking here in Japan, we must as well refer to the great injustice inflicted on Canadians of Japanese ancestry between 1941 and 1949. The Canadian government forcibly removed this community from their homes, imprisoned them in internment camps, and confiscated and liquidated their property.

Many of you know so much better than we the results of the explosion of Japanese military and economic imperialism in Asia. Millions of civilians in China and other parts of Asia were killed, and millions of others were subjugated under brutal military rule. The degradations suffered are incalculable, not least of them the horrors suffered by Asian women who were forced into sexual slavery, the live human medical experimentation, and the use of fatal and disfiguring biological warfare. The rape of Nanking was not an isolated incident of war policy gone awry. It was only a precursor to the more comprehensive enslavement and destruction of massive numbers of innocent civilians. By reason of your activism, which in part has been inspired by the courage of the survivors and the penitence of a few brave former Japanese soldiers, the international community is now finally beginning to take notice of the trauma inflicted on Asia during those dark years.

In the conflict in Europe, the Holocaust (or *Shoah* in Hebrew), was the culmination of 2,000 years of anti-semitism that subjected Jews to the teachings of hate, forced conversion, torture, expulsion, massacre, and finally—under Hitler's regime—annihilation. With the assistance of sophisticated technology, the Nazis devised instruments of mass murder par excellence: the extermination camps. And dehumanization did not end with death. The bodies of Jewish victims were treated as industrial and consumer products to be mined for their by-products—gold crowns from teeth; hair, skin, and bones. And all of this was conceived by one of the most so-called advanced of European societies.

The Nazis were animated by an ideology at whose very center was Jew hatred. Germany, one of the most modern, best-educated and technically competent nations in the world, with the complicity of collaborator states, enlisted its massive human and material resources for the singular purpose of annihilating the entire Jewish people simply because of who they were. Every aspect of German society was complicit, including the legal and medical professions, the major business and industrial enterprises, academic institutions, the military forces and the civil service.

Of course, we also now know that simple greed, the prospect of dispossessing an entire people of its wealth, was a powerful motivator resulting in the largest mass robbery certainly in modern history.

Two-thirds of Europe's Jewish population, including over two million babies and children, were destroyed along with a 2,000-year-old culture. But the Nazi murder machine did not stop there. It included among other incomprehensible tragedies, the Nazi brutalization of the Polish nation, the attempted genocide of the Gypsies, and the enslavement and killing of Slavic peoples. As the Nobel Laureate survivor and writer Eli Wiesel so rightly put it, "All Jews were victims, but not all victims were Jews."

The memory and history of these last 100 years make for a sorrowful list of mass murders, and our enumeration is by no means all-inclusive.

And as in the case of the Holocaust, it is not only precious lives but the entire complex of an ancient culture that is destroyed as part of a systematic campaign and that is lost to humanity forever. It compels us to refer, as the genocide scholar Israel Charny has, to "the rotten cannibalism and sadistic cruelty that is, tragically, a serious part of human nature and potential."

Yet we know there is that noble and altruistic potential to being human that compels us to reject pessimism as the final answer. Our presence here is a testament to our collective belief that even after unmitigated evil there is the possibility of redemption. And we must resist those who listen to our century's litany of horrors and argue that every war-related death is identical. For the innocent who were made refugees and haphazardly murdered, the precise and unique animating historical and political forces are irrelevant. But for those of us continuing to live and advocating for human rights, it is vital that we do not capitulate to the belief that everyone is equally guilty—for if everyone is guilty, then ultimately no one is guilty. Relativism and rationalization are too often used by those who would prefer not to face the past.

Redemption from evil through atonement is very much a Jewish belief. The most sacred holy day of the Jewish calendar is Yom Kippur—the Day of Atonement. It is a day wherein each Jew annually takes stock of his actions and atones for misdeeds as a prelude for a reconciliation with God. Peoples and states in the same way must take account of their past, reviewing it and confronting it honestly. This is what defines accountability, and only with accountability can there be the possibility of reconciliation.

We want now to touch upon one aspect of Jewish historical consciousness that we think is very relevant to our Forum.

We ask you to consider how it came about that a marginalized, inconsequential rabble like the ancient Jews, who were held in contempt by every mighty conquering empire, including the Assyrians, Babylonians, Persians, Greeks and Romans, have been able to survive to contribute to the world and joyously celebrate their peoplehood both outside and inside the restored State of Israel.

The answer in part must surely be found in the Jewish commitment to memory and in its collective form, the writing of an authentic history. What do we mean by authentic? We mean a history that reflects the degradations of a people as well as its great achievements; a history which reveals that even its greatest leaders were flawed and capable of committing acts of evil.

We ask you for example to look at the great master story of the Jewish people: the central collective memory found in the Biblical book of Exodus that recounts the slavery of the Israelites, who were the ancient Jews, and their subsequent liberation from slavery by their leader Moses with God's guidance.

The words that Moses hurled at the ruling Pharoah of Egypt to "Let My People Go" have reverberated throughout the millenia, inspiring enslaved peoples everywhere to strive for freedom. But when this history was first being written there was no nobility in the story. Slaves were sub-human; to root your past in a slave history was seen by Near East belief systems of the time as shameful. But the Jewish Bible, the Torah, did not shirk from an honest confrontation with reality, for there was the profound realization that a sanitized history, a history depleted of reality, is inauthentic and will never be seen as vital and sufficiently transcendent to be transmitted from one generation to the next as a living history.

Jewish history teaches that we must begin with the truth no matter how painful or humiliating. Accurate rendering of a collective past permits a society to escape the inevitable catastrophe arising out of living in worlds of illusion. Those who write purposefully distorted histories give to their fellow citizens illusions: illusions of grandeur, illusions of superiority, and illusions of absolute power that all too often have erupted into murderous frenzies orchestrated by ultra-nationalist and power-intoxicated leaders who feed their peoples a disfigured past. We know all too well that the illusions of Axis superiority set in motion a worldwide tragedy on a scale previously unknown to mankind. Clearly our reference to authentic history is intended for those in Japan who would resist confronting the ugly past of the Pacific War years. Our point, if we need to make it any clearer, is that the Jewish people did not go down to psychological or cultural defeat just because they recorded painful parts of their history, and neither would Japan.

But we want to go further and suggest that the accurate recording of memory is not sufficient to ensure that the past is emotionally understood by subsequent generations. For the people subjected to onslaught, what is needed is not only authenticity in the preservation of memory but also memory anchored in purpose and meaning. A cataloguing of catastrophes, while absolutely essential, runs the risk of numbing those who were not directly involved. Therefore the search for meaning in the transmission of history becomes an essential, perhaps the most essential, of all tasks.

We submit that the principal reason the past has been preserved as a living force in Judaism, despite overwhelming odds, is because of the absolute insistence by our rabbis and other communal leadership that we find meaning and context when confronted with the face of evil.

The Jewish community is still searching for the right formula, the right balance, between cataloguing the horrors of the Holocaust and maintaining optimism for the human spirit. Only time will tell if we will be successful. But we have a great precedent to guide us by looking at the Jewish slave history to which we have already referred.

Over and over again in the Torah, the people are reminded by God to love the stranger in their midst; for God reminds them, prods their memory, that they were once strangers in the Land of Egypt who were enslaved because they were seen as the not fully human outsider. The message, loud and clear from ancient Jewish history, is that notwithstanding enslavement and persecution, when liberation comes you must not turn inwards but always maintain an open and ethical approach to the world. *"Love the stranger in your midst."* Time and again the biblical writer makes clear that while one is creating peoplehood, creating national pride and history, one must at the same time remember first and foremost our common humanity and our obligation to act ethically to all.

One of the most compelling demands placed on the Jewish people by their leadership was that of one of the great Biblical prophets when he thundered the words "Justice, Justice ... Justice thou shalt pursue" over and over and over again. But Justice can only be pursued if a people has the capacity to remember and the commitment to engage in the writing of authentic history. So memory, accountability, and ultimately ethics, purpose, and meaning are linked together in a complex dynamic.

The great challenge for those of us involved in this Forum is to somehow insist on the recording of the details of history as an absolute imperative and then, despite this record, move to a place where we affirm that it is possible to have a world where warmth, caring and compassion and not terror, death and destruction will ultimately reign supreme. This Forum's leadership has already begun to create meaning by highlighting the need to move to reconciliation and into an era of peace. But also, by looking at those righteous ones during the war who would not march to the party line and emphasizing their readiness for self-sacrifice in the cause of goodness we make sure that we do not fall into the pit of despair.

By focusing on our common humanity rather than our differences we will ensure that while we remember and mourn the loss of our own relatives and people and work on their behalf, our concerns are also with other peoples so they do not share a similar fate.

If a commitment to working on behalf of all those who are persecuted because of their race, ethnicity, or cultural background arises out of our efforts, then the memory of those we commemorate today will continue to be kept alive for generations to come.

We want to thank the organizers of the Forum, members of the Global Alliance, and Alpha and Thekla Lit of Alpha British Columbia for extending their invitation to the Canadian Jewish Congress, the Canadian affiliate of the World Jewish Congress. Our National President, Moshe Ronen, conveys his regrets for not being able to attend and has asked us to bring heartfelt wishes from the Canadian Jewish community for a most successful Forum. Indeed many, many Canadians of every background wish us much success in our work over the next several days.

It is especially encouraging that this Forum is taking place in the great city of Tokyo, principally organized by Japanese citizens. The movement towards "overcoming the past," therefore, is in part and very importantly coming from within. Segments of leadership in this great and wondrous country of Japan do understand that accountability is vital, first and foremost for the victims, but also for the benefit of the Japanese people, for the sake of the new Japan that emerged after the war, and for humanity as a whole.

Let us now conclude with one final observation. Accountability and justice have the potential to redeem evil and therefore have the potential to be massively transformative experiences; for these are the only paths to rescue humanity from the depths of inhumanity. All peoples, as members of a single human family, must commit and re-commit themselves to the post-Holocaust cry of "Never again!" We hope this Forum will one day be seen as a great human rights watershed; but irrespective of the immediate outcomes, it is clear to us that the Forum organizers and all of you as participants have embarked on the most challenging road of attempting to extract goodness from evil; and for that, this Forum, even if it accomplishes nothing else, stands as a beacon of light to the victims, to present and future generations of Asians, and to all citizens of the world.

References

Barkan, Elazar. 2000. *The Guilt of Nations: Restitution and Negotiating Historical Injustices*. New York: W.W. Norton.

Buruma, Ian. 1995. *Wages of Guilt: Memories of War in German and Japan*. New York: Meridian Books.

Chang, Iris. 1997. *The Rape of Nanking: The Forgotten Holocaust of World War II*. New York: Penguin.

Friedlander, Saul. 1993. *Memory, History, and the Extermination of Jews of Europe*. Bloomington: Indiana University Press.

Hochschild, Adam. 1998. *King Leopold's Ghost: A Story of Greed, Terror, and Heroism in Colonial Africa*. Boston: Houghton Mifflin.

Honda, Katsuichi. 1999. *The Nanjing Massacre: A Japanese Journalist Confronts Japan's National Shame*. Translated by Karen Sandness. New York: M.E. Sharpe.

Linenthal, Edward T. 1997. *Preserving Memory: The Struggle to Create America's Holocaust Museum*. New York: Penguin Books.

Novick, Peter. 1999. *The Holocaust in American Life*. Boston: Houghton Mifflin.

Schwarcz, Vera. 1998. *Bridge Across Broken Time: Chinese & Jewish Cultural Memory*. New Haven: Yale University Press.

Shermer, Michael, Alex Grobman & Arthus Hertzberg. 2000. *Denying History: Who Says the Holocaust Never Happened and Why Do They Say it?* Berkeley: University of California Press.

Yerushalmi, Yosef Hayim, Elisheva Carlebach, & John M. Efron, (eds.). 1998. *Jewish History and Jewish Memory: Essays in Honor of Yosef Hayim Yerushalmi*. University Press of New England.

Yerushalmi, Yosef H. & William Golding. 1996. *Zakhor: Jewish History & Jewish Memory*. Seattle: University of Washington Press.

Part II

The American POW
Experience Remembered

7

The Bataan Death March*

Lester I. Tenney

Editor's Note: *On April 9, 1942, for the first time in the United States history, an entire army surrendered to an enemy. Subsequent to the surrender of approximately 72,000 United States and Philippino troops to the Japanese, the infamous sixty-five mile-long Bataan Death March carried out in twelve grueling days beginning from the southern tip of Luzon to Camp O'Donnell began. Lester Tenney was among the surrendering American troops who took part in the march. But this was to be only the first test of his survival skills, which continued for three and half more years until the end of the war. In this chapter of his book, Tenney gives a searing day-by-day account of unbridled, brutal recreational killing of the Japanese troops along the march. By the end of the war, of the 72,000 troops that surrendered only 7,500 survived; of the 12,000 American troops only about 1,500 returned home. The survival rate for this long ordeal was roughly one in ten. Lester Tenney was one of the lucky few who survived. When he was released from the labor camp he weighed only 101 lbs. His normal weight is 185.*

Knowing the war was over for us and that it was only a matter of time before we would become formal prisoners of the Japanese, our emotions ran high the night of April 9. Bob Martin, Jim Bashleban, Orrie T. Mulholland, and I sat around our bunks, whispering about our concerns and about what our families would think of us when they found out we had surrendered.

I started to talk about Laura and all she meant to me. There was no doubt in my mind, I told them, that I would return home. I tried to explain how I was going to be decisive, and that my first priority would be to make it back all in one piece. I finally said, "You can do

---

* This chapter is from chapter 4, "The March," of Lester I. Tenney's *My Hitch in Hell* (Washington, New York: Brassey's, 1995), pp. 42-64. Printed with permission of Brassey's, Inc.

anything you set your mind on doing; you just have to set goals and priorities." My words must have had some meaning to these friends of mine, for all three came home.

The men who stayed together that night in our company's biv-ouac area were abruptly awakened the following morning by loud voices obviously speaking Japanese. The Japs had come for us. They stormed our area carrying handguns and machine guns; they were ready for business. My knees began shaking, my hands felt cold and clammy, and sweat broke out on my neck and forehead. We were all scared beyond anything imaginable. What was going to happen now? Were we going to be shot? Was this what happens to soldiers that surrender? I began recalling some of the stories I had heard about how some of our men who were captured early in the war were treated. Then, as a terrifying afterthought, I real-ized that at that moment we were facing the same enemy who only days before we were trying to kill. And, of course, if I knew that, so did these fighting Japanese soldiers who were just now com-ing up the path to us. Their mission, we were praying, was to take us prisoner.

Within seconds, dozens of Japanese soldiers came into our area, some asking politely for a cigarette while others pounded our heads with bamboo sticks whose ends were loaded with sand. These rough soldiers did not ask for a thing; they just took whatever they wanted. They ransacked our bodies and our sleeping area. They were bellig-erent, loud, and determined to act like winners of a tough battle (which they were). Once again we were frightened by what was happening and fearful that our future treatment was going to be worse.

The first Japanese soldier I came into contact with used sign lan-guage to ask if I had a cigarette. Fingers together, he moved his arm to his mouth, and inhaled, making it easy to see what he meant. I had to tell him, I did not have any cigarettes. He smiled and a sec-ond later hit me in the face with the butt of his gun. Blood spurted from my nose and from a deep gash on my cheekbone. He laughed and said something that made all of his buddies laugh too. He walked away from me and went to the GI on my right. He used the same sign language, and this time my buddy had cigarettes and offered him one. The Japanese soldier took the whole pack, and then he and his friends began beating my friend with rifle butts and cane-length pieces of bamboo until he could not stand. Then they left, laughing, laughing at the defeated and weak Americans.

My God, what was next? I wondered how I would stand up to this type of punishment for a prolonged period. If we had known earlier just how we would be treated and for how long, I think we would have fought on Bataan to the last man, taking as many of the enemy with us as possible rather than endure the torture, hunger, beatings, and inhumane atrocities we were to undergo during the next three and a half years.

Unfortunately for us, the Japanese plan for evaluating their captive prisoners was based on three assumptions, all of which proved to be without merit. First, the Japanese assumed that only twenty-five thousand to thirty-five thousand military people were on Bataan. The correct number may never be known for scores of men were killed the day before the surrender and more escaped into the jungle or attempted to reach Corregidor. Besides the Allied personnel, almost twenty-five thousand Filipino civilians also sought the shelter and expected safety of the Bataan peninsula. Therefore, the number of people in Bataan at the time of the surrender was closer to 105,000. The number that actually started the infamous Bataan Death March has been estimated at 65,000 Filipino servicemen, 28,000 civilians, and 12,000 Americans—considerably more than the Japanese had estimated.

Second, the Japanese assumed that the enemy forces were in good physical condition and capable of a sustained march without much food or water. The reality was just the opposite. We men on Bataan had had our rations cut to as few as eight hundred calories a day during the past forty-five days. We ate rice and a small spoonful of C rations (an emergency military field ration of food intended for use under combat conditions and consisting of specially prepared and packaged meats). In some cases we augmented our meals with a snake or a monkey or two, or possibly even an iguana. For all of the men on the front lines, we only had two meals a day. This starvation diet brought along with it scurvy, pellagra, beriberi, and of course the diminished ability to fight off the malaria bug or any other sickness. We were anything but ready to march, with or without water and food. Those of us able to walk should have been in the hospital, and those men in the hospital looked as if they were dead.

Finally, the Japanese thought that all details of our evacuation were planned to perfection and that they knew what had to be done and how to do it. In fact, the individual Japanese units did not know what they were supposed to do. No sooner had one group of Japanese lined us up and told us to start walking than another group would tell us to wait. All of these orders were issued in Japanese, and if we did not respond immediately, we would be hit, spat upon, shoved, or in some cases shot for not obeying orders. Once again, they obviously wanted to "get even," wanted revenge, and wanted to show us they were superior. In some situations, however, the guards were simply ignorant of the outside world and thought that everyone understood Japanese. They became irritated by our slowness to respond and our inability to understand their commands and vented their frustration on us.

So, contrary to the Japanese plans, when the march began from Mariveles there was confusion everywhere. Cars, trucks, horses, and field artillery filled the road, all going in different directions. The Japanese were moving all of their heavy equipment and guns into Bataan for the assault on Corregidor. Figuring out how they could achieve total victory in the Philippines with all of the enemy service personnel in the way was a major problem to the Japanese. Confusion reigned, and it seemed that no specific officer was in charge, which made the task of maintaining control almost impossible.

It is also interesting at this point to note that the men captured on Corregidor never made the Bataan Death March. Instead, after the fall of Corregidor on May 6, 1942, the captives were taken by boat to Manila and from there trucked to Cabanatuan, their first prison camp. Another significant difference between the prisoners from Bataan and those from Corregidor was their overall health condition. None of the men from Corregidor had to suffer the brutalities of the march or our first prison camp, Camp O'Donnell. We men from Bataan were half dead by the time we arrive at the camp. Without any hesitancy I can say that fully 100 percent of the men who arrived at that first camp had at least one, and most of the men had two or three, of these health problems: malaria, dysentery, malnutrition, hunger, dehydration, pneumonia, beriberi, or diphtheria. In addition almost all of us were beaten and tortured beyond the body's normal endurance on the march. Then of course we all suffered psychological damage after our surrendering and then helplessly watching our buddies being killed right in front of us, powerless to stop the slaughter and always fearful that we would be next.

By contrast, the prisoners taken from Corregidor ate well until the last days of fighting. The main quartermaster, with full control of all supplies, was headquartered on Corregidor. As the war continued from December to April, transporting large amounts of food or other supplies to the Bataan peninsula became more hazardous and difficult; therefore, food on Corregidor was plentiful. Thus, while the men on Bataan had fourteen to seventeen ounces of food per day, those on Corregidor had forty eight to fifty-five ounces per day. Furthermore, those who were not wounded during the fighting on Corregidor were in pretty good health. Malaria did only mild damage to those on Corregidor, but it struck 99 percent of us on Bataan, whose jungles were known to have the heaviest infestation of malaria-carrying mosquitoes in the world.

Ultimately, none of the assumptions the Japanese made about the forces on the Philippines were realistic or based on solid intelligence. In the opinion of many, the assumptions, which were discussed at the end of the war at the war crimes trials, were made to justify the treatment meted out to the men on the march. The Japanese had no way of knowing the real situation on Bataan, and they did not really care. At their courts-martial, many high-ranking Japanese officers who served in the Philippines said about the same thing: "I didn't really know the situation or condition of the Americans and the Filipinos."

Actually, after looking at a map of the Philippine Islands and especially of Bataan, it is easy to see that the Japanese could have saved themselves a great deal of trouble. Had the Japanese just kept a small force of fighting men along the Pilar-Bagac line, we would have been our own prisoners of war, under our own command. In fact, we often said, "If they leave us alone now, we will be the first POWs with guns and ammunition, taking orders from our own officers." The bottom line was we had no place to go. Going north we would have come into contact with the enemy. Going south, east, or west, we would have ended up in the water. If the Japanese had just left US alone, we would have starved and would eventually have been forced to surrender. This strategy would have allowed the Japanese a two-month head start on their conquest of Australia and their dreams of ruling the entire Southeast Asia territory. The Japanese ego, however, insisted upon a clearly defined defeat of the U.S. forces in the Philippines. They were then faced with the problems of dealing with almost eighty thousand disorganized and diseased military prisoners, as well as twenty-five thousand civilians.

That morning of April 10, the Japanese marched us to the main road, a distance of about half a mile. During this short march, the

Japanese soldiers hollered and prodded us with their bayonets to walk faster. Once at the main road, we waited for three hours, standing, sitting, or resting any way we could; but talking was not allowed.

Down the road, we saw a cloud of dust from which a group of walking and shuffling U.S. and Filipino soldiers emerged. When they passed us, we were told to join them and to start walking. For our group the Bataan Death March began at kilometer marker 167, about two miles east of Mariveles. It had originated at the tip of Bataan in the barrio of Mariveles, where many of the U.S. and Filipino soldiers had congregated and where the Japanese had made their main landing on the Bataan peninsula.

If only we had heeded General King's message to save some vehicles for moving our forces to another location, if we had not destroyed all of our trucks, maybe we would have been able to ride to prison camp. For some unknown reason, or just being in the right place at the right time, a few of the American prisoners ended up riding all the way to our first prison camp, Camp O'Donnell. We walked.

The road we marched on was about twenty feet wide and constructed of rock covered with crushed stone, then a layer of finely crushed rock, and a final coat of sand. The sand, when put down, was intended to make the road hard enough for small automobiles, Filipino carts pulled by carabao, and of course, pedestrians. By the time the march started, the road had already been overused, not only by all of our heavy trucks but also by our tanks and half-tracks whose metal and hard rubber tracks made the road a shambles for driving, much less for walking. The entire road was now nothing more than potholes, soft sand, rocks, and loose gravel. Walking on this terrain for short distances would have been bad enough, but walking for any long distance or for any extended period of time was going to be a painful and difficult experience.

We started our march in columns of fours, with about ten columns in a group. By the end of the first mile we were walking, not marching, and not in columns at all but as stragglers. What was at first an organized group of about forty men was now a mass of men walking or limping as best we could. We had no idea what our final destination was. Many of us felt that we were headed for death. It was just at this time that I decided if I were to survive it would be necessary to have a plan of survival. I thought back to the night before, before we were captured, when I determined that I had to really believe that I was going to survive and get home. To do so I had to set attainable goals, like making it to the next bend in the road or to the herd of carabao in the distance. And of course I had to dream, for It was my dream that kept me going.

After watching everyone being stripped of just about everything we owned, I placed my picture of Laura in my sock, on the ankle side of my boot. She gave me inspiration for my dream, and I reasoned that without a dream, no dream could ever come true and my resolve would weaken. I did not want the enemy to take away the very thing I was dreaming about, the reason why I had to live, to see Laura again, and to make my dream become a reality.

We did not march very far before we found out what kind of treatment was in store for us. After the first shock of being taken prisoner wore off, we realized that how we were outfitted when we were taken from our bivouac area was how we were going to spend the balance of our march. For instance, those who left without a canteen had no means of getting water, even if it was available. Those who left without a cap or headpiece walked in the broiling hot sun and midday temperatures well above one hundred degrees without any head protection. They also suffered the pain of stinging rain during those periods when it would pour down in buckets and the wind-blown dust made seeing difficult.

After the first few hours of marching, however, the men who did have a few extra items with them started discarding them along the road. Some of the men carried knapsacks loaded with a variety of gear: toothbrushes, toothpaste, shaving cream and razors, blankets, and pup tents. The road out of Bataan was strewn with a sampling of these various articles, thrown away at random after the first few miles.

The Japanese guards also began hollering at us in Japanese, which we did not understand. Because we did not respond to their commands as fast as they thought we should, they started beating us with sticks that they picked up from the side of the road. They were trying to get us to walk faster or to walk at a slow trot would be a better description. It made no difference to the guards that we could not understand what they were saying; they just continued repeating the same words over and over again. It dawned on me then that our guards were not the brightest members of the Japanese army. In fact, I concluded, they were most probably the poorest educated and could not connect the fact that we did not respond with our inability to understand what they were saying.

After four or five hours of this constant harassment and beating and of being forced to march in their poor physical condition, many of my fellow prisoners just could not go another step without rest; but the guards did not allow us to rest under any circumstances. One man in my group, Hank, finally limped over to the side of the road and fell in the brush. Within seconds a guard ran over to him. Some of us passing our fallen friend hollered as loud as we could, "Get up, get up!" It was too late. With his bayonet aimed at Hank's body and while screaming something in Japanese at the top of his voice, the guard bayoneted the exhausted American soldier. After five or six jabs, Hank struggled to get up. With blood trickling down the front of his shirt, he hobbled back into the line of marching prisoners and joined a different group of prisoners who were marching by at that particular moment.

Hank survived, but not for long. That evening I was told by another friend of ours that Hank had passed out while walking, fell to the road, and was shot by one of the guards. I could not cry; it seemed I was all cried out. All I had left were just memories, memories of a fine young man who did nothing wrong but who was in the wrong place at the wrong time. Nothing could be clearer: taking a rest while on the march was impossible, that is, if we wanted to live. But what would we do when we had to defecate? Or urinate? We sadly and quickly found out. In order to live, we had to go in our pants.

On the second day of the march, I saw a Japanese truck coming down the road. In the back of the truck were guards with long pieces of rope that they whipped toward us marching men. They tried to hit any prisoner who was not marching fast enough. They snapped a rope at one of the marchers on the outside of the column, caught him around his neck, and then pulled him toward the back of the truck. They dragged him for at least one hundred yards down the road. His body just twisted and turned; he rolled this way and that way, bumping along the gravel road until he was able to free himself from the whip. By then he looked like a side of beef. As he crawled on his hands and knees and slowly raised his bleeding body off of the road, he screamed at them, "You bastards! I'll get even with you for this. I'll live to pee on your graves." In spite of his physical condition, the welled-up anger gave him new strength. He pulled himself up to his full height and began marching with a new spirit.

Also on that second day, when we stopped at the Cabcaben barrio, I watched a Japanese soldier finish eating rice from his *bento* box (mess kit) and fish from a can he had just opened. He had about two spoonfuls of fish left in the can, and as he turned in my direction, he looked me in the eye and pushed the can toward me. He must have seen a pitifully hungry looking soldier, staring, not at him, but at his can of fish. I had not eaten in almost two days, and I was hungry, tired, and demoralized. Without a moment's hesitation, I took the can. Using a piece of tree bark I found on the side of the road, I scooped out just enough for a good taste. I then turned to my buddy Bob Martin, took one look at his face as he sat there staring at me, and gave him the makeshift spoon and the can of fish. From that moment on, Bob and I were close friends.

Always happy-go-lucky, nothing ever seemed to bother Bob. Maybe the word nonchalant would better describe him. Although only five foot seven inches tall, he was a big man when it came to giving of himself, and nothing was ever too much to ask of Bob. His smiling face always made people feel warm and friendly, and his brown hair and green eyes complemented his effervescent personality. Whether wearing his dress uniform hat or his fatigue cap, Bob always perched it jauntily on the back of his head; it was one of his trademarks.

Watching Bob keeping up his own spirits while at the same time trying to make the rest of us on the march feel better made all of us realize that Bob Martin was someone special. Bob and I shared many experiences together on the march and throughout the war. As of this writing, I am glad to be able to say he is alive and well, and we are still very close friends.

I also clearly remember a good-looking and clean-shaven lieutenant from the 194th Tank Battalion, a man about twenty-eight years old with blond wavy hair. He was a large man, about six feet tall, and I guess before the war he had weighed at least 200 pounds but now, on the march, was closer to 150. He appeared to be quite strong but he walked slowly carrying a large bundle—first under his arms, then as we walked farther, over his shoulder. Then he tried walking with the bundle on his head. None of us knew what was in the bundle, but we assumed it was the usual type of gear any good soldier would take with him for emergency purposes.

Our group was walking a little faster than the lieutenant, and as I got closer to him, I saw his eyes were bloodshot and glassy, almost as if he did not know where he was. As I passed him, I asked if he needed any help; I got no answer. Then, as I looked toward him again, I realized he was not walking but staggering, first to the left, then to the right. He was not going to make it, that I knew, and I felt awful not being able to help someone who obviously needed help and was going to die. If any of us had stopped for him, we would have had to accept whatever punishment the guard near us felt appropriate.

As the march continued, he fell farther and farther back, hardly able to walk. We had tried to persuade him to throw away unnecessary items, for his pack was too heavy a burden for him under these conditions. He refused and, after stumbling along for several hundred feet, fell to the ground. The Japanese guard overseeing our marching group stopped and looked at the fallen figure. He yelled something in Japanese and without a moment's hesitation shoved his bayonet into the young officer's chest. Then with a mighty scream, the guard yelled what we interpreted to mean, "Get up." Of course it was too late. That bayonet had finished the job the march started, and another good U.S. soldier had died in the service of his country. I could not help but think, there but for the Grace of God go I. As I witnessed one after another of these atrocities, I became more and more convinced that what was going to happen to me was, to a great extent, going to be up to me.

While walking forward, we looked back at the sickening scene. There the lieutenant lay in the middle of the road. Within minutes we heard the rumble of trucks coming down the road; the Japanese were moving some of their fighting men in position against Corregidor. Making no attempt to avoid the fallen body, they ran over the dead man, leaving only the mangled remains of what once was a human being.

No sympathy, no concern for us as humans, no burials—the Japanese were treating us like animals. We had no doubt as to how we would be treated as prisoners of war.

We had thought that the first few hours of captivity would probably be the most dangerous, but the horrors we witnessed continued well after the surrender. For the Japanese, their sweet taste of victory should have overshadowed the bitterness associated with their strenuous fighting on Bataan, but it was obvious to us that the Japanese soldiers were committing acts of revenge. Many of them had seen the death of close friends only days before, and they wanted to get even with those who killed their comrades. Emotions ran high during the battle, and now their elated feelings of victory coupled with their vengeful reactions associated with close physical contact with their enemy, made many of the Japanese soldiers barbarians. The warrior philosophy associated with the traditional Bushido code was reawakened when the victorious Japanese achieved the surrender of the forces on Bataan. All Japanese soldiers were indoctrinated to believe that surrender was the coward's way out, and a soldier who was captured was expected to commit hara-kiri at the first possible opportunity.

Our ignorance of the Japanese language, their customs, and their military discipline contributed heavily to our casualties on the Bataan Death March. While few of us spoke Japanese, we were aware that many Japanese soldiers spoke a little English but did not dare reveal this ability in front of their comrades, for fear of being accused of having pro-American sympathies.

On the march the guards seemed to have most of their fun with prisoners who seemed to be weak. Later, in the prison camps in Japan, the guards and civilian workers seemed to seek out those prisoners who appeared to be big or strong for punishment. Many times the Japanese guards would boast, "Americans are big but weak; Japanese are small but strong." They had a severe psychological hang-up about being small.

The guards also forced us to go without water on the march, making it one of the most difficult and painful physical experiences I had ever encountered. My stomach ached, my throat became raw, and my arms and legs did not want to move. Words cannot properly explain the mental and physical abuse the body takes when in need of liquid. By the third day, marching without food and water caused us to start screaming about food and drinks we had consumed in the past. Simple things like hamburgers covered with cheese and smothered with onions, milkshakes, a beer or even a Coke made our mouths water. Our minds played tricks on us, but eventually we came back to reality—to hunger and thirst and not knowing where or when our next meal or drink would come from. Still, we were forced to push on and to keep going, one foot in front of the other, with our bodies going in the direction of our feet.

Although there were many free-flowing artesian wells located in and around Bataan, the Japanese had no set policy on giving water to us prisoners. Some of the guards would let a few men go to a well for water but would deny others the same benefit. One day our tongues were thick with the dust kicked up from the constantly passing trucks, and our throats were parched. We saw water flowing from an artesian well, and after a long, hard look at the water being wasted and given the fact that there was no guard right at our side, a marching buddy, Frank, and I ran toward the well to drink what we could and to fill our canteens for future use. We reached the well and started to swallow water as fast as we could. First I took some, then Frank took a turn, then I drank again, and then Frank. We took turns until some other marchers saw us at the well.

Within a few minutes, another ten to fifteen prisoners ran to the well for water. At just that time a Japanese guard came over to the well and started to laugh at us. The first five of us drank, and when the sixth man began to drink, a guard suddenly began to stab the man's neck and back. The American prisoner fell to his knees, gasped for breath, and then fell over on his face. He died without ever knowing what happened—killed, murdered, slaughtered for no apparent reason.

All of us at the well ran as fast as we could to get back into the marching line. Fear filled each of us. My heart pounded like a jackhammer, my eyes popped opened to twice their normal size, and I could not help but think once again, There but for the grace of God go I. Tears streamed down my cheeks as I thought about this young man, murdered and cut down in the prime of his life by a maniac who felt that killing was a game.

About two hours later, we passed a carabao wallow about fifty feet off the road. After one look at the water, I could see it was not fit to drink; green scum floated on top and two carabao were in the water cooling themselves off. The men were dying of thirst, however, and ready to do anything for a drop of water. Not only were we thirsty, but many of us had malaria and were burning up with fever. In addition, most of the men on the march had severe dysentery and felt that water would heal all of their problems. One of the men motioned to a nearby guard and in sign language asked if he could get some of the water. The guard started to laugh and made a hand movement that indicated it was OK.

In a matter of minutes dozens of half-crazed men ran toward the carabao occupied water. The men pushed the green scum away and started splashing the infested water all over themselves and drinking it. Some thought that using a handkerchief to filter the filthy water was going to make it safer to drink. How foolish they were! Nothing could have filtered that dirty scum-laden, bacteria-infested water, swarming with blowflies, to make it fit for human consumption.

Only a few minutes went by before a Japanese officer ran to the wallow and began hollering at the Americans in the water. Once again, none of us understood him, yet he continued to shout. He did not use any sign language to indicate there was trouble, but the fellows in the water ran back into line to continue the march. Then the unbelievable happened. The officer, with a big broad smile on his face, began prancing around the area where the Americans were lined up and ordered the guards to search our ranks for any men who had water soaked clothes. The guards picked them out of our group of marching men and lined them up on the road. Then the officer ordered the guards to shoot all of them. What a horrible massacre! And those of us forced to watch had to stand by helplessly. We knew if we attempted to interfere with the orders of the Japanese officer we also would be shot.

These past few horror-filled days helped me to evaluate my chance for survival. What would my priorities be? How would I deal with these overzealous conquerors of Bataan if they came for me? How would I be able to stay alive on what seemed to be a never-ending march to nowhere?

Hope is what kept most of us survivors alive on the death march. Hope that the starvation, the disease, and the agonizing effort to put one foot in front of the other would end when we got to wherever we were going. Some of us heard rumors that we would be exchanged for Japanese prisoners and that we would be taken care of in a U.S. hospital or other facilities. Others hoped that our capture was a brief bad dream and that we would soon be on our way home. Those were the optimists. Everyone, however, hoped at least for a destination where food and fresh water would revive us and where a shelter would protect us from the sweltering tropic sun and the stinging, slashing precipitation made up of rain and gritty sand.

Again, the one thing that kept me going was my determination to make it to that banana grove or mango tree or whatever I could see down the road. I had to have a goal, a place to march to. Most of the time we walked without thinking of where we were going, with our heads down, dejected. We're real failures, I thought to myself, but I must go on.

Many of the men on the march were just too weak and had too many illnesses to continue. If they stopped on the side of the road to defecate, they would be beaten within an inch of their lives or killed. Of course, with the small amount of food we were getting, we did not worry very much about having a bowel movement. Those men who had a bad case of dysentery, however, never knew when they would have to defecate.

On the fourth day of the march, I was lucky enough to be walking with two of my tank buddies, Walter Cigoi and Bob Bronge. Cigoi looked like a typical southern Italian. He was over six feet tall, with jet-black hair, a heavy beard that always seemed to need shaving, and a full head of wavy hair that made his strong, handsome, elongated face look sinister. His dark brown eyes were sunken a little, almost as if he had just awakened, but they seemed to dance from left to right, then back to the left again. Wally was very soft-spoken and never raised his voice, even when irritated or angry. From the day of the surrender, though, he was notably on edge about what was taking place.

Bronge, on the other hand, looked like he was from the northern part of Italy. With blond hair, bright blue eyes, and a firm, strong body, he had a loud voice that could be heard a block away. The life of the party, Bronge always had something funny to say and was liked by everyone; he was included in all get-togethers. Bronge stood just short of six feet and was built like a bear, with strong arms and a barrel chest that portrayed power. Everyone in Company B liked both Bronge and Cigoi. They were known throughout the entire battalion as the "Meatball Twins."

I was walking with Bronge and Cigoi when a Japanese officer came riding by on horseback. He was waving his samurai sword from side to side, apparently trying to cut off the head of anyone he could. I was on the outside of the column when he rode past, and although I ducked the main thrust of the sword, the end of the blade hit my left shoulder, missing my head and neck by inches. It left a large gash that had to have stitches if I were to continue on this march and continue living.

As the Japanese officer rode off, Bronge and Cigoi called for a medic to fall back to our position. The medic sewed up the cut with thread, which was all he had with him, and for the next two miles or so, my two friends carried me so that I would not have to fall out of line. We all knew that falling out of line meant certain death.

Cigoi and Bronge saved my life; I only wish I could have saved theirs. Military records show that Bronge died in Cabanatuan Prison Camp on July 31, 1942, of dysentery, and Cigoi died of the same disease in Formosa on November 3, 1942. Upon coming home, it was very difficult for me to see both of my friends' families and to answer questions about how their sons acted as soldiers and how they died. The emotional meetings with their parents left an indelible mark on my mind and heart that I will never be able to erase.

Each day on the march we trudged along like zombies. We walked from 6:30 in the morning till 8:00 or 9:00 at night. Most of the days we would get a few minutes' rest when the Japanese changed guards; otherwise it was hit and miss regarding a rest period. The guards were always fresh, for they only walked for about three miles and were relieved for the next three or four miles. This constant changing of the guards kept us always on edge because we never knew what the new group would want us to do or not to do. Moreover, the new guards were always trying to impress their fellow soldiers and, of course, the officers. In addition, being well-rested, they were able to walk at a faster pace than we were. Thus, we were fearful and apprehensive every hour of the march. I also made sure that I never again walked on the outside of the column of marching men.

Due to the poor road conditions, our deteriorating health, the lack of food and water, and our overall defeatist attitudes, we were able to walk only about a mile, or two at the most, for every hour on the march. With the added constant screaming and the beatings by the Japanese guards, we could merely trudge along the road at a snail's pace. I would wonder, where were they taking us? If they were going to kill us, why not do it where we could be buried along the side of the road and no one would ever know the difference? Walking with a destination in mind would have been much easier. If the Japanese had only told us to walk for seventy miles before we could rest or that we were going to a prison camp so we could work for them, it would have been better than walking for what appeared to be eternity.

Once again, we had not eaten in days, and we were nearly going out of our minds from thirst. We were all slowly becoming completely dehydrated, and we realized that we would die soon without water. The Japanese, we were told, planned on feeding us once we arrived in the town of Balanga, which was thirty-five miles from where we were taken prisoner. Under normal conditions, for a well-rested, properly trained, and adequately fed army, a march of this distance could be made in about nineteen hours. We prisoners were not in the condition necessary for a march of this type, or any type. We were tired, worn out, and in need of prolonged rest and medical attention. Also, the heat of the day seemed to suck any energy we had left.

Finally, on the fourth day, as we entered the town of Balanga, Filipino civilians stood along the sides of the road, throwing various food items to us: rice cakes, animal sugar cakes, small pieces of fried chicken, and pieces of sugar cane. At that moment, the sugar cane was more important to us than anything else. By peeling the bark off with our teeth and chewing the pulp, we were able to get enough liquid to satisfy our thirst and get the energy and nourishment found in its natural sugars. These Filipinos' gestures lifted our sunken spirits to a new high.

Suddenly, we heard shots ring out from somewhere in the middle of our marching group. Within seconds, the people along the side of the road scattered in all directions, for the Japanese soldiers were shooting at them for offering food to us prisoners. Two of the Filipinos started to run across the field, heading for a water hole. Three of the guards turned, aimed at the running Filipinos, and fired round after round in their general direction. The Japanese guards were not very good marksmen, so they just continued firing until the two men fell to the ground. The guards then ran over to the fallen men and began hollering at and kicking them, first in their backs, then directly in their heads. Next, the Japanese guards fired several shots at point-blank range into the men's prostrate bodies.

The guards watching over our marching group made us stop and watch the proceedings. Watching this made me feel woozy. I almost started to vomit, but there was nothing in my stomach to come up, so I just stood there with my eyes fixed in the direction of the slaughter. Then I tried to wipe away the scene from my mind as fast as I could. I knew what was happening; I did not have to watch it any longer to have another indelible memory barbarism. Once again, in the blink of an eye, more innocent people were slain by the conquering Japanese.

During the shooting and hollering, the Filipino civilians were running to get as far away as possible. Many of the Filipino prisoners on the march with us broke away and ran with their countrymen. Their goal was to enter the barrio, change clothes, and become just another civilian. Because it was starting to get dark, the escapees had a good chance of succeeding.

We continued marching into the center of town, and when nighttime finally came we were herded into a large warehouse. About 75 feet wide by 160 feet long, the building was used for storing grain, rice, sugar, and other agricultural products. Those men who could not find room inside the building were herded back outside into a large open area. I ended up inside the building. When the warehouse was filled to capacity, the guards pushed and shoved another couple hundred men inside. We were so tightly packed together that we sprawled on each other. When one of us had to urinate, he just did it in his pants, knowing that the following day the heat from the sun would dry them out. Those who had to defecate found their way back to one of the corners of the building and did it there. That night, the human waste covering the floor from those who had dysentery caused many others to contract this killing disease.

The stench, the sounds of dying men, and the whines and groans of those too sick to move to the back of the building became so unbearable that I put small pieces of cloth into my ears in a feeble attempt to drown out some of the noise. Nothing could be done about the smell. The air inside became putrid from the odors that accompanied the abnormal body functions associated with dysentery and the urine-soaked clothes the dirty men were wearing. The Japanese guards, also unable to bear the horrible smell, closed the doors to the warehouse, put a padlock on them, and kept watch from outside.

Getting accustomed after a few hours to both the noise and the smell, I allowed my mind to drift away from this nightmare and back home to Laura. Was she aware of what was happening? How was she standing up to the news of our capture? Or did she think I was killed? Did she think I was a coward? Did she still love me and want me as much as I wanted her? After I pondered all these questions, I began daydreaming about our life together. Oh, I thought, when would this nightmare come to an end? Then sometime in the middle of the night, I shook my head, got rid of the cobwebs, and began facing reality.

The following morning when the guards unlocked the doors, we staggered to the door of the warehouse totally dazed. We exited the dark and dreary warehouse with the quickness of scared animals. We lunged to get away from the smell of death that permeated the air around us. That morning, at least twenty-five men were carried out and thrown in the field behind the building. I was mesmerized by what I had seen. All I could do was cry and say to myself, "Oh God, please have mercy on their poor souls." I felt they deserved more than being left to the elements. Would it have been so hard to have allowed some of us to bury those poor men who died so miserably during the night?

In the courtyard of the warehouse, we saw a group of Japanese guards milling around. Within minutes, we were herded in their direction. There, to our surprise, in the center of all this activity we found three large kitchen pots, each containing rice. Those men without a mess kit received one ball of rice about three inches in diameter. Those with a mess kit were given one large scope of rice equivalent to the rice balls. At the far end of the field, another group of guards was rationing out hot tea. A man who had no container would borrow a friend's canteen or cup just long enough to obtain his ration of this most welcome liquid.

After the hunger of these last four days, we relished the food, however sparse. The Japanese reminded us how lucky we were that they had provided so much food and tea for us. As soon as we received our rations, they ordered us back on the road leading out of Balanga. The Japanese guards began laughing at us, and their grins and acknowledging nods showed that they were having fun taking advantage of us. We were pushed back into a marching column heading north. The march, obviously was going to continue. But where were we going and when would it end?

On many nights the Japanese guards would just stop the marchers and yell for them to sleep right on the rocky, dirty, dusty road, strewn with items discarded by the marchers and of course reeking with human waste. However, after the ordeal in the warehouse the previous night, my first choice would be to sleep outside even though the guards would roam around at all hours, prodding and kicking us and generally not allowing us more than a few minutes' uninterrupted rest.

During the first four days of the march, not only did we have to contend with the guards' physical abuse but we had to endure constant psychological torture that sapped our strength. Of course, the lack of food and water did not make things any better. There were also times during this ordeal that we suffered the pangs of loneliness. I thought back to when I was ten years old and I went to camp. That first night I had cried myself to sleep because I was so lonely and had lost the sense of security I had while at home. Now, many years later and ten thousand miles from home, I had the same feelings of alienation that I had had as a child. During the grueling, lonely hours of marching down that long road, my thoughts often turned to my past happy home life and to Laura. For what seemed like an eternity, but was actually only four days, I kept saying, "This is a bad dream; it can't be for real." When my spirits were low, I would think of Laura being there to comfort me and to tell me everything would be all right. In my thoughts, my family gave me hope, my friends showed me compassion, and my loved ones gave me the warmth and understanding I needed.

On the march we were always ready for a good rumor. We told each other, "When we reach Balanga, we will be taken by ship to Manila and then traded for Japanese prisoners. We'll be home soon," or "We'll be fed as soon as we get to the next barrio." In spite of persistent contradictory evidence, we lived on these rumors for the entire twelve days of the march.

On that fifth day of the march, I witnessed one of the most sadistic and inhumane incidents on the entire march and I did see some of the worst. We had just stopped for a brief rest while waiting for another group to catch up with us. When the other group finally arrived, the guard ordered us to stand up and start walking. One of the men had a very bad case of malaria and had barely made it to the rest area. He was burning up with fever and severely disoriented. When ordered to stand up, he could not do it. Without a minute's hesitation, the guard hit him over the head with the butt of his gun, knocked him down to the ground, and then called for two nearby prisoners to start digging a hole to bury the fallen prisoner. The two men started digging, and when the hole was about a foot deep, the guard ordered the two men to place the sick man in the hole and bury him alive. The two men shook their heads; they could not do that.

Once again without warning, and without any effort to settle the problem any other way, the guard shot the bigger of the two prisoners. He then pulled two more men from the line and ordered them to dig another hole to bury the murdered man. The Japanese guard got his point across. They dug the second hole, placed the two bodies in the hole, and threw dirt over them. The first man, still alive, started screaming as the dirt was thrown on him.

A group of about five or six of us witnessed this slaughter of innocent, unarmed men. As for me, I turned away and hid my face in my hands so that the Japanese could not see me throw up. It was one of many experiences I will never forget, one that made me sick for days. I asked myself over and over again, "Is this what I'm staying alive for? To be executed tomorrow or the next day, or the next? How will I be able to continue to endure these cruelties?" The strength of my resolve was once again challenged. After wiping away the tears and the vomit, with my eyes focused along the winding road in front of us, I sought another landmark to use as my objective. I had to have a goal; I had to go on.

Under normal conditions, in the real world, only two possible courses of action are open to us: either we can try to make our lives conform to our beliefs, or we can modify our beliefs to conform to our lives. Although true contentment may depend a great deal on which path we choose, under the conditions I faced on the march, I quickly found that in order to survive emotionally and physically I had to choose a little of each. Therefore, to survive I had to modify my beliefs to conform to what the Japanese wanted and at the same time try to make my life conform to my beliefs. For example, if the Japanese guards forced me to assist in burying a man who might still be alive, I quickly realized that although obeying the guards' commands did not conform to my beliefs, I still had to make my life conform to their demands in order to continue living. Had I insisted on conforming to my beliefs and on not burying a man who may still be breathing, then I too would have been killed, as were so many other prisoners, for disobeying a Japanese order. By altering my beliefs, I rationalized, I could increase my chances of being around later to help others. When a man is able to be successful without compromising his morals, it is a blessing, a blessing I had to forgo in order to survive.

I could not forget or understand the guards' actions. I had observed that the Japanese soldiers were well disciplined and obeyed their officers without question. I thought the officers would have known the Japanese army regulations pertaining to the handling of prisoners of war. These regulations can be found in Japanese Army Instruction Number 22, issued in February 1904. Chapter 1, article 2 states, "Prisoners of war shall be treated with a spirit of goodwill and shall never be subjected to cruelties or humiliation." The Japanese guards in the Philippines did not adhere in any way to these written instructions of their emperor. In fact, the Japanese interpreters told us on more than one occasion, "You are lower than dogs. You will eat only when we choose to feed you; you will rest only when we want you to rest; we will beat you any time a guard feels the need to teach you a lesson."

These Japanese army regulations were not followed at any time— not on the march or in any of our prison camps or on any of the work details. Obviously, these regulations were just words—not meant to be taken seriously—intended to influence world support and to show that the Japanese were "humane and caring" people. We found out the hard way that the Japanese guards were just the opposite. They seemed to revel in watching men being tortured, in the mistaken belief that they were superior and could do any thing they wanted to us.

Immediately after witnessing the execution-style burial, my mind turned to the positive side for survival. What, I wondered, can I do to overcome the total despair I felt when I was forced to witness these brutalities? Or, for that matter, forced to participate in the very march itself? What can I do to better prepare myself for survival?

First, I had to become determined and convince myself of what I can do. Second, I had to keep a positive attitude, and I had to realize that I could do anything the Japanese wanted me to do. Then, I quickly understood the importance of having the "smarts," or knowing when to do or not do certain things, such as when to walk faster and to become a part of another column of men. I vowed to walk with determination, my head high, shoulders back, and chest out. This posture would make me feel righteous, and the guards did not harass or belittle the men who looked healthy and in control of themselves.

We walked for several more days and often right into the night as well. Only twice were we offered food and water, and then very little of each. The four- or five-mile march from the town of Lubao became another nightmare. We did not know why we were being hurried the way we were. The guards yelled more and louder than ever before. We prisoners were subjected to constant hitting, pushing, and prodding every few minutes by a different guard.

At one point on this section of the march, we were ordered to double time, or run, and try to keep up with a fresh group of guards. As we passed a group of Japanese soldiers, our guards ordered us to stop. When we looked over to where the group of soldiers were, we saw an American soldier kneeling in front of a Japanese officer. The officer had his samurai sword out of the scabbard, and he was prancing around the other soldiers, showing off his skills in moving around the kneeling American while swinging his sword in every direction. Up went the blade, then with great artistry and a loud "Banzai," the officer brought the blade down. We heard a dull thud, and the American was decapitated. The Japanese officer then kicked the body of the American soldier over into the field, and all of the Japanese soldiers laughed merrily and went away. As I witnessed this tragedy and as the sword came down, my body twitched, and I clasped my hands in front of me, as if in prayer. I could hardly breathe. I could not believe this killing, just for pure sport, was happening again.

I have relived this scene hundreds of times since that day; I will never be able to get that scene out of my mind. At the time, however, despite my horror, I was determined to go on. I knew I had to survive this ordeal in order to let the world know what had happened.

It took two more days to reach the barrio of Orani, a distance of about fifteen miles. During these two days we again went without food or drinking water. Along the route, we witnessed more of the same kind of treatment we had seen the first four days. The Japanese were trying very hard to humiliate the Americans any way they could in front of the Filipinos, as if to prove Japanese superiority. Each time they killed or tortured an American, they would seek out some of the Filipinos on the sides of the road and force them to watch. Men, women, and children—there were no exceptions—all had to do whatever they were commanded by the guards. The Filipino people watched in stunned silence the many atrocities. They did what they had to do; but they watched with tears in their eyes and a prayer on their lips.

While marching through the town of Orani, we came to a group of Japanese standing on the side of the road. They would scream at us, *"Hayaku, hayaku"* (faster, faster). Before long we were almost running. Then as we passed the guards, the Filipinos standing on the edge of the road threw us balls of rice. If we caught one, we ate it on the run. If it dropped on the ground, then that meal was gone forever. Luckily most of us were willing to share, so no man went without some of the tidings our Filipino friends threw to us during the days on the march. Unfortunately, once we arrived at our first camp, there was no longer an opportunity to share. We each received only a small ration of rice for our early meal and another for our evening meal, with nothing more to share, no Filipinos throwing food at us, and no food growing on the side of the road that was easy picking. Our spirit of comradeship deteriorated. While I tried on many occasions to talk some of my tank buddies into eating their rice and not trading it for a cigarette, other prisoners preyed on sickly men and tried to convince them to trade away their life for a cigarette that supposedly would make them feel well again. It became a dog-eat-dog existence.

Finally, exhausted and barely able to stand, we were forced to continue the double-time march until we entered the city of San Fernando, about two kilometers away. What now, we wondered? Which one of us would be the next to die? How much more of this can our bodies endure?

Upon our arrival in San Fernando, the largest town on the march, we found a bustling little city scarcely touched by the soldiers and equipment associated with war. We Americans, on our withdrawal to Bataan, had not stopped in San Fernando long and neither had the Japanese in their hurry to locate and annihilate us. Some fairly large factories were located in this capital city of the Pampanga province. We noticed many Japanese soldiers milling around town in groups of four or five, all of them armed and all having a good time at the expense of the Filipinos.

We marched to the local railroad station, where we were told to rest. In the distance we could just see a group of boxcars being pulled by an old engine. We sat for about an hour along the railroad tracks before the train finally chugged its way into the little station. We were going to Manila, we heard, to be traded for Japanese prisoners. We would be home soon, we reasoned. We found out soon enough that these were all rumors, just rumors.

We were herded onto small railway boxcars. Cars that would normally hold ten animals, or perhaps twenty-five or thirty people, were jammed with eighty to one hundred men. We had to take turns just to sit down because there was not enough room for all of us to sit at the same time. Even sticking our feet out of the car did not leave enough room for the rest of the men. Some of the men were unable to breathe and were so tightly packed in the middle of the car that they suffocated while trying to get a breath of fresh air. The lucky ones were those who were able to get to the outside door and breathe some of the air that seeped in. We all stood shoulder to shoulder for most of the five-hour ride to Capas, the town near our final destination, a POW camp.

I was one of the lucky ones. I got a place at the door, and I was able to sit down with my legs dangling out. Enjoying fresh air with a little breeze and resting without a bayonet at my back provided such a relief. But then along came one of the guards, swinging a large cane like piece of bamboo. He swung the bamboo toward my feet and hit me just above the kneecap. I was taken by surprise, and I yelled out in pain—exactly what I do not remember, but it was not complimentary toward the Japanese guard who hit me. Then, without warning, he grabbed the handle of the sliding box car door and slammed it shut, once again striking my legs. My pain proved not in vain, however; my legs stopped the door from closing all the way. Because of this small opening, we were able to get a little fresh air, and while the train was moving, a significant breeze flowed into our boxcar.

As the train slowly rolled along with its cargo of thousands of diseased and dying soldiers, Filipinos stood along the track and threw rice balls wrapped in banana leaves, rice cakes made with sugar and spices, and pieces of cooked chicken to us in the boxcars. When I saw the Filipinos throwing food toward us, I shoved the door open another couple of feet, allowing us to retrieve much of the food. Little did they know at the time that their actions and generosity saved many of us from starvation. Their show of concern helped us get through another stage of this living hell.

Finally, the train stopped, and for the next ten minutes we stayed where we were. No one said a word; the quiet of the day was broken only by the moans of dying men. At this point, we still did not know what was going to happen to us. Were we going to be executed and placed in a mass grave out here in the country where no one would witness this? We were all afraid of the quiet. Even the Japanese guards said nothing. I barely heard a whispered prayer from within the boxcar. Oh God, I thought, please give us a chance. Do not let us die like animals in this remote section of the Philippines where we would never be found.

Only the living finally got off this train; the dead, we were instructed, were to remain inside the boxcars. Those men who could jumped out of the cars while the others slowly sat down at the edge of the door and slid off. I slowly jumped out of the boxcar, and as I tried to start walking, I fell on the side of the tracks. I realized that my cramped legs would not cooperate with my brain. I did not get up as fast as one of the guards thought I should, so he started beating me with the butt of his rifle on my back, legs, and neck. At one point, he made a thrusting movement toward me with his bayonet, a threat meaning death if I did not move. I got the message, and I got going.

We started to march again, not knowing where or for how long. All we knew was that we were being herded like cattle into a slaughtering bin. I felt like my body was burning up when I got out of the boxcar. After walking about two miles, I started to feel faint. I began wobbling back and forth across the column of marching men, and before long I dropped to my knees from sheer exhaustion and fever. Luck was with me once again, however, and I found myself being carried by my two friends, Cigoi and Bronge. They carried me for about a mile before I got my strength back and was able to make it on my own. How often in one person's lifetime will he be saved by the same people twice and within only a few days?

The columns of haggard, half-dead men—our dirty bodies drained of almost all fluids, our clothes tattered and torn, our faces unshaven—continued down the road. Along this narrow, unfinished road we admired the beautiful and tall, full mango trees and other rich green foliage. Then, every so often, we would see the body of a fellow American sprawled near the side of the road, the rich green foliage near his body splattered with dark brown blood.

Mobubiko Jimbo, author of *Dawn of the Philippines*, was a Japanese soldier who served in the Philippines during the Philippine campaign. In his book, he states that on the day Bataan surrendered all of the Japanese troops were told that at least seventy thousand prisoners were in the hands of the Japanese Imperial Army.

The following Japanese order, issued in Manila, explains in detail the reasons for many of the atrocities suffered by the prisoners who were forced to march out of Bataan.

> Every troop which fought against our Army on Bataan should be wiped out thoroughly whether he surrendered or not, and any American captive who is unable to continue marching all the way to the concentration camp should be put to death in the area 200 meters off the highway.

This order may be the justification the guards used during the march to kill any American who dropped out of the marching line for any reason. Once General Yamashita accepted the surrender of Bataan, his only interest was not in our welfare but in the final capitulation of all fighting forces in the Philippines. Then he could direct all energy and supplies toward Corregidor. Without a shadow of doubt, I am convinced that the slaughter of our surrendering troops was premeditated and authorized by someone with considerable authority, someone in the Japanese military high command in the Philippines.

Meanwhile, what ended up as the last day on the march nearly ended my life as well. My feet had swollen to about twice their normal size, and I had trouble keeping up with my column. I found out later that this problem plagued many of the men.

We had just been turned over to a group of well-rested Japanese guards, who got a kick out of yelling, pushing, and clubbing those of us who could hardly continue walking. The weak were their chosen prey. One of my walking buddies, seeing my swollen feet, suggested that I cut the sides of my boots. This seemed like a good idea, so not only did I cut the sides of my boots, but I also removed the shoestrings to allow for continued swelling. By this time I was so weak, hot, and tired that I seriously doubted whether my fever would permit me to continue any farther. As my health problems threatened to overwhelm me, I quickly realized that I had to continue and that I had to make it to wherever they were taking me. Then, like a miracle, my fever seemed to disappear. After what seemed a lifetime, but was in reality an excruciating eight miles, we finally saw the faint outline of barbed wire and typical Philippine huts in the distance. I felt as if the end of this forced march might at last be in sight.

8

Mitsui: "We Will Send You to Omuta"*

Linda Goetz Holmes

Editor's Note: *During the war, when Mitsui Mining Company had to keep up its war production quotas, it was eager to get as many white prisoners as possible as workers because they were more highly skilled laborers. Several thousand American POWs were shipped to Japan after their surrender in the Philippines and elsewhere and made to work in the mines of Japanese corporations such as Mitsui, Mitsubishi, Kawasaki, etc. that have now become some of the world's riches conglomerates. In this chapter Ms. Holmes describes the brutal treatment of a number of American POWs who were sent to do work as "slave" laborers in Japan's largest and most dangerous coal mines in the town of Omuta. These mines were owned by Mitsui Mining Company. Ms. Holmes has interviewed hundreds of ex-POWs to get their stories. Now Mitsui, the richest integrated trading company in the world, operates a large container fleet. The tremendous growth and prosperity of these companies were due in part to the help of American POW slave labor during the war. But to this day these companies have refused to compensate the former POWs who worked in their mines and factories for little or no pay. One of the ex-POWs now suing the Mitsui Company is Lester I. Tenney who was captured in the Philippines and worked in the Omuta mines (information supplied by Ms. Holmes). His account of the Bataan Death March is included in this volume (see chapter 7).*

"If you don't do exactly as you are told, we will send you to Omuta." Japanese guards at Cabanatuan, on the Philippine island of Luzon, would taunt their exhausted American captives, prodding the prisoners to do work they were already too weak from hunger and disease to perform. Most had barely survived the brutal, sixty-five-mile Bataan Death March—nine days of forced marching on empty stomachs with no water and very little rest. The remnants of Gen. Douglas MacArthur's Army of the Pacific mingled with sailors, Marines, and airmen as they stumbled around their second prison camp in the late spring of 1942.

---

* This passage is from chapter 5, "We Will Send You to Omuta," of Linda Goetz Holmes' *Unjust Enrichment: How Japan's Companies Built Postwar Fortunes Using American POWs* (Mechanicsburg, PA: Stackpole Books, 2001), pp. 44-53. Printed with permission of Linda Goetz Holmes.

The largest number of survivors was from the 200th Coast Artillery Regiment, a New Mexico-based unit that was the first to fire in World War II, and the last full unit to surrender in the Pacific. They were also the last army cavalry unit to use horses in battle. Fewer than 20 of the 1,800-man unit died in battle, but only half came home alive from Japanese captivity. None of the horses survived; one by one they were slaughtered and consumed for food in the last desperate weeks on Bataan. "We didn't know until after the war that we had eaten our horses," Leo Padilla remarked wistfully.[1]

Most Bataan survivors say theirs was a medical defeat, even more than a strategic one. "We were starved by our own people," is a bitter phrase one still hears at reunions of the American Defenders of Bataan and Corregidor, referring to the supplies that never came as they held out for five months. None had eaten anything close to a decent meal for two weeks when they finally ran out of ammunition too, and were forced to surrender.

So now they were at Cabanatuan, dispirited, sick, and watching comrades die at the rate of 100 a day. As many as 3,000 died at the Cabanatuan camp and "hospital" complex (which the men nicknamed the "Zero Ward" in a grim reflection of the survival rate) while it was the main holding center for American prisoners in 1942. By the time six months had passed, 5,000 Americans had died in Japanese captivity. Everyone at Cabanatuan was sure he would die if he stayed there.

Agapito "Gap" Silva remembered guards at Cabanatuan making the threat about Omuta, and wondering what place could possibly be worse than where they were now, still numb from the long march of death they had just endured, and faced with daily fear of being summoned for a work detail by the "white angel," a Japanese officer who wore a white uniform. Silva, from the 200th Coast Artillery, seemed to recall each day of captivity as if it were yesterday.

"We called him the 'white angel' because he was like the Angel of Death," Silva explained in a 1998 interview. "Each day we prayed the wouldn't pick us—because no one ever came back from his work detail." Could some place called Omuta really be more terrifying than a summons from the "white Angel?" Silva wondered. The answer, which their guards knew and many American prisoners would soon discover, was yes.

So when a group of Americans, including Silva, were told in the summer of 1943 that they were going to Japan, they were actually relieved, because by that time, they all believed staying at Cabanatuan was a certain death sentence. They had no idea lay ahead.

Japanese soldiers goading American captives with threats about Omuta knew their country's largest coal mine, operated by Mitsui Mining Company near the town of Omuta in Japan's Fukuoka district, was a hazardous and frightening place to work—even for an experienced miner. This had been especially true since 1923, when a devastating earthquake shifted the bedrock of Japan's home islands, and Mitsui had to seal off some of the deep mine's shafts and tunnels, declaring them too unsafe for anyone to work in. Despite that caution, cave-ins and explosions could happen unexpectedly anywhere in the vast mine, and all the workers knew it. So the threat of being sent to Omuta, used in more than one POW camp to keep prisoners in line, seemed like a strong one to a soldier assigned to guard POWs. There may have been some former Mitsui coal miners among those guards; by 1942, most able-bodied miners, along with factory and shipyard workers, had been conscripted into the Imperial Japanese armed forces.

The Mitsui family is the most powerful dynasty in Japan, outside of the Imperial Palace. Baron Takanaya Mitsui, who headed the vast Mitsui shipping, mining, and heavy industry empire, had studied in the United States; he was a 1915 graduate of Dartmouth College in Hanover, New Hampshire. Two years after his graduation, the family opened its huge coal-mining complex, the Miike mine at Omuta. Built by American engineers, it was for many years the largest coal mine in Japan, and operated until 1997. At its peak, the mine had nine levels, and its tunnels extended 700 feet under Omuta Bay.

Since the production of coal was vital to Japan's war effort, Mitsui's urgent request for the use of white prisoners was no doubt given a priority. Sure enough, in August 1943, the first group of 500 American POWs from Cabanatuan, including Gap Silva, arrived at Omuta, not because they had misbehaved, but because skilled workers were desperately needed if monthly production quotas were to be met, and Americans were a likely bunch to have many useful skills. Few, if any, had ever worked in a coal mine, but they had to learn on the job, in the pitch dark, working the already worked-out tunnels, which had been sealed off for the past twenty years. And if one was injured or killed, he could always be replaced. Or so the prevailing philosophy of the POWs' new "employers" seemed to be, judging from the brutal treatment and minimal training and equipment the prisoners were given.

When the first 500 Americans arrived at Mitsui's Omuta coal mine in mid-August 1943, still dazed from their voyage aboard the *Clide Maru* (nicknamed Benjo "toilet" *Maru* by the POWs) and a long, stifling ride from the port of Moji crammed into railroad boxcars, the bedraggled prisoners were the first white POWs townsfolk had seen, and their greeting was a barrage of stones and catcalls.

The POWs also got a bittersweet taste of home at Omuta. Army staff sergeant Harold Feiner, a New York electrician by trade, remembered noticing the familiar labels of General Electric, Honeywell, Joy drilling equipment, and Ingersoll-Rand compressors. Mitsui had hired American engineers and purchased almost exclusively American equipment to build its Omuta mine in 1917. Little did those American engineers know that a quarter century later, their fellow American citizens-soldiers and civilians-would be forced to work on American equipment in this now-hostile land with no choice, almost no food, long hours, no pay, no safety gear, and next to no clothing.

The Omuta site had been designated as Fukuoka Camp No. 17, and Mitsui had built flimsy, wooden barracks on company property for the POWs, with no heating. Despite the fact that coal was all around, there was apparently not enough available to warm the prisoners, except for one hour a day. At the end of the hour, a company employee would walk through the long barracks to the small coal stove, open the door, and remove the few warm coals with a small scoop—even on the coldest winter nights.

Soon the barracks were crawling with fleas, lice, and other vermin. Prisoners slept on mats on the bare floor, seven to a chamber. They were separated from one another by a flimsy curtain, which Amado Romero of the 200th Coast Artillery remembered, "Might as well have been electrified...prisoners who touched [it] were severely beaten."[2] Blankets were thin and infested with vermin. No one had warm enough clothing; the winter of 1943 to 1944 was the coldest in forty-two years in Japan.

Harold Feiner recalled the irony of being handed woolen uniforms, which had been looted by the Japanese from British supplies in Hong Kong. "But as soon as we got them, we were told to put them on the shelf for 'special occasions.' We were never allowed to wear them, except during a rare visit by a Red Cross inspector." Feiner did not hide the bitterness in his voice, even though he told the story with a little chuckle, when he described one of those rare

Red Cross visits. It was Christmas 1944, and the men were told to put on those still freshly creased British uniforms. "By that time we were pretty skinny," Feiner says. "They made us wear scarves so the inspectors wouldn't see how scrawny our necks were." Then, Japanese officers broke open some of the locked-up Red Cross boxes, and placed food in front of each starving man, which he was not allowed to touch. "After the inspectors left, the Japanese took all the food away from us. We never got to eat even one bite!" Feiner exclaimed, shaking his head at the memory.[3]

Dr. Marcel Junod, head of the International Committee of the Red Cross in Tokyo during the latter part of the war, wrote a chilling description of such a visit: "The prisoners, British and American, did not dare to speak, but bowed low to the Japanese, their arms kept tightly to their sides until their heads were almost on a level with their knees."[4]

One ex-POW said he wished the Swiss inspectors could have seen the Japanese guards eating the Red Cross food. Prisoners remembered that when the Red Cross inspectors visited the clinic set up by POW physician Dr. Thomas Hewlett at Omuta, the Mitsui employees put the camp cooks in the beds as patients, and hid the sick men in the mines. So the Red Cross report read: "Sufficient clothing; good medical care."[5]

Perhaps the most bizarre aspect of barracks life for the prisoners was the staff who was in charge of them. "Most of them were wounded or disabled veterans from the China occupation, and the Rape of Nanking," Feiner said. "They must have been driven a little crazy because of what they had seen and done in China," he speculated, "because their behavior was completely unpredictable. One minute they were in their quarters; the next minute they would rush out and start screaming at us or beating us for no reason. Then they would go back to their quarters. It was very nerve-racking!" Some POWs wondered if perhaps their barracks supervisors were listening to radios, and when they heard of yet another Allied victory, they would vent their wrath on the nearest prisoners.

Once the workday started, POWs were completely under the control of Mitsui employees, who arrived at the barracks each morning to escort the prisoners to the mine and order them to meet an impossible quota of output. Some of the most severe beatings any prisoner received were administered on the job, by company employees. If a prisoner was injured while working—a frequent occurrence in such hazardous conditions—the accident would be the excuse for a relentless thrashing. The most brutal beatings were handed out by a company superintendent in charge of explosives, whom the POWs nicknamed the "dynamite man" because he had a temper that matched his specialty. To the great relief of many POWs, the "dynamite man" died in an accident in the mine, when he became caught in a conveyor belt and was crushed.

In fact, the injury rate was so high at Omuta that an investigator for the War Crimes Trials told Mel Routt that Omuta was put at the top of his list, to visit first, for that reason. The investigator, an attorney from Greenville, Kentucky, named Robert Humphrey, Jr., took a series of twenty-four photographs of the POW camp facilities at Omuta, as the company was dismantling the buildings and covering the site with dirt in early 1947. He offered them for sale to ex-POWs who had been at the camp, and Routt purchased the set.

Harold Feiner spent 1,243 days as a prisoner of the Japanese, most of them at Omuta. Even fifty-five years later, when he walks he leans slightly to the left, because he suffered permanent skeletal damage from being forced, day after day, to hoist loads too heavy for his emaciated body to carry. In a room where Feiner's fellow members of the American Defenders of Bataan and Corregidor are gathered, one can almost pick out the ones who toiled at Omuta. Many walk bent slightly forward; for the rest of their lives, these men have been unable to stand fully straight. This is their legacy from Mitsui employees who forced them to work twelve- and fourteen-hour shifts, day after day, in tunnels barely four feet high-or less.

"Sometimes the ceilings were so low, we had to crawl on our bellies like a snake, wearing nothing but a G-string," Frank Bigelow, a sailor from the *USS Canopus* recalled, the disgust plain in his voice as he described wiggling his six-foot-six frame along dank passages. "You had a little rubber band for your head, with a little battery light at the forehead—that was our 'hardhat miner's cap,'" Bigelow sneered. Gap Silva said the prisoners were issued rubber split-toe flip-flops, and when those wore out, no new footwear was issued. Most POWs were forced to work barefoot in the mine.

And always there was the fear. When the POWs discovered that Mitsui was opening tunnels that had been sealed off, and ordering the prisoners to enter those tunnels for the first time in two decades, they were terrified. "You have no idea how scared we were, every day, to go into that mine," Bigelow explained in a 1996 interview.

Mel Routt said the prisoners were given just ten days to learn the names of tools, and the various job assignment orders in Japanese. But what they needed most, and didn't have, was experience—and the skills needed to do such hazardous work with some degree of safety. Army master sergeant Frank Stecklein recalled: "We rode a cable car down [the shaft]. I felt as though I was going to Hell and prayed all the way down."[6]

"We were 'pulling pillars'—the most dangerous work you can do in a mine," Frank Bigelow remembered. "In this country a miner would get paid a high premium for doing such work, if you could get him to do it. And we were made to do that kind of thing every day. When a tunnel is all worked out, just a thin pillar of coal is left. It's all that's holding up a ceiling. We were supposed to pull down those pillars as we left the tunnel, and the ceiling would collapse behind us."

But one day part of a ceiling fell on Bigelow's leg, because he didn't quite move fast enough. He found himself pinned under a rock, 1,600 feet below the mine's surface. Bigelow wondered how his friends carried him up so many vertical levels to the top of the mine on that awful January day in 1944.

> The Mitsui foreman wouldn't let my buddies carry me to the "hospital." He made them lay me on the stone floor in what we called the "Buddha" room, a small shrine at the entrance to the mine, where we had to go in and bow to Buddha every morning. Then he ordered them back to work, and I lay there in the freezing cold for another five hours, till the work shift was over. Later Dr. Thomas Hewlett, our camp doctor, told me the only thing that kept me from bleeding to death was I got so cold my blood coagulated. He tried to save my leg, but with no medicine, and no anesthetic, eventually he had to cut it off. I remember asking him, "Doc, you got an aspirin or a shot of whiskey or something you can give me?" He answered, "If I had a shot of whiskey, I'd take it myself." Then a couple of men held me down while he did the job. But he saved my life![7]

Gap Silva was also made to wait without assistance after the mine ceiling collapsed on him in September 1944, on orders of the Mitsui foreman. Silva suffered four broken ribs, a fractured right pelvis, and two crushed vertebrae on the lower part of his back. "For the first eight weeks I could not walk. Two corpsmen were assigned to help me. I was given massage and hot tubs. Gradually, I was able to walk; gradually I recovered. I was sent back into the mine."

Silva also described injury inflicted by a Mitsui employee, for a minor infraction:

> Another time prior to the mine injury, another POW and I were late in getting in line to go to the mess hall. A Japanese guard caught us, took us to the guard house where he

swatted our buttocks with a pole two by two [inches] by six feet. He swung the stick three times like a baseball bat. We cried out each time because the pain was excruciating. Each time we cried he would swat us again. Our buttocks got so swollen we could not sit for three weeks.[8]

Army corporal James Stacy described the daily working conditions at Omuta:

I worked in water from ankle deep to waist deep. [I] had cold water dripping on my head, back and shoulders all the time.... Our labor there was anywhere from ten to fourteen hours daily.... I was forced back to the mines to work with [my] left hand swollen up so big I couldn't even bend or move my finger. I was beaten [by a Mitsui employee] with a pick handle and a 2 x 2. This time I had such a beating that my whole buttock was as bloody as a piece of beef steak. I had to be carried to camp.... I was beaten on several occasions.[9]

The word "hospital" requires quotation marks when describing what passed for medical facilities at company-owned POW worksites in Japan or, for that matter, any of the 170-odd places where Allied prisoners were held by the Japanese during the war. Despite the dedication and daily miracle-working by POW doctors (when a camp was lucky enough to have a medical doctor or corpsman), the lack of medicine, supplies, and surgical equipment was heartbreaking— specially because Red Cross boxes containing such vital and life-saving equipment remained locked up in warehouses at just about every place where POWs were confined. Omuta was no exception. In a postwar report, Dr. Hewlett wrote:

Following the exodus of the [Japanese] guard detail in August 1945...we found several warehouses packed with Red Cross food and medical supplies. The dates of receipt and storage indicated that these items had reached Japan prior to August 1943. Thus while we suffered from lack of food, essential medicines, surgical supplies and X-ray equipment, these items, gifts of the American people, were hoarded in warehouses during our two years in Japan. The reason we were denied these essentials remains a top secret of the Imperial Japanese Army.[10]

Still, the POWs were lucky to have a multinational team of physicians, headed by Dr. Hewlett, who credited Baron Mitsui with seeing to it that the clinic at least had adequate space for beds, even if medicine, equipment, and supplies were sadly lacking. The company had a fairly well-equipped hospital on the property, but the prisoners were afraid to be treated by Japanese doctors, and requested their own facility.

If the fear of death from injury was ever-present, the fear of starvation was a daily reality, as these prisoners felt their bodies gradually weakening. Once again, the meticulous record kept by Dr.

Hewlett tells the grim, graphic story. Dr. Hewlett notes that the minimum daily caloric requirement, a balance of protein, carbohydrates, fat, and vitamins, is 2,800 calories for a young male aged twenty to twenty-five doing "moderate labor." But the diet at Camp No. 17 in Omuta in 1943-44 was 80 percent rice and 20 percent filler, and amounted to 597 calories for the men being sent out to work, 469 calories for men confined to quarters, and just 341 calories for men in the camp "hospital." (The Japanese during World War II had a practice of not feeding sick prisoners at all in most locations; those at Omuta were lucky to be allocated anything. What they got was usually sneaked in by comrades.)

By 1944-45, the last year of their captivity, Dr. Hewlett's records show that the food allocation for prisoners had become 60 percent rice and 40 percent filler, with just "traces" of vitamin content; caloric intake for the men had dropped to under 500 calories for men going to work, 408 calories for men in quarters, and just 153 calories for men too sick to work.[11]

Little wonder that the average weight loss for prisoners in Japanese captivity was between 70 and 100 pounds; most said they weighed between 80 and 90 pounds when the day of liberation finally came. Their families never saw these POWs at their worst, because by the time they were transported from camp, they had been eating air-dropped real food, courtesy of the U.S. Navy and Air Force, for at least two weeks. But half a century later, their bodies and eyes are still struggling with the long-term effects of such severe malnutrition.

An incident referred to by the ex-prisoners as "the truckload of oranges" illustrates just how precarious their nutrition was; as told by Harold Feiner:

> In the summer of 1944 many of us began to go blind. Dr. Hewlett told the camp commander we needed vitamin C. A truckload of small oranges [mikan] appeared, and we ate them up, skin and all. And we began to be able to see again![12]

Harold Feiner also recalled how persistently Dr. Hewlett tried, every day, to pry loose medical supplies and food for his comrades. "Each day, the Mitsui company doctor would accompany Dr. Hewlett on his rounds," Feiner said softly. "Dr. Hewlett would say 'We need this, we must have that,' and the Japanese doctor would say, 'tomorrow, tomorrow'—always, it was 'tomorrow.' But tomorrow never came," Feiner added, shaking his head as his voice trailed off.

For the survivors of Mitsui's Fukuoka Camp No. 17, their tomorrows began when the emperor of Japan broadcast his message of surrender on August 15, 1945. For many of their comrades, it was already too late. For those who came home, their postwar lives have been marked by the effects of malnutrition, breathing coal dust, and post-traumatic stress. Not one was restored to full health in which to enjoy his hard-won freedom. A total of 1,859 prisoners, including 821 Americans, were sent to Mitsui's Omuta coal mine. Despite the high injury rate, 1,733 survived. Forty-nine Americans died. Fewer than 200 of those Americans who toiled at Omuta were still alive in 1999.

When Gap Silva finally returned home in September 1945, he was met with a painful example of what life over the past three years had been like for families who had received no word from or about their loved ones. When he ran to greet his father, instead of a joyful smile of recognition, the elder Silva traced his fingers over his son's face. Doctors told him that the windy nights he had spent crying for his son as he worked in the rail yard at Gallup, New Mexico, had dried his tear ducts and eye moisture, eventually causing blindness.

"In my whole experience as a prisoner of war, that was the hardest thing to bear," Silva said.

Notes

1. Conversation with the author, San Antonio, Tex. May 22, 1999.
2. Letter to the author, June 22, 1992.
3. Series of interviews with the author, Louisville, KY. May 1998.
4. Marcel Junod, *Warrior without Weapons: The Story of Dr. Marcel Junod of the International Committee of the Red Cross* (Geneva: International Committee of the Red Cross, 1982).
5. Swiss inspector's report August 15, 1944, on file at New Mexico National Guard headquarters, Santa Fe, N. Mex.
6. Frank Stecklein, unpublished memoir, sent to the author July 1998.
7. Series of conversations with the author, March 1996-March 2000.
8. Statement written to the author June 18, 1998.
9. Extract from service record, sent to the author July 1998.
10. Extract from report by Col. Thomas Hewlett, M.D., to a reunion of the American Defenders of Bataan and Corregidor, August 1978. In 1997 the author discovered the reason for undistributed Red Cross boxes. It is the subject of the next chapter.
11. Ibid.
12. Conversation with the author, September 14 and December 8, 1999.

Part III

Psychological Responses

9

The Nanjing Massacre:
The Socio-Psychological Effects

Zhang Lianhong (translated and edited by Peter Li)

The savage cruelty of the Nanjing Massacre was an event seldom seen in human history. The physical and spiritual injury inflicted on the people by the invading Japanese troops were deep and massive. Using historical documents and close to 100 interviews with surviving victims and eye-witnesses, the author of this article attempts to study the socio-psychological effects on the citizens of Nanjing.

I. On the Eve of the Attack

Fears of the upcoming battle for Nanjing actually began on 15 August when the Japanese initiated air raids on the city. The bombings not only incurred heavy damage to property, but more importantly, they were an assault on the sense of security of the people of Nanjing. According to the reports of the Japanese Imperial armed forces, from 15 August to 13 December when Nanjing fell, the planes of the Japanese Navy flew more than fifty missions over Nanjing, using more than 800 airplanes, and unleashing 160 tons of bombs.[1] Other sources, however, indicate that the actual number of missions may be as great as 110. If we were to count the average number of times that the air raid sirens sounded on any given clear day during that period, it would be more than three times.

Almost every day the newspapers would write about the number of people killed and wounded. All the big newspapers in Nanjing reported that on the morning of 27 August, from 1-3 AM when Japanese planes bombed Nanjing, 400–500 houses were destroyed, over a hundred people killed, and several hundred injured.[2] Bombs exploded everywhere, and the constant reporting of the devastation caused by the air attacks increased people's fears steadily.

119

The constant air raids made it intolerable for many people. The residents of Nanjing began to flee in large numbers. The wealthy ones loaded their belongings on boats and headed to the interior up the Yangzi River. Those less wealthy headed for northern Jiangsu and Anhui province to stay with friends and relatives. The poor planned to flee to the countryside if and when the Japanese began to attack the city. There were also those who believed that war had nothing to do with the common people; no matter who's in power, the common people will be allowed to live. But this was not an ordinary civil war, it was a war between two nations. By the latter part of November, the majority of the people had already fled Nanjing. According to the records, the population of Nanjing was more than a million before the war. By the end of November, however, the population was down to about half a million.[3]

Because the population was reduced by half, there were few people on the streets. Many houses were empty, so the landlords voluntarily stopped collecting rent from many of their tenants. Goods exceeded demand, so the prices began to drop. For example, *The New Citizen*, a Nanjing newspaper, advertised special reduced prices for pasteurized milk, newsprint, oils, and ink, etc. Many stores and businesses closed down. Along Taiping Road only one-fourth of the stores were doing business.[4] The larger hotels were also closed down. Only the bars continued to do a thriving business despite the dangers of the war. For example, "the Lingnan Tavern along Zhongshan North Road, the Houdefu at the Zhongyang Shopping Center, the Bieyoutian by the Fuzi Temple continued to do business as usual. Many of those who loved eating and drinking were not afraid to die; they gathered there like ducks."[5]

During the month of September, the number of marriages and engagements suddenly increased compared to previous years. The Nanjing newspapers were full of marriage announcements. Advertisements seeking marriages also began appearing even in the large papers, such as *The New Citizen*. According to Minnie Vautrin, an American professor at Jinling Women's College, the reason for the sudden increase in the number of marriages was "principally because many parents whose daughters were already grown or engaged wanted their daughters to be married before anything unfortunate happened to them."[6]

Under continuous aerial attacks and constant propaganda from the newspapers about the ability of the Nationalist forces to defend

Nanjing, the people who were terrified of the attacks gradually became more calloused. The newspapers wrote "the people of Nanjing are now used to the Japanese air-raids. Almost every day, when the sirens sound, they routinely head for the air-raid shelters without any sense of fear or panic."[7] But for most of the people, war was still a frightening experience. The exploding bombs and speeding bullets did not distinguish civilians from soldiers. After the middle of November, due to the establishment of the wartime capital in Chongqing, the evacuation of government personnel, the rumors of Japanese cruelty, the intimidating propaganda from the Japanese military, the influx of panicky refugees from the Shanghai-Ningbo Railway, and the withdrawal of large numbers of foreigners from the city fueled the psychological fears of the people. On the main roads there were lots of desperate people looking for safety: "People in the northern part of the city were moving to the southern part, people in the south were moving to Xuanwu Lake (located in the north); the people in the Xuanwu region were moving to the countryside, and those in the countryside were moving back into the city. Just by moving from where they were before made them feel safer."[8]

At this most desperate moment, the foreigners who remained in Nanjing decided to follow the Shanghai model and set up several Nanjing Safety Zones to take in refugees. Starting on 4 November 1937, refugees began moving into the safety zones. On the 8th, the Committee of the International Safety Zone officially announced that the refugees should go to the safety zones. The announcement said, "The people within the zone will be much safer than people elsewhere." In Rabe's Diary for the 11th, "The streets in the safety zones were filled with people. They were no longer afraid of the sound of bombing in the city; they have more faith in the 'safety zone' than I do." On the 12th, many of the refugees crowded into Rabe's home, "thirty people were sleeping in my study, three people were in the coal room in the basement, eight women and children were sleeping in the servants' bathroom, the remaining one hundred people were either in the air raid shelter, under the open air in the yard or on the pebbled walkways."[9] The safety zones organized by the Westerners became a haven for the panic-stricken refugees.

II. During the Nanjing Massacre

Even before the attack on Nanjing, the Japanese first waged a campaign of fear to try to break down the people's psychological line of defense and destroy their determination to resist. Originally "many inhabitants of the city earnestly felt relieved when the Japanese troops entered Nanjing, because they thought the threat of war was over and the air raids would end."[10] However, once the Japanese troops entered the city, they did not distinguish between civilians and the military. The widespread slaughter and rape quickly dispelled any dreams that the refugees might have had about the Japanese. The refugees of the entire city were thrown into panic and fear.

All the alarmed, frightened, and helpless refugees began to seek safety in their own ways. Those who stayed in their own homes began to flock to the International Safety Zones set up by the Westerners. Except for those refugees who were protected by the Westerners, all the rest wore the rising sun insignia on their arms, or held up Japanese flags. Almost all the young women had their faces smeared with soot from the bottom of cooking pots, and dressed in old, ragged oversized jackets making themselves look dirty, old, and ugly. Some of the girls cut their hair and disguised themselves as young men.[11] All the women interviewed by the author had similar stories to tell. One 82-year-old woman, Ding Rongsheng, told the author that when she was hiding in the safety zone she did not wash her face for a whole month.[12] Many of the other women, "in order to avoid being raped, pasted lots of medicinal plasters (*gaoyao*) all over their bodies. When the Japanese soldiers saw them, they turned away with disgust. At first this worked, but later this trick didn't work either."[13]

Faced with the unbelievable cruelty of the Japanese troops and constant threat of death, the refugees lost all sense of reason and logic. Very few resisted; they were mostly just passively waiting for inevitable death. One military correspondent reported that 100 to 200 Chinese watched paralyzed as their compatriots were bayoneted to death five at a time.[14] When one or two Japanese soldiers were raping Chinese women in front of large numbers of Chinese men, the majority did not interfere.[15] In the face of evil, justice became cowardly, and the goodness of human nature in the face of terror took an ugly twist.

During the massacre, the line of psychological defense became very fragile; just the sound of the Japanese soldiers' boots set off pangs of fear in the hearts of the refugees.[16] On 1 January 1938, the Japanese established the puppet Autonomous Association by the

Drum Tower of the city. The refugees were herded onto the square to celebrate the occasion. When firecrackers were set off, many of the refugees thought the Japanese had opened fire on them. They immediately fell to the ground and did not get up until it was all over.[17] No matter how hard the Japanese tried to assure them, the refugees no longer trusted the Japanese. When the Japanese tried to recruit coolie workers, the coolies all believed that they were going to be shot, so they tried to escape at every opportunity.

As the massacres and rapes became more violent, the people's hopes for the Nationalist forces became more desperate. A rumor, poster, slogan, or rapid gunfire in the middle of the night would create much unfounded hope. According to Mr. Jiang Gonggu's diary for 5 January 1938, "Recently, our guerilla forces were attacking fiercely close to the city walls. We could hear their mortar fire during the night. During this time of helplessness, we would go to the backyard and listen to the sound of the shooting and try to determine how far they were from the city."[18] Some of the incidents would bring tears and laughter at the same time. On 8 January, "there was a rumor that Chinese troops had already entered the city to liberate the people. The Chinese washerwomen working at the Japanese Embassy carried arms-full of stuff to bring home. When they reached Jinling Women's College, rumor has it that the Japanese had already left the Embassy, and these women raided the place and were returning home with their loot. In a flash, a group of women climbed over the barbed-wire fence surrounding the embassy to take their turn at looting the embassy."[19]

When the Nationalist government's defending troops deserted the city, the refugees trapped in the city turned to the twenty-some Westerners who stayed in the city as their only hope. The residences and offices were the best places to hide. Jinling University and Jinling Women's College, during the height of the onrush, accommodated 30,000 and 10,000 refugees respectively. Even the Japanese themselves believed that these were the safest places. On 20 January 1938, a young Japanese officer, who had to leave Nanjing, went to see Minnie Vautrin and asked her to shelter his twenty-year-old Chinese girlfriend and her fourteen-year-old sister.[20] In the eyes of the refugees, the Westerners became the only true "saviors." Wherever the Westerners went, they were surrounded by refugees like a brood of young chicks flocking around the mother hens. Before the Nanjing Massacre, whenever the Chinese saw Westerners, they would call them condescendingly "foreign devils." But after the massacre, they had a thorough change of heart. Vautrin and Rabe were now given the name of "Living Buddhas." On 17 February 1938, when Minnie Vautrin held a farewell tea party for John Rabe, two to three thousand refugees from Jinling Women's College kneeled on the lawn crying and begging Rabe not to leave.[21] "When the Japanese announced that they were going to do away with the refugee camps, thousands of women knelt down in front of us, and swore that they would die in the camps rather than return to their homes to be raped and killed by the Japanese."[22] The original intention of the Japanese was to make the Chinese less dependent on the Westerners, but in the end they discovered that their policies made the Chinese more dependent on the Westerners than before. Even the Chinese policemen under the Japanese puppet regime could not help but regard the Westerners with respect.

III. The Aftermath of the Massacre

The six weeks of continuous burning, killing, raping, and looting that followed the taking of Nanjing created a gigantic psychological wound. The people were filled with unspeakable fear. In the author's interviews with the survivors, many told us that during daylight hours, people all gathered on the streets. There was safety in numbers. Only after dark, did they dare go back to their homes to sleep. For a long time after the "pacification" there were very few young women to be seen on the streets of Nanjing. Only old women dared to appear on the streets. During the period of Japanese occupation, everyone lived in great fear and stress. When you entered or left the city gates, the slightest mistake could result in punishment by kneeling on the ground or standing with a brick on your head. Among the males interviewed by the author, almost all of them had been physically punished by either the Japanese soldiers or the Japanese merchants.

After six weeks of unceasing brutality, the family social structure also changed greatly. Life became increasingly more difficult. According to a survey made by Professor Lewis S. C. Smythe in 1938, 11.7 percent of the families remaining in Nanjing, or 5,500 households, could be considered to be incomplete households; of these, 26 percent were headed by women. In the safety zones, the numbers were much higher, reaching 35 percent. The report also pointed out that in March 1938, only 9 percent of the people in the entire city were employed. Families that were inadequately provided for reached a total of 94 percent.[23] In addition, the Japanese troops stationed in Nanjing constantly seized the homes and property of the residents. In 1938, Japanese troops occupied more than 4,000 homes; the number of those uprooted as a result reached 7,617. In 1939, the various units of the Japanese army occupied more than 500 acres of land; this affected more than 1,463 families.[24] The occupation of homes and property, as well as Japanese control of the economy, brought added hardship to the people.

During the period of the Japanese occupation, the brothels and opium houses, which the Nationalist government tried to eradicate, were promoted by the Japanese on a large scale. The Japanese established many "comfort stations," which provided sexual services to the troops; government-operated newspapers placed large advertisements for houses of prostitution in order to attract customers. According to the latest figures compiled by the author, the Japanese established more than forty comfort stations in Nanjing. For a country with a strong emphasis on traditional morality with regard to sexual behavior, to have this open display of sexuality was extremely disturbing and damaging to the moral well-being of the people.[25] In addition, "before the Japanese came, the Nationalist government and others before it had outlawed opium smoking and the punishment for drug dealing was death, but within a year of Japanese occupation, the number of opium dens grew like reeds along the river bank." "The Chinese coolies between the ages of 10 and 30 years of age were paid with heroin."[26] According to a survey conducted by Miner Searle Bates in 1938, the number of legal opium houses numbered about 175, and there were another thirty stores just for selling opium. A conservative estimate of the number of people addicted was 50,000, or about one-eighth of the population of Nanjing at the time. Along the street from Jinling Women's College to the South Gate, there were twelve stores that sold "official opium."[27] The comfort stations brought relief to the Japanese soldiers, and the brothels and opium houses were important means of implementing the policy of colonization. They were not only profitable, but, more importantly, they weakened the determination of the people to resist and to better themselves.

No matter how strong the Japanese may have seemed, most Chinese believed that Japanese rule would not last long. They looked down on those who became the henchmen of the Japanese. Even those traitors and collaborators who joined the puppet government often revealed their sense of inferiority. According to the observations of the German Ambassador Rosen, "in his conversations with his Japanese colleagues, he understood that the newly formed government in Nanjing was not regarded highly. It had a difficult time dealing with the Japanese authorities, especially with regard to food which was desperately needed by the residents."[28] Some of the women who were raped by the Japanese, when they discovered that they were pregnant, immediately went to the hospital or took other measures to abort the pregnancy. In the eyes of the residents, the Japanese in Nanjing were like "monkeys without tails."

The tragedy brought on by the massacre cannot be expressed in words. And the high-pressured occupation tactics and senseless looting made the people of Nanjing hate the Japanese with a vengeance. In 1939, Professor Miner Searle Bates conducted a survey of eighty individuals in different occupations, of different ages, and with different educational backgrounds. The results indicated that "in the next fifty years, the inhabitants of this region would not believe anything good said about the Japanese. The effect of the Japanese soldiers on the lives of individuals and their families—including those who worked for the puppet government—were unspeakably painful."[29] The diaries of Minnie Vautrin verified this. Among the nine people in her neighborhood, "not one person had anything good to say about the Japanese, they hated the Japanese to the bone."[30]

IV. The Unforgettable Images of the Nanjing Massacre

When Japan surrendered in August 1945, the day finally came for the people of Nanjing to reclaim their country. The inhabitants were prepared to give the Japanese a beating but were thwarted because the Nationalist government announced a policy of "return enmity with kindness." After 1949, England and America became arch enemies of China, and after that all political movements were directed toward exposing the crimes of British and American imperialists. As a result, those who suffered the holocaust of the Nanjing Massacre had to bury their sorrow and memories in their hearts.

But in the eighties, after the textbook controversy, the Japanese rightists' denial of the Nanjing Massacre became more vehement. The words and actions of the Japanese rightists fueled widespread renewed interest in this long-forgotten period of history. This led to the establishment of special non-governmental research organizations and academic institutions for the study of this period of history. In 1985 planning began for a Memorial Hall Commemorating the Victims of the Nanjing Massacre. At 10 o'clock, on every December 13th, a remembrance service is held for those that were killed during the massacre and survivors. News of the textbook controversy, the confessions of the Japanese soldier Azuma Shiro, the discovery of John Rabe's diaries, and Li Xiuying's case against the Japanese government, all received widespread coverage in the press and became part of the public memory of the Nanjing Massacre. Using the Azuma Shiro case as the focus, the author conducted a sociological survey and found out that 89 percent of the people understood the Azuma Shiro case and that 84 percent continue to pay attention to the case.[31]

It is unfortunate that the events of the Nanjing Massacre have been catapulted from the past into the present. The aged victims and survivors of that event must once again experience those painful moments. For the many wives who lost their husbands, orphans who lost their parents, husbands who lost their wives, mothers and fathers who lost their children, and the thousands upon thousands of women who suffered humiliation and degradation it is like reopening an old wound to hear Rightists say the Nanjing Massacre never happened. Every time the aged survivors heard in the news that the Japanese denied the Nanjing Massacre, they could not sleep at night. It was as if the sounds of the boots of the Japanese soldiers were once again being heard. The tragedy that had occurred sixty years ago was going to be replayed. There was Meng Xiuying, who, after being interviewed by the author, begged the author not to reveal her name or picture because she was afraid that the Japanese would still come to kill her.[32] For the older generation, who had suffered at the hands of the Japanese in the past, to hear the denial is like suffering the pains once again.

Of the some 800,000 elderly people in Nanjing today, about 2,630, according to the author's unfinished survey, have experienced the Nanjing Massacre. According to psychologists, the elderly have good long-term memory. They remember incidents and personal experiences from their distant past. And regarding traumatic experiences, either physical or psychological, their memories of them are particularly clear and long lasting. They often sit in the sun and tell their children or grandchildren about their experiences, and sometimes even their neighbors. In the author's surveys, the interviewees were all agreed that the Japanese were ruthless and had no con-

science. Almost all those interviewed had nothing good to say about
the Japanese. They refuse to buy Japanese products, because every
item brought them pain. Those who experienced the Nanjing Massacre or those who lived under Japanese occupation, the influence
of their views on their families and society should not be underesti-
mated. If a Westerner were to commit an act of impropriety in China,
it would not attract much attention, but if a Japanese were to commit
the same act, it would arouse widespread indignation.[33] When the
Japanese Rightists repeatedly deny the occurrence of the Nanjing
Massacre, is this beneficial to the future of Sino-Japanese political
and economic relations?

While the far-sighted Japanese are trying to soothe the hearts and
minds of the survivors of the Massacre, at the same time, there are
those who are using thick black ink trying to cover up the bloody
tracks, and using irresponsible lies as substitutes for truth. We should
let the tragedy of history be a lesson to us, rather than leading us to
more hatred. The Japanese government and the Japanese people
should reflect thoroughly on the responsibilities of war. The longer
this issue remains unresolved, the greater the burden and the greater
the cost will be.

Notes

1. Harold John Timperley, *Qinhua Rijun baoxing lu* (*Japanese Terror in China*), translated by Ma Guangping, Wan Gaochao, et al. (New China Press, 1986), p. 111.
2. See Nanjing newspaper, *Xinminbao* (*The New Citizen*), 29 August 1937, p. 2.
3. *"Nanjing shizhengfu junshiweiyuanhui houfang qinwubu han* (Letter from the In-terior Affairs Department of the Military Affairs Committee, Nanjing Muncipal Government)" dated 23 November 1937. Nanjing Muncipal Archives.
4. *Riben diguozhuyi qinhua dangan ziliao xuanbian: Nanjing datusha* (Selected Docu-ments from Documents on the Japanese Imperialist Invasion of China: Nanjing Massacre) (China Press, 1995), p. 14.
5. Tao Jinghuan, *"Shoudu kongxizhong de xingxingshishi* (Nanjing under the Air Raids)," in the Nanjing newspaper, *Xinbao*, 19 October 1997.
6. Hu Hualing, *Jinling yongsheng: Wei Telin nushizhuan* (*The Biography of Minnie Vautrin*) (Taiwan: Jiuge, 1997), p. 79.
7. Xu Ziling, *"Nanjing zai kongxi xia* (Nanjing under the Air Raids)," *Xinbao*, 19 October 1937.
8. *"Women gangtieban de guodu* (Our Steel-like Capital City)," *Shishi* Semi-monthly, Vol. 1, no. 3.
9. *Labei rije* (*Rabe's Diary*) (Jiangsu People's Publishing House, 1997), p, 165, 170.
10. M.S. Bates, *Tianli nanrong—Meiguo chuanjiaoshi yanzhong de Nanjing de datusha* (*The Nanjing Massacre seen from the Eyes of an American Missionary*). Translated by Zhang Kairuan (Nanjing University Press, 1995), p. 5.

11. *Qin-Hua Rijun Nanjing datusha shiliao* (*Historical Records on the Nanjing Massacre by the Invading Japanese Troops*) (Jiangsu Antiquities Press, 1985).
12. Interviewed by the author and Wu Xiaojing on 31 December 1998.
13. *Historical Records*, p. 12.
14. *Nanjing datusha yu sanguan zuozhan* (*The Nanjing Massacre and the Three-All Tactics*) (Sichuan Educational Press, 1984).
15. In the interviews by the author, the survivors explained that, to this day, they could not understand why they were so cowardly.
16. In the interviews, many of the survivors mentioned the sound of the Japanese soldiers' boots, especially the women who trembled as soon as they heard the sound of the boots.
17. Xu Zhigeng, *Nanjing datusha* (*The Nanjing Massacre*) (The Liberation Army Press, 1998), p. 217.
18. *Historical Records*, p. 83.
19. Bates, *American Missionary*, p. 458.
20. *"Wei Telin riji* (Minnie Vautrin's Diaries)" for 20 January 1938. Xerox copy.
21. "Vautrin's Diaries," 17 February 1938.
22. Rabe's letter to his wife quoted in Bates, *American Missionary*, p. 32.
23. Lewis C.S. Smyth quoted in *Historical Records* (1985).
24. Document 1002-2-928 in Nanjing Muncipal Archives.
25. Zhang Kairuan, *Nanjing datusha de lishi jianzheng* (*Historical Evidence for the Nanjing Massacre*) (Hubei People's Press, 1995), 132-133.
26. Zhang, *Historical Evidence*, p. 224.
27. "Vautrin's Diaries," 29 January 1940.
28. "Rosen's Report to the German Ministry of Foreign Affairs," 20 Jan. 1938 quoted in *Kang-Ri zhanzheng yanjiu* (*Studies on the Sino-Japanese War*), no. 2 (1991).
29. Zhang, *Historical Evidence*, p. 155.
30. Hu, *Biography of Minnie Vautrin*, pp. 180-181.
31. Nanjing edition of the *Xinhua ribao* (New China Daily News), 23 January 1999.
32. Author's interview on 20 September 1999.
33. Recently on 15 November 1999 there was the case of a Japanese tourist who forced a Chinese female manager to kneel on the floor. Public indignation was aroused throughout Hubei province. Within one day the local paper received more than 300 phone calls. Throughout the nation more than fifty newspapers reported the story in great detail. See *Xinhua ribao* (New China Daily News), 19 November 1999.

10

One Army Surgeon's Account of Vivisection on Human Subjects in China

Noda Masaaki (translated by Paul Schalow)

Translator's Preface: *The Redress Movement generally asks that the Japanese government admit its responsibility for war crimes and provide just compensation to survivors. The unfortunate result is that many Japanese have the sense that their government is being unreasonably attacked by outside forces over issues they thought were resolved long ago. The major contribution of Noda Masaaki's book,* Senso to Zaiseki *(War and Guilt,* Iwanami, 1998) *is to redirect the focus of the issue of war responsibility to the Japanese people themselves, not their government. By shifting the focus to individuals, Noda succeeds in making the idea of "war responsibility" a concrete, personal issue, instead of a political abstraction. The book is structured around interviews with men in the imperial forces, ranging from common foot soldiers to elite army surgeons, who participated in atrocities during the Pacific War. Men of conscience among them have continued to suffer from the emotional consequences of their crimes. Noda emphasizes the importance of soldiers and surgeons accepting individual responsibility for their misdeeds as a prerequisite for their emotional healing. Noda thereby shows the extent to which perpetrators of war crimes are secondary victims of their own monstrous acts. Noda's thesis is that before a society-wide discussion of war responsibility can occur in Japan, the individuals who participated in atrocities must be willing to tell their stories and express their remorse. Noda has provided a valuable record of individual Japanese voices of conscience that will continue to be heard long after the individuals themselves have passed on. Noda also clarifies how the continued failure of the guilty to face their misdeeds has caused lasting harm to Japan's social health. Ultimately, Noda argues, it is in Japan's self-interest to respond to the calls for justice coming out of the Pan-Asian Redress Movement. What follows is a complete translation into English of the Introduction and first chapter of Noda Masaaki's* War and Guilt.

Introduction

When human beings live within small groups and spend their days close to the rhythms of nature, their change of mood follows a predictable pattern. When illness strikes or when someone they love dies, their instinctive response is to grieve. When they sit before a warm fire with friends, they instinctively experience feelings of pleasure. Grief and pleasure arise spontaneously in response to the momentary events of their lives, but their underlying sense of well-being is stable and ongoing.

When people live as part of a nation state, however, the historical time in which they live exerts its own influence on them. People are easily swept up in the mood of the times and lose sight of the gentle rhythms of life.

The first time I became cognizant of the existence of a historical mood was in the 1980s.

In the 1980s, Japanese society became materially affluent and began to move beyond the anxieties of defeat and post-war reconstruction even as it continued on its path of complete denial of the past. One night in the spring of 1985, I emerged from a Tokyo subway station into the street and became swept up in a large crowd of people waving "Rising Sun" flags and holding flashlights. The flags and flashlights of the crowd of several thousand, no, tens of thousands of people, completely filled the brightly lit Ginza street as it pushed its way from the direction of Kyobashi toward Nihonbashi. It was a parade commemorating the 60th year of the Showa era. There were old people from all over Japan, along with a few young and middle-aged people. This was the gist of their repeated cry as they swept forward: "We fought a war in the name of the Showa Emperor, and defeat was followed by chaos and poverty; even so, the Showa reign has been a good one."

My memories of that night are muddled because of the confusion I felt. What period of history had I stumbled into? Was I watching a parade from my youth, celebrating National Physical Fitness Day perhaps, or Arbor Day? Or was I in a darkened movie theater watching a pre-war newsreel, narrated by a solemn-voiced announcer? The color of the bright red "Rising Sun" and the glare of the flashlights shimmered in my mind like the cool flame of a devil's flare. Though the image itself was enigmatic, at that moment I clearly sensed that I had been swept up in the mood of a historical time.

The mood of those times was characterized by a faint and superficial sense of "happiness," or, perhaps more accurately, I should call it "euphoria." It was an empty feeling of pleasure that lacked solid basis and involved a willingness to believe that everything was "going fine" despite all the evidence to the contrary. Behind the happy mood was a reduced ability to make independent decisions and an increase in impulsive behavior.

Japanese people worked at a frenetic pace buoyed by false confidence in the bubble economy, always striving for an illusory happiness but never stopping to question what they had done in the Emperor's name during the Pacific War. The increasing irrelevance of politics, the failure of financial markets, the bloated bureaucracy, the complicity with dictatorial economic development throughout Asia, the explosion in pointless information, the sense of alienation among young people—these and other problems were dealt with ineffectively, and if a few people shed tears in an occasional spasm of conscience, none ever showed deep remorse or sadness.

People became compulsive readers of books that can only be called euphoric, containing the message that "If we just try to live cheerfully and positively, our natural morphines will kick in and make all our dreams possible." Was modernization nothing more than a path to morphine addiction?

Prior to the "period of euphoria" in which we live today, there was a "period of anxiety." A society that was rushing to modernize as it built a rich country and strong military with the greatest possible aggressive potential was basically unhealthy. The mood of the people was volatile, authoritarian, and hypersensitive as it continually sought a target for its aggression. People responded to others from a simultaneous sense of superiority and inferiority depending on the other person's rank, function, role, or sex; they were always prepared to humble themselves toward certain people, to be domineering toward others, and magnanimous toward still others. The peculiar blend of superiority and inferiority, humility and arrogance, began with relations among family members, friends, and neighbors and extended to relations with the peoples of other Asian countries. People who could not treat others as equals mistook their own anxious feelings for virtue. Every action was taken from an intense feeling of anxiety, and anxiety was the main characteristic of prewar society.

Why did the mood of the times change from anxiety to euphoria? Did Japanese society have no other choice?

Why have the Japanese people's emotional lives become so monotonous, and why is there such pressure to appear happy? The full range of emotions cannot be abandoned in favor of emphasizing one emotion over others. Only someone who can grieve fully and completely is able to rejoice fully and completely. Someone who learns to laugh before he has felt joyful will never be capable of honest feeling.

What is it that the Japanese have failed to grieve for?

In the mid-1970s, I had the chance to read *Die Unfähigkeit zu trauern* (*The inability to grieve*) by the West German psychologist Alexander Mitscherlich and his wife Margarete Mitscherlich,[1] subtitled *Grundlagen kollektiven Verhaltens* (*The basis of group behavior*). The authors ask, "What in the world is a group of people to do once they confront the fact that they have killed six million human beings for no better reason than that they wanted to satisfy their own aggressive desires, and have lost the moral foundation that once was theirs? Their only choices are increasingly complete denial of their motives or, barring that, retreat into clinical depression," and since, of course, Germany did not choose the latter course of melancholy, its "political and social barrenness is a product of its denial of the past. The communal desire to protect itself from bearing responsibility for what happened—whether for sins of omission or sins of commission—could not help but leave its traces on the German character," they argued, also pointing out that, nonetheless, "Germany has now set out to establish a commercial Democratic Republic from exactly the same basic position it occupied when it joined the National Socialist (Nazi) movement."

In other words, failing to grieve sufficiently, Germany chose to bury the past and plunge headlong into economic reconstruction. But what exactly did Germany fail to grieve for? Was it the failure of the Nazi philosophy? The deaths of six million Jews? On this point the Mitscherlichs' analysis is vague.

When I read *Die Unfähigkeit zu trauern*, I could agree completely with the authors' statement that denial of the past leaves its traces in a society.

Ten years passed, and the spirit of the times became even more euphoric and superficial, and I began to wonder again what it was that the Japanese had failed to grieve for.

I was born in the final years of the Pacific War and was raised in the world of post-war democracy. My youth coincided with a time when post-war ideals were gradually being replaced by materialistic values. I became a doctor of psychiatry in the years of high economic growth and thereafter entered the ranks of the intelligentsia. In my present middle age I have tried to maintain a critical perspective on the times but, not infrequently, I sense in myself a strange inability to experience deep emotion, and this troubles me. Why is it that I cannot have a richer emotional imagination and a greater ability to empathize with others? Why do I always treat events and knowledge as important but fail to show interest in the flow of emotions and the motives that inspire them? Why do I always act as if paying attention to the feelings of myself and others is of secondary importance to knowing about outcomes and results of various matters? And this is the case even though I know perfectly well that what is fulfilling in life is not the attainment of knowledge or success but in the experience of emotions.

The problem is more than a personal issue, however. It is also a communal issue. Why? Because it is culture that surrounds the individual and unconsciously directs him or her to respond emotionally in certain ways to events. In Japan, the vast majority of older and middle-aged people have lost the ability to feel deep emotion and are unable to maintain open relations with others. The heads of major firms, government bureaucrats, scholars, journalists, in fact the entire Japanese elite, is not a group endowed with deep emotional insight. Far too many of them lack empathetic or imaginative skills. The same is true of the average individual who has dealt his whole life with Japanese society. Their children who comprise the next generation are even more superficial in their emotional range and can only experience personal relations in terms of the exchange of information or physical contact.

We make no effort to know the facts about what happened during the Pacific War, but ignorantly make sophisticated-sounding excuses for ourselves. "We were the victims of war. It wasn't a war of aggression but a war of self-preservation. We cannot justify a self-critical view of history." What have we lost, I wonder, by denying the past in this way? When we deny our life experiences, we invite psychological self-destruction. When wounds to the spirit are repressed they eventually explode in the form of emotional dysfunction and mental illness. Are the Japanese living in a spiritual state any different than the one we lived in during the war of aggression? Through our denial of the past, what sort of future have we destined for ourselves?

Clearly, the Pacific War is now an event from a half-century ago. As a result of it, we now have a peace movement whose goal is to eradicate nuclear weapons from the earth. But the former culture that had no respect for the individual, encouraged competitiveness at the same time it demanded a high level of personal sacrifice for the sake of the group, and stressed hierarchical relations, remains just as it was. We still have a pedigree-based society, we have elite universities, we have uneven systems of justice, we have an infatuation with rank and title in business, and we have ways of applying pressure to anyone who harbors doubts about these values. Throughout the country there is bullying in schools and in the workplace, and the emphasis on loyalty to the company deprives Japanese people of the pleasures of family life. The pressure to work after-hours and to socialize with colleagues makes it impossible to be fully human. In short, the culture that drives people onward towards achievement and promotion remains as it was during the Pacific War.

The present situation does not differ significantly from the spirit of the Japanese people during the war of aggression (15 years beginning with the Manchurian Incident in 1931 until the end of the war in 1945), when new recruits were bullied in the Domestic Affairs Corps and soldiers vied to kill Chinese people with bayonets, oblivious to the suffering of those under attack, as a way of impressing senior officers and moving up in the ranks. It is the same mechanism that nowadays encourages competitiveness from an early age and, by means of rites of passage involving envy and humiliation, increases feelings of aggression and turns those feelings into an organized force that targets others.

After the defeat of August 15, 1945, the Japanese people who survived the war could no longer believe in their grand slogans: "Eight Great Lands, One Universe," "Five Peoples Living in Harmony," and "The Rule of Right in a Paradise on Earth." It was also no longer possible to believe that "Manchuria was crucial to Japan's survival," as Matsuoka Yosuke (1880-1946) argued in parliament in 1931. Once the post-war shock of defeat, emotional numbness, and ensuing chaos had subsided, there were two basic ways the Japanese people responded to losing the war.

The first response to defeat was to blame no one. From this viewpoint, the Pacific War's perpetrators and its victims were equally blameless, since war is miserable whether you win or lose; what was important, they said, was the call for peace. This response found expression in the peace movement. The peace movement itself was divided into two schools of thought, one group which emphasized absolute peace based on a psychology of universal forgiveness that rendered themselves guiltless, and another group which having absolved itself of guilt insisted from an ideological viewpoint that a distinction should be made between antiwar forces (the Socialist bloc) and pro-war forces (America). In any case, there was no attempt by either group to confront what Japan had done during the war or address what had been lost in the defeat.

The second major response to the defeat was materialism resulting from a process of psychological displacement. The emotional wounds of war were hidden by materialistic values based on the logic that since America won the war because of material superiority, Japan could recover by reconstructing the economy, rebuilding industry, and working to catch up and surpass America economically. That approach was based on a traditional refusal to admit Japan's complete eclipse historically by Chinese civilization. Reactionary forms of materialism and obsessive faith in the economy were simply displaced forms of the extreme emphasis on Japanese spiritual superiority during the war. It was not a practical, functional economic principle but simply another manifestation of the extreme belief that the Japanese are spiritually superior. It was no more than a transformation of the ideology of the "rich and powerful military state" into a capitalist ideology focused on economic growth at all costs, convinced that the only thing that mattered was achieving material wealth.

The materialistic response to the war was further strengthened by post-war developments such as the economic boom during the Korean War, high economic growth, the economy of financial assistance to rural agricultural and lumber enterprises essential to the building industry, centralization in Tokyo, and restructuring of manufacturing industries; and it has now become the dominant mindset of the Japanese people. This determination to overcome the defeat of war through materialistic means is exactly what I believe has created the culture of Japan today, a culture that still refuses to recognize its emotional wounds.

But are the Japanese people entirely without conscience? Did no one experience a sense of guilt? Whether or not they feared the shame of others finding out what they had done, did no one agonize because they knew that they themselves had personally done something terribly wrong?

I would like to believe that is not the case.

For example, eight years ago I met a beautiful old man on a farm in Omi. Kawasaki Tajiro and his wife had been growing almost all of their own food on the farm for most of their lives. "There is no better livelihood than farming," he insisted at age 79 when I saw him as he jotted down a memo to himself on a faded old blackboard in his chicken coop: rice husks, 10 kilos; fish meal, 2. 5 kilos; oyster shells, 10 kilos. Next to it he had written a poem.

> Hello, little blossom of cock's comb.
> I recall a child picking herbs in a Shanghai field.
> "What are you doing?" I asked.
> She smiled up at me and said, "Food, food."
> There was a red bandage on her shoulder.
> "What is this?" I asked, and she answered only
> "I am a girl."
> If she is still alive she would be fifty years old,
> Holding a grandchild in her arms,
> telling tales of war
> without end.
> It was not a red camellia that you wore
> for your underrobe.

Under the blackboard was a single stem of camellia blossoms in a vase filled with water. I think of the poem as an expression of the old man's sense of guilt, kept quietly in a corner of his mind all these years due to his participation in the war. I later found out that he had been in China during the Shanghai Incident between 1931-1934, was next sent to the South Pacific from 1940-45 during the Pacific War, and was in the Philippines when the war ended.

There may not be many of them, but at least some Japanese people have found a way of their own to live with their sense of guilt. But their feelings have existed for half a century now without being adequately acknowledged or understood by society at large. The anti-war peace movement in post-war Japan was built upon a sense of Japan as a victim of war. Even the anti-nuclear peace movement in Hiroshima and Nagasaki and the work of journalists in collecting and passing on stories of wartime experience treat war as something that makes victims of both friend and foe, thereby circumventing the issue of blame.

Even so, there are those who have spoken of the Nanking massacre, reported the massacres in Manchuria (Northeast China) and the South Pacific, confessed to crimes committed as members of the

Kempei security police and Tokumu special forces, or recorded that in the flight following defeat they were guilty of leaving family members and comrades behind to their fates. However, their voices were silenced by the overwhelming power of the post-war refusal to place blame.

In addition, those who survived student mobilizations at the end of the war suffer from the sense that the truly good and beautiful among them did not come back alive (this is called survivor's guilt). Their stories, too, have never been properly heard or analyzed.

I have always wanted to study the way in which, through denial and amnesia, Japan's refusal to face the war of aggression and its unwillingness to ascertain the multiple forms of war crimes committed by the Japanese people has impoverished the Japanese culture. I decided to approach the problem by telling the story of individuals who lived their life since the war unafraid to acknowledge their guilt, and by their example show how the majority has failed to confront its own guilt.

I began the process of searching for precious evidence of a sense of guilt in Japanese individuals like someone panning for gold.

Just about that time, I read a book called *Legacy of Silence: Encounters with Children of the Third Reich*, which contained interviews with the children of Nazi perpetrators of crimes in Germany, on the other end of the Eurasian continent from Japan. [2] The author is Dan Bar-On, who was taken by his father from Heidelberg in Germany to safety in Israel before the war and is now a psychologist. In the book, he explores how the children of Nazi leaders had accepted or denied their parents' guilt 40 years after the end of the Second World War.

West Germany in the 1980s was teaching children about the crimes of the Nazis and was making it clear that an understanding of the past was the basis on which to build the present. As a result of Germany's deep sense of regret for having brought the Third Reich into the world, the countries of Europe were able to accept the rapid reunification of East and West Germany after the breakup of the socialist bloc. Had Germany not gone through its aggressive period of education in the 1980s, the rest of Europe would surely have had far greater misgivings about German reunification.

Nevertheless, even in West Germany until the middle of the 1970s there was little attempt to educate its people fully about the Nazi past. The only role most schools fulfilled was to preserve complete silence about the past of the parents' generation, and history lessons ended with Bismarck in the 19th century.

Most of the middle-aged men and women whose fathers had been close to Hitler declined to be interviewed by the Israeli psychologist who traveled tirelessly throughout Germany in search of a "legacy of silence," but a few came forward and began to tell the story of their emotional histories for the first time, albeit with some trepidation. Their fathers had been instrumental in ordering and carrying out mass murder from various positions of power in the central government such as extermination camps and forced labor camps, special military units, euthanasia programs, the Gestapo, and the network of deport and transport systems. Among those interviewed were the nephew of security chief Reinhard Heydrich, the son of Nazi party chief Martin Bormann, and the daughter of army chief Hermann Göring.

Though these men were the primary movers in a program of genocide, they were men who at home showed a love for their families and for music. Many of those interviewed wondered if their fathers really knew what was going on. One remembered his father as a gentle man who, just before committing suicide after the defeat, took his child for a walk as he hummed a favorite tune. Others lived in fear of the possibility that they carried genocidal DNA in their own blood.

For example, one man whose father had assisted in the death selections as a doctor at Auschwitz refused to follow the path towards membership in the intellectual elite that his family had followed for generations, and instead became a cook. He says, "It is unfortunate that nothing was taught about it in our schools after the war. The word Hitler did not even exist. Our generation had to dig up information by itself. As a result, we ended up with a situation in which some people believed there was an Auschwitz, others did not." Thus, the stories unfold of 11 people who lived in the silent generation of the postwar period.

Then, finally, the author is relieved to hear the story of a man who was once a member of the Hitler-Jugend (Hitler Youth) and whose father was a member of Hitler's inner circle, but who tried and failed to save the Jews in the ghetto and subsequently became mentally deranged as a result. In the midst of his suffering, he kept crying "Christ was himself a Jew. We must have respect for the Jews." The longer Bar-On stayed in Germany, the more he found himself search-

ing together with the children of the Third Reich for a sense of hope
for humanity in the second generation after the Nazis. The book
ends with a suggestion that the children of Nazis who are attending
a conference at which the author's research is being addressed should
form a discussion group to explore the structure of their self-identi-
ties. Afterwards, Bar-On invites all of them to Israel to spend four
days with the children of people who were killed in the extermination camps.

Bar-On's research shows that it is possible even half a century
after the war to conduct a scientific study of people who lived through
the war. Unfortunately, for those of us living in Asia, the conditions
do not exist for the children of the perpetrators to enter into a meaningful discussion with the victims or their children. The citizens of
China and several other Asian countries are limited politically in
what they can say. Nevertheless, the Japanese people could convey
the meaning of the 20th century to the rest of Asia if we were able to
convey the sense of guilt of those involved in the war and undertake
a detailed analysis of it. The awareness of guilt that still lingers in
Japan is a valuable part of our human culture, and by understanding
how Japanese culture has suppressed a sense of guilt about the war,
we can come to an understanding of who the Japanese really are.

Chapter One: War and the Japanese Medical Profession
(The Story of Dr. Yuasa Ken, an 80-year-old Doctor)

Post-war medical schools in Japan have preserved the exact same
instructional program used in the pre-war period and have followed
a philosophy of antagonistic competition, rigid hierarchy, and urban
centralization of hospital services. As part of the health care insurance system, the two main concerns of doctors who attend academic
medical conferences have been how to improve methods of treatment and how to increase their profits. This sort of medical practice
and treatment has been successful in establishing enormous medical
centers and operating high-tech medical equipment, but it has failed
to respond to the emotional needs of patients. Why is this the case?

Post-war medical care in Japan is directly linked to wartime Japan. There was no evidence of careful soul-searching by the medical profession after the war. For example, the very same doctors
who developed germ warfare in China and carried out medical experiments on humans as members of the Army Disinfection and
Water Provision Corps (Unit 731) later, in the post-war period, be-

came professors at medical schools (Kyoto National University, Kyoto Prefectural University of Medicine, etc.) and chief officers of public hospitals, or found work in government as policy makers in the Ministry of Welfare and set up businesses such as the "Green Cross" specializing in the manufacture and distribution of blood products. The wartime legacy of the medical profession's failure to respect human life is apparent in the current corporate culture that led to the "Green Cross" AIDS scandal involving contaminated blood and in the special relationship between the Ministry of Welfare and the medical profession.

However, germ warfare was the least of the crimes committed by the medical profession. On the Chinese mainland, military doctors performed vivisection and medics used Chinese people for surgery practice. The vivisection of captured American soldiers at Kyushu University Medical School in the final days of the war are well known, but they were just the tip of the iceberg. There has been almost complete silence about the "work" done by numerous military doctors during surgical demonstrations or for purposes of education. One man who has spoken out unflinchingly about the crimes he committed as a medical doctor is Yuasa.

Yuasa Ken was born in October, 1916 (Taisho 5), the son of a medical practitioner, and grew up in the neighborhood of Echizenbori in the Kyobashi section of Tokyo. His father received his medical training and became a doctor after great hardship, and perhaps for that reason he took the greatest pleasure in caring night and day for his patients as the local neighborhood doctor. Yuasa was the third of nine children, with an elder sister and an elder brother. When he was in the first grade of elementary school, he came close to dying when his home was destroyed by fire in the Tokyo Earthquake of 1923. For a while his father treated patients in a temporary facility outdoors, and during that time Yuasa was evacuated to his grandmother's in Chiba for two and a half years. There, the little boy from Tokyo was often bullied by local children who refused to play with him. It was the same kind of mistreatment that would be directed at children who would later end up in the countryside as a result of wartime evacuation of the cities.

After his return to Tokyo, Yuasa's homeroom teacher during fifth and sixth grades at Meisho Elementary School was a hardworking man originally from Okinawa. This man had become a teacher after experiencing discrimination and great hardship, yet Yuasa remembers well being told by him that "The Japanese people are a superior race. They must conquer China and become the masters of all of Asia."

In 1929 (Showa 4), Yuasa entered Tokyo First Public Middle School (currently Kudan High School). On the way to and from school each day, he stopped to pray at Yasukuni Shrine, which was next door to his middle school. The previous year (1928) saw the "event of March 15th" (the mass arrest of Japan Communist Party members), and in the month Yuasa entered middle school, the "event of April 16th" occurred (likewise, a roundup of Communist Party members). It was a period when Japanese society began to lean heavily towards militarism under new laws promulgated to preserve internal security. Then, in 1931, came the Manchurian Incident, and in the following year, 1932, came first the Shanghai Incident and finally the "event of May 15th." Receiving a certain amount of military instruction at school, Yuasa was just an average middle school student of the time, trusting the story of three brave heroes who acted as human bullets that came out of the Shanghai Incident (and which proved to be a lie), thrilling to the lyrics of the song of the Mounted Bandits that announced "I am going; you come, too; crowded Japan is no place for us," and believing that Chinese and Koreans were inferior races capable of little more than peddling noodles.

In 1934 (Showa 9) Yuasa, who excelled in his studies, was admitted as a young man to the preparatory school of the medical program at Tokyo Jikei Hospital. He recalls that "I naively believed that if I studied hard and became a doctor, I could make a good living anyone would be proud of. I was completely unaware that the nation and the times might have a profound influence on me."[3] A friend of his, Hayashi Toshikazu (now at Oji Seikyo Hospital), was arrested for anti-war activities and expelled from First High School before he entered medical school. This friend once told him that after the war large land ownership would be abolished, but no one took what he said very seriously.

In 1937 the Marco Polo Bridge Incident occurred, and that winter Nanking was attacked. Of course he heard nothing about the massacre, nor did he have any interest in finding out about it.

In 1941, he graduated from medical school and became a doctor of internal medicine at Komagome Hospital in Tokyo, specializing in contagious diseases. This was because he felt that knowledge of contagious diseases would be beneficial if he were ever sent to war.

In October of that year, he applied for short-term deployment as an army surgeon and was assigned to Asahikawa Infantry Squadron 28. At the time of the June enlistment examination, he was encouraged by the officer in charge to apply for full status as an army surgeon.

After two months of training in the general infantry, he was promoted to the rank of First Lieutenant Army Surgeon along with two or three of his classmates from medical school. This is the way that army surgeons were made. To Yuasa, who believed in a superior class of beings made up of the imperial family and the descendants of samurai, it made perfect sense that medical doctors should be commissioned officers. Even so, the satisfaction of enjoying success in his career was tempered by the realization that he would likely die on a battlefield somewhere. Yuasa was a man who faced reality and did his best to adjust to it. He was not one to flee from the facts, but neither was he one to let himself be brainwashed. He was a fine young man who had grown up in the environment of a medical school education in which the only important things were memorization and practice, and who had been completely deprived of his ability to voice criticism.

On December 8th of 1941, the year Yuasa joined the army, the Japanese military attacked Pearl Harbor, signaling the beginning of the wider Pacific War. At the end of January the following year, 1942, Yuasa was assigned to the Luan Army Hospital near the city of Taiyuan in China's Shanxi Province. During his period of service there, he remembers being impressed by how hard the Chinese coolies worked. "Even Chinese people are capable of hard work," he thought in amazement, but he felt no particular pity for them. He also remembers seeing a Chinese person riding in the first class section on a train and thinking, as a Japanese commissioned officer, "Who does that person think he is?" but he was sophisticated enough not to put the thought into words.

In Taiyuan, the Shanxi version of the Monroe Doctrine held sway and was the home of the only regional warlord who managed to survive into old age, Yan Xishan [Yen Hsi-shan] (1883-1960). In October of 1937, Taiyuan fell as a result of the Nikka (Japan-China) Incident. Yan Xishan's soldiers avoided confrontation with the Japanese army, thereby retaining their power. Instead, the Japanese army fought a bitter battle against the 8th Army (the liberation army organized by the Chinese Communist Party), which entered from the west.

The staff of the Luan Hospital consisted of the director of the hospital, who was a Lieutenant Colonel, and eight army surgeons. Yuasa was assigned to the Contagious Diseases Ward, Pathology Testing Unit at the hospital. There were approximately 30 patients being treated in the Contagious Diseases Ward suffering from infectious tuberculosis, intestinal cholera, para-diptheria, dysentery, diptheria, and recurring fevers.

In the middle of March, about 40 days into Yuasa's assignment at the hospital, the director of the hospital, Lieutenant Colonel Nishimura Keiji (surgeon and graduate of Okayama Medical School), announced one day after lunch that he would be conducting a practice surgery session from 1:00 p. m. and wanted everyone to assemble in the autopsy room.

Yuasa received the news with a sense of resignation. He had heard already as a student at Jikei Hospital Medical School that army surgeons performed vivisections, and he knew that it was unavoidable. At that time his only reaction was a feeling of fear, coupled with a sense of curiosity to see what it would be like.

Now that it was imminent, he felt strong resistance to the idea. Yuasa usually approached his work eagerly, but that day he arrived late at the autopsy room. It was a room he knew well from several autopsies he had conducted on patients who died from tuberculosis, dysentery, and intestinal cholera, but today his footsteps were heavy.

He saw no one in the courtyard of the hospital. Usually coolies who worked in the hospital were lazying about, but today he did not see a soul. There was something unusual about the place that day. At the entrance to the autopsy room armed soldiers stood guard with fixed bayonets.

In the cavernous autopsy room, about 30 feet square, were assembled not only surgeons from Luan Army Hospital but also surgeons from the army division. The chief of the divisional medical corps, Colonel Otake, was engaged in friendly conversation with Hospital Director Nishimura.

Yuasa bowed to both of them and took his place next to his immediate superior, Lieutenant Hirano Koji, head of the Contagious Diseases Unit, and slowly surveyed the room.

In a corner to his left were two farmers with their hands tied behind their backs. The strong, well-built one stood there in silence. The other was a smaller, dark-skinned older man, and he was crying out in terror "Aiya, aiya."

On a cart next to the operating table, nurses lined up instruments such as scalpels, amputation knives, and bone-cutting saws. Along with the clatter of the instruments, the surgeons and nurses exchanged jokes and indulged in loud laughter. Theirs was a professional act, designed to convey normalcy and the sense that there was nothing to be nervous about.

Yuasa took his cue from the commissioned officers around him and maintained his composure. Even so, he could not help asking Lieutenant Hirano beside him whether the two men had committed some crime deserving death.

"The 8th Army would kill them anyway," was his reply.

"Oh, yes. I had forgotten," Dr. Yuasa nodded lightly in agreement.

"Shall we get started?" came the signal from Hospital Director Nishimura. Prodded by guards, the larger man walked calmly to the operating table and laid himself down on it. "A brave man, even if he is Chinese," Yuasa remembers thinking admiringly. But when he considered that the man was submitting to the power of the Japanese army, the man's behavior struck him as the only sensible way.

The scrawny-looking man, however, was wailing loudly and refused to come forward. The more the armed guards prodded him with their bayonets, the more desperately the man tried to avoid approaching the operating table. Finally, the filthy man backed right into Yuasa.

Surgery Practice

Yuasa Ken, army surgeon, was no longer capable of imagining what human beings who were about to be vivisected might be feeling. The two men who were to be operated on were nothing more than medical objects to him. To some extent he understood the feelings of the man who climbed onto the operating table by himself, that he was a brave man, and that he was submitting to the power of the Japanese army. But this was simply a reflection of Yuasa's impoverished value system. In his mind a man either lived manfully or he was a coward—those were the only choices. He could imagine neither the bitter humiliation of the Chinese men, their land invaded, who were going to be killed, nor the horror they felt at facing the most miserable death any human being could suffer—to be butchered alive. If he had believed in an afterworld, surely it was the sort of death that would turn a man's soul into a restless ghost seeking vengeance.

To First Lieutenant Yuasa, the only human relations that existed in that room were those involving his fellow army surgeons. He had no relationship as a human being with the Chinese men who were to be killed.

The man with the dirty face continued to moan "Aiya, aiya" as he backed away from the operating table towards Yuasa.

When the now 80-year-old doctor reached this point in his story, he gritted his teeth and his eyes filled with tears.

"I feel so ashamed of myself."

It was perhaps the first time I had ever heard words spoken from such deep remorse.

The young surgeon, Yuasa, was also thinking at that moment that he had to be careful not to do anything he would later regret.

I must not do anything shameful. Why did I have to choose this place to stand? How brave is the novice army surgeon?—that's what they are all thinking. If I have to wrestle with this dirty fellow, I'm going to soil my hospital whites.

These thoughts raced through his mind as he shouted in a majestic voice "Move forward!" and pushed the man towards the operating table.

The old farmer who had backed into Yuasa must have lost his balance when pushed from behind, for he fell forward and was forced onto the operating table, still moaning "Aiya, aiya." Army surgeon Yuasa was proud of himself for avoiding having to wrestle with the man.

For the act of pushing the man, and for thinking that he must be careful not to do anything he would later regret, Yuasa now shuts his eyes in sorrow. Fifty years ago, when he thought, "I have to be careful not to do anything I'll regret later," it was based on a morality aimed only at his army surgeon colleagues. Now, when Yuasa takes a deep breath and says he is ashamed of himself, it is in relation to all human beings, to himself as a human being. That is morality in its true form. But for the Japanese people of that day morals were something that changed depending on person, place, and circumstance.

We must return repeatedly to Yuasa's first vivisection, so let us continue with the story.

The man held onto the operating table and stretched his body in resistance.

A nurse approached the man and comforted him. *"Sui jo"* (lie down). *"Ma yao gei, bu tong"* (I'll give you some anesthetic; it won't hurt).

Perhaps hearing his mother tongue dissipated his fear, for the man allowed the nurse to place him flat on his back. The nurse glanced back at Army Surgeon Yuasa with what he took to be a smug look of professionalism on her face. He was appalled that she could speak such lies.

After the intravenous anesthetic was administered, the man would never get up again. The 20 army surgeons present in the autopsy room divided into two groups and placed themselves around the two operating tables. They cut off the crude hempen clothes the men were wearing, leaving them naked.

Army surgeon Yuasa noted that the farmer's body bore no bruises or evidence of torture. This struck him as strange. It meant that the man had not undergone interrogation of any kind. He had simply been arrested and brought in.

Later, when he himself was put in charge of carrying out these things, he learned that vivisection for educational purposes did not take place spontaneously. Even though Hospital Director Nishimura had only announced it at lunch that day, preparations had naturally been made in advance. Initial orders were issued by the First Army (one of the regional armies in North China that occupied Shanxi Province) and sent to the various army division medical corps, mobile medical units, and army hospitals to be carried out, and it was the chief of general affairs at the hospital who took care of making the actual arrangements for the vivisection.

Notification by higher authorities was not the only way vivisections were arranged, however. All the Army Hospital had to do was tell the Security Police [Kempeitai] how many subjects were needed, and it could rely on getting exactly that number of Chinese captives on the day specified; the Security forces always obliged with the number requested. For example, if someone informed on a Chinese man, the man could immediately be arrested. Since the arrest was not based on proven facts, false accusations inevitably occurred and innocent men were almost certainly among them. In any case, it is not true that the choice of subjects for vivisection was based on the rationale that they were prisoners already condemned to death, as is generally believed.

"It was never the case that we used prisoners for vivisection just because there were extra prisoners available. It was always 'We need them, so get them for us. ' They were necessary for surgery practice in order to save the lives of Japanese soldiers, you see. Chinese people were arrested for that purpose alone."

Army Surgeon Yuasa learned all this because he later became chief of general affairs at the hospital and was himself in charge of making arrangements for practice surgeries, but at the time of the first vivisection what most impressed him was the fact that there was not a mark on the farmer's body.[4]

In order for one of the surgeons to practice piercing the lumbar vertebra for spinal anesthesia, the first man was placed on his side and the surgeon began inserting a needle.

"Is it disinfected?" Yuasa asked.

"What's the point? We're going to kill him anyway," Lieutenant Hirano answered with an annoyed expression.

After spinal anesthesia was administered, they placed the man on his back and bound his arms and legs. Next, they practiced administering total anesthesia using chloroether.

They covered his nose with a mask and began administering the anesthetic. They held down the struggling man until he fell asleep and began to snore.

The first practice surgery involved an appendectomy (removal of the appendix) performed by two surgeons from the divisional army. Since antibiotics were not yet widely used in those days, it was important that the incision be as small as possible. They made an incision in the abdomen just big enough to insert two fingers, but a healthy appendix is smaller than an infected one and therefore they had difficulty locating it. They made a second incision and still could not locate it. With the third incision they pulled out the entire caecum, removed the appendix, and sutured the wound.

The practice surgery continued with an upper-arm amputation performed by First Lieutenant O. Amputation is the only option when limbs are severely damaged by bullet fragments. He inserted the amputating knife deep between the upper arm and torso, then twisted forcefully to cut through the skin and muscle in one circular motion. This was First Lieutenant O's first attempt at an amputation, and he cut through the muscle only with great difficulty.

Once the blade of the amputation knife had reached the bone, the arteries were clamped shut with forceps. Then the flesh around the amputation site was pushed up as far as possible and the bone was cut. This was done so that the cut bone surface would be deep inside at the end of the operation. The large bone heated up from the sawing motion and bone dust rose like smoke. The First Lieutenant sprinkled salt water on the bone to cool it as he cut, and then smoothed the cut surface with a file. Next he pulled the nerves out as far as possible from the amputation site and severed them to prevent future problems with nerve pain. He sutured the arteries and then gradually eased the clamps on them to make certain there was no bleeding. The final step was suturing of the muscle and skin. The farmer's arm was now gone.

The next pair of surgeons continued with practice surgery to repair damage to the intestine. When a bullet enters the abdomen, infection to the abdominal lining results from the intestinal perforation, unless the damaged section of the intestine is removed and the two healthy ends are reconnected. The two army surgeons made an incision in the center of the abdomen, removed the intestine, and cut out a section of it at random. They then reconnected the two ends of the intestine, reinserted it into the abdomen, and closed the incision. This ended the exercise. The farmer who had lost his arm earlier and now had a section of his intestine removed was breathing shallowly.

Next came a tracheotomy. If a bullet strikes the chest, blood fills the trachea and causes suffocation. Using a hook-shaped surgical tool called a "field combat tracheotomer," one of the army surgeons made a quick incision from the top of the neck to the larynx. Red blood mixed with saliva came gushing out with the sound of each breath. This was carefully cleared away with a feather. Gradually the blood subsided and all that remained was a quiet wheezing sound, like someone blowing gently on a flute.

Three hours had passed. Surgery practice ended at 4:00 p. m. The surgeons from the army division left, and the only ones in the autopsy room were the doctors belonging to the hospital and some of the officers from the medical corps, about seven or eight men altogether. The nurses had also left.

"The two Chinese men on the operating tables were still breathing, although weakly. It would be humiliating for us to toss them that way into the hole that had been dug behind the autopsy room. Hospital Director Nishimura therefore took a 2cc syringe and injected air directly into their hearts five or six times, but there was not the slightest change in their breathing. I strangled one of them with my hands and applied pressure to the carotid artery, but I still could not get him to stop breathing. Finally, First Lieutenant O and I tied the man's belt around his neck and strangled him by pulling hard on both ends, but still his breathing did not stop.

"Just then, Sergeant-Major Otani Misao, a doctor who had entered the autopsy room after the operations, told us 'If you inject anesthetic directly into a vein, that will do the trick.' Following his directions, I took up 5cc of the remaining chloroether in a syringe and began injecting it into a vein in the man's left arm. I had injected about 2-3cc when he coughed quietly five or six times and then stopped breathing. I dealt with the other man the same way. I assume, of course, that the medics then took care of disposing of the bodies, for we army surgeons left the room after that."

That night, Yuasa felt restless and went out with his colleagues for a drink.

The above practice surgery took place in March of 1942 on behalf of the army surgeons of the 36th Division field hospital. Yuasa remembered it well because it was his first such experience.

As I listened to his story, I was dumbfounded. I thought of the total anesthesia, tracheotomies, and intestinal reconnections I had practiced on dogs; of spinal anesthesia and appendectomies I had performed after becoming a doctor and I had gained experience as an assistant at various surgeries; and the emergency amputation of a leg I had assisted in. All of these things that a doctor experiences over the course of an extended period of time were carried out on a human subject in the space of three hours. Moreover, Yuasa's account was completely different from the human experiments I had read about—things such as removing liver cells through an incision, measuring how low the body temperature must fall before death occurs, or inducing death by injecting air into an artery, etc. The army was using human subjects merely to produce army surgeons as quickly as possible. Saddest of all, it had no affect whatsoever on these young doctors as human beings.

The Medical Profession, a Product of Its Times

In the three years from that point until the defeat, Army Surgeon Yuasa participated in a total of seven vivisections, including the first. Five of them were practice surgeries for divisional army surgeons, one was for the education of freshman medics, and one he participated in for the education of army surgeons of the Taiyuan Army Surgeons Corps. Fourteen Chinese people were butchered in these vivisections.

In accordance with secret orders issued from the North China Regional Army, practice surgery was to be carried out in each and every division twice annually for the education of army surgeons. The second one took place in autumn of that year. Assembling the army surgeons of the 36th Division, Hospital Director Nishimura served as the person in charge and, as usual, two Chinese men were made available for surgery practice. This time, Army Surgeon Yuasa was among those who operated, performing his first tracheotomy. Nearby, Doctor of Dentistry First Lieutenant N performed lower jaw surgery on a simulated jaw fracture, and a young urologist Second Lieutenant Ando performed a testicular extraction, exclaiming excitedly "Hey, I got it out!"

Not all army surgeons were necessarily educated as specialists in surgery like Yuasa, and being a specialist in surgery was no guarantee that a doctor was equipped to handle the entire range of specialties that were required when dealing with injuries that occurred in battle. Practice surgery was the quickest and easiest way to educate them.

The third vivisection took place in December of 1942. This time, in response to orders from the First Army, all 50 army surgeons from each division in Shanxi Province received instruction in military medicine at Taiyuan. In the afternoon of the second day, led by Second Lieutenant Shukichi, director of the surgery office of the First Army, they fired bullets into the abdomens of four Chinese men and then practiced removing them without the use of anesthesia, in addition to the usual tracheotomies and amputation of limbs.

First Lieutenant Yuasa became the officer in charge of general affairs at the hospital in April, 1943. This placed him second-in-. command. From then on it was his responsibility to make arrangements for vivisections. The war was at a standstill when orders arrived from the North China Regional Army in Beijing: "The quality of army surgeons has deteriorated. They are no longer able to perform adequately in battle conditions. Implement frequent surgery practice." In response, First Lieutenant Yuasa drew up plans to increase the frequency of practice surgery from two to six times annually, or every other month. In actual fact, however, due to circumstances involving troop movements that several times prevented the divisional surgeons from assembling, only three practice surgeries were performed.

At one of them, a practice surgery that took place on a cold day in November, attendance was so poor that only one Chinese man was needed for vivisection, so Hospital Director Nishimura's successor,

Hospital Director S, took the opportunity to behead the other Chinese man with a Japanese sword.

At another practice surgery, after the divisional army surgeons were finished and had left, he had a medic help him open the skull, extract the brain, and then took it to Hospital Director S, who had requested it. He learned that Hospital Director S had been asked to provide it by a former army surgeon, Regimental Commander Sugino of the 9th Regiment Telegraph Corps, and that the healthy brain would be sent to a Pharmaceutical Company in Japan.

A few months later, he was again asked by Hospital Director S to surgically remove a brain. In response, Army Surgeon Yuasa decided to conduct the next anatomy class, scheduled for a new group of reserve medics from Yamanashi Prefecture, on a living body. He thought, "Instead of relying on anatomical charts, I think I will surprise them with something new. It will toughen them up." So he contacted the Security Police [Kempeitai] and had them bring him one Chinese man. Army Surgeon Yuasa performed the vivisection himself, removing the internal organs and showing them to the reservists. Afterwards, he opened the skull and cut out the fresh brain.

Since the very first vivisection, Dr. Yuasa felt very little psychological resistance. He was a bit nervous the first time because it was a new experience, but he went out drinking with his colleagues afterwards and felt better. After that, he never questioned what he was doing nor did he suffer mentally from it. He never once had a nightmare involving vivisection. He is able to describe his first vivisection in detail only because he was forced to recall it later when he was accused as a war criminal. Vivisections were a part of his business, and he performed them with the same inborn seriousness of purpose with which he approached the care of sick and injured soldiers. In the beginning, it could be argued that he performed them under orders from the North China Army or the First Army, but the later ones were done on his own initiative. The removal of brains and the use of a living body to teach reservists their anatomy lesson was entirely unrelated to surgery practice, but by then he was incapable of making such distinctions.

Doctors encounter death every day. As soon as we enter medical school we start our study of anatomy with the dissection of cadavers, and through the study of pathology, daily clinical evaluation, and research we grow accustomed to looking at human beings as physical bodies. For that very reason, if we are to avoid degenerating into practicing a "medicine of death" or a "medicine of the physical body," it behooves us to learn first a "medicine of life" which recognizes people as living beings. How are a mother and her child linked? How do infants develop and grow? What does it mean to suffer emotional problems? How does aging affect one's relationship to society? To the extent that medicine fails to base itself upon a "medicine of life" that pays close attention to mental and emotional development and personal lifestyle, its focus will be limited to the mere mechanics of internal organs and illness.

If we trace the process whereby Yuasa adapted so easily to being an army surgeon who performed vivisections, what we discover is that Japanese medicine never succeeded in creating an independent philosophy opposed to militarism. A strong society is a society that is structured with each of its components having a distinct philosophy not easily compromised by the whole, but mutually antagonistic to each other. As far as Yuasa's medical education went, he learned only to be interested in the human body, and to adapt himself to the medical profession in order to have a successful career.

Moreover, in addition to vivisections, Yuasa was involved in sending dyptheria and dysentry germs collected from his patients to the Disinfection and Water Provision Corps of the army. He was unaware how these were to be used, but the Water Provision Corps asked for cut only the freshest and most potent germs in order to use them in germ warfare. The germs were cultured and delivered to the army. The army then scattered them as part of their attack strategy.

Furthermore, in the autumn of 1943 he received a request from the First Army Commander of the Medical Corps, Major General Ishii Shiro (1892-1959), founder of the infamous Unit 731 to participate in a mock exercise to exterminate air-dropped fleas infected with the bubonic plague. He also attended a class taught by Commander Ishii in which Chinese subjects were used to demonstrate the effects of frostbite on the human body. Another time, he took part in a study of venereal disease among Korean comfort women in March, 1945, when he was assigned to the Southern Shanxi Province Battalion as battlefield surgeon.

Self-Justification and Rationalization

Yuasa began his assignment at the Shanxi Province Luan Army Hospital in February, 1942, and three and a half years later in Taiyuan, Shanxi Province, on August 15th, 1945, he received word of Japan's defeat. In Taiyuan, there was much debate among the Japanese expressing opinions such as "There's no point in returning to Japan when it is in chaos," and "Let's remain here and work on behalf of China." This turned into a full-fledged movement to remain in China. The movement was fueled by self-serving considerations of the continental Japanese, such as "I do not want to lose all of my investments in China," and "I am not sure what awaits me if I return to Japan." The head of the People's Society to Remain in China, Komoto Daisaku (1883-1955)—staff officer of the Guandong Army who planned the assassination of Zhang Zuolin (Chang Tso-lin), and who afterwards became president of Shanxi Industries, Ltd. in Shanxi Province—and others like him are prime examples. In the end, 2,700 armed soldiers and 3,000 technical personnel responded to conscription into the army of the Nationalist Party and remained in China with their families.

Yuasa decided that "If Japanese people are remaining behind, I will stay, too, and take care of them as their doctor. For a while, at least, they will be needing me." Tokyo was completely burned out, and he had no idea what he would do if he went back there. In the back of his mind, he also may have felt that by seeing Chinese patients he would be able to atone for his misdeeds. Yuasa established a medical facility called the Nikkyo Clinic and began examining and treating Japanese and Chinese patients. The officers and soldiers who remained behind continued to battle the Communist 8th Army, and Yuasa was sent out on occasion to assist them as army surgeon.

However, as they continued to suffer defeat at the hands of the 8th Army, from the fall of 1947 to the spring of 1948, most of the Japanese people returned to Japan. Yuasa thought, "Even if we are defeated, with my skills as a doctor I should be able to survive somehow. As long as there are even a few Japanese people left, I cannot leave them," and he continued to examine and treat patients at the clinic. During this time, he married at the end of 1947 and eventually had two children.

In April of 1949, Taiyuan finally fell to the Communists. He was ordered to the provincial hospital where he continued his treatment of patients. Each day he spent his mornings making house calls, and in the afternoons he made the rounds of the hospital wards and gave instruction to young Chinese doctors.

In January of 1951, however, he was sent without warning to a prison camp in Yunnan, Hebei Province. His family was also taken into custody.

At the time, Yuasa had absolutely no sense of having done anything wrong. All he thought was that "Crimes were committed by the Security Police [Kempeitai] and by people like Ishii Shiro with his frostbite experiments, but even in wartime conditions we regular doctors did nothing particularly wrong." Neither did he feel that surgery practice on living human beings was evil. For a while, he thought of prison camp as little more than a place where he would receive instruction in Communist ideology. It was when he was asked to make a confession of guilt that he began to feel uneasy about vivisection for the first time. He was assailed by doubts and fears: "How many people in the prison camp know about it?" or "I wonder if they are keeping their mouths shut?" The Korean War was growing more intense, however, so he did not take his plight that seriously. "There is no way they could be victorious against the powerful United States," he thought. "Conditions will change soon, and anything I may have done will no longer be an issue."

Over the years I have met many officers and soldiers who were imprisoned in Chinese camps for war crimes, and the one thing they had in common was a complete lack of fear of retaliation. No one is worried that, "I murdered Chinese people. Therefore, no matter what the situation, I, too, might be killed by the Chinese." Along with the lack of a morally-based sense of guilt, they have a strong expectation that the Chinese will forgive them. Since they do not recognize that they have done anything wrong, it never occurs to them that they should take responsibility for it. However, even if they do not feel they have done anything wrong, one would expect that since they murdered large numbers of Chinese people, they would fear being killed in retaliation whether they deserved it or not. Nevertheless, none of them ever expressed such fears.

Yuasa also might be expected to fear that, having conducted vivisections (apart from the issue of whether it was right or wrong to do so), he would also suffer vivisection. But the thought never even occurred to him.

"Inside, I was making all sorts of rationalizations to justify what I had done. 'I was just following orders. There was nothing I could do about it. There was a war going on. It was not the first time something like this had been done. Everybody was doing it.' Things like that. Plus, the war was already over."

Here, we see clearly an example of how mentally "strong" people are who live their lives conforming to the group and who possess only the weakest sense of themselves as individuals. People with no sense of self are comfortable only as long as they belong to a group. When the group panics, they panic, but the feeling soon passes. Groups always make it unclear how much responsibility individuals bear for their actions, and they function on the premise that all actions are agreed to by everyone in the group.

Another reason he was not overly uneasy about his fate even though he was confined to a prison camp had to do with the attitude of the Chinese government. Over and over again, the prisoners were told, "The people of China are a generous people. If you truly repent of your misdeeds and reform your way of thinking, you will be forgiven and you can return home. If you stubbornly resist and make a false confession of guilt, you will inevitably be exposed and punished." Inside the prison camps, this was called the "Policy of Generosity." It was essentially the same policy as "Ideological Reform," applied in this case to Japanese war criminals.

Nevertheless, it is important to understand that there were several types of ideological reform practiced by the Chinese Communist Party at this time. Towards wealthy Chinese farmers, urban commercial capitalists, members of the Nationalist Party, and collaborators with the Japanese Army, China was anything but generous. This fact is apparent from a series of government documents produced during the period after the People's Republic of China was established on October 1, 1949, when China turned inward after finishing the fight against outside forces such as Japan and the Nationalist Party.

The "PRC Land Reform Law" dated June 30, 1950, states the following:

In order to guarantee the implementation of land reform, people's courts shall be established in each province during the period of land reform and, employing circuit courts, those corrupt bosses who have committed heinous crimes and are despised by the people, as well as criminals who oppose the land reform law or try to destroy it, shall be tried in accordance with the law and punished. Indiscriminate arrest, assault, murder, and any other physical punishment or surreptitious physical punishment is strictly forbidden.

Nevertheless, four months later in the "Instructions Regarding the Suppression of Anti-Revolutionary Activities from PRC Central" dated October 1, 1950, the government had turned to vicious oppression.

Anti-revolutionary elements which refuse to repent but continue in their evil ways in the post-liberation period, particularly after receiving generous dispensation, shall be sup-

pressed in conformation with regulations governing the punishment of anti-revolutionary activities as promulgated by the Committee of State of the Central People's Government. Those deserving of execution shall be sentenced at once to death. Those deserving
imprisonment and reform shall be arrested and imprisoned at once and made to reform. In
enforcing these matters, the court's decision shall be made public by announcement in the
printed media (placed prominently where it will be noticed) or disseminated widely
among the masses by other means for the purpose of political education.

Not a few Communist party leaders and committee members have become puffed
up with pride due to the victory and have grown complacent about the enemy threat, or
in the new political environment have come under the influence of corrupt ideas about
personal freedom. As a result, they have confused the issue of opposition to isolation-
ism in the context of the battle for national unification with the issue of resolute suppression of anti-revolutionary activities in the context of the battle with the enemy, and have
confused the correct, severe suppression of anti-revolutionary activities with indiscriminate murder, thereby misapprehending the policy of 'Combining Suppression and
Generosity' as only a policy of 'Generosity.'

In this way, it is said that anti-revolutionary elements totaling 700,
000 people were sentenced to death.[5]

In addition, the ideological reform of Christian missionaries was
severe and included torture. The American medical psychologist
Robert J. Lifton has conducted a detailed analysis of missionaries
and intellectuals expelled to Hong Kong in *Thought Reform and the
Psychology of Totalism*.[6]

All of these policies belonged to a single Chinese Communist
Party and were carried out during one period of time, but Japanese
prisoners in their isolated environment were unaware of this.

Confessing Guilt in a Protected Environment

In any case, China embraced a policy of generosity toward Japanese prisoners. They were provided with meals surpassing in quantity and quality those offered Chinese (Nationalist) soldiers in custody. Doctor Yuasa even received compensation for the diagnosis
and treatment of Japanese prisoners he performed under orders.

It was a period of work, education, and confession of guilt within
a collective. He heard the story of the "Long March" encompassing
25,000 miles, and of the sad lives of China's farmers. Or, from a
Japanese prisoner, he heard the story of how, after the liberation, a
soldier of the liberation army whom he had been fighting as the
enemy carried him on his back through the mud. The collective stories had a powerful emotional effect and induced each individual to
reflect on his misdeeds. Weeping, they admitted remorsefully that,
"The Chinese people bore such suffering and lived so virtuously,
yet we killed them mercilessly." Their regret for misdeeds and their

trust of the Chinese side led them to make confessions of guilt. To use the metaphor of the sun and the north wind from Aesop's *Fables*, the confessions came in response to the warmth of the sun. There was also the threat that, if they did not confess their guilt, the north wind could be made to blow.

Yuasa confessed to his involvement in vivisections. He could not bring himself, however, to write that he had extracted brains from living bodies or that a urologist had removed a living man's testicles. He felt that those acts were too dirty, too shameful, and too despicable for him to claim that he had been able to rationalize them to himself because they were his orders. His written confession was immediately returned to him as inadequate, filled with excuses and showing a lack of genuine remorse.

At the end of 1952, as the Korean War reached a stalemate, Yuasa and several hundred other war criminals were transferred to a prison in Taiyuan, Shanxi Province. They were blindfolded and transported by train, and because they arrived at night he had no idea where it was, but he later learned that he was in the Taiyuan Prison. Taiyuan Prison: was that not the place where Yuasa and the other surgeons had performed vivisections on four Chinese men?

For the first three months in prison they were housed 10 men to a room, which was about 15 feet square, and apart from interrogations by prosecutors they were not allowed outside their cell. In March their treatment changed and they began to get cooked rice with fish or meat with their meals. In June, Yuasa collapsed from tuberculosis of the lungs. He was infected because he slept side by side in his cell with fellow inmates who were infected with tuberculosis. He had a high fever and coughed blood. The Chinese doctors conscientiously treated him with antibiotics acquired from the Soviet bloc. Yuasa battled his serious illness inspired by one thought: that he wanted to return to Japan and be with his children. Eventually the progress of the disease was halted and he recovered.

At this point, Yuasa had already confessed guilt for all of his misdeeds, including the ones he had omitted earlier. By the time he received a letter from the mother of the man who had been vivisected for the education of the medical reservists, he was finally able to picture the man he had killed as not merely one man sacrificed to medical vivisection but as an individual human being with a family, and the realization had caused him unspeakable suffering and grief. This is what the mother wrote.

Yuasa, I am the mother whose son you killed. The day before his death, my son was picked up and taken away by the Security Police. I went to the gate of the Security Police Headquarters and waited and watched. The next day the gate opened suddenly. My poor son was placed on a truck and taken away somewhere. I followed on my bicycle, but because I have bound-feet there was no way I could keep up and soon I lost sight of him. I looked everywhere, but I had no idea where they had taken him. The next day, someone I knew came and told me what had happened to him. "Old lady, your son was taken to the army hospital and dissected alive," the person said. I was sad, so sad I thought my eyes would burst from weeping. I could not tend the rice paddies I had been cultivating. I could not eat. Yuasa, I hear that you are now under arrest. I asked the government to please punish you severely. (The contents of the letter written in Chinese as rendered by Yuasa.)

Doctors show little interest in the social relations and personal histories of their patients. They ask for an absolute minimum of information pertaining directly to the illness. In fact, they tend to think that if they know too much about a patient's personal history it may cloud their judgment regarding treatment. They have been trained in this way to see patients as living objects. How much more so the man he dissected alive. All of his mechanisms of repression were at work to forget what the man's face and hands looked like. Even when the image of the butchered man's internal organs floated in front of his eyes, he still could not recall the look of helpless horror etched on the man's face. But as soon as he read the mother's letter, he could see the man as an individual human being, surrounded by the family he loved. Moreover, the letter informed him that the man was taken into custody without just cause and turned over to Army Surgeon Yuasa the next day without investigation. The man was arrested solely because Yuasa had asked the Security Police to supply him with material for live dissection.

In his dimly lit prison cell, lost in solitary thought, Yuasa began to recall all sorts of forgotten details. Originally, in confessing his guilt, he had simply been thinking of how much he wanted to go home to Japan, and he wrote his confession out of his desire to pass the investigation of the prosecutors. Now those selfish considerations faded away and he began to realize what a twisted path he had followed as a medical doctor. Intending always to become a doctor who, like his father, lived alongside his patients as their equal, he had somehow ended up becoming the complete opposite. This happened not from his own will but because he had been swept along by forces in Japan that sent him in a mistaken direction, away from his true self. In the process, he had become a man without a self. Yuasa felt this from the bottom of his heart.

The Inability to Recognize One's Own Guilt

Afterward there was great improvement in the treatment of inmates at Taiyuan Prison. The jailers continued to eat rice with chestnuts, but the war criminals were served cooked rice with side dishes of fish or meat. It was explained to him that this was because prisoners were required to be treated as closely as possible to the lifestyle of their mother country. They were also able to play volleyball in the athletic field. In the spring of 1956 they were even divided into several groups to make a tour of the new China.

In June of 1956, Yuasa received a stay of prosecution and was released. The Chinese side had decided to distinguish the deeds he had committed from the orders he had received, and on that basis they considered him responsible for the deeds. Even so, they gave him a stay of prosecution.

In July, he arrived in Maizuru, Japan, and returned by train to his home in Shinagawa, Tokyo. He had been away for 14 years. Though many people were on hand to welcome him home, he was shocked not just by the extent to which Japan had recovered from the war but also by something else.

Among those gathered to welcome him were army surgeons and nurses with whom he once worked. One of the army surgeons who had returned to Japan immediately after the defeat said this to him.

"Yuasa, why were you labeled a war criminal? I bet you insisted that the war was correct, didn't you? All you had to do was hide your feelings and go along with things, you know."

"No, that's not it at all. Remember what we did?"

"Huh? What do you mean?"

It was a full 11 years since the war had ended, and only now, for the first time, was the former army surgeon forced to recall performing vivisections. There was a wide gulf separating Dr. Yuasa, who had faced the past, and the doctors who had come to welcome him.

Yuasa discovered that all the army surgeons who had returned to Japan from North China took exactly the same stance. The North China Regional Army numbered 300,000 men, and there were at least 20 hospitals there to serve them. The hospital surgeons and combat surgeons combined must have numbered in the thousands. There were also thousands of medics and nurses. But not one of them said a word about guilt. Had even a single voice admitted, "We did terrible things here, so the best move is to get out of China," all the army surgeons would have left Taiyuan immediately in those days after the defeat. Given that no one thought of what they did as evil, there was no necessity even to deny it. Under the catch-all excuse that "war is a terrible thing," the events had been utterly forgotten without a trace even in the deepest recesses of their minds.

Immediately upon his return to Japan, Yuasa entered the Red Cross Hospital in Tokyo. He received treatment for the holes in his lungs left by his bout with tuberculosis. The following year, in March of 1957, he returned to his alma mater Jikei Medical School and restudied internal medicine. From 1958 he started working at the Nishi Ogikubo Clinic in Suginami, Tokyo, and he remains there today. In addition to his diagnosis and treatment of patients, he has participated in the Japanese peace movement.

For six years after returning to Japan, however, he said nothing about the crimes he committed in China. For a while, he was concerned mostly with his survival. If what he had done became known, patients would stop coming for treatment, he worried. Eventually he won the trust of patients in the area and felt able to speak about them at rallies in support of the peace movement. Even so, his wife is still opposed to his speaking about war crimes. "My wife suffered in the containment camps in China. She doesn't want to remember any of it, I suppose. But, her resistance makes me feel very lonely," Yuasa says.

Yuasa published an account of the war crimes he committed in China in *Kesenai Kioku* (*Indelible Memories*), as told to Yoshikai Natsuko. This book continues to be widely read.

Let me introduce here three responses to the publication.

One of them was from Dr. O, the doctor who had amputated the arm of the Chinese man at Yuasa's first vivisection. Perhaps he had recalled the past after being admonished by Yuasa, for he sent the following letter.

> Regarding the publication of the reminiscences you told me about, to be honest I feel extremely threatened by it. A coward such as myself, through pure circumstance, was assigned an evil role, and I have suffered a tortured conscience each time I think of it ever since.
>
> Unlike myself, you lived inside the Shanxi and Communist armies, you experienced a situation where you could suitably reflect on your misdeeds, and now your conscience is clear. I, on the other hand, live every day filled with deep anxiety. Please, I beg you on my hands and knees, lead me by your generous spirit away from these stormy seas (October, 1980).

Dr. O's forgetfullness was shaken because Yuasa persistently spoke to him over a long period from the 1960s to 1970s. But what sort of "tortured conscience" does the man really suffer? He possesses an abstract knowledge of the idea that the vivisection he performed is condemned by society today. However, he has not held imaginary conversations with the spirits of the dead as Yuasa did while in prison. It was on the basis of repeated lonely conversations with the spirits of the dead that, reading the letter from the mother of one of the dead men, Yuasa was able to bring them back from the realm of medical objects into the realm of humanity as people who had lived in a certain time, were connected to the people they loved, and whose faces showed all the human emotions. It was a process that also involved self-discovery, turning Yuasa himself from a medical object into a human being. It was not that he had a clear conscience, but that he had chosen to live each day bearing his burden of guilt.

As to be expected, Yuasa also received anonymous threats. One postcard read:

I saw your report regarding vivisection and cannot contain my anger. It is impossible to understand what motivated you to speak out about something like that at this late date—publicity? You are the epitome of stupidity. With international relations as delicate as they now are, are you enough of an idiot not to realize what damage speaking about such things will inflict on relations between the two countries? Figure out the difference between things that can be said and things that must not be said . . . . You are a disgrace.

The letter, written in old-fashioned script, was from a man of the wartime generation. Its concern with "damage to relations between the two countries" is worlds removed from the spirit of humanity that Yuasa seeks. It clearly reveals the emotional limitations of the old man who wrote it, educated as he was always to consider people's actions in terms of his own interests.

Let me introduce one more letter that came from Yuasa's own brother, Minoru, a doctor of internal medicine. After the war, Minoru established himself in Hokkaido as a medical practitioner.

The book arrived 3-4 days after your postcard. For some reason I felt a moment of uneasiness. Maybe it is a feeling common to all of us who went to war. I opened the pages and began to read. Earth-shaking! I felt I had to brace myself. This was what everyone had been afraid would come, and here it was. As your brother, I am prepared to suffer the consequences with you. It was brave of you to express yourself so honestly. It must have felt like spitting up blood to say those words. I do not have one ounce of your courage. Like you, I was forced to experience the bitterness of war, though not of the extreme sort you write about. They are the dark, dirty scars of my youth that I will never be able to wipe away completely. Even now, there are times when I cannot control feelings that make the blood rush to my head.

You were just a youth trained in samurai values in a household under the care of our middle-class parents in downtown Tokyo, and out of a sense of duty you obediently followed the orders of your superiors because they came from the army—no, from the emperor himself—and for the sake of your family and colleagues you blindly and without complaint submitted to ridiculous orders that you could never justify rationally. Some people would go to church and make a Christian-style confession of sins in order to express everything in their hearts, but you are one who puts things down in writing. It is something that requires great courage. For Japanese people immersed in the teachings of Buddhism, such courage is doubly difficult.

I realize that I completely misunderstood the word 'brainwashing' that returnees from China brought back with them. I thought it meant only to be converted to communist ideology. [Author's note: Returnees did not bring the word back with them from China. Others used it to label them.] Years ago, when we were boys, I read a story titled "The King's Ears Are Donkey Ears" in a book of Aesop's fables, about a timid barber who spoke the words of the title to a tree, and when the tree was made into a violin it sounded those words when played. I am just like that barber, and have been speaking all these years to nature for relief, and maybe I can only continue to speak to nature for the rest of my life.

I remember buying a camera in China and, fearful lest I dirty the lens, taking pictures of nothing but natural scenery. The fact that this year I made my third trip to post-war China is because I wanted to look at it with friendly eyes, praying for the recovery of the China we laid waste and searching for atonement. Maybe the reason I came to Hokkaido was because I thought its wide, open spaces and cold northern climate made it the right sort of place for me to rid myself of the awful experiences of my youth.

[portion omitted]

I telephoned right away to order your book for my daughter and her husband, and for my eldest son. It will be our bible. I have it with me now in Sapporo and am asking them to read it.

This letter was extraordinarily precious to Yuasa Ken. His brother, separated by less than a year in age, shows that he understands—as someone who lived through those times—the work his younger brother is trying to do in manfully bearing the weight of his guilt. The elder brother speaks to his younger brother in his own words, infused with his own sense of sorrow.

Individual Human Beings Have But One Chance at Life

Yuasa has always thought of his past actions as a personal issue. If he insisted on making excuses such as "I was forced to do it," or "Everyone took part in it, so there was no way for me to stop it," in the end he would have had no life of his own. In that case, he would have been unable to live a life of his own making as an individual, and would have had no choice but to spend his life as a mere member of a collective, confined within that collective. By taking personal responsibility for his actions, both the good and the bad, and questioning the meaning of what he had done, he reclaimed his life for himself. This is the way Yuasa chose to live his life after the war.

Yuasa's story was the first time I had ever heard about practice of surgery conducted in North China by army surgeons. My own father was an army surgeon, but he never spoke of it. He lived his life to the end believing that war was folly while rigidly maintaining his status as a male authority figure. When I went to medical school, the older doctors who returned from China never spoke about it either. The only thing I remember hearing from one of the professors was something he said in an unguarded moment: "We did terrible things in China, but we also did some good."

Medical schools are still run on an authoritarian model just as they were before the war; professors, who are far from expert in every field of medicine, present themselves as omnipotent; and graduates spend their careers working within a medical office system. Medical schools, public hospitals, and medical entrepreneurs join forces to create powerful factions, pursue research without questioning its meaning, and learn to skillfully manipulate the health care system. These factors have led to the development of a twisted form of medical care in Japan that is unconcerned with the plight of the socially disadvantaged, the mentally ill, or those suffering from Hansen's disease (leprosy) and other such diseases and that remains oblivious to the spiritual needs of patients, believing without question that the cutting edge of medicine is to be found in organ transplantation and reproductive medicine.

The extent to which Japanese medicine is built upon the legacy of silence about wartime crimes was made painfully clear in the case of AIDS transmission through medical blood products (*yakugai eizu*), which came to light in 1996. It showed that the Ministry of Welfare, medical researchers including Abe Hide (vice-president of Teikyo University), and the Green Cross were a three-faced monster with one body created by the evil deeds of the Japanese army medical corps.

The predecessor of the Green Cross, the "Japan Blood Bank," was founded in 1951 immediately after the onset of the Korean War. At the time when Yuasa and others were being questioned about their guilt in conducting vivisections on the Chinese mainland, the company was being set up by three major proponents of vivisection and human experimentation, Kitano Masatsugu and Niki Hideo, formerly key men in Unit 731 (Guandong Army Disinfection and Water

Provision Corps), and Naito Ryoichi, formerly professor in the Disinfection Unit at the Army Medical School. Those men used the methods of freezing and drying blood learned from wartime experiments on human subjects to turn blood they bought cheaply in slum areas such as San'ya, Kamagasaki, and Kotobuki-cho into dried-blood products that they sold to the United States Army at an enormous profit. The emergency demand for medical products generated by the Korean War turned war criminals in the medical profession into rich men. By 1964, the company had grown into the "Green Cross" and was busy importing large quantities of purchased blood from the United States and, with the full cooperation of the Ministry of Welfare, made Japan into one of the major consumer nations of blood products (albumin, globulin, and congealing agents).

Meanwhile, it turns out that the vast majority of former directors of the central research institute of the Ministry of Welfare, the National Institute of Preventive Hygiene, and heads of smaller specialized research centers were formerly doctors in the Army Hygiene and Water Provision Corps or in the Army Medical School. Moreover, the leader of the "Research Group Concerning the Status of AIDS in Japan," Professor Abe Hide, had in 1958 as a member of the Office of Internal Medicine at Tokyo University come in contact with Naito Ryoichi of the Green Cross and afterwards was named a member of the Board of Trustees of the "Naito Foundation for the Promotion of Medical Research." For them, the lives of individual patients were of minor concern. Knowing full well the danger of using unheated blood products, the collusion of those three entities led to large numbers of people becoming infected with the AIDS virus.

Moreover, none of those involved within the medical establishment has shown remorse for the tragedy. For example, Teikyo University has not questioned the nature of their organization that could name a man like Professor Abe Hide to a position of responsibility as vice president. Medical students likewise raise no questions. On the contrary, the medical school professors I know are bold enough to argue that "The medical profession is based on trust. If patients found out our medical care could not be trusted, the next thing you know they would stop coming for treatment."

The Japanese medical profession has pressed forward with its gilded medicine and medical care by forgetting the misdeeds of wartime doctors. Doctors have failed to accept Yuasa Ken as a prophet of Japanese medicine and go on practicing medicine with the same impoverished spirit they possessed since wartime. And the people of Japan continue to believe that the medical care provided by such men is among the most advanced in the world.

Notes

1. Published 1967; Japanese translation *Ushinawareta hiai* by Hayashi Shun'ichiro and Baba Ken'ichi, Kawade Shobo Shinsha, 1972; reprinted 1984.
2. Published 1989; Japanese trans. *Chinmoku to iu na no isan* by Himeoka Toshiko, Jiji Tsushinsha, 1993.
3. From *Kesenai kioku—Yuasa gun'i seitai kaibo no kiroku [Indelible Memories: Army surgeon Yuasa's record of vivisection]*, as told to Yoshikai Natsuko, Nitchu Publ., 1981.
4. In the description of the dissection which follows, in sections where my interview with Yuasa was vague I rely on the description he gave to Yoshikai Natsuko, in *Kesenai kioku [Indelible Memories]*.
5. *Genten Chugoku Gendaishi [Primary Sources in Chinese Modern History]*, vol. 1 "Seiji" *["Government"]*, eds. Mori Kazuko and Kokubun Ryosei, Iwanami Shoten.
6. Published 1961; Japanese translation by Ono Yasuhiro, *Shiso kaizo no shinri— chugoku ni okeru senno no kenkyu*, Seishin Shobo, 1979.

Part IV

Artistic Responses

11

Reunion: A Play in 2 Acts, 5 Scenes, and an Epilogue (Excerpts)*

Yoshiji Watanabe

Reunion, a powerful play written by the playwright and actor Yoshiji Watanabe in 1991, explores the terrible pain, suffering, and complexity of the war's aftermath—consequences of the acts of human cruelty in war. The protagonist of the play, Shinzo, age seventy-nine, must confront his past as an army officer in China, when his first wife, Haru, abandoned in Manchuria, sojourns to Japan in search of her ex-husband. Shinzo, in the mean time, founded and heads the Fujita Machinery Company, has remarried, and has started a new life and family in Japan. Now he lives with his son, Tomoyoshi, age forty, after the death of his second wife. Upon the return of his first wife, Shinzo must relive his past in Manchuria and, for the first time, his son learns about this chapter of his father's hidden life. As Shinzo struggles with whether to be a guarantor for Haru, his son, Tomoyoshi, vehemently objects. Father and son clash and results in physical violence.

In real life, Watanabe's father was an accused Class C war criminal, and his family was ostracized by the community. Yoshiji, his father, and mother all suffered terribly for many years. His father never spoke about his experiences in China, but suffered in silence and often took it out on his wife and son in acts of violence. He took his silence to his grave. In the "Confessional" preface to the play, the playwright tells of his attempts to understand the violence of his father and the ghosts that haunted his household. In his need to uncover the past, he journeys to China, to the places where his father had lived and spoke with the Chinese people who had suffered under the Japanese occupation. Finally, his meeting with a group of Japanese women who had been abandoned in China brought home the full extent of the suffering of all the participants in the war—the aggressors and victims, the dead, and the survivors.—Editor

Preface: "A Confession"

Manchuria was Japan's new frontier, her colony on the Chinese mainland. Japan invaded the territory in 1931 and poured in not only a huge amount of military personnel, but mobilized a large number of Japanese farmers to develop military facilities, industry,

---

* Printed with permission of Yoshiji Watanabe and Kazuko Yokoi.

171

and agriculture in Manchuria. The Japanese government tried to persuade families to migrate, but farmers were reluctant to leave their villages. So the government offered inducements for people to join what they called "development groups."

Manchuria became home to more than one million Japanese—300,000 of them farming families. Most of the farmers were the poorest people from their villages in Japan, who followed a promise of escape from poverty. Manchuria came under the control of the Japanese Imperial Army. Army leaders pushed the invading forces inland from Manchuria to the rest of China, and as Chinese resistance fighters struggled against the invaders, Japan found itself in a quagmire. In December 1941, Japan also plunged into war against the Allies in the Pacific.

By August 1945, it was obvious that Japan's only future was surrender. On the ninth of August, Soviet troops stormed across the Manchurian border and advanced rapidly. The Japanese Army abandoned the Japanese settlers and retreated to save themselves. Army leaders also reasoned that the civilian population would act like a buffer to slow the Soviet advance. Many of the settlers died. Some survived and remained in China. Many were women who looked for whatever means they could to stay alive.

It is strange that when the Japanese government asked the conquering Army and Japanese settlers to respect and worship the imperial family, there was no request that the imperial family and Japanese Army look after the Japanese farmers who were abandoned in Manchuria. Instead, they retreated earlier than anyone else.

More than fifty yeas later, some of these people were able to return to Japan. One day, I met with a group of Japanese wives who were stranded in China. It was on July 6, 1991 in Nagano Prefecture in a place called Yasuoka Village. I will never forget the emotion of that day. And I never realized how that one day would change my life.

The women spoke of their escape from the ugliness and flames of war. At times they were agitated, other times they let tears fall with no attempt to hide them, and at times they even laughed. I wondered how they could still smile after being discarded and left to the horrors and hardships of the past half-century. I wanted to know more about them, and I also realized that there was something inside me that compelled me to go to Yasuoka Village. I had to make sure why I came and what I was really looking for from these women. In front of these women, who talked about their horrible past as if it happened only yesterday, I felt a dark cloud of guilt that kept hanging over my head long after I left the village.

My father went to Manchuria in 1934, a commissioned officer in the Imperial Japanese Army. His assignment was to crush anti-Japanese resistance fighters—Japanese called them "bandits," who were, in fact, only guerrilla bands fighting for their invaded Motherland. My father and mother married in Manchuria in 1938 and in 1939 my elder brother was born. That same year, after the four-month war against the Soviets broke out on the Mongolian border at Nomonhan, my father became an official of Japan's puppet government in Manchuria. Then, when the Japanese military expected the Soviets to come into the war, my father was once again drafted and given a military officer position with the Japanese Army. In the summer of 1945, my father received early warning that Japan was about to surrender. All members of the imperial family had been sent back to Japan a month earlier for their safety. My father, as well as other military officers, used their position to put their own families on a train for a port, blasted the rails one after another after the passage of their train, and returned to Japan by ship. The ship was able to dock at a port in Japan only three weeks after Japan's surrender to the Allies. My elder brother, who remembered those times, told this story:

> The Japanese Army, including my father, deserted the Japanese settlers, not only by leaving them behind, but also by destroying their access to any escape route. Many of them did not even know that the Soviet Union had entered the war. I could imagine their fate afterwards being abandoned by their own country and army.

My father would, after the war ended, wake up suddenly in the middle of the night, sit up, and stare into the darkness with glaring eyes. He lived in emotional agony. He argued and fought constantly with my mother. He would grab her by the hair and throw her down, then pull her along on the floor by her hair. Perhaps he was remembering the past—those Japanese settlers who were left behind running for their lives, those Chinese who were killed by him. By hurting himself and his family, he was trying to reveal his troubled-soul. Our home was a battlefield—until my parents died.

Peace came to our household, but a disturbance grew in me. I wanted to know more about my parents. Ten years after they died, on September 16, 1991, my wife and I went to China. I carried photographs of my parents with me. For some strange reason, each time I put a piece of the historical jigsaw puzzle together, there were thunderstorms. I arrived in China in a thunderstorm. Later, when I went to Yasuoka Village to speak with the abandoned women, there was a thunderstorm. Again, when I went to speak with my elder brother about the past and to visit my parents' graves, there were thunderstorms. I had an uneasy feeling that my father was trying to tell me something.

On the journey to Manchuria, I arrived on September 18 at the city that used to be called Harbin. It was the anniversary of the Manchurian Incident of 1931 when Japan started its invasion of the territory. Lightning and thunder greeted us as my wife and I went to the hotel. I turned on the television and was astonished by the program: it was about Unit 731, Japan's military organization that conducted experiments on humans for biological warfare in localities near Harbin. Afterwards, I trembled even more when I learned that any program about Unit 731 would be a guaranteed hit in China.

On September 20 we took a night train from Harbin to Mishan, where my parents stayed right before their repatriation back to Japan. It was a fifteen-hour journey. On the morning of the twenty-first, we were eating noodles for breakfast in the dining car when the chef came to us and said "Unit 731 and the Japanese military took many Chinese from this area. They never came back. As a Japanese, what do you think of that?" My mind was a complete blank; I had no answer...

In four days we reached Changchun. We began searching for the house in which my parents lived. Our interpreter, Mr. Lee, searched with great effort and found a house that seemed to be the one. There was a very kind Chinese woman living there and she invited us in. It turned out that her son was studying in Japan and a letter from him had just arrived. She showed me the letter, in a typical brown-colored Japanese envelope with the Chinese address written on it. I was in the house where my parents had lived and I was heartened by the fact that I was being treated so kindly by the Chinese person who now lived there.

We walked around the city. We saw General Tojo's former vacation house, the old government buildings, and the palace that was supposed to be for Emperor Hirohito—a very large building indeed that had been turned into a university.

Finally, we went to the museum of the last emperor of China, Pu Yi, who later became the puppet emperor of Manchuria, manipulated by the Japanese Military in Manchuria. I saw a photograph there that made me stare transfixed in horror. A Japanese officer was laughing as he held his sword high during an execution of Chinese people. About twenty severed heads were lined up for the photograph. I stood there, unable to move, unable to breathe, staring at the scene in the photograph. I saw the heads come alive and stare back at me. In that moment of shock, I also saw the answer to a family riddle that had been with me since childhood.

Ever since I was a small child, people in our neighborhood avoided us. My father was designated a Class C war criminal, and in a Japan that was trying to make the transition to an era of peace, we were an unfortunate reminder to our neighbors of the past.

Raised in that kind of environment, I felt that I had been searching throughout my life for a place where I could feel secure. I think that is why I entered the world of the theater. Yet deep inside, I always had the feeling that I could never be happy, and I refused any help offered me. As I stood frozen before this photograph, I understood why I came here and was staring at this photograph: I was still looking for a place where my soul could find the security I wanted, and I still had not found it.

During the "Fifteen-year War," starting from Japan's invasion of Manchuria in 1931 and ending with Japan's surrender to the Allies in 1945, my family participated in a war on the side of the aggressors. They murdered Chinese people, just as in this photograph, and they abandoned their fellow Japanese. The souls of the dead and murdered still wander, drifting among those who are considered "normal families." The suppressed fear reached out, encircling me as a child, stirring in the deepest part of my soul.

As a child of one of these aggressors, my soul was in distress. As I stood there, emotionally paralyzed, I realized that the root to all that I had experienced in my life was here, in the faces of the Chinese people I saw in this photograph. This was why I felt I could never find happiness. This was the cause of my fear.

The secret of my father's role in history died along with him. My mother's hatred for him weighed heavily on top of my father's own postwar hatred for himself. After my father died, my mother took her own life, as if she had followed him into death. I had hated them both and had not forgiven them, but at that moment standing in front of the photograph, for the first time, I began to understand the deep conflict of my father and mother as human beings in the days of the postwar era.

After I came back to Japan from the trip to China I could not but feel for those millions of Chinese who became victims of Japan's aggression. I began questioning my own existence. I was living, but I was also denying my life. I decided I needed to examine my life in its entirety.

Did my parents think they were the only ones suffering? I realized that the war of aggression had also robbed me of my childhood. My parents came to realize this and therefore were very lenient with me, and allowed me plenty of freedom. I often think that if they were alive, I'd like to put our lives back together.

I think about the abandoned women who talked with me in Yasuoka village. As farmers, their lives in China then, compared to army families, were relatively harsh. They had to work hard to grow rice for the Japanese Army. Then, after the war, these women, who were left behind, were punished by the Chinese as they represented the Japanese invaders who committed war crimes. Yet they lived honestly with the Chinese people. The lives they led were those of the aggressors as well as the victims, and their lives atoned for the wrongs that people like my father had committed during the war.

The labyrinth of fate made me go to China to find the source of my fears, the specter that haunted me from within. For this understanding, I owe much to a large number of people, because now I can escape from that fear and finally face my postwar history as a Japanese.

I wrote this play for the people of Yasuoka village and for my father and mother. If possible, I would also like to convey my feelings to the people of China. After I met the abandoned women and after I went to China, I was finally able to look at my life and question whether I was living it the right way. I was also able to experience deep gratitude. I realized that my life could not end with my guilt unresolved. I wrote this drama to return and heal—as well as possible—the souls that were torn apart in China. This is my way of facing my family's role in Japanese history.

*   *   *

After a separation of fifty-five years, Haru (age seventy-six), the female protagonist, returns to Japan to visit her home country and see her former husband, Shinzo (age seventy-nine). She was one of many women and children left behind in China by the Imperial Army after Japan's surrender in August 1945. With no means to support herself and straddled with two young children, Haru married a Chinese peasant and started a new family. In this excerpt, Haru and Shinzo, at their first meeting, exchange experiences after their separation on August 9, 1945.—Editor

ACT I, SCENE 2

Two weeks have passed [since Haru's return to Japan]. It's a hot afternoon. In the grounds of a temple in Yasutani Village, Shinzo is sitting by himself. As soon as he sees or hears something he jumps to his feet and then sits back down again. Some time passes.

Shinzo realizes that a person has come and he stands up. Haru enters from stage left. Their eyes meet. Shinzo holds his breath and is momentarily struck dumb. Haru, who is five years younger than him, looks much older. Shinzo is full of emotion. Haru shifts her gaze upwards. Quite a long time passes.

Shinzo: It's Haru...isn't it?

He moves towards her. Haru moves away. Shinzo stops. Haru tries to maintain the distance between them.

Shinzo: (without really meaning to speak) ...I see you're well. (He is surprised at the silliness of what he has just said.)
Haru: Yes. (She replies firmly as if she is speaking about someone else.)

Shinzo falters. Awkward silence as words run out.

Shinzo: You're still...alive...

Haru looks directly at Shinzo for the first time. PAUSE

Haru: (suddenly) Shinzo...
Shinzo: Yes.
Haru: ... I knew you were alive.
Shinzo: (shocked) You knew?
Haru: When I came back to Japan after a little while I went to your house...

Shinzo:	You did?
Haru:	Shizuko Tanaka took me by the hand and dragged me there.
Shinzo:	(shocked)...

Awkward silence as words run out again.

Haru:	When I reached Kawasaki station, I went out the gate and looked at the city...all the bright neon lights seemed to be flying towards me...and suddenly...I thought: "Shinzo is alive somewhere in this city, he is living with his family." Then I started running. Before I realized it I was on a train. Everything finished at that point.
Shinzo:	...

PAUSE

Shinzo:	Do you resent me?
Haru:	...No. I'm very glad to see you looking so well.
Shinzo:	...
Haru:	(kindly) Please, I wish you continued good health.

Haru bows very sincerely. Shinzo keeps standing. Haru prepares to leave.

Shinzo:	What about the children! Yaeko! Minoru!

Haru stops.

Haru:	...
Shinzo:	(comes closer to Haru) Are the children alive? (fervently)

Haru looks long and hard at Shinzo and silently shakes her head.

Shinzo:	(goes into a daze) Oh...!

Shinzo moves away from Haru.

Shinzo: Please, if nothing else, please tell me what happened. (He bows deeply.)

LONG PAUSE

Haru: I don't know where to begin.

PAUSE

Haru: Well...it was August 2, 1945, right?

Haru begins to speak mechanically, almost as if she was talking about someone else.

Haru: You were drafted into the army without even a draft notice...

Shinzo: ...

Haru: Only women and children and the sick and elderly of our corps were left...but we felt it was our duty to give the army even our last grain of rice or last bean. And then that day...August 11!... Without knowing at all what has happened, we went to our fields. Our commander came and he looked as if something was wrong. "Bring enough food for ten days and gather at Enja Station," he says. I went straight to the station with the children, taking only my good luck charm from the Suwa Shrine and your fountain pen that you liked so much. There were thousands of people from different districts waiting at the station—it was bedlam! We waited, but no train came. Finally a train arrived the next day...but it left empty.

Shinzo: Empty?

Haru: If we started to get on the train, people would call out "Traitor!" "You'll be taken to the Soviets" and in the end no one got on. Apparently it was the commander's orders.

Shinzo: ...

Haru: So we watched the empty train leave and I suddenly felt that I would like to see the house and fields again. So we went back, but the house and the fields had been wrecked. We just went into a daze and wandered around aimlessly. A coolie told us that bandits were coming, so we ran. The whole corps formed a line and we made it to the river, but the bridge had been destroyed. That year the rains had been very heavy and the river was swollen. It would have been hard for even a strong person to cross it. Behind us the rebelling Manchurian army was catching up, so we had to cross the river—that muddy flow...

PAUSE

Haru: We...had to leave the sick and elderly behind. Remember our next door neighbor, Miyoko?

Shinzo: Yes.

Haru: Tuberculosis. We had to leave her behind too. "You go first," she kept saying, gesturing with her hands. "Just go! Go! Goodbye, Goodbye!"...she just kept saying it and saying it...waving her hand. Her mother was frantic. She kept leaping into the river then dragging herself back, over and over...

Shinzo: And what happened to her to Miyoko?

Haru: Not one single person said they would help the family...

Shinzo: (nodding) ....

Haru: And after that we just walked. We walked and walked...through the pitch-black night like lost souls—hundreds of us, trudging and trudging. I don't know how many days we walked... One day we were completely surrounded by bandits. Knowing that we would probably die, we headed right back into the enemy... Then the sound of gunfire stopped...

Shinzo: ...

Haru: After awhile, we started trudging again. Yaeko and Minoru were getting weak, so I tied a rope around them and pulled them along.

Shinzo: (nodding) ...

Haru: And then, that day...Japanese soldiers... (suddenly becomes agitated)

PAUSE

Haru:	Soldiers. About 100 of them.
Shinzo:	So you were joined by Japanese soldiers?
Haru:	...I was so happy. Now everything will be okay. These soldiers will protect us...that's what I thought... But what seemed like their Commander...

PAUSE

Haru:	(takes a deep breath) Ahhh. (shakes her head) ...they said if the children cried, enemies would discover us...
Shinzo:	What happened?
Haru:	They ordered us to kill the children...
Shinzo:	Kill the children? (shocked)
Haru:	(It is all she can do to keep talking) We couldn't do that. If they were going to kill the children, we decided to all die together. So...we all made a circle, sat down and asked them to throw hand grenades at us. I was holding Yaeko and Minoru close to me...but for some reason we weren't hit. We missed our chance to die, I thought, so I asked them again...
Shinzo:	...
Haru:	...I lost consciousness at that point...then I heard the sound of children crying and screaming, voices and when I came to...Minoru...his chest was... (Haru tries to pull herself together.)
Haru:	I heard Minoru's voice very clearly; he said, "Mommy, it hurts, Mommy, I don't want to die." And then the commander stabbed Minoru's chest with his bayonet!... Minoru's face became paler and paler...and...he stopped breathing... (Haru sobs.)

Shinzo looks into the distance. PAUSE

Haru:	...Mass suicide becomes contagious. It spread like wild-fire from person to person. Yaeko...Yaeko took one look at my face and fled. She thought I was going to kill her.

Shinzo gasps as he listens.

Haru:	The fact is, I did try to kill her... I tried to... I chased her...
Shinzo:	Haru...
Haru:	Then a bullet shot by just in front of me. It shocked me back to my senses... (Her eyes are wide and she speaks clearly.) I tried to kill our child. I was set on it. Nothing mattered any more. I ran around like a devil. I ate weeds and tree roots—whatever I could find. I drank my own urine...
Shinzo:	...
Haru:	One day I realized that Yaeko wasn't there. But then, I felt little feet bumping against my back. Someone had tied her onto my back...maybe I did it myself...

PAUSE

Haru:	Soon we were discovered by Soviet soldiers and taken to a prison camp. There I heard for the first time of Japan's defeat.
Shinzo:	(Nodding) ...The faint sound of thunder in the distance can be heard.
Haru:	...It was a prison camp, but there was no food, no clothing. And winter had come... People just kept dying... I thought "Ahh, this is where Yaeko and I are going to die together." All that was left was to wait for death.
Shinzo:	...

PAUSE

Haru:	Even more terrifying, every night the Russian soldiers came for women. I can't explain the fear I felt at that time...the only thing that got me through was a Korean woman—she was a "comfort woman"...
Shinzo:	...
Haru:	...but, one night she didn't come back.
Shinzo:	...

PAUSE

Haru: One day a Chinese man came. He was called Wang Kei Rin. He told me, "If you come to my home, I'll make sure you get fed." Yaeko was very ill—she could hardly breathe. I thought if I went with him, it might help Yaeko, so I went along.

Shinzo nods vigorously.

Haru: It was a poor farmer's house. But I remember the warmth of the stove so well. Tears just overflowed and I couldn't stop them. And the rice porridge was so delicious. I'll never forget that taste. I finally felt as though I had been brought back to life.

Shinzo: Yes, yes.

PAUSE

Haru: But Yaeko...

Shinzo: What happened to her?

Haru: She did recover briefly, but...

Shinzo: Yes.

Haru: ...she passed away within the year. If only I had died along with her...

Shinzo: Haru!

Haru: I was ashamed to be alive. My children were dead, and I had let myself be rescued by people from the enemy country...but I didn't die!

Shinzo: ...

Haru: And then I...

Shinzo: ... (looks at Haru's face)

Haru: became pregnant.

Shinzo: ...

Haru: Accepting myself and my situation took a long time. I found myself constantly thinking "I'm going to get out of this place and return to Japan!" But after awhile I gave up on that idea. I could hardly abandon the child I was having. And after letting Yaeko and Minoru die, how could I possibly go back to Japan?

Shinzo: Haru, don't think about that—you can let it go, now.

Haru: And what I did was I told myself that I wasn't Japa-
             nese.
Shinzo: ...

PAUSE

Shinzo: It's truly a miracle that you're still alive.
Haru: ...
Shinzo: Are your husband and children well?
Haru: Yes, very well, thank you. I have three children.
Shinzo: I'm glad.
Haru: ...fifty-five years have past since then; it has been a
             long time!
Shinzo: ...

The sound of thunder.

Shinzo: I was taken off to defend the northern border of Man-
             churia against the Soviets. On August 9 we were told
             that the Soviets would attack and my commander or-
             dered me to burn all the division documents. I went to
             the nearby mountains to do that, and during that time
             my division was attacked and completely wiped out. I
             was lucky to have survived. But I was soon caught by
             the Russian soldiers and taken to a prison camp in Si-
             beria. I came back to Japan in spring 1947.
Haru: So that's what happened.
Shinzo: I wanted to fly straight to China, but diplomatic rela-
             tions between Japan and China had been broken off
             and I couldn't go. When I heard about people who had
             come back, I immediately went to see them to find out
             if they had heard any word of you and the children. I
             went all over the place searching. Finally I met Shizuko
             Tanaka and she told me about the mass suicide...
Haru: ...
Shinzo: I went back to the village at first, but I couldn't live
             there—I just didn't get along with the village people
             any more.
Haru: Why not?

Shinzo:	They were very cold toward the people who had returned. I left the village and came to Kawasaki. I began working at one of the factories in town. And I remarried. Her name was Hiroko.
Haru:	Where is she now?
Shinzo:	She died fifteen years ago. It was the same with lots of people after the war. The pressure of not having enough food just caught up with them.
Haru:	...I see...did you have any children?
Shinzo:	Yes, just one. He's called Tomoyoshi.
Haru:	I see...
Shinzo:	If I hadn't gone to Manchuria...I want to say...I want to say...please... please...

Shinzo bows his head low.

Haru:	Shinzo...
Shinzo:	(Desperately trying to keep the flood of emotions under control) I was so stupid. I really wanted to help raise the Japanese flag in Manchuria.
Haru:	Everyone did...
Shinzo:	It didn't even occur to me at the time...that we were invading another people's country. Using military strength to get our way, stealing land and houses. And worse than that treating the Chinese as if they were slaves. And getting you involved in all that, and even our children.
Haru:	That's not what happened.
Shinzo:	And it wasn't just us—I dragged the entire youth group into that mess...they all died, you know...now I'm the only one left.
Haru:	You mustn't say things like that, Shinzo.
Shinzo:	I'm sorry!
Haru:	No matter how much you want to forget—it's impossible. The things you want to forget most of all are the ones you remember the most, don't you think? Often Chinese people who were complete strangers would yell at me. They screamed "Japanese Demon" and threw rocks. I would suddenly wake up in the middle of the night. Someone with a sword is chasing me, but no

	matter how much I try to run away, they would chase after me. We were invaders. It was only to be expected that we would be hated. During the Cultural Revolution...
Shinzo:	...
Haru:	I thought I'd be killed. Everyone said I was a Japanese spy.
Shinzo:	...
Haru:	I was thrown into an internment camp and everyday they tried to force me to admit that I was a spy. But I was completely innocent, so I kept telling them I was not a spy.
Shinzo:	(nodding) ...
Haru:	They finally released me after six months...and just when I was feeling relieved about being free, I developed amnesia.
Shinzo:	Amnesia?
Haru:	Yes... My family was very surprised. My mother-in-law brought in another Japanese woman and she would sing songs.
Shinzo:	Sing songs?
Haru:	Yes, Japanese songs—every day we would sing folk songs, popular songs... (Haru begins to sing "Usagi Ouishi.") After the fifth year, I was finally back to normal.
Shinzo:	Haru, when I found out that you were still alive, at first I couldn't bring myself to come and see you. It was as if the peaceful life that I had finally managed to put together would crumble away. I was scared.
Haru:	(looks tearful) ...Japan has become very rich. But coming back to Japan this time, I realized people like me have been thrown away. Even my own brother thinks that having me around is somehow awkward. Maybe I shouldn't have come back.
Shinzo:	Haru!

PAUSE

Haru:	Shinzo, sometimes I think that my soul is still wandering...around the district where we lived...and where the mass suicides took place... For the past fifty-

五 years, I always imagined that if I could see you again, if I could somehow get back to Japan, that people would be sympathetic, that they would say "that must have been terrible," "how awful for you." That was always how I imagined it would be.

Shinzo: ...

Haru: (suddenly becomes more frantic) I want to return to Japan! I'm Japanese and I want to die in Japan. In Japan! Do you hear me? In Japan!... (She cries violently.)

Shinzo stands in a daze. As if to call the souls of the people who died in the mass suicides, the sound of a small bell can be heard, at first in the distance. It comes closer and then slips away again.

(End of Scene 2)
Sound of bells while scene changes.

In this excerpt, after Haru has been introduced to Shinzo's new family, the father (Shinzo) and his son (Tomoyoshi) are in total disagreement with regard to inviting Haru and her family to Japan. The younger generation does not want to have anything to do with the actions of the previous generation. The two engage in a heated exchange that ends in blows. In this episode, while the women are happily trying on new clothing, the father and son are seriously confronting each other.—Editor

ACT I, SCENE 3

Tazaru (Tomoyoshi's daughter) takes Haru's hand and pulls her over to her room. Misako (Tomoyoshi's wife) goes with them. Shinzo and Tomoyoshi are left and they are silent.

PAUSE

The sound of the women laughing comes from the room.

PAUSE

Shinzo suddenly becomes formal.

Shinzo: Tomoyoshi, regarding Haru...

Tomoyoshi, as if he'd expected this, pours a beer and drinks it.

Shinzo: This time I want to bring Haru back to Japan, along
               with her family.
Tomoyoshi: ...
Shinzo: I will never be able to die in peace if I cannot get them
               to Japan.
Tomoyoshi: ...
Shinzo: I want to be her guarantor.
Tomoyoshi: ...

PAUSE

Tomoyoshi: What do her relatives say about this?
Shinzo: ...They don't even want to see her...
Tomoyoshi: If even her close relatives feel like that, why should
               you have to go to so much trouble? It seems like Misako
               and Tazuru feel like they're related to her, but she has
               nothing to do with me. All I see is some woman who
               was abandoned in China, that's all.

Misako goes to a back room.

Tomoyoshi: Look, Dad, have you thought about how are you going
               to take care of her? Becoming her guarantor is a huge
               responsibility... You know that we can't take that on at
               the moment. Don't you even understand that?
Shinzo: ...Sure, Haru might mean nothing to you, but for me...
               She used to be my wife.
Tomoyoshi: You're nothing but an opportunist, Dad.
Shinzo: ...
Tomoyoshi: And what about Haru herself? Her home is in China,
               she has a family there. If they all come to Japan now,
               they won't be able to speak the language, they won't
               be able to get jobs... I don't think it's a good idea at all
               for her to return to Japan. Don't you agree, Dad?
Shinzo: Somehow I'll manage to look after her living expenses.
Tomoyoshi: Oh sure! How can you? Get a grip on reality, Dad. This
               is the dividing line between success and failure.
Shinzo: What do you mean by that?

Tomoyoshi: I've ordered the work robot. I just spoke with Toa now.
Shinzo: (shocked) What? How could you just decide something as major as that without telling anyone?
Tomoyoshi: Nothing would ever get done if I had to talk to you about every detail.
Shinzo: I won't let you do this!
Tomoyoshi: I don't care what you say, I'm going ahead.
Shinzo: Since when have you been such a mean-spirited merchant?
Tomoyoshi: Merchant?
Shinzo: Making products, producing them...what on earth do you do it for? Tomoyoshi, listen to me, human beings always want to be free and to be able to express their creativity. A real craftsman will make things that are expressions of his soul—truly created. Just pushing a button to make products, with the sole aim to make money...this way of thinking is wrong...
Tomoyoshi: Think about those closest to you for once. Think about how they are struggling. As for the soul of the craftsman and pride in your work, I'm sick of hearing about it.
Shinzo: As for money—all you need is the minimum to live on—that's enough. (With anger) If it's just a matter of money, go ahead, rip down this factory and build condominiums or something.
Tomoyoshi: You're so righteous... Mom was killed by that righteousness of yours.

Suddenly Misako appears.

Shinzo: (His body is shaking) Killed? Are you saying I killed Hiroko?!

Tomoyoshi regrets saying what he knows he shouldn't have said, but refuses to back down.

Tomoyoshi: Who was it that said they had work to do and wasn't even there when Mom died in the hospital?
Shinzo: ...
Tomoyoshi: If it was to help your craftsmen pals, you would even pawn Mom's family jewelry. It was the same with

Mr. Ichikawa! Even though you knew it was highly risky, you became his guarantor and of course he went bankrupt and we're still paying it off. Am I right? Mom died because of your hypocrisy.

Misako tries to stop Tomoyoshi, but she is overwhelmed by this force. Shinzo's whole body is shaking.

Tomoyoshi: I'm a victim of you, too, Dad. When I was in Junior High, I couldn't even go on the school trip. Because you had used the money for something or other—helping someone probably. Can you understand how lonely and upset I felt about that? I bet you can't!

Shinzo: ...

PAUSE

Tomoyoshi: (calmly, reasonable) I always thought it was so strange... You were always too good, always trying madly to help others. Why?! That's what I always wondered. And the day I heard about Haru, I understood why.

Shinzo: ...?!

Tomoyoshi: To you, Mom and I were just incidental. In your heart of hearts it was Haru and your dead children, your comrades from the war. There was no room for us. By looking after other people all the time, you're trying to fill in the emptiness inside you. That's all it is, am I right?

Shinzo: ...

Tomoyoshi: When you thought of Haru and the children, you could never love me, and Mom. The war and the past had nothing to do with me, but they made my life hell.

Shinzo: The other day I went to meet Haru. But the Haru that was standing there was a different person. I was stunned. I was overwhelmed by the experiences of her life. Please, I'm begging you—I don't care if I lose all my worldly possessions, but this time I want to protect Haru—and her family who have also taken on the pain and suffering. Please. (bows his head) Please!! (bows again, very deeply)

PAUSE

Tomoyoshi: Leave out the lies!
Shinzo: What?!
Tomoyoshi: What Haru needs is not fake love. All she needs right now is to face up to the fact that you abandoned her. That's all.

Shinzo fades into a daze and heads for the factory. The sound of Shinzo's groans come from the factory. Misako is holding her breath. Suddenly Shinzo comes out.

Shinzo: Tomoyoshi! Tomoyoshi! Think anything you want of me. I just have this to say: I never looked for pleasures in life. Since I survived the war, my work has been my whole life. Working for the people who died, to build a peaceful Japan. And I believed that was for both you and Hiroko. Of course when you played as I worked, laughing and running around, sometimes images of Yaeko and Minoru would overlap and I would start to cry. When we would eat watermelon in the evenings, I'd remember one of my dead comrades who loved watermelon...but how can you know anything about the war!!

Tomoyoshi: (calmly) Why don't you realize your biggest mistake?
Shinzo: What?!
Tomoyoshi: You all cry about your dead friends and tragedies of the battlefield, but you never mention that you were part of the invading forces and that you killed tens of millions of Chinese...you never mention the "comfort women." Not one soldier has ever expressed regret about the shameful things he did to those women.

Shinzo: ...
Tomoyoshi: If Haru hadn't turned up, you might well have been able to die without saying anything at all. Maybe you think it might have been better that way. But as your son, I would have had to pick up the burden, handed to me in the dark, without a word. That would have been okay with you. (Matter-of-factly) Could you really call us father-and-son?

Shinzo: (body and voice shaking) Listen to me, Tomoyoshi, I have given my all to making things. Production has given shape to my life. That's all one needs in life.

Tomoyoshi: Yeah, that's right, your generation has produced magnificent things...and left everything else ambiguous.

Shinzo: What the hell do you know?

Tomoyoshi: (calmly) If you really want to become Haru's guarantor, then forget you are my father—do it by yourself.

Shinzo: Okay—that's fine. All I need is just one press—I'll build a barracks in the parking lot and live there!

Tomoyoshi: Go ahead—do what you like...

Suddenly they notice Haru standing there.

Shinzo: Haru!

Haru: ...

Tomoyoshi goes straight to his room. Misako follows directly. Their voices can be heard arguing. Tomoyoshi comes out carrying an envelope containing two to three hundred thousand yen.

Tomoyoshi: (to Haru) You decided of your own accord to remain in China. I understand your feeling that as a Japanese you would like to come back to Japan. But do you think your husband and children, who helped you so much, would be happy in Japan? There's the language barrier and difference in customs to think about, and in this highly competitive society, how do you think your family would survive in Japan? My father abandoned you. I think it would be much better for you to stay in China with your family, the people who helped you when you were abandoned. This is all I have right now—please accept it.

Tomoyoshi takes Haru's hand and gives her the envelope. Shinzo leaps on Tomoyoshi. Locked together, they fall to the ground. Shinzo is on top of Tomoyoshi, punching him.

(End of Scene 3)

In this scene, the attention shifts to the younger generation that has not experienced the war directly, but suffers from the after-effects of the war through the previous generation. Tomoyoshi and his wife, Misako, and a friend, Kobayashi, recount their experiences as children of the war generation.—Editor

ACT II, SCENE 4

Evening in a park. Tomoyoshi, after leaving the house, has come to the park and is sitting on a bench by himself. Misako comes.

Misako: I don't understand anything.

Tomoyoshi: ...

Misako: You said you were going to cut all ties with your father, but you're not serious, are you?

Tomoyoshi: ....

Misako: "Shaping his life." That's what father talked about. I never thought of it like that. Wouldn't it be nice to have a bit more money, wouldn't it be nice if life was a bit easier...that's all I ever thought of. And after a while I found I was pressuring myself... And as I was doing that, I didn't even think about how Father was feeling, or Tazuru, or Manalo...or even you. Perhaps I didn't want to hear the screaming that was really going on...deep in everyone's heart. I don't deserve the name of 'wife' or 'mother.' You know, it was good that this happened.

Tomoyoshi: I'm moving out.

Misako: ...

Tomoyoshi: I'm going to start over, right from the beginning.

Misako: ...You mean you're running away?

Tomoyoshi: Running away?

Misako: That's right—that's what it would be—running away!

Tomoyoshi: What? (He sobs uncontrollably, his whole body shaking.) What can you expect? I was born in deception.

Misako: Tomoyoshi...

PAUSE

Misako: (a little angry) What are you talking about?!! (She's clutching Tomoyoshi as if her, or his, life depends on it.) I think you already realize this, but your father wants you to help him, even if it means exposing your own foolishness. You criticized Father's new start after the war but anyone can criticize. I agree with you— Father's generation tried to avoid the whole issue of responsibility for the war, maybe they did try to blame everyone else. But Father is honestly trying to take responsibility now—he's staking his life on it. If that weren't the case, then he would never have gone to meet Haru.

PAUSE

Misako: If Father's life after the war really were a complete fake...he wouldn't have gone to meet Haru like that. He remarried with Mother and they had you and brought you up. There was nothing fake about that. That's what he wanted to say to you with pride. That's why he's trying so hard. And if that's true...then this is our problem, too. Those of us born after the war may have problems, but nothing compared to Haru and Father...where irreversible wounds of the soul remain unhealed. That means our lives are fake as well. If Father and the others are not healed, then we can't truly live either. And there will be no real peace. The war is not just something of the past. By hurting each other now, we're perpetuating the cycle... I never knew our family history was this heavy.

Tomoyoshi gazes into the distance. PAUSE

Misako: You know, I think the person who is happiest about Haru being alive and coming back to Japan is your mother.
Tomoyoshi: What?
Misako: When your father told her about Haru...I think, for the first time, I understand how she must have felt. Even though it was hard on her, by telling her what really

happened, they became happier because now the truth was shared. The basis of their life together was a small life inside your mother's belly—it was you.

Tomoyoshi: ...

Misako: And I bet your mother's biggest concern when she died was Haru.

Tomoyoshi: ...

Misako: You know, for some reason, I feel close to your half-brother and sister, Minoru and Yaeko. Maybe the souls of all those people who were killed have been reborn into our generation.

Misako has moved closer to Tomoyoshi.

Misako: I was born in peaceful times and I was proud of that, but I had no idea.

Tomoyoshi: ...A child of peace, huh?

Misako: Since I met Haru, I've been able to understand, for the first time, about my older brother who died, too—I'm very happy about that.

Tomoyoshi: You mean the brother that nearly died in the Bashi Channel?

Misako. ...Yes... It's made me want to go to the Philippines. All the pictures my brother used to draw were always so dark. People's faces would be floating in the water. And I asked him—why do you always draw such depressing pictures? He said that the sea in the picture was in the Philippines. I had no idea at the time!

Tomoyoshi: Your brother sang that song he liked at the time for us at our wedding, didn't he?

Misako: Ta ta-ta ta, Ta ta-ta ta, I'm singing in the rain, just singing in the rain... He died so young. My brother was the only one who was really happy about our marriage. I'm going back home, Haru and the others will worry.

Misako leaves. Tomoyoshi goes to the bench. Kobayashi enters.

Kobayashi: You know, when I first met Haru near the river...I thought that it was my father that had brought us together.

Tomoyoshi: Your father?

Kobayashi: It was like I'd finally met the person whom I had to meet, for my father's sake as well. (Suddenly straightens his shoulders) My father was an officer in the Kanto Army. And it was really people like my father who abandoned the development laborers and their families like Haru.

Tomoyoshi: ...

Kobayashi: My family was already back in Japan by September 1945. Very early... On the day the Soviet Union joined the war, August 9, my father's unit was in Seishin, a city that borders on Russia, China, and Korea. Russian troops were attacking and the army met with the mayor about what to do about the Japanese settlers. The mayor wanted them to be evacuated as soon as possible. But the army said that wasn't necessary—that the army may need the cooperation of the civilians, so they ordered them to stay where they were! But the next morning, August 10, the officers quarters were empty. The officers and their families had escaped first. My family! As they retreated, my father and the other officers blew up bridges and railroads behind them so people like Haru were left with no way to escape...all they could do was wander through the fields.

Tomoyoshi: ... (moves away from Kobayashi)

Kobayashi: This is very hard for me to say this as a son...but it's the truth. My father changed the fate of Haru and your father.

Tomoyoshi stares at Kobayashi.

Kobayashi: Please, please become Haru's guarantor... And please let me help you.

PAUSE

Kobayashi: Meeting Haru has given me a chance to pay back the terrible debt I inherited from my father...that's how I feel about it. After my father came back to Japan, he was tried for war crimes.

Tomoyoshi: ...
Kobayashi: Yeah, GHQ—the American Occupation Forces.
Tomoyoshi: ...
Kobayashi: A photograph was submitted to GHQ and it showed
my father with a Japanese sword cutting the heads off
Chinese POWs from behind!
Tomoyoshi: Oh!
Kobayashi: Life in my family wasn't very happy after the war. My
parents fought endlessly. My father would suddenly
wake up in the middle of the night, screaming and he
drank heavily. He used to beat my mother all the time....
It was terrifying... Everyone suppressed their feelings
in front of a father like that. I just curled up into myself.
Tomoyoshi: ...
Kobayashi: After the war, the Japanese talked about the hardships
and tragedies they suffered during the war, but they
never mentioned responsibility for their own crimes, or
that they were aggressors. My father always used to
say, "If only we hadn't lost the war, we never would
have been reduced to this. One day we'll get revenge!"
But he never used to talk about the terrible things he
did. He called the Chinese "Chinks" and the Koreans
other derogatory names. The Japanese killed 20 or maybe
even 30 million innocent Chinese, Koreans, and other
Asians in that war. The anguish of those people continues
today. You can hardly blame those Asians for looking at
us as a nation of people who're looking away from the
truth, trying to forget by burying ourselves in materialistic wealth. Perhaps we are a cursed people. At least,
mine is a cursed family—I learned that much.
Tomoyoshi: It's the same with my family. Whatever you say, they
abandoned Haru. And all that stuff about "developing
the country," was really stealing Chinese land—forcing them off their own land. My father never told the
truth about it either.

PAUSE

Kobayashi: I think it must have been very hard for my father to try
to work out his feelings overnight for a nation that sud-

denly claims its people are such pacifists that they wouldn't even kill a fly. I don't think he ever did. My father was accused of war crimes at the trials, but from his point of view, he must have wondered why he was tried when some people who had done much worse things went free. Not only were they free, they were living amongst the leaders of a peaceful society. The anger he must have felt about that...he let it out on my mother, I'm sure that's why he was violent to her. He just couldn't keep it inside. In the end, she became a manic depressive and committed suicide. I think my mother's suicide was the result of our cursed family.

PAUSE

Kobayashi: Deep in my heart, I always felt that I was a child of the war. I was someone that everyone else would try to avoid. The son of someone who survived the terrible Kanto Army and returned from Manchuria. And on top of that a war criminal! That was enough to make everyone shun us. Well, of course, in the new peaceful Japan, we were a great inconvenience. I was always anxious, always scared of something, threatened by something. I always thought "I will never be happy." How can I justify my life in this world? This is what I was looking for.

PAUSE

Kobayashi: So I met my wife and we got married. But I was really scared of getting married. Bringing into the world a child with my blood... I wanted to be the end of that blood-soaked line. A silent dinner table! A mother that only complains! Beating up a wife who ignored him... that's all I knew of my father. The worst was when my mother's mental sickness began, I went to the hospital to visit her. And when she looked at me, her face was grotesque. I had to run away from there. It was too much. I felt like I was being sucked into a deep darkness, like I might loose my very self. I was so scared. I thought my

fate was the same as my mother's—to just rot away.
But my wife told me I must not fall victim to that. She
challenged me to live. One day I got a letter from my
mother. It was written in blood. She had cut her wrist
and written, "You are my son. You can't ever change
the blood connection between us, even if you want to."
I abandoned my mother and got married. And then
Hiroshi was born. But I wasn't pleased. In fact I couldn't
stand him. I think I was only happy at the bank. Chas-
ing all those figures somehow gave me a sense of reality—it was fun. The competition made me feel liber-
ated from everything.

Tomoyoshi stands up.

Kobayashi: I'm very ashamed of this, but I have hit my son—my
handicapped son. If I fight with my wife, my hands
seem to react before my mouth. When that happened I
was so scared of myself. But Hiroshi doesn't know hatred and he would come to me as if nothing had happened. My wife would go crazy, and not care if she got
hit. She would snatch Hiroshi away from me and hug
him. That happened every day. When I looked at
Hiroshi's innocent face, I would become uncontrollably angry. One day I went to Hiroshi's sports festival
for the first time. Hiroshi was in the fifty-meter race.
"Ready, get set, go!" and everyone started running slug-
gishly. Suddenly a little girl fell down. And then—I was
really surprised, the children all stopped running and
picked her up. When she was on her feet again, they all
started running again until they reached the finish line.
And then...and then Hiroshi caught sight of me and ran
over shouting, "Daddy, Daddy." The other kids came
with him. "Is that your Dad, Hiroshi?" "Hello, Mr.
Kobayashi." "Can I come to you house and play one
day soon?" They all came milling around me. I felt
uncomfortable at first, but for some reason, I felt tears
in my eyes. I couldn't stop crying! So I picked up
Hiroshi and gave him a big hug... No, actually he was
hugging me. Tomoyoshi, I was the one being hugged.

Hiroshi's body was so warm. I quit my job at the bank because I wanted to be with Hiroshi. He was sent by God to give me hope, that was the first time in my life I'd ever felt such warm hope.

Tomoyoshi: Really...

Tomoyoshi moves slightly away from Kobayashi.

(End of Scene 4)

In this final excerpt, after Haru returns to China, Tomoyoshi, her step-son, has gained a much better understanding of the pain and suffering of his parents' generation, and he himself has become more humanized.—Editor

Epilogoue

Haru is climbing stairs one at a time. She is going to a very high place. From here is an abstract world. Sound of a severe winter. Snow is falling.

Tomoyoshi: Dear Haru, how are you? It's been almost three months since you left, but I think of you all the time. I thought that I didn't have any brothers or sisters but now I know I did, but they died. I realized that our whole life since the war has been lived in that blank space that we weren't told about. Dad felt that if he loved me, he would somehow be betraying his dead children, so he was always hesitant. He didn't even realize what he was doing. But he became so confused when he met you. His selfishness when he said he would disown me made me shudder and I couldn't forgive him for that. At the same time, I was amazed when I saw him being so honest about his pain—the pain he never showed us before. I realized that Dad's generation didn't even have the freedom to feel their own pain. Yet even in the crucible of pain, Father seemed to shine.

Growing up with a father who was so restrained was beyond my understanding. And the crime of aggression...how after the war they were taught to conveniently put it aside. When Father was forced to confront the enormity, the weight of all the years after the war, he did not look at crimes he was subjected to but he chose to take responsibility for his own crime and in doing so, for the first time, experienced the brilliant light of his own life. For the first time, Dad woke up to the brightness in his own life. For the first time, as his son, I was able to accept fully into my heart the reality of the times into which my father was born. The moments that were lost were not of the past.

Maybe living means to know the fear of constantly living in those lost moments. When Kobayashi and Misako and I were in the newspaper club together as students, we used to discuss Louie Aragon, the French poet who lived through fascism. I suddenly feel like I'm reliving that youthful period. Aragon said "There is no such thing as happy love, but that is what our love is!" Aragon was then caught up in the storm of fascism, in the middle of his despair. We were born to a generation that left the past unaccounted for and raced into the future too rapidly. That's what I've come to think.

Horizontal lighting gives the impression of a harsh winter.

Haru: Ahhh, this is my Japan. This is the Japan that I dreamt of. For a long time, I was obsessed about my Japanese blood. Now, I've finally let go of that. My home countries are both Japan and China. My children and myself have two home countries—and we're proud of this. I have hope in this new age.

Looking back, from the day Japan lost the war, we wandered through fields practically naked, like beggars. But at that time, we experienced the deep sadness and despair of a hated people. There was the depth of the crimes Japan had committed, and the wounds inflicted on Chinese hearts that could not be healed. For those of us who were left behind in China, we groveled in that huge continent and we were taught how to be reborn. I will walk the road of new relationships and common ground between Japan and China—no, the whole world—beyond racial bloodlines. Japan, please somehow remember us—"the forgotten women."

Storm sounds. Bells.

CURTAIN

Translation team:

Caitlin Stronell
Deirdre Tanaka
Hal Gold
Kevin Chiang

12

Cinematic Representations of the Rape of Nanking

Michael Berry[1]

The Rape of Nanjing was not only one of the most horrid and tragic moments of twentieth-century Chinese history, but may very well be remembered as an incident ranking "among the most brutal in modern warfare."[2] On December 13, 1937 the Japanese army entered the Chinese capital of Nanjing, beginning a six-week bloodbath where an estimated 300,000 Chinese citizens were killed.[3] Although the incident was largely marginalized in the west until the 1997 publication of Iris Chang's *The Rape of Nanking* and consistently underplayed in China for political reasons, it was not until the mid-eighties, when the Nanjing Massacre suddenly began to reenter the Chinese consciousness—via a changing PRC political agenda—that a handful of cinematic depictions of the Rape of Nanjing began to appear in theaters and classrooms in China. Although much of the body of film on the Nanjing Massacre has been produced in the documentary mode, such as Peter Wang's *Magee's Testament,* the PRC produced *The Massacre of Nanjing—The Surviving Witnesses (Nanjing datusha—Xingcunzhe de jianzheng)*, and Christine Choy and Nancy Tong's *In the Name of the Emperor,* there were also three full-length dramas representing the Nanjing Massacre produced between 1987 and 1995.

Although the painfully tragic black and white images of brutalized Chinese children taken by John Magee during the massacre and other footage filmed by the Japanese themselves, obtained after the allied victory, have become virtually ingrained on the Chinese collective unconscious through their continual reuse in a series of pedagogical documentaries, it is arguably the trio of dramatic features produced between 1987 and 1995 that have reached the widest Chinese audience in recent years. These three films serve not only as cinematic depictions of the Rape of Nanjing, but also as a means of recreating that tragic historical moment in the context of popular culture. Like the documentaries, these films not only attempt to address history itself, but also the wider viewing public. It is here that the burden of history clashes with the burdens of the market, where art and economy, politics and propaganda combine to create a group of complex and challenging recreations of perhaps the most notorious "rape" of the twentieth century.

Through a close reading of the PRC director Luo Guanqun's 1987 film *Massacre in Nanjing* (*Tucheng xuezheng*), Hong Kong-based director T.F. Mou's (Mou Dunfei) docu-drama *Black Sun: The Nanjing Massacre* (*Hei taiyang: Nanjing datusha*), and another PRC director Wu Ziniu's 1995 release *Don't Cry, Nanking* (*Nanjing 1937*), I will examine the strategies each work uses to reconstruct the historical nightmare that is the Nanjing Massacre. Through a survey of the narrative, formal, and technical aspects of each film, and close readings of several key scenes, I hope to explore the different, and at times startlingly similar, ways in which the Rape of Nanjing has been depicted on the Chinese screen, and relived in the eyes of millions of moviegoers.

Massacre in Nanjing: Proof and Consequences

PRC film critic Zhang Xuan (1996: 102) has noted three distinct ways in which filmmakers have approached (or proposed to approach) the Rape of Nanjing: 1) to deal with the incident from the perspective of the Tokyo War Crimes Tribunal, 2) to look at the Massacre from the perspective of the foreigners at the International Safety Zone, and 3) to present the perspective of an average Nanjing family. Luo Guanqun's film, *Massacre in Nanjing,* the first major motion picture to depict the event, falls somewhere between Zhang Xuan's second and third categories. In terms of narrative and structure, the film bears a deep artistic debt to the Xie Jin model of melodrama,[4] a mid-eighties cinematic form that has been described as dwelling "excessively on innocent victims' traumatic experiences of political persecution so as to invoke in the viewer an acute sense of injustice as well as a profound feeling of sympathy." (Zhang & Xiao 1998: 241) *Massacre in Nanjing*, however, fails to fully escape the pre-76 PRC cinematic tradition of socialist realism aesthetics, especially those of political martyrdom. Co-produced by the Fujian

Film Studio and the Nanjing Film Studio, the film was awarded the 1987-88 Ministry of Film & Broadcasting award for Outstanding Picture and the 1991 Tokyo World Peace Film Festival award for best drama, which was a surprising recognition, in light of the sensitivity of the subject matter in Japan.

Beginning on December 13, 1937, the first day of the massacre, Luo's film follows the lives of a group of individuals and their respective fates as the atrocity develops. At the center of the story is Dr. Zhan Tao (played by Zhai Naishe) and his love interest Bai Yan (Shen Danping); Fan Changle, a photographer who develops photos for the Japanese in a desperate attempt to save himself and his family; Katy, the daughter of an American doctor who stays behind to aid the wounded; a battalion of Chinese soldiers, a second rate sing-song girl and her corrupt lover/manager, a Japanese lieutenant named Zhuyuan (played by mainland Chinese superstar Chen Daoming); and his former lover Liu Jingjing (Wu Lijie). This group of characters in many ways makes up a microcosm of Chinese society in the thirties—an ensemble approach that is startlingly similar to the "group film" model that was prevalent in the late 40s. Although the ensemble cast of characters all come from different social and economic classes, during the ensuing chaos of the massacre, the lives of these very different individuals cross paths in a tragic, yet markedly patriotic, way.

The main plot line, which brings these characters together, involves Dr. Zhan's efforts to recover photos Fan Changle developed of Japanese soldiers committing atrocities in order to provide proof of the massacre.[5] In this sense, embedded into the very plot line itself, there lies the film's political/ideological message, which is that the Rape of Nanjing *did* in fact occur. Although it might seem self-evident to many western viewers, after living in the shadow of Japanese denial of the massacre for more half a century, much of the Chinese discourse on the Rape of Nanjing focuses on trying to "prove" that it actually happened. The true tragedy of the film is that just as the characters portrayed in the film struggle to prove that the massacre actually happened (through a group of photos), so *Massacre in Nanjing*, which was made on the fiftieth anniversary of the tragedy, is still struggling with the same issues—only this time, the film itself replaces the photographs as the chosen medium.

During the quest to retrieve Fan Changle's photos, no fewer than four major characters die, including Mr. Fan, Liu Jingjing, the sing-

song girl, and eventually Dr. Zhan. However, because of the addition of the subplot of "recovering the photos," none of these characters die meaningless deaths (as, arguably, the vast majority of the
Nanjing Massacre victims indeed did). Instead they are all trans-
formed into martyrs, especially so in the case of Dr. Zhan and Liu
Jingjing, who are portrayed throughout the film as Lei Feng-esq
everyday heroes. Ever pure and upright, as evidenced by Dr. Zhan's
berating of Mr. Fan for selling out to the Japanese (even if it was to
save his pregnant wife's life), and Liu's outright refusal of Zhuyuan's
advances (even though we know that she once loved him). Zhan
and Liu could have walked directly out of one of Jiang Qing's Cultural Revolution-era (1966-1976) model operas; this not-so-subtle
injection of revolutionary, socialist realist discourse into the film links
it up with the tradition of pre-78 PRC film, but simultaneously, push
it even further away from the brutal reality of the Rape of Nanjing.

In one fascinating scene that both proves Liu's purity and brings
in the photo motif, Zhuyuan, during his reunion with Liu Jingjing
(she is in fact his prisoner), admits to her that he has loved her ever
since their time together in Manchuria. He proves his love by men-
tioning a treasured photo of the two of them: "I've carried it with me
for six whole years." He removes the photo to show Liu, but she
does not accept his affections and the photo is never actually shown
on camera. This photo of love is not only the direct antithesis of the
atrocity photos, around which the plot revolves, but by never actually showing the photo (the proof), the relationship is negated, thus
metaphorically functioning as the negation of Sino-Japanese love/
friendship.

Even the film's Chinese title, *Tucheng xuezheng,* a literal translation of which would read as something like "The City of Massacre—Evidence in Blood," hints at the underlying intent behind, or
rather, transparent in, the film's narrative. The key word here is the
final character in the title, *zheng,* "authentication, proof, or evidence,"
which points to the series of black and white photos, but also to the
film itself as a vehicle for proof against the Japanese denial of the
event. In an attempt to enhance the authenticity of the history that
his film portrays, Luo Guanqun, also uses an array of cinematic techniques. The most blatant of these is the use of actual vintage black
and white documentary footage from the thirties to open his film.
By bracketing his film with a forty-five-second montage of actual
archival footage of Japanese bombers, followed by a nearly two-

minute segment where the opening credits are run against a back-drop of fire, the director is trying to draw the audience into *his* vision of wartorn Nanjing and convince them of its authenticity. This is enhanced by ending the opening credits with the transitional title, "December 13, 1937" in red and immediately cutting to Luo's staged version of 1937 Nanjing, complete with burning buildings and refugees flooding the streets—the direct result of the actual bombing footage just shown.

As the film progresses, Luo Guanqun undertakes a series of highly dramatic juxtapositions of images in his attempts to highlight the cruelty of the invading Japanese army. The first such scene occurs approximately thirteen minutes into the film when a wall of wounded, unarmed soldiers are summarily executed outside the gate of Chaotian Palace in western Nanjing. To draw attention to this scene, Luo draws on a virtual arsenal of cinematic techniques as the soldiers are being gunned down: slow motion, removal of all sound and background music to highlight the images, periodic stills, and random insertions of ghostly black and white negative snapshots (the images that Fan Changle will later develop?). The scene concludes with the image of a traditional stone lion—a symbolic rendering of China herself—bathed in blood and the sound of a baby crying silenced by a single gunshot.

The director goes all out in his attempt to pull the viewers' heartstrings in this scene by making all of the captured Chinese soldiers wounded—virtually every one of them is wrapped in bloodied bandages. This feeling of victimization is heightened by the inclusion of the crying child, the ultimate symbol of innocence. Luo, however, goes one step further by juxtaposing this scene with the sinister laughter of gloating Japanese soldiers.

Later in the film, this motif of juxtaposing radically opposing images to produce an emotional effect in the viewer is repeatedly rehashed. One after another, we are presented with images of utterly irreconcilable qualities: smiling geisha girls handing out candy to dejected Chinese children (with bayonets pointed at them), Zhuyuan's execution of a Chinese prisoner is immediately followed by the image of a holy cross, sounds of gunfire and tortured screams are matched with images of biblical murals and Jesus on the crucifix, a baby bayoneted and a mother's look of horror as she watches and faces an impending rape is again juxtaposed against exaggerated evil snickering of Japanese soldiers. Although a powerful tool when used sparingly, Luo Guanqun's overuse of these juxtapositions in the end brings a staged, contrived quality to the film.

It is only towards the end of the film, after Dr. Zhan has sacrificed himself delivering the photos to Katy, the American girl, that these all-important photographs are finally shown on camera. It is also interesting that the necessary guardian of the photos is not the Chinese "victim" nor Japanese "perpetrator," but the mediating figure of Katy—the detached "witness" of the West. Somehow, the filmmaker is not only confident in the West's identity as a neutral and objective party, but allocates to the West the exclusive power to wield the gaze of atrocity. Perhaps this serves as an attempt to rationalize China's own historical amnesia regarding the Nanjing Massacre, but in placing such emphasis upon the legitimizing power of the West (through an invented character), the filmmaker simultaneously undercuts his own attempt at providing "cinematic testimony" to the massacre. As Katy flips through the images, the viewer instantly recognizes the set of photos—the very site of atrocity—as the most well known collection of photographic images associated with the Rape of Nanjing. This group of black and white photos effectively works to finalize the bracketing or framing of the film (the other side being the black and white film of Japanese bombers that opened the movie). In a sense, this presents Luo Guanqun's film as a conscious attempt to reconstruct or fill in the blanks of what happened between these two concrete, documented historical junctures—the Japanese air raids and the atrocities depicted in the photos. This bracketing is further enhanced by the reoccurrence of another number in bold red print (the first being the date "December 13, 1937" which immediately followed the opening credits), this time the number is not a date, but a death toll—300,000. As this death toll, etched in large, ominous blood-red roman numerals lingers onscreen, an offscreen narrator declares: "Let us always remember this number."

Black Sun: Two Faces of a Violent Docu-Drama

Seven years after the release of *Massacre in Nanjing,* two other Chinese-language feature films dealing with the atrocities committed by the Japanese in 1937 were released. *Black Sun: The Nanjing Massacre* and *Don't Cry, Nanking*[6] were both released in 1995 to correspond with the fiftieth anniversary of the Allied victory over fascism (which also marked the conclusion of China's eight year War of Resistance Against Japan). This in itself gives both films an inherent political slant, further enhanced by the fact that each work was openly marketed as a visual commemoration of the event.[7]

For better or for worse, the first of these two films never got a chance to live out its cinematic life as a work of propaganda/commemoration. Although partially funded by a well known Beijing-based government organization and filmed on location in Nanjing, Hong Kong-based producer and director T. F. Mou's *Black Sun* never made it past the PRC censors, consequently limiting its release to a short run in Hong Kong and a small handful of international screenings.[8] The film was most likely banned because of its overly violent content (especially in the wake of Tiananmen) and to avoid straining current Sino-Japanese political and economic relations.

In order to capture the terror and violence of the Rape of Nanjing, Mou tries to recreate some of the most horrid incidents of the massacre in his film. Combining the bullets and blood of John Woo with Chang Che's penchant for swords and severed limbs, T. F. Mou brings the blood and violence of Hong Kong martial arts and action cinema (without the martial arts or action) directly into his Sino-Japanese docu-drama. With intentionally weak characterization, the complete absence of any recognizable stars, and the lack of a tangible plot line, *Black Sun* instead tries to serve as a detached witness to the massacre as it chronologically unfolds the events from December 11, 1937 to Christmas eve. Over the course of this fifteen-day bloodfest, Mou's camera bears witness to a monk getting castrated, numerous beheadings, cannibalism, people being buried and burnt alive, multiple firing squad style executions, a child being boiled alive, a woman disemboweled (and the subsequent removal of her intestines by a bayonet), dogs gnawing on human corpses, and the rape of a pre-adolescent girl. Although Mou prefaces his film with a dedication to "all war victims to commemorate the 50th Anniversary of the successful conclusion of the Campaign of Resistance," his vulgar and contrived portrayals of violence often make the movie seem closer to an exploitative horror film than a solemn cinematic memorial to victims of war.

In his groundbreaking study of exploitation films from 1919-1959, Eric Schaefer defines atrocity films as "essentially about death and disfigurement; their spectacle centered on violent, 'inhuman' behavior such as war, massacre, mutilation, and other grisly topics (1999: 254)." Schaefer then goes on to describe the function of these films as "primarily to repulse with images of violence, carnage, or bloody ritual (1999: 258)." In this context we can read *Black Sun* as a contemporary reinvention of the atrocity film. The film recreates a carnival-like spectacle of "war, massacre, mutilation, and other grisly topics"—such as dismemberment, torture and rape. The way in which *Black Sun* freely mixes documentary newsreel footage with dramatic reenactments is also almost identical to Schaefer's description of early American atrocity films such as *Hitler's Reign of Terror* (1934) and *The Love Life of Adolph Hitler* (1948). It is here that the depictions of blood and gore in *Black Sun* become a double-edged sword—turning away a more serious audience, while attracting a new one by nature of its inherent sensationalism.

The exploitative element of the film is enhanced by the film's "non-portrayal" of the victims. Although the history itself takes center stage in *Black Sun,* the failure to build an emotional link between *any* of the Chinese characters and the audience, in the end, makes much of that history appear cold and dehumanized. Most Chinese characters who appear on screen do not even have names, whereas when each major Japanese character first appears, there is a momentary still and the character's name and official position appears in titles on the screen. In all, this occurs eleven times during the course of the film, all the characters named are Japanese (except for one enigmatic case of an American from the International Safety Zone who is also identified in this way). The director's strategy in attaching real names to the Japanese characters is undoubtedly an attempt to bring accountability to the perpetrators. However by naming the perpetrators and focusing most of his attention on them (the vast majority of the dialogue in the film occurs amongst Japanese officials), Mou runs the risk of silencing the voices, identities, and ultimately, the humanity of the victims—the very group he purports to be dedicating his film to.

Although *Black Sun* lacks the melodramatic components of *Massacre in Nanjing,* it does bear a series of uncanny similarities to its cinematic predecessor. The most startling of these similarities occurs in the opening scene of *Black Sun,* setting up an unavoidable parallelism between Mou and Luo's films. Luo's film, as discussed earlier, opens with a forty-five second montage of documentary footage immediately followed by the credits being run against a background of fire. T. F. Mou's work also opens with just under one minute of vintage documentary footage—some of which actually overlaps with the footage used in *Massacre in Nanjing*—followed by a close-up of yet another flame image, this time in the guise of a candle.[9] Basically, the structure is: black and white documentary footage of planes, cut to fire imagery, cut to dramatic footage of film proper. The fire imagery is manifested as burning flames in *Massacre in Nanjing* and a candle close up in *Black Sun*. The stunning structural similarities between the formal techniques utilized in the films' respective opening sequences is so striking that one could conjecture that it is more than a mere coincidence.

What distinguishes the first two minutes of *Black Sun* from *Massacre in Nanjing* is the presence of a voiceover narration. This objective unseen narrative voice combined with the vintage black and white film clips makes the first moments of Mou's film virtually indistinguishable from a documentary. Also, unlike *Massacre in Nanjing*, which only uses documentary film footage in its opening scene, *Black Sun* effectively laces the body of its dramatic footage by constantly integrating vintage photos and film clips into the narrative fabric. All told, there are at least nineteen different scenes in the film where T. F. Mou augments his film with the inclusion of actual photos and footage of the Rape of Nanjing. Just under half of these scenes (eight in total) are accompanied by the same documentary-like voice over narration. The most startling of these documentary interruptions occurs about eight minutes from the end of the film where, for the first time, the documentary-style narration actually *spills over* from the black and white footage and runs over into the color footage of the film proper. At this moment the two bodies of film (the documentary footage and Mou's footage) are linked not only spatially and contextually, but also narratively. At once the historical stakes are raised and the lines are blurred between documentary and fiction, staged reenactment and actual history.

Black Sun not only incorporates documentary photos and archive film footage into the narrative, but in what are without question some of the film's most fascinating moments, it tries to meticulously restage specific historical moments.[10] Filmed on location in Nanjing, many of the recreations were staged at the actual sites where the atrocities occurred. The most moving of these images occurs thirty minutes into the movie when a Japanese soldier executes an elderly Chinese monk. Just as the monk drops to his knees and the soldier draws his gun, the frame freezes. Then, corresponding with the sound of a gunshot, the staged image is replaced with the actual photo on which the scene is based upon. Underlying T. F. Mou's painstaking recreations of these fleeting moments of this historical tragedy is the same obsession to bear testimony and prove the truth of the Rape of Nanjing that we see in *Massacre in Nanjing*. Besides the incorporation of documentary footage, black and white photos, and dramatic re-staging of particular events, *Black Sun*, like Luo Guanqun's film, also uses the presence of photos and cameras within his dramatic reenactments to stress the validity of the version of history they are depicting.

T. F. Mou's extensive appropriation of archival film footage and photographic images is, however, not without its problematic dimensions. Aside from film footage taken by the American missionary John Magee and a handful of other exceptions, the vast majority of all extant visual records of the massacre were produced by the Japanese, the very perpetrators of the violence. Needless to say, the motivations behind the production of the images were very different from those of contemporary filmmakers like Mou who have appropriated these photographic and filmic visions some sixty years after the event. Holocaust survivor and Nobel Prize winning writer Elie Wiesel addresses this very issue in his short introduction to *Indelible Shadows: Film and the Holocaust*. Although Elie Wiesel is addressing a historical tragedy of a different milieu, his criticism on the usage of documentary footage bears enough relevance to our current discussion to deserve being quoted at length:

> For the most part the images derive from enemy sources. The victim had neither cameras nor film. To amuse themselves, or to bring souvenirs back to their families, or to serve Goebbel's propaganda, the killers filmed sequences in one ghetto or another, in one camp or another: The use of the faked, truncated images makes it difficult to omit the poisonous message that motivated them...will the viewer continue to remember that these films were made by the killers to show the downfall and the baseness of their so-called subhuman victims? (Insdorf 1989: xii)

Although, as Wiesel concludes, "we [nevertheless] can't do without these images, which, in their truthful context, assume a primordial importance for the eventual comprehension of the concentration camps' existence" (Insdorf 1989:xii). In our context, the comprehension of the Nanjing Massacre as historical fact, one cannot easily escape the problematic at hand. Ultimately, the perspective of horror and pity assumed by the viewer as he or she views the images of atrocity is not terribly far away from the gaze of the executioner.

The many faces of *Black Sun*—docu-drama, gore-fest, exploit-ative atrocity film, historical tragedy, pseudo-documentary, cinematic commemoration, and war epic—merge together, creating a decep-tively challenging pastiche of sounds and images. All at once the film seems to live a double life as a serious historical docu-drama (no doubt the filmmakers' original intention), while at the same time building up a cult following of sorts among fans of grade-B horror movies. These two self-contradictory and seemingly irreconcilable identities that *Black Sun* has taken on are evidenced in the market availability of the film.

Black Sun can be obtained through the Alliance in Memory of Victims of the Nanjing Massacre (AMVNM), a nonprofit organiza-tion based in New York, for a donation of $75. AMVNM also dis-tributes the film in a boxed set entitled "Can Japan Say No to the Truth?" therein marketing the film as an educational lobbying tool. In this context, *Black Sun* is presented as "evidence" (along with the two other straightforward *documentaries* in the boxed set) of the massacre. However, at the same time, the film is also widely avail-able on the Internet from horror film distributors where it is sold alongside such titles as *Cannibal Apocalypse: Vietnam Vets Eating Flesh, Model Massacre* and *Caligula Reincarnated as Hitler* and described as: "Very horrific! People are tortured and killed in ways that you never knew existed."[11]

In recent years popular Hong Kong cinema has expanded its once primarily entertainment-based viewership, and has begun to meet with ever-increasing enthusiasm abroad, at international film festi-vals, and in academia. The complexity, poignancy, irony, and to some extent, blasphemy, of this dual identity is perhaps displayed nowhere better than in T. F. Mou's *Black Sun*, where an attempt at a serious historical docu-drama is combined with the cinematic aes-thetics of a shock-infused carnival of gore.[12]

Don't Cry, Nanking: International Melodrama

The third and final film based on the Rape of Nanjing released to date is Fifth Generation director Wu Ziniu's *Don't Cry, Nanking.* Wu's film clearly won the largest viewership among the three films exam-ined here. Not only was *Don't Cry, Nanking* shown across China, it also had a coveted theatrical run in Taiwan.[13] Although *Don't Cry, Nanking* was released in 1995, the same year as *Black Sun,* Wu's approach couldn't have been more different from T. F. Mou's. In fact, when asked to describe his film, Wu Ziniu's response seemed to be, at least partially, directed at the kind of violent aesthetics and cold, historical reconstruction undertaken by Mou, while at the same time, addressing Luo Guanqun's obsession with authenticity:

> I hope to make a sincere, dignified, and solemn literary work (*wenyi pian*). I began to realize the difficulty in choosing an angle [from which to approach the material] last May when I first began to brainstorm. If I try to present a cinematic record of what actually happened, [the film] will come off too bloody and violent. Then again, using my film as a means to confirm the authenticity of the event is also not what I am interested in—that's work to be left to the historians.
>
> The Rape of Nanjing is China's national shame, the Chinese people were slaughtered without putting up any kind of resistance. Because of this, it is extremely difficult to find the proper angle [from which to approach the subject matter]. Simply filming images of desperation and desolation will be nothing more than a kind of vulgar exhibition. So I have decided to focus on the human element and stick with a more humanistic approach. (Jiao 1998: 184)
>
> ...Nakedly exposing blood and violence, as far as I'm concerned, is nothing more than selling out for money and a betrayal of one's conscience. (Jiao 1998: 185)

This conscious break from the internal aesthetics, historical perspectives, obsession with authenticity, and portrayal of violence in the previous two films is, however, only the tip of the iceberg when it comes to the differences between Wu Ziniu's film and the others.

Not only is Wu Ziniu the most famous of the three directors, but his film was also by far the biggest budget production for any historical drama based on the Rape of Nanjing to date. More than nine thousand extras were used—some of whom were actual survivors of the Massacre[14]—and the final budget exceeded 25 million yuan (roughly three and a quarter million dollars U.S. and more than twice the initial budget). The Nanjing municipal government also gave the crew virtually unprecedented liberties by allowing them to film on location at several Ming dynasty historic sites.

The cast and crew behind *Don't Cry, Nanking* reads like a veritable who's who ensemble of big name figures. The film was produced by Hong Kong-Hollywood superstar action director John Woo (who coordinated most production efforts from Hollywood), beautifully scored by American-based composer Tan Dun (of *Crouching Tiger, Hidden Dragon* fame), and starred Taiwanese pop singer/actress Rene Liu along with an international cast from China, Japan, and Taiwan. The screenwriting team included the PRC best-selling writer Liang Xiaosheng and Hong Kong-based screenwriter Hong Weijian (Tsui Hark's longtime collaborator). This international creative team not only brought the work a higher profile and wider audience than the previous two films, but also reached a level of depth and reflexivity unmatched by earlier cinematic depictions of the massacre.[15]

The main storyline revolves around Cheng Xian (Qin Han), a doctor working in Shanghai, who returns to his hometown of Nanjing with his family as refugees on the eve of the massacre. As a widower, Cheng Xian has remarried a Japanese woman named Rieko (Saotome Ai) who is pregnant with their child. Reiko, like Cheng, also has a child from a previous marriage and the film explores the family's struggle to stay together and retain their dignity amid the ensuing Rape of Nanjing.

Unlike the interracial Sino-Japanese romance portrayed in *Massacre in Nanjing*, which is all but refuted (and eventually ends with the Japanese lieutenant Zhuyuan executing his former Chinese lover), the love story between Cheng Xian and Rieko forms the basis not only for the story but also for the optimistic worldview and humanistic quality that Wu Ziniu works to convey. Although the previous two films both include the presence of Japanese characters who take a somewhat sympathetic stance towards China, *Don't Cry, Nanking* develops this to the point that a Japanese character actually shares the same fate as the Chinese. The innocent, naive, almost angelic, light in which Rieko is portrayed works against the tendency to universally vilify the Japanese, enhancing the humanistic mood of the film. It is details such as these that enable the film to function as a more general denouncement of war and the brutality man is capable of, rather than a simple defamation or vilification of the Japanese.

The complications of the wages of guilt are further developed with the inclusion of the supporting character, Ishimatsu (Jiang Guobin). Ishimatsu is a Taiwanese draftee sent by the Japanese to China where he serves as a military cook. Ishimatsu's presence marks an attempt on the part of the director to address the complex, precarious position Taiwan played in the Second Sino-Japanese War. Although forced into service for the Japanese, Ishimatsu's allegiance remains with the greater China as is demonstrated by his willingness to sacrifice himself so that Cheng Xian can escape. From a political perspective, Ishimatsu's martyrdom is not only a symbolic act of atonement, but a patriotic reappraisal of Taiwan's role in the war. If my hypothesis is correct, Ishimatsu's presence in the film (like the array of Taiwanese actors, who dominate the lead roles) is indeed a direct result of influence exerted by the Taiwan-based production company—Long Shong International Co. Ltd. Where even the most subtle reference to Taiwan remained markedly absent from the previous two films, here we are presented with a concrete example of how politics, the market, and international investment shapes, complicates, and perhaps even compromises, our cinematic presentation of history.

Like the example of Ishimatsu's death, Wu Ziniu adds to the depth of his film through the inclusion of a number of subtle, yet carefully thought out, symbolic gestures. "Cheng Xian's profession being that of a physician is naturally symbolic," as is "the new life Rieko is pregnant with, which symbolizes the once good relationship between these two nations...[equally symbolic is the scene wherein Japanese soldiers] kick her pregnant body." (Jiao 1998: 185) Another brilliant moment of the film's symbolic imagery occurs as Shuqin (Rene Liu) is teaching her students Li Bai's famous poem "Thoughts on a Silent Night" (*Jing ye si*). The inclusion of this particular poem carries strong symbolic resonance due to the fact that the scene takes place in a refuge camp where everyone has been uprooted from his home—separation from home is the key theme of the poem. The interruption of this poetry lesson by a Japanese air raid not only represents the interrupted education of countless children during the War, but also because Li Bai's *Jing ye si* is often read as the poetic quintessence of Chinese culture, the air raid actually symbolizes the destruction of the Chinese cultural and historical heritage.

Although heavy symbolism is also present in *Massacre in Nanjing* (Zhan Tao was also a doctor) and *Black Sun* (as seen in the John Woo-esque juxtaposition of Christ images with violence and death), neither reach the level of subtlety and complexity expressed by Wu Ziniu. While *Don't Cry, Nanking* tries to use the Rape of Nanjing as a springboard to address larger issues, T. F. Mou and Luo Guanqun's films never seem to get past trying to prove that the incident happened. This can also be seen in the temporal trajectories that each film respectively follows. While both *Massacre in Nanjing* and *Black Sun* are temporally trapped in the actual massacre (both beginning and ending amid a flood of seemingly never-ending violence), *Don't Cry, Nanking* is the sole film that actually begins *before* the arrival of the Japanese army. This allows for a level of character development absent in the earlier films and a more complex portrayal of the city struggling to continue functioning amid the growing chaos brought on by the flood of refugees and the looming Japanese threat.

For instance, we are allowed to bear witness to the sudden influx of refugees into the seemingly impregnable capital city (among these new refugees are the main protagonists) on the eve of the massacre. Rather than a simple documentary-like recreation of the gory incident, this slightly wider historical perspective also allows for a more complex and introspective look at the forces at work leading up to the massacre.

Even in the arena of spoken language, *Don't Cry, Nanking* presents a much broader and genuine representation of the linguistic heteroglossia of wartime Nanjing. In Luo Guanqun's *Massacre in Nanjing* all dialogue, whether be it spoken by Chinese, Japanese, or American characters, was dubbed into perfect Mandarin—although far from accurate, it was at least consistent. *Black Sun* also dubbed all dialogue into Mandarin (including lines spoken by Japanese, Germans, and Americans), however, special efforts were made to dub all lines spoken by Westerners into a choppy, almost pidgin Chinese, while all Chinese and Japanese characters speak standard Mandarin.[16] Wu Ziniu's film, by far, achieves the highest degree of linguistic accuracy. Barring the fact that several of the actors have trouble entirely covering up their Taiwanese accents, for the vast majority of the movie Chinese actors speak Chinese, Japanese speak Japanese, Westerners speak English (or pidgin Chinese), and interpreters actually interpret into two different languages.

The only flaw with the linguistic diversity of Wu Ziniu's film, which may very well be a crippling one, occurs in the dialogue scenes between Cheng Xian and his Japanese wife Rieko. It is obvious from the film that both Rieko and Cheng understand only a smattering of each other's languages, yet they repeatedly carry out long conversations with Cheng speaking Chinese and his wife answering back in Japanese. Although Rieko tries to compensate by throwing occasional lines of broken Chinese, the contrived nature of their exchanges repeatedly compromise the illusion of a real relationship between the two characters. As the two lead actors, this naturally carries larger implications for the film as a whole.[17] With elaboration of dialogue being one of the key components of the melodramatic form, the linguistically closed world in which Cheng Xian and Reiko live poses a significant hurdle in realizing the illusion of a genuine relationship. Wu Ziniu's melodramatic vision ultimately lies contingent upon his viewers making an unconscious "leap of faith" when it comes to communication between the main characters.

Don't Cry, Nanking marked the culmination of a decade-long cinematic meditation on war by Wu Ziniu (and the beginning of a five-year hiatus from filmmaking). Since his 1984 feature *Secret Decree*, Wu Ziniu directed more than half a dozen war films, including *Evening Bell* (*Wan zhong*), *Joyous Heroes* (*Huanle Yingxiong*), *Between the Living and the Dead* (*Yinyang jie*), and the banned Vietnam War epic, *The Dove Tree* (*Gezi shu*).[18] At the time of its release, *Don't Cry, Nanking* was hailed by critics, audience, and government censure boards (although Wu Ziniu was eventually forced to make some alterations) and today stands among Wu Ziniu's strongest cinematic contributions. As an exploration of, and meditation on, wartime atrocities, *Don't Cry, Nanking* presents an unquestionably more complex and introspective vision than Luo Guanqun and T. F. Mou's films. However, it unfortunately does not rise to the aesthetic, visual, and narrative standards set by Wu's classmates Zhang Yimou, Chen Kaige, and Tian Zhuangzhuang.

All three films analyzed here work in very different ways, but they do bear a surprisingly large number of similarities. Among these similarities are the incorporation of the International Safety Zone as a major line in the respective narrative threads and the attempt to offset Japanese war crimes with the presence of "good-hearted" Japanese characters. Other recurring images include that of a single weeping Chinese child after a mass execution, a pregnant woman being kicked in the stomach (which occurs in two of the films), and the concluding image of children escaping into the night which also occurs in two of the films. And just as the first image seen when visiting the Nanjing Massacre Museum in the western outskirts of the city is a massive "300,000" carved into stone at the museum entrance, all three films end with subtitled captions stating the 300,000 death toll (*Black Sun* actually breaks the numbers down, in an attempt to enhance the credibility of this controversial tally). On this level all three films collectively and individually function as cinematic memorials working to inscribe the still debated death toll into the collective memory of the audience—and, at the same time, into history.

Luo Guanqun's noble effort to readdress the atrocities committed during the Rape of Nanjing deserves credit for being the first to face the burden of history, at a time when it was not terribly popular to do so. In order to bring his vision of the massacre to a large Chinese audience, he appropriates the popular cinematic form of the melodrama. However, by using his film as a blatant vehicle to "prove" or "authenticate" the event itself, Luo must also face a new set of problematic consequences. By borrowing the formal strategies of the melodrama, a genre which often relies upon sensationalism and extravagance of emotion (along with other cinematic conventions, such as the "group film" model), as a means to not only portray but *legitimize* the authenticity of the massacre, the film falls into an internal trap. In the end, Luo Guanqun fails to address the problematic implications of using a highly stylized, dramatic, and inevitably convoluted form—the melodrama—to bear objective testimony to actual history, as the film seems to attempt.

Black Sun escapes this issue by avoiding the melodramatic structure—the only film of three that does so—and attempting to bear detached witness to the cold, brutal events as they unfolded. However, Luo Guanqun's lack of plot, structure, and character identification and development combined with his bloody aesthetics of violence create a new problematic—a problematic demonstrated most poignantly by the two conflicting, contradictory (and one would think mutually exclusive) ways in which the film has been appropriated by the market. From the gory shock-cinema to pedagogical propaganda, viewers have created two very different readings of this disturbing text. Naturally any cinematic portrayal of the Nanjing massacre is bound to be unsettling in terms of the inherent nature of the subject matter. But *Black Sun* is doubly disturbing, owing to the exploitative strategies it employs to present historical atrocity as a blood-and-gore spectacle for an entertainment-thirsting audience, under the pretext of a commemoration.

Although Wu Ziniu has tried to escape the issue of authenticity dealt with by Luo Guanqun and T. F. Mou's bloody representation, the inherent nature of the subject matter makes either one a difficult task. Wu has stated that his film was not intended to be vulgar or a bloody exhibition of the Rape of Nanjing, but like the other two movies, his film remains, by nature of the subject matter, nonetheless a very violent depiction of the incident. In fact, the scene in Wu's film depicting the Japanese raid and subsequent gang rapes of Chinese women (including Rene Liu's character, Shuqin) in the International Safety Zone stands as one of the most violent moments in the history of Chinese cinema. But even if the depictions of violence in both *Massacre in Nanjing* and *Don't Cry, Nanking* never reach the level of vulgarity of *Black Sun*—whose spectacles of violence leave viewers in disbelief, or to simply walk out of the theater in disgust[19]—they both remain much more effective depictions. This is due to an increased sense of empathy on the part of the viewer because of the more developed characters in *Massacre in Nanjing* and *Don't Cry, Nanking*. At the same time, although Wu consciously tries to stay away from the issue of authentication, the screenplay to his film does feature the subtitle "historical record" (*lishi jishi*). And like the other filmmakers, he cannot avoid a final gesture of proof, the 300,000 death toll that is shown at the end of film.

Luo Guanqun, T. F. Mou, and Wu Ziniu each attempt to pay homage to the victims of the Rape of Nanjing through films released on symbolic anniversaries.[20] However, through their respective cinematic strategies, docu-drama styles, and depictions of violence, each film, to varying degrees, compromises the subject matter. From *Massacre in Nanjing*'s politically-charged melodramatic form and aesthetics of authenticity and martyrdom, to *Black Sun*'s faceless victims and exploitative docu-drama violence, and ultimately to *Don't Cry, Nanking*'s mass-market strategies and contrived Sino-Japanese romance, each of these films illustrate in their own way the various problematics associated with cinematic portrayals of atrocity. None of the films have fully escaped the shadow of Japanese denial and, to a lesser extent, the fear that representing Japan in an overly negative light will result in the film's being banned—as was the case with *Black Sun*. Perhaps the greatest tragedy of the Rape of Nanjing is that even today, some six decades after the fact, the Chinese cultural, and cinematic, memory of the massacre continues to be dictated by Japan's denial.[21]

Notes

1.   I would like to thank Professors Peter Li, James Shamus, Richard Pena, Ban Wang, Robert Chi, and David Der-wei Wang, who took time to read various versions of this paper and offer several helpful and constructive comments.

2.   *New York Times,* December 12, 1996.

3.   Official PRC historiography has placed the number of deaths at around 300,000. Some even take this number as conservative and place the number closer to 450,000. Some Japanese revisionists claim that as few as 5,000 died; others claim the entire incident was a fabrication. Most western scholars have generally accepted the 300,000 death toll, although some scholars, such as America's high profile Yale historian Jonathan Spence, who has placed the number of deaths at 50,000.

4.   Renowned third generation director of such classics as *The Red Detachment of Women, Hibiscus Town,* and *The Opium War,* Xie Jin has long planned on making a film about the Rape of Nanjing. His initial plan was to focus on the Tokyo War Crimes Tribunal, however, in recent years he has instead talked about tackling a film based on the diary of John Rabe, a German and member of the Nazi party who played a key role in the Nanjing International Safety Zone.

5.   Although this incident is significantly dramatized and politicized in the film (as evidenced by Fan Changle's initial motivations for retrieving the photos and his subsequent martyrdom), it is in fact a fictionalization of an actual event that occurred during, or perhaps in the aftermath, of the Nanjing Massacre. The incident is retold in a essay by Daqing Yang who writes: "a Chinese clerk working in the shop secretly made an extra set of prints, which were hidden until the end of the war and then admitted as evidence no. 1 at the Nanjing Tribunal." (Fogel 2000: 146).

6.   *Don't Cry, Nanking* is just one of the many titles used for the film, which was marketed under different titles in different regions. In Chinese the film is known as *Nanjing datusha, Nanjing 1937,* and *Bie ku le, Nanjing.* In English, the film is known as *Nanking 1937, Don't Cry, Nanjing,* and *Don't Cry, Nanking* (there is arguably some political and symbolic significance behind the use of "Nanking" in some regions and "Nanjing" in others). Oddly enough, even the film credits significantly change in different prints of the film. For instance, Hong Weijian was credited as the sole screenwriter when the film was screened in Taiwan, whereas a team of several co-writers was credited in the PRC cut.

7.   This is the same in the case of Luo Guanqun's *Massacre in Nanjing,* which, as mentioned earlier, was released to correspond with the fiftieth anniversary of the massacre itself.

8.   *Black Sun's* Hong Kong theatrical run lasted from July 7-21, 1995, grossing HK $902,488.00. It was screened in New York and Palo Alto on December 13 and 16 1995 respectively with the director present as part of a series of events organized by the Alliance in Memory of Victims of the Nanjing Massacre in commemoration of the fiftieth anniversary of the end of WWII.

9.   Other similarities in the two films include the focus of both works on the International Safety Zone, the presence of a Japanese character who sympathizes with the Chinese (Zhuyuan in *Massacre in Nanjing* and Takayama Kenshi in *Black Sun*), the attention to photographers, the punishment-like death of Chinese collaborators who appease Japan, etc.

10.   *Black Sun* was also marketed as documentary of sorts. The cover of the videocassette features an actual photograph from the 1937 massacre (rather than a movie still) and only the cast roster makes the tape distinguishable from a documentary.

11.   This description was taken from a recent online eBay action of *Black Sun: The Nanking Massacre* http://cgi.ebay.com/aw-cgi/eBayISAPI.dll?ViewItem&item= 524499876.

12.   *Black Sun* is actually the second installment of Sino-Japanese shock cinema by the director. Mou's first offering on the subject was his 1988 feature *Men Behind the Sun (Hei taiyang 731)* which deal with vivisection and other medical experiments carried out by the Japanese on Chinese subjects.

13.   The Chinese government, did however, pull the film from the Venice film festival. According to Wu Ziniu's biographer, Zhang Xuan, the decision to pull the film was made by the Taiwan based Long Shong Production Co. for financial reasons.

14.   This fact bears an eerie resemblance to the famous Ming play, the *Peach Blossom Fan*—which was also set in Nanjing. In the play, the storyteller who introduces the work notes how he (who actually took part in the events portrayed) himself had a small role in a play produced several decades after the event.

15.   It should be noted that although the producers of *Don't Cry, Nanking* went to great lengths to create a superstar cast and crew and market the film as a serious historical drama, not unlike *Black Sun,* Wu Ziniu's film also took on a double life in the Asian film market. Thanks primarily to Asian bootleggers, *Don't Cry Nanking* appeared throughout Asia (often under various alternate titles) with black and white atrocity photos replacing the original cover art featuring color stills of Rene Liu and Qin

Han, the featured actor actress and actor of the film. Obviously, in some regions, especially where Taiwan actors are not well known, atrocity is more marketable than star-power.

16.   This is especially ludicrous when the Chinese interpreter, who is working as a collaborator for the Japanese, translates the Japanese general's orders from Mandarin to the Chinese crowds in Mandarin.

17.   From the perspective of a filmmaker, this inconsistency of dialogue has the same effect as an actor looking directly into the camera in that all illusion of genuineness is broken.

18.   The film also marks an interesting point in the political transformation of Wu as a filmmaker. From his early controversial war films like the aforementioned *The Dove Tree,* which Deng Xiaoping is said to have personally criticized (Jiao 1998: 173) to his most recent offering, 1999's *National Anthem (Guoge),* a film which, according to Hong Kong-based film critic Paul Fonoroff, qualifies for nothing more than "creative propaganda." See Fonoroff's review in the 10/01/99 edition of the *South China Morning Pos).* In this context, *Nanjing 1937* marks a middle ground in Wu's trajectory as a political filmmaker.

19.   As Wu Ziniu did after sitting through the first ten minutes of *Black Sun.* Interview with Wu Ziniu, November 2000.

20.   Wu Ziniu's film was not only released in the summer of 1995 to correspond with the fiftieth anniversary of the end of WWII, but actually started filming on December 13, 1994, the date on which the massacre began. By incorporating these two anniversaries into its shooting and release schedule, the film itself functions as commemorative symbol, beginning with the date (and site) of the atrocity and concluding with the date of the Allied victory.

21.   Iris Chang has well documented the Japanese tradition of denying the occurrence of the Nanjing Massacre. Citing such incidents as politician Ishihara Shintaro's now infamous 1990 *Playboy* interview, Chang go so far as to interpret Japan's denial as a "second rape." (Chang 1997:199-214). Not surprisingly, Chang's book was also "denied" by Japanese revisionists, as evidenced by the revisionist website *The Rape of Nanking: looking for truths in the sea of war-time propaganda* (http://www.jiyuu-shikan.org/nanjing/). The site not only goes to great lengths to challenge the accuracy of and discredit Chang's work, but even resorts to revenge-like tactics by including exposé essays on "Cannibalism in Chinese History" and "Chinese Execution Methods." The concerted effort to deny the massacre has continued with the 2000 publication and mass distribution of Tanaka Masaaki's book *What Really Happened in Nanking: The Refutation of a Common Myth.*

Filmography

Luo Guanqun (director). 1988. *Tuchang xuezheng (Massacre in Nanjing).* Fujian Film Studio, Nanjing Film Studio.
T.F. Mou (Mou Dunfei) (producer and director). 1995. *Hei taiyang: Nanjing da tusha (Black Sun: The Nanking Massacre).* T.F. Films Hong Kong.
Wu Ziniu (director). *Nanjing 1937 (Don't Cry, Nanking).* 1995. China Film Co-production Corporation, Long Shong Production Co. Ltd.

Bibliography

Brook, Timothy. 1999. *Documents on the Nanjing Massacre.* Ann Arbor: Ann Arbor Paperbacks, The University of Michigan Press.

Chang, Iris. 1997. *The Rape of Nanking: The Forgotten Holocaust of World War II.* New York: Basic Books.

Cheng Shuan (editor). 1997. *Zhongguo dianying mingpian jianshang cidian (Encyclopedia of Appreciation of Chinese films).* Beijing: Long March Publishing House.

Fogel, Joshua A. 2000. *The Nanjing Massacre in History and Historiography.* Berkeley: University of California Press.

Fonoroff, Paul. 1988. *At the Hong Kong Movies: 600 Reviews from 1988 Till the Handover.* Hong Kong: Film Biweekly Publishing House (Distributed by W.W. Norton & Co.).

Honda, Katsuichi. 1999. *The Nanjing Massacre: A Japanese Journalist Confronts Japan's National Shame.* Armonk: M.E. Sharpe.

Insdorf, Annette. 1989. *Indelible Shadows: Film and the Holocaust* (Second Edition). Cambridge University Press, Reprinted.

Jiao, Xiongping (Peggy Chiao). 1998. *Fengyun jihui: Yu dangdai Zhongguo dianying duihua (Dialogues with contemporary Chinese directors).* Taipei: Yuanliu Publishing House.

Landy, Maricia (editor). 2001. *The Historical Film: History and Memory in Media.* New Brunswick: Rutgers University Press.

Long Shong International Co. Ltd. 1995. *Nanking 1937.* Taipei: Wanxiang tushu.

Schaefer, Eric. 1999. *"Bold! Daring! Shocking! True!" A History of Exploitation Films, 1919-1959.* Durham: Duke University Press.

Sharrett, Christopher (editor). 1999. *Mythologies of Violence in Postmodern Media.* Detroit: Wayne State University Press.

Tanaka, Masaaki. 2000. *What Really Happened in Nanking: The Refutation of a Common Myth.* Tokyo: Sekai Shuppan, Inc.

Zhang, Junxiang and Cheng Jihua (editors). 1997. *Zhongguo dianying da cidian (China Cinema Encyclopedia).* Shanghai: Shanghai Cishu Publishing House.

Zhang, Xuan (editor). 1996. *Wan zhong wei shei er ming: Wu Ziniu (For Whom the Evening Bell Tolls: Wu Ziniu).* Changsha: Hunan Arts & Literature Publishing House.

Zhang, Yingjin and Zhiwei Xiao. 1998. *Encyclopedia of Chinese Film.* New York: Routledge.

Part V

History Will Not Forget

13

The Nanking Holocaust:
Memory, Trauma and Reconciliation

Peter Li

As Auschwitz has become a symbol of the Jewish Holocaust and Nazi atrocities in World War II, the Nanking massacre has become the symbol of the Japanese military's monstrous brutality and savage cruelty in the Asia Pacific war from 1931 to 1945. But in comparison to the Jewish Holocaust, relatively little has been written about the atrocities committed by the Japanese military in China, Korea, the Philippines, Singapore, and Indonesia, where close to 50 million people died as a consequence of Japanese aggression. In China alone, an estimated 20-30 million people lost their lives. While thousands of volumes have been written, numerous museum exhibits have been mounted, and documentaries and feature films have been made about the Holocaust, literature about the Japanese atrocities committed in the Asia Pacific region has been scarce in the fifty years since the end of the war. In fact, Eugene B. Sledge has written that, "the best kept secret about World War II is the truth about the Japanese atrocities." (Sledge, 297)

Why has this part of World War II been kept from the world, and why has the present-day Japanese government not faced up to its militarist past and eluded justice? Firstly, the Japanese government has utilized its position as the one and only country in the world to suffer the devastation of the first atomic bomb in human history. Secondly, because of the United States government's feelings of guilt and responsibility for dropping the atomic bomb, it helped Japan rebuild, nurtured Japan's victim status, and swept her war crime responsibilities under the rug. Thirdly, the Cold War made it necessary for the United States to cultivate Japan as an ally to counter the Soviet and Chinese threat; therefore, its past transgressions were overlooked. Fourthly, China also played a significant part in not publicizing the wartime atrocities because it was engaged in a vicious civil war of its own after World War II. And after the civil war ended, both China and Taiwan wanted to play Japan off each other and subsequently needed Japan as a trading partner. Therefore, no reparations were demanded of Japan.

Perhaps the most important reason for Japan's historical amnesia, lack of remorse, and continued denials is because of the Showa-era continuum, or the transwar continuities in Japan. The most important symbol of this continuity is the reign of Emperor Hirohito after the war. He was exonerated from any responsibility for war crimes through a secret arrangement with General MacArthur, who engineered the surrender of Japan and the subsequent U.S. occupation. Emperor Hirohito, therefore, remained in power until his death in 1989. Along with the emperor, a large number of people in politics, the economic-industrial complex, military doctors, and scientists soon became active again in the public sector soon after the occupation was over. Several who were accused Class A War Criminals rose to high positions in Japanese politics. They received a slap on the wrist and then returned to run the government and industries. It was because of this continuity that Japan would never assume full responsibility for the atrocities committed in Asia, preferring to regard them as lies, fabrications, or just a part of war and downplaying their significance.

It is equally regrettable that in Emperor Hirohito's Imperial Rescript, delivered on August 15 on the occasion of Japan's surrender, he never mentioned remorse, guilt, or assumed any responsibility for the war in the Pacific. He denied any aggression on the part of Japan, stating that war was declared on America and Britain "to assure Japan's self-preservation and the stabilization of East Asia"; nor did Japan intend "to infringe upon the sovereignty of other nations or embark upon territorial aggrandizement." Therefore, he admitted to no wrongdoing or the commitment of any war crimes. In the last part of his speech to the nation, he never mentioned defeat or surrender. He said, "However, it is according to the dictate of time and fate that we have resolved to pave the way for a grand peace for all generations to come by enduring the unendurable and suffering the insufferable." It was the consequence of "the dictate of time and fate" that Japan must face defeat and surrender. It was not due to any faults of its own.

However, as the new century begins to dawn, there are renewed calls to bring Japan to justice. Japan must face its past, its war time atrocities. As the Nobel Laureate for literature, Oe Kenzaburo, aptly noted: "[Japan's] unwillingness to come to terms with its past is not just *morally offensive*, it prevents Japan from playing its proper role in Asia" ("Denying History Disables Japan," *New York Times,* July 2, 1995).

Japanese designs on China began as early as the 1890s, after Japan's successful program of modernization during the Meiji period (1868–1912), culminating with China's defeat in the first Sino-Japanese War of 1894-95. From that time on, China lost all respect and dignity in the eyes of the Japanese, who looked upon China as territory to be exploited as a colony in a manner similar to Asia and Africa, as a result of European and American claims of "manifest destiny."

In the 1930s, at the height of the worldwide depression, Japan's expansionists and militarists once again looked at China as their rightful claim and as a solution to their internal problems. Lt. Colonel Ishiwara wrote in 1930: "Japan's survival depends upon a favorable resolution of the problem of Manchuria and Mongolia," "Japan must expand overseas to achieve political stability at home," "[t]he future of Manchuria and Mongolia will only be satisfactorily decided when Japan obtains those areas," and "Japan must be willing to fight America to achieve our national objectives" (Ienaga, 11). Thus, the blueprint for the Asia Pacific war was laid. On September 18, 1931, the Japanese staged an incident in Mukden (the present-day city of Shenyang), later called the Manchurian Incident, that led to the seizure and occupation of the whole of Manchuria. For the militarists, Manchuria was still not enough; they eyed the whole of China. Again, in 1937, the Japanese instigated the "Marco Polo Bridge Incident" outside Beijing, which led to all-out war with China and subsequent occupation of about one-third of the country. There is no question that the eight-year war that ensued from 1937-1945 was one of the bloodiest in human history. Wherever Japanese soldiers went, they committed atrocities of indescribably cruelty and barbarism against the military and innocent civilian population indiscriminately.

While these events have not occupied headline news for many years, within the past ten years there has been a gradual awakening of interest in the history of the Asian-Pacific region, and a flurry of books films and documentaries have appeared about the Asia Pacific war. However, it is Iris Chang's recent volume, *The Rape of Nanking: The Forgotten Holocaust of World War II*, that has ignited a groundswell of interest in the Asia Pacific war, and even shocked the Japanese ambassador to the United States, Kunihiko Saito, who, at a press conference on April 21, 1998, criticized the book and the attention it was getting.

Trauma and Remembrance

For over half a century the Chinese and other Asian nations have remained relatively quiet about the Japanese atrocities. This should not be taken to mean, however, that there has been any lack of pain, suffering, and anguish among the surviving victims, and friends and/or relatives of those victims who succumbed. In fact, Iris Chang's family is a good example of how memories of the war were kept alive and passed on from one generation to the next. Iris Chang received her inspiration to write about Nanking from her maternal grandparents, who escaped the Nanking massacre by just one month, and from her own parents. Since the war experience was an integral part of the family memory, it was frequently the subject of conversation at the Chang family gatherings. However, it was not until 1992 that the ideas about the subject began to coalesce, and two more years of gestation before the ideas were galvanized into a book. The immediate cause was a conference sponsored by the Global Alliance for Preserving the History of World War II in Asia, held in Cupertino, California, which displayed poster-sized photographs of the Rape of Nanking. Chang described them as "some of the most gruesome photographs I had ever seen in my life." This sparked her interest, and after more than two years of intensive research and writing, the final product was *The Rape of Nanking: The Forgotten Holocaust of World War II* (Basic Books, 1997).

During the course of her research, Chang would have nightmares. She woke up in the middle of the night shaking with anger, she lost weight, lost hair, and had trouble sleeping and eating. There was also an urgency about Chang's book, in that the survivors and witnesses to the massacre at Nanking were dying fast.

However, the publication of *The Rape of Nanking: The Forgotten Holocaust of World War II* in November 1997, on the sixtieth anniversary of the fall of Nanking to the Japanese in 1937, has brought about a sea change. It was ranked number eleven on the *New York Times* bestseller list in February 1998. The book has initiated a gradual awakening of the world at large, that aside from the horrors of the Jewish Holocaust under Nazi Germany, there had been another awful tragedy perpetrated by the Japanese during the Asia Pacific war in which victims of slaughter, rape, and savage brutality numbered in the millions—some estimate 30 million in China itself. The numbers killed in the city of Nanking alone, in a period of seven weeks from December 13, 1937 to February 1938, according to the International Military Tribunal of the Far East (IMTFE), was an estimated 260,000. The Memorial Hall of the Victims of the Nanking Massacre in Nanjing, established in 1984, claims that at least 300,000 Chinese were killed. Japanese sources significantly underestimate the numbers; one of Japan's leading historians of the war, Hata Ikuhito, wrote in 1986 that "illegal murders" at Nanking ranged from 38,000 to 42,000. The important point is not the numbers, but the fact that illegal killings did take place.

"Hell on Earth"—The Fall of Nanking

The city of Nanking took on special significance for the Japanese because at the time Nanking was the capital of China, and victory there would have meant the symbolic defeat of China as a whole. A few weeks earlier, Japan had just taken Shanghai after more than three months of fierce fighting. The Nationalist army had lost 300,000 troops and ten generals. Shanghai was a great prize for the Japanese, but the greater prize would be the capture of the capital. But the Japanese had come to realize that taking China would not come as easily as some had predicted earlier—that China could be conquered in just three months.

In the march from Shanghai to Nanking during the month of November, the Japanese troops had already begun their bloodthirsty spree of indiscriminate killing. Their 200,000-man force advanced on Nanking with a vengeance, killing, looting, raping, and burning as they proceeded. Wherever they went, they left a trail of devastation and dead bodies. It is estimated that another 300,000 civilians were killed along the three routes taken by the Japanese troops (Yin, 21).

Upon entering Nanking, the Japanese were shocked at the number of soldiers who surrendered without firing a shot. The surrendering Chinese soldiers often outnumbered the invading forces by ten to one. Japanese soldiers, who had been trained in a military culture in which suicide was infinitely preferable to capture, found it incomprehensible that the Chinese soldiers would surrender rather than fight. Thus, the Japanese regarded the Chinese prisoners with great contempt.

The perspective of the Japanese soldier probably can be garnered from the diary of a Japanese soldier, Azuma Shiro, who was in Nanking and felt secretly ashamed that he had been afraid of the Chinese. Azuma wrote in his diary: "They [the surrendered Chinese soldiers] all walked in droves, like ants crawling on the ground. They looked like a bunch of homeless people, with ignorant expressions on their faces.... They hardly looked like the enemy who only yesterday was shooting at and troubling us. It was impossible to believe that they were the enemy soldiers. I felt quite foolish to think we had been fighting to the death against these ignorant slaves. And some of them were even twelve or thirteen-year-old boys" (Chang, 44).

The massacre, arson, looting, and brutal assaults on women that ensued are graphically depicted in James Yin and Shi Young's *Rape of Nanking: An Undeniable History in Photographs* (Innovative Publishing Group, 1997), which contains some 450 photographs that leave an indelible record of the Japanese atrocities. The order from above was: "Kill All Captives." The methods of killing ranged from beheadings to bayoneting, live burials, burning, and freezing. Killing had become a form of entertainment and recreation. "There seemed to be no limit to the Japanese capacity for human degradation and sexual perversion in Nanking. Just as some soldiers invented killing contests to break the monotony of murder, so did some invent games of recreational rape and torture when wearied of the glut of sex. Perhaps one of the most brutal forms of Japanese entertainment was the impalement of vaginas. In the streets of Nanking corpses of women lay with their legs splayed open, their orifices pierced with wooden rods, twigs and weeds" (Chang, 94).

Among the different methods of execution, beheading with the sword seemed to bring the most satisfaction to many Japanese soldiers because of the association with the military culture of the samurai, *bushido* (the way of the warrior). It was also used as a method of building up courage and stamina in the novice soldier inexperienced in killing. Corporal Sone Kazuo, reporting on his first decapitation, wrote:

> Of course I was reluctant to show my weakness in front of others. My last bit of courage was brought out when I screamed "Kill!"—and brought down the sword against the prisoner's neck.... The severed head dropped to the ground and rolled like a

ball down the embankment to the water. The whole process lasted only a few seconds. But it seemed like hours to me. Thus, I had now obtained the unusual experience of a beheading. (Yin, 110)

If the image of the samurai sword had once evoked heroic acts of bravery and courage, the numerous souvenir pictures taken by Japanese soldiers of themselves wielding swords about to behead the bound, helpless, kneeling victims should dispel any romantic conceptions. The swords have now become symbols of something much more sinister. There were contests devised to see who could behead the greatest number of persons in the shortest time. Photographs of severed heads lined up neatly in a row or placed on fence posts were taken for souvenirs.

Other methods of killing included the bayoneting of local civilians and POWs. Tens of thousands of Chinese prisoners were used for live bayonet practice. They were tied to posts with ropes or wires, and new recruits were forced to practice stabbing their victims to death with their fifteen-inch bayonets to build up their morale and courage. Again Sone wrote in his *A Japanese Soldier's Confession*, "This kind of killing experience was every soldier's test and ordeal. After this they would be fearless in real battle, and would glory in the act of killing. War made people cruel, bestial and insane. It was an abyss of inhuman crimes" (Yin, 132). We often read about the terror of a soldier's first experience in hand-to-hand combat or his first experience in killing another human being written about in war literature. In the Japanese case, on the other hand, the soldiers were already conditioned before combat by live bayonet practice.

Live burial was another method of getting rid of captives. This method of killing was slow and excruciating: "...Chinese captives were also bound hand and foot and planted neck deep in the earth, leaving their protruding heads to terrorize people...some were jabbed with bayonets, some trampled by horses, some doused with boiling water, some crushed under tank tracks" (Yin 144). The terrified screaming and miserable howls of the victims could be heard up to several miles away. Some of the captives were buried up to their waists in the ground, then set upon by German shepherds.

There were also burnings, committed by first dousing the prisoners with gasoline and then shooting them, thus igniting the fumes, and ending with a spectacular conflagration. The Japanese also derived great joy from devising new ways of killing; they laughed and applauded as the victims struggled in agony. In this respect, the Japanese surpassed their German counterparts in the cruelty and ingenuity in devising their methods. A Japanese soldier wrote in his diary: "...Recently, when we were very bored, we had some fun killing Chinese. We caught some innocent Chinese and either buried them alive, or pushed them into a fire, or beat them with clubs, or killed them by other cruel means" (Yin 152).

The worst of the atrocities were the brutal assaults on the unfortunate Chinese women who crossed the paths of the Japanese. It is estimated that upwards of 80,000 women were raped by the invading Japanese soldiers, and this is the reason why the Nanking massacre is often referred to as the "Rape of Nanking." The women were not only assaulted and brutalized, but also humiliated and insulted. Case after case was enumerated at the International Military Tribunal of the Far East (IMTFE), totaling some 436 documented instances of rape and subsequent mutilation and many times that of undocumented cases. The undocumented cases remain buried with the victims themselves. Occasionally, instances of fierce resistance paid off, as in the case of Ms. Li Xiuying, who survived to tell of her ordeal. Li was eighteen years old at the time, and she fought back with such ferocity that the Japanese soldiers were shocked. But finally, outnumbered,

> The soldiers aimed their bayonets at her head, slashing her face with their blades and knocking out her teeth. Her mouth filled with blood, which she spit into their eyes. "Blood was on the walls, on the bed, on the floor, everywhere," Liu [Li] remembered. "I had no fear in my mind. I was furious. My only thought was to fight and kill them." Finally a soldier plunged his bayonet into her belly and everything went black for her. (Chang, 98)

Now 79, Ms. Li has brought her case to a Tokyo court, demanding compensation from the Japanese government, together with nine other survivors of the massacre. Her indomitable spirit was still very much in evidence as she told reporters, "I want to tell the world that [the Nanking Massacre] really happened.... The Japanese people must tell their children the truth and let them know that war must never happen again between our two nations."

Another survivor told how he refused to lead Japanese soldiers to the women they desperately wanted. Xue Jialin recounted that day in December 1937 when Japanese soldiers appeared in his village: "They came to our village and forced me to lead them to where the 'flower girls' hid. I would rather die than do this kind of inhuman thing. I refused and angered them. An officer cut my lips open with his sword and chopped off my teeth" (Yin, 182).

A valuable lesson was to be learned from the Japanese occupation of Nanking. After the experience of Nanking, the savage brutality of the Japanese Army became known and their promises of good treatment for those people who surrendered peacefully were never to be believed. When the Japanese first took Nanking, they dropped leaflets saying, "Those Chinese soldiers who are not willing to fight and who are holding up white flags or both of their hands to surrender to the Japanese Army with this certificate [Preferential Certificate], will be treated leniently by the Imperial Army. No harm will come to them; no one will be killed. Jobs will be offered to them. Intelligent soldiers, come!" (Yin, 30). This turned out to be a total lie; those who surrendered were indiscriminately shot and killed. From this point onward, few Chinese soldiers ever surrendered to the Japanese. They would fight to the end rather than surrender.

To be fair, if the Chinese Army had been better organized and led, there would not have been such a large-scale disaster. The Chinese command was marked by chaos and disorder. In the midst of the fighting, General Tang Shengzhi, who had been earlier ordered by Chiang Kai-shek to defend Nanking at all cost, was suddenly ordered to retreat. Chiang seemed to be playing dice with the lives of his own troops. "Not surprisingly, the order to retreat threw the Chinese military into an uproar. Some officers ran about the city haphazardly informing anyone they came into contact with to pull out.... Other officers told no one, not even their own troops.... In their haste and confusion to leave the city, at least one Chinese tank rolled over countless Chinese soldiers in its path, stopping only when blown up by a hand grenade" (Chang, 76). It must be admitted there was also a callous disregard for human life on the part of the Chinese Army, but there was no deliberate cruelty. Often the surrendering troops outnumbered their captors; if there had been any organized resistance, the Japanese soldiers would have been overcome and killed. But there was no resistance. Most of the prisoners watched passively as their comrades were killed by the Japanese, knowing all the time that they would be next.

The Perspective of Foreign Nationals

The foreign nationals who remained in the International Safety Zone provided a valuable third-party perspective on the Nanking massacre. Some two dozen foreigners, mostly American, but also German, Danish, Russian, and Chinese, including doctors, educators, missionaries, and businessmen stayed behind to protect and care for the 250,000 Chinese who sought refuge in the International Safety Zone that was set up in the heart of Nanking. Chief among them were John Rabe, a German Nazi who also came to be known as the "Living Buddha of Nanking" because of his heroic stance to establish the International Safety Zone; Robert Wilson, an American surgeon who elected to stay behind in Nanking while other doctors left; and Wilhelmina (Minnie) Vautrin, known as the "the living Goddess of Mercy of Nanking," who was dean at Ginling Women's Arts and Science College and the only woman who remained to face the brutal Japanese invaders.

While researching the life of John Rabe, who went to China in 1908 and worked for Siemens China Company selling telephones and electrical equipment to the Chinese government, Iris Chang discovered he had kept an extensive diary of the daily events that took place during the Rape of Nanking. She went to Germany to seek out Rabe's granddaughter and secured the diaries that are now available to the public.[1] This has become the most recent and most important of the incontrovertible corroborative evidence regarding what had happened in Nanking. But Rabe did more than just set up the Safety Zone and supervise the activities; he roamed the city streets as well to prevent atrocities through his personal intervention. He was appalled by the rapes in the city and personally intervened to stop them. "There were girls under the age of eight and women over the. age of seventy who were raped and then, in the most brutal way possible, knocked down and beat up. We found corpses of women on beer glasses and others who had been lanced with bamboo shoots" (Rabe's diary quoted in Chang, 119). But not all his attempts to save the Chinese were successful. Rabe persuaded thousands of Chinese to lay down their arms, believing the propaganda of the Japanese posters: "Trust Our Japanese Army—They Will Protect and Feed You." But much to the soldiers' and Rabe's dismay, the Japanese never kept their word. The soldiers were rounded up and shot.

Another heroine of the Rape of Nanking was Wilhelmina (Minnie) Vautrin,[2] who became virtually the head of Ginling College when most of the other faculty fled the city. She was an avid diarist and left an invaluable record of her days in China. At the height of the terror, one thousand refugees a day were passing through the city. In three days, the compounds of Ginling College were filled with three thousand women. Because Ginling was a women's college, Minnie Vautrin specifically looked after women, girls, and children. She herself also became vulnerable to the rapacious Japanese soldiers, who were on the lookout for women for military prostitution and rape. Vautrin was, like Rabe, at times duped by the deception of the Japanese. She was tricked into sending innocent women into the hands of the Japanese soldiers believing that they were to wash clothing and cook; she was slapped by Japanese soldiers more than once.

When the Rape of Nanking began on December 13, there were also reporters from Japanese, British, and American newspapers on hand who reported on the events. Yoshio Moriyama of the *Asahi Shimbun*, Tillman Durdin of the *New York Times*, and H. J. Timperley of the *Manchester Guardian* wrote in their respective newspapers reporting on the terrible events occurring in Nanking. The Japanese, American, and British reporters were all in agreement regarding the mass exterminations that were taking place. Moriyama reported on December 14: "At one time, after Nanking was captured, more than 30,000 Chinese were driven to the foot of the city wall. Machine guns then swept the crowd and grenades were thrown from atop the wall. The 30,000 people were all killed, most of them women, children, and the elderly" (Yin, 48). Durdin telegraphed an urgent dispatch to the *New York Times* on December 17, stating: "During the first three days of the occupation, the situation developed in an unpredictable fashion; large-scale looting, sexual assault on women and tyrannized killing of innocent people, civilians driven out of their houses...all of these turned Nanking into a city of terror" (Yin, 50). George Fitch, an American and a longtime resident of Nanking, wrote: "a city laid waste, ravaged, completely looted, much of it burned. Complete anarchy has reigned for ten days—it has been hell on earth" (Yin 52). The atrocities had been so horrendous that even Prince Mikasa, the youngest brother of Emperor Hirohito, wrote a report, "Reflections as a Japanese on the Sino-Japanese War," in which he revealed to his brother the atrocities he had witnessed in China and wished desperately to bring the war to a close (Yin, 54).

The horrors of the Rape of Nanking and the moral questions raised to this day remain unresolved and not completely understood. The reasons for the savage brutality of the Japanese soldiers are many, ranging from the Japanese military culture stemming from the traditional training of the Japanese samurai and the highly disciplined military training in the army, to long years of indoctrination on the superiority of the Japanese race and the Japanese contempt for the Chinese after the First Sino-Japanese War of 1894–95. Generalizing on human nature, the Japanese movie director and comedian Takeshi Kitano has stated: "I believe that even the most normal-seeming people have the potential for violence. The most extreme example might be found among the Japanese soldiers during World War II who committed atrocities in China. Most of them were probably the sons of farmers" (*New York Times*, March 15, 1998).

Others believe human cruelty will never cease to exist even with the progress of civilization: "It is an error to imagine that civilization and savage cruelty are antitheses.... In our times the cruelties, like most other aspects of our world, have become far more effectively administered than before. They have not and will not cease to exist" (Bauman, 9). Probably the most ingenious explanation came from General Matsui Iwane himself, the general nominally in charge of the Nanking campaign: "The struggle between Japan and China was always a fight between brothers within the 'Asian Family.' ...It had been my belief during all these days that we must regard this struggle as a method of making the Chinese undergo self reflection. We do not do this because we hate them, but on the contrary we love them too much" (Chang, 219). The irony of this statement boggles the human mind. If this is the way the Japanese show brotherly love, then the Chinese people could certainly do with less of it.

In the Foreword to Yin and Young's *The Rape of Nanking: An Undeniable History in Photographs*, the Most Reverend Desmond Tutu wrote: "To sweep under the carpet the atrocities which occurred in Nanking in 1937-38 and turn a blind eye to the truth is at best a gross disservice to future generations and at worst to be criminally negligent and irresponsible. A record such as this book is an essential part of our history. However horrible, we must not be sheltered from the evils of our past" (Yin, ix).

Forgiveness and Reconciliation

Is it possible to overcome the feelings of anguish and hate after having been captured, tortured, and brutalized by the Japanese? The case of Eric Lomax is a moving example of how reconciliation can be achieved. Eric Lomax was a British soldier who became a POW under the Japanese and survived two years of brutal torture by the Kempeitai (the Japanese equivalent of the Gestapo). Lomax was captured while serving in Singapore and subsequently sent to work on the Burma-Siam Railway in a camp called Kanchanaburi [Kanburi for short], in present-day Thailand. Arrested and interrogated for having secretly built a radio, Lomax had to suffer two years of dreadful torture, starvation, and physical beatings at the hands of his English-speaking interrogator, Nagase Takashi, and his subordinates.

After the war, for fifty years, Lomax suffered from the aftereffects of his two years of torture, humiliation, and dehumanization, and he often thought of confronting his hated interrogator with murderous intent. By coincidence, while visiting a friend he was given a photo-copy of the *Japan Times* for August 15, 1989, which had a picture of and an article about Nagase Takashi, who was described as devoting much of his life to "make up for the Japanese Army's treatment of prisoners-of-war." When he first heard about the good deeds that Nagase was performing, Lomax was filled with disbelief. His hatred of the Japanese was so strong that he did not care to see another Japanese for the rest of his life. And he doubted Nagase's sincerity:

[My friend Henry Cecil Babb] gave me some information about his correspondent Nagase Takashi, who claimed to have become active in charitable causes near Kanburi in the post-war years, and who had just built a Buddhist temple close to the railway there. *I read about his activities with cold skepticism and found the very thought of him distasteful. I could not believe the idea of a Japanese repentance.* He had organized a meeting of "reconciliation" at the River Kwae Bridge... *I had not seen a Japanese since 1945 and had no wish ever to meet one again. His reconciliation assembly sounded to me like a fraudulent publicity stunt.* (emphasis added, Lomax, 232)

Lomax had a total distrust of the Japanese and had no desire to meet him. However, through more coincidences, they corresponded and fi-nally arranged to meet in Kanburi in Thailand. Lomax had learned that Nagase's repentance was genuine and sincere, and not merely words. Mr. Nagase had gone back to Thailand more than sixty times since 1963, and his reparations were not an occasional thing but had become a way of life. He built a Temple of Peace on the River Kwae Bridge and became a devout Buddhist. He often spoke out against militarism and is known to have said critically of Japan: "Japan is a very strange country, truth cannot prevail. So I am a citizen of the world and not a Japanese." He accuses the Japanese royal family of being a family of war criminals and claims that 80 percent of the Japanese today do not know that Japan had ever invaded another country.

Because of Nagase's sincere remorse and demonstration of his repentance with good deeds and actions, Eric Lomax was finally moved to give Mr. Nagase the forgiveness he desired. They met alone in a hotel room in Tokyo, and Lomax handed the tense Nagase a handwritten letter. He tells the reader what he had written in the letter: "The war had been over for almost fifty years; that I had suffered much; and that I knew that although he too had suffered throughout this time, he had been most courageous and brave in arguing against militarism and working for reconciliation. I told him that while I could not forget what happened at Kanburi in 1943, I assured him of my total forgiveness" (Lomax, 275).

Lasting Distrust of Japan

"Unlike many in the West who have come to see Japan as a reformed militarist nation, a 'civil power,' many East Asians, in varying degrees, still view Japan with suspicion in terms of its militarist past. In other words, unlike those in the West who see the Japanese militaristic culture of the 'sword' has given way to an anti-militaristic culture of the 'chrysanthemum,' many East Asians see the revival of militarism as by no means a foregone scenario of a future Japan" (Deng, 5). Distrust of Japan dating back to the days of Pearl Harbor was echoed in Ruth Benedict's classic anthropological study of the contradictory nature of Japanese personality and character, *The Chrysanthemum and the Sword* (1946). For East Asians, particularly those who had directly suffered the brutality of Japanese militarism and occupation, the memory is still painfully sharp; it is especially important for Japan to make a sincere, unambiguous apology and pay reparations to its victims even though the compensation will not erase the pain and suffering.

At the moment a decision is pending in a suit representing 33,000 U.S. POWs, 14,000 civilian internees, and thousands more Dutch, Australian, and New Zealand survivors, filed in the Tokyo District Court on January 30, 1995. The suit asks for an official apology and compensation of $20,000 per individual from the Japanese government. Ms. Li Xiuying, the Nanking massacre survivor, and nine others have also filed suit in the Tokyo District Court asking for an apology and compensation. Her quest is supported by a courageous group of 200 Japanese lawyers, scholars, and others who wanted the Japanese people to become better informed about Japan's past actions. Individuals such as Azuma Shiro, a retired veteran of World War II, historian Ienaga Sabura, Eric Lomax's Kempeitai interrogator, Nagase Takashi, and Nobel Laureate novelist Oe Kenzabura have all spoken out courageously about the fact that the Japanese government has not faced up to its past.

Recently, a bill was introduced in the U.S. House of Representatives, HCR 126, which condemns the Japanese for their wartime atrocities and calls for (1) the Japanese government to formally issue a clear and unambiguous apology, and (2) immediately pay compensation to all victims of World War II Japanese war crimes. With her book *The Rape of Nanking*, Iris Chang has now added her voice in challenging the sixty years of denials and deceit by the Japanese government that have kept its own people and the world from knowing the truth about the atrocities committed by the Japanese military in China and elsewhere in Asia.

Many complex factors came into play to bring about the conflict in the Pacific: the worldwide economic depression in the 1930s, Japan's late adoption of imperialism and colonialism, racism and prejudice, cultural conflict, modernization, militarism, expansionism, and Japan's perceived need for self-preservation. However, in order to close this bloody chapter of modern history, Japan must come to terms with her past. In order to achieve a meaningful reconciliation, a fuller discussion of the complex and multifaceted issues of the Asia Pacific war perhaps will help provide a common ground upon which to build a satisfactory settlement among the Pacific rim countries. Furthermore, the dialogue must continue not only among the many voices of the Pacific region, but needs to include also the voices of the Western allies—Americans, Canadians, English, Dutch, Australians—and all those who have suffered the pains of hunger, torture, and disease under the Japanese military. The issue is not merely an East Asian one, but a transnational one that involves the international family of nations.

Notes

1. See John Rabe, *The Good Man of Nanking*, *The Diaries of John Rabe*. Edited by Erwin Wickert. Translated from the German by John E. Woods (Alfred A. Knopf, 1998).
2. For her recent biography, see Hua-ling Hu, *American Goddess at the Rape of Nanking: The Courage of Minnie Vautrin* (University of Southern Illinois Press: 2000).

Selected Bibliography

Bauman, Zygmunt. 1989. *Modernity and the Holocaust*. Ithaca, NY: Cornell University Press.

Chang, Iris. 1997. *The Rape of Nanking: The Forgotten Holocaust of World War II.* New York: Basic Books.

Daws, Gavan. 1994. *Prisoners of the Japanese: POWs of World War II in the Pacific.* New York: William Morrow.

Deng, Yong. 1997. "The Asianization of East Asian Security and the United States' Role." *East Asia: An International Quarterly,* 16.3.

Dower, John D. 1986. *War Without Mercy: Race and Power in the Pacific War.* New York: Pantheon Books.

Ienaga, Saburo. 1968. *The Pacific War, 1931–1945.* New York: Pantheon Books.

Karnow, Stanley. 1992, November 22. "Collective Amnesia in Tokyo." *New York Times.*

Oe, Kenzaburo. 1995, July 2. "Denying History Disables Japan." *New York Times Magazine.*

Sledge, Eugene B. 1998. "The Old Breed and the Costs of War." In *The Costs of War.* New Brunswick, NJ: Transaction Publishers.

Yin, James and Shi Young. 1997. *The Rape of Nanking: An Undeniable History in Photographs.* Chicago: Innovative Publishing Group.

14

The Great Asian-Pacific Crescent of Pain: Japan's War from Manchuria to Hiroshima, 1931 to 1945*

Werner Gruhl

Today the memory of the Allied Asian death toll and destruction of World War II has been relegated to the attic of history; the suffering goes unrecognized or treated as if it counted for little. Most of the American public is not aware that the fourteen-year war in the Asia Pacific theater (1931-1945) caused far greater pain and suffering than generally realized. While academia and the media have focused their attention primarily on the casualties suffered by the Western allies, Germany, the United States, and Japan—particularly the victims of the atomic bombing of Hiroshima and Nagasaki—few mention the tremendous loss of life and property of the other Asian countries. This myopia extends to focusing only on American lives saved—and excludes the Asian and other Allied lives spared—when considering the use of atomic bombs to end World War II.

---

* This essay is based on the author's synopsis of a book-length study entitled *Japan's War from Manchuria to Hiroshima, 1931-1945: The Great Asia Pacific Crescent of Pain* (forthcoming). The author has employed an abundance of sources to derive the figures presented here. They include the United Nations' Report of the Working Group for Asia and the Far East and the International Military Tribunal for the Far East records, and from institutions around the world, such as the National Archives at College Park, Maryland, the University of the Philippines, the British Imperial War Museum, and the Netherlands Institute for War Documentation. The two volumes of Michael Clodfelter's *Warfare and Armed Conflicts: A Statistical Reference*, and R.J. Rummel's *China's Bloody Century: Genocide and Mass Murder since 1900* and *Democide: Nazi Genocide and Mass Murder* have been used extensively. The author has used his years of statistical experience gained from working as chief of NASA's Cost and Economic Analysis Branch to add another dimension to the understanding of the Asia Pacific war and the U.S. and Allies' policy decisions.

The Asia Pacific war was traumatic if not devastating to over 700 million people directly in its path—one third of the world's population. (See Figure 1) Japan invaded, among others, China, Burma, South East Asia, and a number of Pacific Islands. More than 300 million people in Japanese occupied areas were terrorized. Some 90 million were severely affected and approximately 24 million lost their lives. Those severely affected include the wounded, raped, tortured, biological war and forced-slave labor victims, refugees, war orphans, Japanese-caused opium addicts, victims of severe war-caused malnutrition and diseases, POWs, internees, and most Asian military conscripts. In comparison, Imperial Japan's attempt at expansion cost her about three million lives. Ninety-nine percent of all Allied dead in the Asia Pacific theater were Asians. About one percent were Americans, British, Australians, Canadians, New Zealanders, Dutch, and French. The scale of death, suffering, and destruction experienced by our Asian Allies demands as much remembrance as do our Western Allies in Europe. We also need to recognize the victims of Imperial Japan in the same way we do those of Nazi Germany.

Often overlooked is the fact that the Asia Pacific war, as part of World War II considered in its worldwide context, was started in 1931 by Japan's invasion of Manchuria and, later, China proper. The war in China, marked by the "Marco Polo Bridge Incident" of 1937, raged in full fury for over four years, 1937-1941, before Japan's surprise attack on Pearl Harbor extended her grasp for a larger empire to the rest of Asia and the Pacific. Lyman Van Slyke, in *The Cambridge History of Japan*, makes the point: "...the Manchurian incident, the war in China, and the war in the Pacific should not be viewed separately but as one continuous war. The only occasion when war was formally declared in accordance with international law was in December 1941, but after 1931 not a day passed without gunfire in the areas where Japanese forces operated."[1]

This study stresses the fact that the United States was allied with fifteen Western and East and Southeast Asian nations and territories that were attacked by Japan. They were all part of the United Nations, which was initially formed in 1942 to defeat and demilitarize the Axis. President Roosevelt explained this common cause in a 1942 speech:

> The United Nations constitutes an association of independent peoples of equal dignity and equal importance. The United Nations are dedicated to a common cause. We share equally and with equal zeal the anguish and awful sacrifice of war. In the partnership of

Figure 1

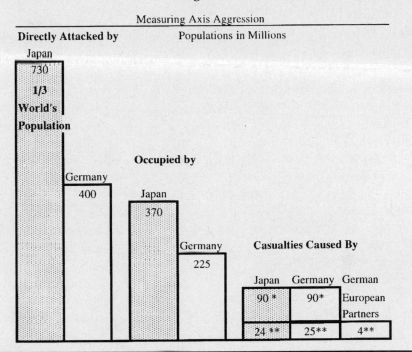

Measuring Axis Aggression

* Casualties/severely affected include: wounded and maimed, rape victims, refugees, forced labor, war orphans, tortured, opium addicts, depressed health, diseased.
** Deaths from atrocities, fighting, war: famine, starvation, and disease. (App.1&2)

World War II Cost in Lives

Allied	In Millions	
Soviet Union and Poland	25	40%
China, East & S.E. Asia	24	38%
Balance of European Allies	3	5%
U.K., Commonwealth 1/ & U.S.	1	2%
Allied Total	53	
Axis		
Germany	5	8%
German Partners in Europe 2/	2	3%
Japan	3	5%
Axis Total	10	
Grand Total	63	100%

1/Less India, Burma & Malaya, counted with East Asians. (App. 2)
2/ Italy, Hungary, Bulgaria, Romanian, Austria (as part of Germany) Finland.

our common enterprise, we must share a unified plan in which all of us must play our several parts, each of us being equally indispensable and dependent one on the other.[2]

Any objective recounting and analysis of the World War II must include *all* nations and territories affected from beginning to end, from 1931 to 1945.

As it is, the Asian nations do not receive nearly the same coverage by academia, World War II histories, popular literature, and the media as do the European nations. Germany's genocide is well remembered; Japan's nearly equal atrocities are hardly mentioned. Even the tough battles fought by the United States forces in the Pacific, the extreme suffering of Allied POWs, and civilian internees play second fiddle to their counterparts in Europe. Over the fifty years of remembrance of VJ-Day there was significantly more coverage on how the war affected the Japanese than how it affected their victims. A careful review of media coverage over that time frame will show this imbalance.

A typical example of the state of public knowledge is displayed in an article in the *Baltimore Sun* from September 1, 2000 entitled "War to Preserve Civilized World Won 55 Years Ago." It listed the World War II dead of the Soviet Union, Poland, Germany, Japan, and the United States. It remarked on the death camps in Europe, and the atomic bombs dropped on Japan. Not a word was offered in memory of other Asians who perished in numbers approximating the extraordinary loss of life in Poland and the Soviet Union combined, and eight times the loss of Japanese lives.

Robert Newman, one of the few historians to bring up this inequality in remembrance, gave this view: "Had John Hersey visited Nanking or Manila and written about these catastrophes; had there been no competing and overshadowing spectacle in Japan fueled by supernatural science; had Hiroshima not become a shrine to the peace-minded, the anguish of Japan's victims might be more on our conscience."[3] Richard Frank adds: "Any accounting of the charnel house must begin with China—the original cause that drew America into the war."[4] The data demonstrate the growing casualty rate as the war progressed. The huge casualty numbers clearly indicate that there was an urgent need to end the Second World War as soon as possible *and under lasting terms.*[5]

The atomic destruction of Hiroshima and Nagasaki has rightly been held up as a reminder of the unthinkable consequences of nuclear war. This emphasis on the atomic bomb casualties, the fact China is now communist, and a Euro-centered focus on World War II, allows apologists to portray Japan as the victim of the war and overlook her responsibility for what happened from Manchuria in 1931 to Hiroshima in 1945. The influence of apologists, and the insufficient historiography about the Asian part of the war, permits a growing body of academic work to imply that the United States and Japan were essentially equally culpable in the Asia Pacific war.

Japan, under the control of its military, became an aggressor nation when it attacked fifteen nations and territories, starting with the 1931 invasion of northeast China, known as Manchuria. Soon Japan pressed into other provinces, and then began a full-scale attack into China proper in 1937. Many historians consider either 1931 or 1937 to be the beginning of World War II. From 1931 to 1941, the first ten years of the war, the Japanese army drove through Mukden, Peking, Tientsin, Shanghai, Soochow, Nanking, Hankow, Swatow, Amoy, Canton, Nanchang, and other cities. This included thousands of villages and hamlets. The Chinese military and civilian casualties in these battles and in their aftermath often exceeded the worst casualty levels in the horrendous World War I battles or Germany's World War II assault on the Soviet Union.

Japan's invasion of Manchuria and China proper caused the League of Nations and the United States (not a League member) to condemn Japan. The League and primarily the United States were in an escalating cold war with Japan over her invasion of China. In July 1941, Japan saw new opportunities because of Germany's successful invasion of Eastern Europe in 1939-41, and thus occupied Indochina with large forces. This move directly threatened Western colonial possessions in Southeast Asia, as well as Australia and New Zealand. That led to the freezing of Japanese assets and embargo on exports of critical war materials, including oil, on which Japan was highly dependent. Americans were growing incensed at the sale of scrap iron and other raw materials of war to the Japanese for use in their invasion of China and the killing of civilians.

Tensions were further intensified when the United States insisted that Tokyo remove its forces from Indochina and China. When Japan would not accede, the United States and the West continued their embargo. With only a limited supply of raw materials to feed its war machine, Japan attacked Pearl Harbor on December 7, 1941, without warning, and then invaded Malaya, Thailand, Burma, South-

Figure 2

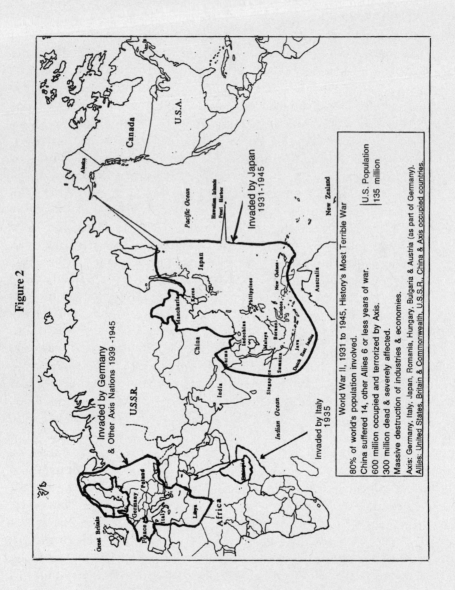

World War II, 1931 to 1945, History's Most Terrible War

80% of world's population involved.
China suffered 14, other Allies 6 or less years of war.
600 million occupied and terrorized by Axis.
300 million dead & severely affected.
Massive destruction of industries & economies.

Axis: Germany, Italy, Japan, Romania, Hungary, Bulgaria & Austria (as part of Germany).
Allies: United States, Britain & Commonwealth, U.S.S.R., China & Axis occupied countries.

U.S. Population
135 million

Invaded by Germany
& Other Axis Nations 1939 -1945

Invaded by Japan
1931-1945

Invaded by Italy
1935

east Asia, and the islands in the Pacific. (See Figure 2) Japan thus forced the United States, Britain, her commonwealth, and the Dutch into the Asia Pacific war. This action provided alternative sources of oil and other raw materials, and allowed Japan to have a defensive perimeter around itself and its newly expanded empire.

By the time Japan attacked Pearl Harbor in December 1941, it held about a third of China, including the major cities, rivers, roads, and railroad arteries. This eliminated 95 percent of the Chinese army's source of domestic industrial production. The Chinese fighting for their survival were cut off from most foreign assistance and virtually isolated in central China, the poorest and least economically viable part of the country. By the end of 1941 China had suffered greatly. *Approximately 45 million Chinese died or were severely affected by the invasion. The toll included roughly 7 million deaths caused by all war related causes.* The mostly civilian dead numbered more than twice the lives lost by Japan in the entire fourteen years of its World War II military pursuits. Further, the Chinese deaths already exceeded forty times the Japanese lives later lost at Hiroshima and Nagasaki. *The count was to double by the end of the war.*

A good case can be made that China, who fought stoically from 1931 to 1945, suffering great losses and disadvantaged by internal problems, nonetheless did contribute noticeably to Imperial Japan's defeat, a shorter war, and fewer American and other Allied casualties.

From the beginning of 1931, Japan's army fought the war with often implacable cruelty and erased the distinction between civilians and military populations during the conflict and the occupation. Starting with Chinchow in late 1931 and Shanghai in 1932, and again in 1937, Japan was the first nation in World War II to employ large-scale bombing of cities, villages, and hamlets in which there was little or no war industry. Merciless ground attacks plus bombing and strafing were used to strike terror in the civilian populations. The International Military Tribunal Far East (IMTFE) records describe an unrestrained punitive war fought against China under the guise of an "incident," i.e., the Manchurian Incident, the Marco Polo Bridge Incident, or more generally, the China Incident, which exempted the Japanese from the accepted rules of war.[6] These military leaders intended to make the war so brutal and savage in all its consequences as to break the will of the Chinese people to resist. In this spirit, the practice of massacring, or "punishing" as the Japanese termed it, the inhabitants of cities and towns in retaliation for actual or supposed aid rendered to Chinese troops was applied. This practice continued throughout the China War.

The list of Japanese atrocities is a long one. Massacres of civilians and surrendering soldiers alike took place across the great Asian-Pacific crescent of pain.[7] Examples of massive war crimes and crimes against humanity include the savage Shanghai/Yangtze Delta Campaign, the Rape of Nanking, "kill all, burn all, loot all," the retribution campaign for the Doolittle bombing of Tokyo, the sacking of Manila, the building of the Thailand-Burma Death Railway, Unit 731 biological agents research with vivisection, and biological weapons use against civilian populations. The slaughter of other Asian innocents, such as at Batangas Province and Lipa Philippines, was not unusual. The infamous Bataan death march was only one example of the high death rate from maltreatment and murder of Allied POWs and internees.

The experience of Cheng Biequan in Changzhou, outside Shanghai, is illustrative of what the war meant to the invaded populations:

> After the coldest days of winter...there were fewer incidents of mass murder and violence, and Cheng's aunt began to worry that bodies of her family members would rot in the open, so the four relatives set out together once again... Several dozen bodies remained unclaimed, some buried in the mud, but most scattered above ground, and the powerful stench of decay was enough to make a person pass out. Unable to bear the stench, Cheng and his party drank some cheap liquor and set about the task half-drunk.[8]

Another example is a report by Philippines Deputy Governor Cesario Golez concerning the murder of 4,300 civilians in northern Iloilo in 1943-44:

> and listed fourteen methods of execution including ripping open the abdomens of pregnant women and killing the babies inside, hanging their victims' heads down...and then cutting them into pieces following the spinal cord, and cutting the male organs and inserting into female organs. The resistance mayor of Alimodian...of the Panay range, counted: 45 deaths between 8 July 1943 and 31 January 1944 of whom only five were shot and the rest were burned, bayoneted or beheaded. The report shows 20 civilians were beheaded in the same small village, Sitio Taban.[9]

From 1931 to 1945, throughout the vast and heavily populated region of Asia, the scale of the tragedy was horrendous. Approximately *20 million* innocent civilians lost their lives to Japanese aggression out of a total of 24 million Allied Asian deaths. They died from murder, forced labor, fighting, exhaustion, malnutrition, disease, and starvation. This was more than all military and civilian lives lost on all sides in the First World War. Civilians and POWs who were caught in the fighting and died from brutality and murder numbered approximated 5 million. Deaths from forced/slave labor maltreatment added approximately 2.0 million, equivalent to about thirty-five Rapes of Nanking throughout the Asia Pacific region. Together these mostly atrocity victims equaled about 7 million.

The war also left tens of millions physically and emotionally scarred from war-related injuries. Large numbers of women, easily in the millions, were raped and others were forced into prostitution as "comfort women." The massive displacement of populations caused unimaginable suffering. Forced/slave labor was employed on a massive scale and brutality and neglect were rampant. The IMTFE records describe forced labor conditions:

> They were all...to be used to the limit of their endurance. The lot of these conscript laborers was made worse by the fact that generally they were ignorant of the principles of hygiene application to their unusual and crowded conditions and succumbed more readily to the diseases resulting from the unsanitary conditions of confinement and work forced upon them by their Japanese captors.[10]

Orphans were the greatest tragedy of the war. There were thousands of them in every bombed city, on the roads, from girls who had to turn to prostitution, to the crippled, the blind, and the insane.[11]

The Japanese often treated prisoners of war and civilian internees with calculated brutality. Ex-American POW Lester Tenney gave this account:

> My God, what was next? I wondered how I would stand up to this type of punishment for a prolonged period. If we had known earlier just how we would be treated and for how long, I think we would have fought on Bataan to the last man, taking as many of the enemy with us as possible, rather than endure the torture, hunger, beatings, and inhuman atrocities we were to undergo during the next three and a half years.[12]

The invasion also brought wide-scale destruction of the economies and infrastructure of many nations and territories, affecting the livelihood of hundreds of millions during and well after the war. William Kirby noted: "No one knows precisely the amount of the losses suffered by the Chinese economy as a result of the war of 1937-45, but there is little doubt that they were staggering."[13] This could be said for the entire Asian-Pacific crescent of pain.

Edgar Snow was a witness to the aftermath of the Imperial Army attack through Shanghai:

> Sometimes I wandered appalled through the enormous devastation of Shanghai, mile after mile of it, with only an occasional chimney or telephone pole left standing. Derelict

wires dangled crazily over the wreckage. Corpses sprouted from the piles of rubble; everything was as still as the death that was rotting in the winter sun. Formerly I knew Chapei and Hongkew fairly well, but familiar landmarks were now completely obliterated. Moving through this ghastly world, burnt-out hell, you could easily become lost.[14]

Militarist Japan was in fact an aggressor, defined as one who makes an unprovoked attack on another with the intent to dominate. The Japanese violated the post-World War I League of Nations covenants and peace treaties against war, to which they were a party during the preceding decade. Peaceful alternatives were clearly available to resolve her domestic and perceived international issues. They also violated the Geneva and the Hague Conventions on the treatment of prisoners and civilians. By its behavior on the battlefield, the Imperial Army created the no-quarter-given fighting that characterized the war in that part of the world.

The Japanese argue that the economic action taken against Japan in 1940 and 1941 by America, Britain, China, and the Dutch (the ABCD countries) forced it to attack Pearl Harbor and the rest of Asia and the Pacific. These "iron chains," as the Japanese described them, were in fact those forged by Japanese aggression. If Japan had not invaded China and then Indochina and threatened the ABD countries and their possessions in the region, there would have been no economic constraints aimed at her war-making ability.

Japan's conquests have been compared to Western imperialism of the nineteenth century. But, by the 1930s this imperialism was on the wane and Japan's leaders knew it. Western imperialism could be harsh and brutal on colonial populations. But these practices could not compare with the scale of force used and the harm done by Japan's World War II imperial expansion.

The propensity of the Japanese military to carry out this conflict with a kind of fanatical zeal, cruelty, and atrocities that violated the accepted rules of war in the West and far exceeded that which could be considered an inescapable part of war, had many reasons. These included the breakdown of discipline, Japanese social structure, attitude of national superiority, educational, military, and ideological indoctrination, and the brutal nature of Japanese military training of the time. Of course, not all succumbed to these influences. A Japanese veteran wrote to the newspaper *Asahi Shimbun* in the mid 1980s:

There were some military men who valued human life above all, despite the foolish deeds of battle. Yet all the officers went through the same officers' training. I wonder how many parted ways in ideology, some to become crazed warmongers, others to respect human life.[15]

On the eve of the use of the atomic bomb in August of 1945, thirty years after the start of the First World War, the Second World War was still being fought and suffered throughout most of Asia and in some parts of the Pacific. Civilians continued to experience the worst of it. Over a quarter billion people were still under harsh Japanese military subjugation.

At the same time, Allied fighting men were still being killed and maimed, even though major fighting had tapered down by mid-1945. However, in September new major campaigns were planned by all the Allies throughout China and Southeast Asia, and the American invasion of Japan itself. Western Allied POWs and civilian prisoners, totaling some 260,000, continued to die from maltreatment, neglect, and disease at increasing rates. By 1945 the Japanese themselves were increasingly becoming victims of their own earlier ambitions and their unwillingness to accept surrender and the end of their militarist state. The rate of loss of life and debilitation were rapidly increasing throughout the war-ravaged region.

From late 1944 into 1945, nearly five million citizens of Allied Asian nations and territories, mostly civilians, perished, not only because of the barbarity and fighting, but also from war-caused widespread famines, malnutrition, exhaustion, and disease. Wartime shortages of medicines like quinine contributed to the death rate. When the loss of Japanese life is included, the toll in the last year of the war *approximated six million lives.*

In August of 1945, the Japanese Supreme War Council, dominated by the military, was not willing to surrender even though the July Allied Potsdam Declaration had implied that the emperor could be retained after surrender. The Japanese military and civilians were prepared to fight to the death in defense of the territories they still occupied and their home islands. The military leadership was counting on these amassed forces, all in essentially a suicidal role, to inflict heavy enough casualties on American troops to force a settlement that would leave Japan's military institutions intact. Only after the second atomic bomb made it clear no such final cataclysmic land battle could be fought did the military accept surrender. After almost thirty years of continuous and ever more bloody war, and the inconclusive end of the First World War, the Allies were determined to ensure Japan was demilitarized to her roots, just as they had with Germany's earlier surrender, through the demand for unconditional surrender.

When the United States acted to terminate the war as soon as possible, she acted also on behalf of her Western and Asian Allies (one-third of the world's population), that is, all those caught in the path of the war. The abrupt end must embrace all their lives saved, all the suffering ended, and everyone's need for a lasting peaceful Japan.

The first atomic bomb was dropped on Hiroshima on August 6 and the second on Nagasaki on August 9, 1945. Both cities were contributing to the Japanese war effort. By the end of 1945, about 150,000, including Japanese military and Korean forced laborers, lost their lives in the two cities. This was a tragedy for the populations of the cities just as each added day and week of war was to the populations throughout Asia and the Pacific. *Every week of non-atomic war at the time added roughly 140,000 more deaths.* (See Figure 3) This weekly total represented the ongoing cost to Allied and Japanese combined, but mostly Allied civilians. *And the rate was increasing.*

There is every indication that the bomb significantly shortened the war. There was no firm evidence then, nor is there now, that the war would otherwise have been over quickly. The bulk of the evidence indicates that the war could easily have lasted at least until October or December 1945. Counting only American lives spared gives a totally inaccurate picture of what the atomic bomb accomplished. My detailed projection, assuming this time frame, *shows that throughout Asia and the Pacific from one to three million would have died had the bomb not been used. Millions more would have carried physical and psychological wounds into the postwar years, many for the rest of their lives.*[16]

The United States' decision to use the atomic bomb responded to what was at stake at the time. *The war Japan started and refused to end on terms that would assure the world that it would not threaten its neighbors again led to the use of the atomic bomb.* The price exacted from Japan to bring her war to an end from all American bombing, including the atomic bombs, came to approximately 400,000 Japanese civilian deaths. *All* Japanese civilian deaths from *all* causes during the fourteen year war equaled about 4 percent of all Allied, including Asian, civilian deaths.

There is a tendency among apologists for Japan to point to Nazi Germany's genocide in order to gloss over Japan's culpability for atrocities committed. While there were differences between Japan and Germany in their policies, and how the wars unfolded, Japan, it

Figure 3

"The Whole goddamn War was a Horrible Thing"*

Deaths per Year and Week Average

	Mukden	Marco Polo Bridge				Pearl Harbor				Hiroshima	Projected
	1931-33	1937 (Six months)	1938	1939	1940	1941	1942	1943	1944	1945 August	1945 to End Oct,

Projected 1945 to End Oct: **187,000**, *2 million Spared (App. 17)*

Hiroshima 1945 August: **148,853**, *6.6 million*

1944: **97,116**

1943: **87,967** *5.1 million*, *4.6 million*

1942: **57,398**, *3 million*, *Total Allied 24 million*, *Total Japanese 3 million*, *Total 27 million*

Per week **   39,440   31,679   31,679   31,679   31,679

Per year ***   1.0 milli 1.6 million   1.6 millio 1.6 millio 1.6 million

990
84,000   About half of all U.S. military deaths in the A-P Theater took place from August 1944-1945

China	800	38,461	30,700	30,700	30,700	30,700					
Allied (Including Chinese)							52,961	82,199	81,447	103,265	91,000
Japanese	190	979	979	979	979	979	4,437	5,768	15,669	45,588	96,000
Total	990	39,440	31,679	31,679	31,679	31,679	57,398	87,967	97,116	148,853	187,000

* George Elsey, an aide to President Truman, made this comment on the decision to use the atomic bomb (McCullough '92, 442): "It is all well and good to come along later and say the bomb was a horrible thing, the whole goddamn war was a horrible thing."

** Weekly average death rate for Allies and Japanese with uncertainty range of +30% to -30%. App. 11.

*** Annual average death rate for Allies and Japanese with uncertainty range of +30% to -30%. App. 11.

Hiroshima and Nagasaki in Perspective

1945	War Deaths Projection Cumulative*	Atomic Bomb Deaths	Ratio Spared
Aug. 15-31	350,000	150,000	2
September	1,100,000	150,000	7
October	2,000,000	150,000	13
November	2,800,000	150,000	19
December	3,600,000	150,000	24

*Shows approximate Allied & Japanese lives saved each month the A-bomb may have shortened the war.

(App. 17)

Figure 4

World War II Deaths*

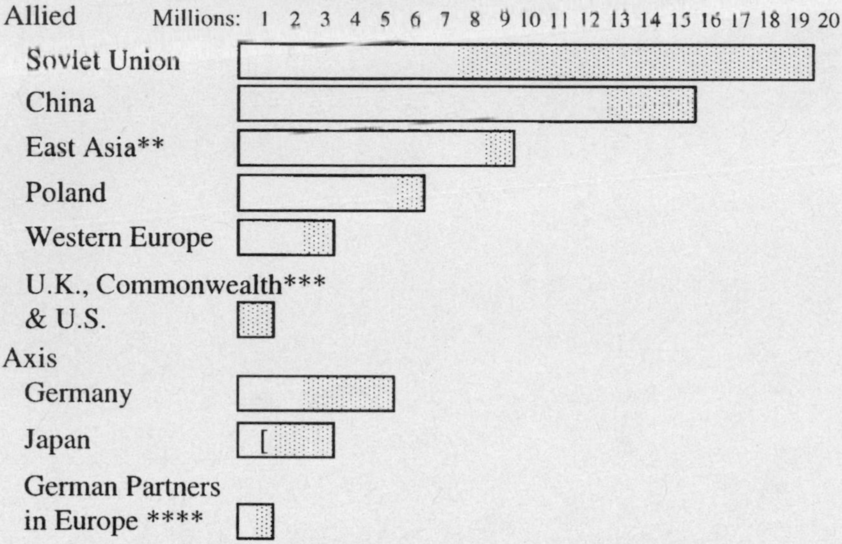

Allied   Millions: 1 2 3 4 5 6 7 8 9 10 11 12 13 14 15 16 17 18 19 20

Soviet Union

China

East Asia**

Poland

Western Europe

U.K., Commonwealth***
& U.S.

Axis

Germany

Japan

German Partners
in Europe ****

Total all WWII deaths: 63 million (39 m civilian. 24 m military) (App. 2)

Key: ☐ Civilian deaths [Hiroshima and Nagasaki deaths ▦Military deaths

* Includes death from all war related causes: combat, war crimes to starvation and disease.
** Indochina, Burma, Malaya, Philippines, Dutch East Indies (Indonesia), New Guinea, India, and Hong Kong, Singapore and Pacific Islands.
*** Less India, Burma and Malaya, which are counted with East Asia dead.
**** Italy, Romania, Hungary, Austria (as part of Germany), Bulgaria, and Finland.

Allied Deaths from Barbarity*

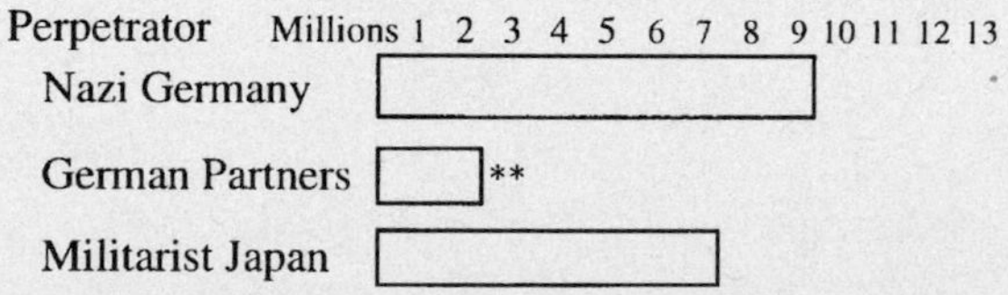

Perpetrator   Millions 1 2 3 4 5 6 7 8 9 10 11 12 13

Nazi Germany

German Partners   **

Militarist Japan

*Civilian & POW deaths from genocide, barbarity, forced labor, and caught in combat.
** Italy, Romania, Hungary, Austria (as part of Germany), Bulgaria, and Finland.

(App. 2)

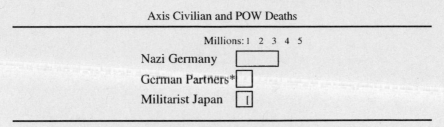

Axis Civilian and POW Deaths

Millions: 1 2 3 4 5

Nazi Germany

German Partners*

Militarist Japan

---

* Italy, Romania, Hungary, Austria (as part of Germany), Bulgaria, and Finland.

(App. 2)

can be argued, was no less guilty than Germany for the war and war crimes. A case can be made that Japan started World War II because the Western democracies were not able to take strong enough steps to stop her in the early 1930s, thus encouraging Germany and Italy to similar aggression in Africa and Europe. In fact, Japan attacked and conquered a far larger population than Germany and caused close to an equal amount of grief, including barbarism.

Asians suffered over 35 percent of all global World War II casualties. In comparison, the cost to Japan was 5 percent. China and other Asian nations experienced the costliest battles resulting in 99 percent of the Allied deaths (one percent were U.S. and Western Allies) in the Asia Pacific theatre, and most of the destruction of infrastructure and economies. (See Figure 4)

Compared to Germany, Japan has been reluctant to face up to its culpability for the war and make necessary amends. An article in the *New York Times* observed: "But while fringe figures who deny the Holocaust exist in Germany and elsewhere, voices here dismissing or greatly playing down Japan's wartime crimes are regularly heard from in the political, academic and media establishment. The governor of Tokyo, Shintaro Ishihara, for one, has frequently called the Nanjing Massacre a lie."[17] Other Japanese have called it a "minor" incident of war.

Western combat veterans, POWs, and civilian internees deserve remembrance and appreciation. Their sacrifice and pain made it possible to win the war, and preserved and extended the freedom that so many take for granted today.

Throughout Asia, those who experienced the horrors of the war deserve the same remembrance and recognition as the other populations who are more prominently featured in contemporary World War II histories and memorials. A detailed analysis of the totality of World War II and the experience of World War I vindicate the United States and its Allies' policies toward militarist Japan from 1931 to 1945.

Notes

1. Peter Duus, ed., *The Cambridge History of Japan: Volume 6, The Twentieth Century* (Cambridge: Cambridge University Press, 1988), p. 302.
2. Russell D. Buhite and David W. Levy, eds,, *FDR's Fireside Chats* (Norman: Univ, of Oklahoma Press, 1992), p. 216,
3. Robert P. Newman, *Truman and the Hiroshima Cult* (East Lansing: Michigan State University Press, 1995), p. 137.
4. Richard B. Frank, *Downfall: The End of the Imperial Japanese Empire* (New York: Random House, 1999).
5. Few countries in the world wars were able to make very precise counts of casualties, particularly those nations and territories in Asia. The numbers shown throughout this work, for the most part, are rough estimates gathered from as many sources as could be found, coupled with the author's organization, analyses, and calculations to provide an approximation of the scale of pain inflicted on the populations in the war zone. Appendix A, "War Statistics," of my forthcoming book explains the nature of the data and provides twenty-three pages of statistics and their sources.
6. B. V. Roling and C. F. Ruter, eds., *The Tokyo Judgment: The International Military Tribunal for the Far East (IMTF)* (Amsterdam: APA-University Press Amsterdam BV, 1977), pp. 386, 388.
7. By mid-1942 Imperial Japan had subjugated Korea, Manchuria, parts of China Proper, Indochina, Singapore, Hong Kong, Burma, the Philippines, the Netherlands East Indies, and many Pacific islands.
8. Katsuichi Honda, *The Nanjing Massacre* (Armonk, New York: M.E. Sharpe, 1999), p. 89.
9. Alfred McCoy, ed., *South East Asia under Japanese Occupation* (New Haven: Yale University South East Asia Studies Monograph Series Number 22, 1985), p. 178.
10. Roling & Ruter, eds., *The Tokyo Judgment*, pp. 416-7.
11. Alvin J. Austin, *Saving China: Canadian Missionaries in the Middle Kingdom 1883-1959* (Toronto: University of Toronto Press, 1986), p. 258.
12. Lester I. Tenney, *My Hitch in Hell: The Bataan Death March* (Washington D.C.: Brassey's Inc., 1995), p. 43.
13. James C. Hsiung and Steven I. Levine, eds., *China's Bitter Victory: The War with Japan 1937-1945* (New York: An East Gate Book, M.E. Sharpe Inc., 1992), p. 185.
14. Edgar Snow, *The Battle for Asia* (Cleveland: The World Publishing Company, 1942), p. 84.
15. Frank Gibney, ed., *SENSO: The Japanese Remember the Pacific War* (New York: An East Gate Book, M.E. Sharpe, 1995), p. 164.
16. Appendix A, "War Statistics," explains the range of uncertainty of all estimates in the book. In this case they are about plus or minus 30 percent. So even if we compare the high end of the range for atomic deaths of 200,000 with the low end of the range of the weekly death rate of 100,000, the lives spared would still exceed the bomb deaths after two weeks of war. Lives-saved estimates would still have ranged from 700,000 to 2,000,000. The low end of the range of dying and severely affected who were spared would still be dramatic. Japan was also unquestionably demilitarized for the sake of future generations.
17. "Japanese Call '37 Massacre a War Myth, Stirring Storm," *New York Times*, January 23, 2000.

15

Women's International War Crimes Tribunal on Japan's Military Sexual Slavery: Memory, Identity, and Society

Yayori Matsui

Aims of the Tribunal

The twentieth century, which has just come to a close, was a century of war and violence. The Second World War brought to humankind destruction and genocide on an unprecedented scale in which vast numbers of women were made victims of sexual violence. Now we are all witnesses to wars between nations and internal armed conflicts that are breaking out one after another throughout the world. Japan's military sexual slavery (the "comfort women" system) before and during the Second World War was one of the most horrendous forms of wartime sexual violence against women known in this century.

In 1998, a group of Japanese women who felt responsible for the crimes their own country committed against women, and who believed that a twenty-first century free of violence against women cannot be realized without a response to the cries of the comfort women for justice and dignity, proposed that a Women's International War Crimes Tribunal on Japan's Military Sexual Slavery be held. In the last month of the twentieth century, from December 8-12, 2000, this Tribunal was held in Tokyo.

The Women's International War Crimes Tribunal is a people's tribunal with two main objectives. Firstly, it aims to confirm that the comfort women system is a war crime against women and a crime against humanity, and to put pressure on the Japanese government to take legal responsibility. This is necessary because the crime of military sexual slavery has never been prosecuted, not by the International Military Tribunal for the Far East (the Tokyo War Crimes Trial), nor by the Japanese government itself. Thus, the Tokyo Women's Tribunal is considered to be an addendum, or a continuation, of the Tokyo Trial.

Secondly, the Tribunal's aim is to end the cycle of impunity of wartime sexual violence against women and to prevent it from happening again in any part of the world. Rape and other wartime sexual violence have gone unpunished for far too long and in far too many places. This is a universal women's human rights issue to be addressed by global women's and people's solidarity.

Structure and Composition of the Tribunal

It was VAWW-NET Japan (Violence Against Women in War Network, Japan) that first proposed the Tribunal at the Asian Women's Solidarity Conference in April 1998. This proposal was accepted by supporting organizations of six victimized countries: North and South Korea, China, Taiwan, the Philippines, and Indonesia. Additional support was offered by female human rights activists and academics in other part of the world who are committed to issues concerning armed conflicts. Women of all three of these categories joined to form the International Organizing Committee and shared the enormous collective task of preparing for the Tribunal. Their first job was to prepare a charter that would stipulate jurisdiction on individual criminal responsibility and state responsibility for military sexual slavery and rape as war crimes and crimes against humanity.

Then, each participating country formed a prosecutors team made up of lawyers, historians, and researchers to draft a country indictment. Two chief prosecutors, Ms. Patricia Viseur-Sellers, legal advisor for gender-related crimes for the International Criminal Tribunal for the Former Yugoslavia and Rwanda (USA) and Ms. Ustina Dolgopol, senior lecturer in international law (Australia), wrote the common indictment based on the country indictments.

Four legal experts on international law and human rights were appointed as judges: Ms. Gabrielle Kirk McDonald, former president of the International Criminal Tribunal for the Former Yugoslavia (USA), Ms. Christine Chinkin, professor of international law, University of London (UK), Carmen Mari Argibay, president of the Internationtal Women's Association of Judges (Argentina), and Mr.

Willy Mutunga, president of the Commission on Human Rights and professor of the University of Kenya.

Survivors' Voices

Responding to the Survivors

The Tribunal was attended by more than one thousand people each day. Some 600 Japanese and 500 overseas participants included sixty-four survivors of military sexual slavery and mass rape from eight different countries, the largest number of survivors ever to meet together for the first time. Most are now advanced in age: one was ninety years old. For the first time, two survivors from East Timor came forward and testified publicly. The opening ceremony, held on December 7, was dedicated to those victims who had passed away, and all participating survivors offered them flowers on the stage.

It was in the early 1990s that Kim Hak Soon, a Korean comfort woman, broke her silence for the first time in nearly half a century. Survivors from other Asian countries and from the Netherlands soon followed her example.

Many women from Japan, the perpetrating country, were deeply moved by their courage, and support groups began to spring up all over the country. The historical role played by these victimized women who spoke up about their painful experience as sex slaves for the Japanese military cannot be overemphasized, for in exposing the horror of wartime sexual violence, they encouraged women all over the world who are currently suffering from sexual violence in armed conflicts, including those from the former Yugoslavia, Rwanda, Bangladesh, and other countries, to come forward. Thus the issue of violence against women in war and armed conflicts has surfaced as an agenda of the global women's movement and of the international human rights movement.

Almost ten years have passed since Ms. Kim first told her story, and now, in each country, survivors of advanced age are dying one after another. In May 2000, VAWW-NET Japan members visited North Korea, only to learn that twenty-one of the forty-three survivors who had agreed to testify publicly had already passed away; the total number of registered survivors in North Korea was 218.

In South Korea, of the nearly 190 survivors who have come forward, more than fifty, including Kim Hak-Soon, have already passed away. In the Philippines as well, many have died, including Maria Rosa Henson, the first survivor to speak out. She was an anti-Japanese guerrilla girl when she was taken by the Japanese military as a sex slave. Hou Chau Lien, a Chinese survivor who was taken to a cave to be gang-raped every day by Japanese soldiers at the age of fourteen, came in a wheelchair to testify at the Tokyo district court in 1998. She died in a remote village in the northwestern part of mainland China the following year.

All these women not only suffered as sex slaves during the war, but have also been forced to endure the hardships of poverty and isolation all their postwar lives. Their lives are now ending without official apology or compensation from the Japanese government, without seeing justice restored. In contrast to their cruel lives, former Japanese soldiers are enjoying their retirement without pain or repentance, and without being punished.

Kang Duk Kyung, an active leader of the Korean comfort women, passed away in 1997, leaving a powerful painting entitled "Punish the Perpetrators!" which expresses the strong aspiration for justice shared by many aged survivors. This painting helped motivate Japanese women to propose a people's tribunal, following the example of the Russell Tribunal on war crimes committed in the Vietnam War by the U.S. and allied countries in the 1960s. VAWW-NET Japan members knew they could hardly expect Japanese courts to prosecute the perpetrators. Not even the International Criminal Court, if the more than sixty countries required ratified the statute to establish it, would have any jurisdiction over crimes committed in the past.

The Power of Survivors' Testimonies

During the three days of the trial (December 8-10, 2001), more than twenty survivors from nine countries, including a Malaysian comfort woman who told her story on videotape, gave testimony about their horrifying experiences as sex slaves. Here are some excerpts:

> I was only twelve years old when I was taken to a comfort station. A Japanese soldier wanted to rape me but my vagina was too small; he cut my private part; it was so painful. I fainted (a North Korean survivor).
>
> I was taken to Manchuria (northeastern part of China); when I resisted, the soldier put a hot iron on my body; the scar is still here. I don't want to die as the ghost of a virgin (a south Korean survivor).
>
> I was an anti-Japanese guerrilla girl and, at the age of fourteen, I was forcibly taken to the enemy garrison and raped many times. Once I tried to escape, I was beaten by a baton, tied to a tree and hung; I was also thrown into a frozen river (a Chinese survivor).

> I'm an aborigine woman of Taiwan. I was raped by many soldiers in a dark cave. I had to get an abortion. I went back to my village and got married without knowing I was pregnant again. My husband beat me violently and divorced me three times (a survivor from Taiwan).
>
> I was thirteen when Japanese soldiers came into my house and took me. My father tried to protect me but was beheaded in front of me. I was raped by three or four men every night (a Filipino survivor).
>
> I cried and cried. The soldier intimidated me "Do you want to live or die?" I obeyed in order to live. My life was like a prisoner in jail. Later I learned my father had been killed (an Indonesian survivor).
>
> The first night, I was raped by ten men and bled so much I couldn't walk. I was treated like an animal. I came to Japan not to see the country but to tell the truth (an East Timorese survivor).
>
> Even after I got married, I could never enjoy sex, because the memory of rape by Japanese soldiers has always haunted me. However, I feel I have to speak up, because I heard the same horrible thing was happening in Bosnia (a Dutch survivor).

Most witnesses told of their own painful experiences in tears; one fainted due to her extreme pain and anger.

All these testimonies illustrated the vast geographical scale, from the Siberian-Chinese border in the north to the Pacific islands in the south, as well as the brutality of sexual slavery and all kinds of sexual violence, including forced and deceptive recruitment, trafficking, deportation, confinement, enslavement, beating, intimidation, gang rape, mutilation, forced pregnancy and abortion, forced labor, unsafe environment, abandonment, and murder on an unprecedented scale.

Criminal Responsibility of the Emperor and State Responsibility

Former Japanese Soldiers' Testimonies and Amicas Curie

In addition to the testimonies of survivors, six expert witnesses gave academic testimony: four Japanese scholars explained the structure of the Japanese military forces, the emperor's responsibility, the comfort women system in general, and Japanese comfort women; Professor Fritz Karlshoven, from the Netherlands, spoke on state responsibility; and Ms. Lepa Mladjenovic, a Serbian feminist and director of the Autonomous Women's Center Against Sexual Violence in Belgrade, gave evidence on PTSD.

Two former members of the Japanese military who were stationed in China also gave testimony as perpetrators. They told of how they gang-raped women anywhere in China, how they used comfort stations, and how they transported Korean comfort women.

"I looked down on Chinese people and thought, what's wrong with raping Chinese women, since we kill them anyway. Comfort stations were pretty expensive for low ranking soldiers. Even if the women never saw the money, the fee took a big chunk out of our small salary. So soldiers would just rape women in the villages and cities instead." They apologized before the survivors and the audience. Their testimonies corroborated the day-to-day sexual violence committed by Japanese soldiers at the front.

Although the Tribunal served notice to the Japanese government, requesting it to defend its position, there was no response. A Japanese lawyer was therefore invited as *amicas curie* to present the standpoint of the defendant, the Japanese government. He gave several points in which the Tribunal was in violation of due process: first of all, it put the deceased on trial, indicting individual perpetrators by name; it criminally applied state responsibility and indicted Emperor Hirohito. He then mentioned the standpoint of the Japanese government concerning postwar reparation, explaining its reasons for dismissing the plaintiffs' claims: that statutory limitations have run out; that individuals do not have the right to sue the state; that peace treaties have already settled the reparation issue.

Thus, during the three days of the Tribunal various viewpoints were presented: survivors' testimonies, legal arguments by prosecutors, *amicas curie*, expert witnesses, and perpetrators" testimonies. Video and slides were effectively used to show live testimony, the background information of each country, various military documents, and even photos of scars on survivors' bodies. In addition, an enormous number of affidavits as well as other written evidence were submitted to the Tribunal.

Emperor Hirohito Found Guilty

On the fifth day of the Tribunal, four judges took more than two hours to read in turn the Summary of their Findings. This was a preliminary judgment; the final judgment would be rendered after March 8.

The Common Indictment, written by two chief prosecutors, prosecuted both individuals and the Japanese government itself for crimes against humanity. Among the ten individual defendants were government officials and wartime field commanders, and, most importantly, Emperor Hirohito, who was prosecuted by all country indictments.

The judges ruled "the Emperor Hirohito criminally responsible for crimes against humanity, because he was Supreme Commander of the Army and the Navy, with the responsibility and power to ensure that his subordinates obeyed international law and stopped engaging in sexual violence. He was not a mere puppet but rather exercised the ultimate decision-making authority as the war progressed." They further stated that, "[Hirohito], rather than taking all necessary steps to prevent rape, including providing meaningful sanction, investigation, and punishment, conducted a massive effort to perpetuate and conceal rape and sexual slavery through the continuing extension of the 'comfort women' system. Moreover, we find that he knew, or should have known, that a system on this scale was not voluntary."

Finally, Ms. McDonald, the presiding judge, stated in the conclusion that "the Tribunal finds the accused Emperor Hirohito guilty of responsibility for rape and sexual slavery as a crime against humanity, and the judges determine that the government of Japan has incurred state responsibility for its establishment and maintenance of the comfort system." At this moment the hall was filled with loud applause and cheers. In tears, survivors climbed onto the stage one after another to express their gratitude to the judges, who were also in tears. Chief prosecutors and country prosecutors in the center and on the left side of the stage also embraced and greeted each other with joy. On the floor, a standing ovation continued for several minutes. This dramatic historical scene demonstrated, above all, that the survivors felt satisfied to hear the judgment that identified those responsible for their suffering, and to see justice restored.

Making Up for the Failure of the Postwar Tokyo Trial

This was the first time the emperor had been convicted publicly. Actually, postwar Japan has been characterized by impunity of war criminals. When Japan surrendered to the Allies in 1945, it accepted the Potsdam Declaration, which demanded that all individual war criminals be severely punished. To that end, the Allied Powers, led by the U.S., established the Tokyo Trial.

Twenty-eight leaders of militarist Japan, both military and civilian, were prosecuted as Class A war criminals. Seven defendants, including Tojo Hideki, prime minister and militarist leader during the war, were sentenced to death and executed; sixteen were sentenced to life imprisonment.

The Tokyo Trial was severely criticized by the right wing as a revenge trial—victors' justice meted out by the Western Powers.

However, the majority of Japanese people found it fully acceptable that Japan's wartime leaders, who initiated a war of aggression and destroyed the lives of 3 million Japanese and 20 million Asian people, should be held responsible and punished.

The Tokyo Trial then began to be viewed critically by progressive scholars and lawyers as well, but for different reasons. They pointed out that the Tokyo Trial had three main defects: it gave the emperor impunity, it overlooked the devastating effects of colonialism, and it neglected the issue of sexual violence, such as military sexual slavery, although this third defect has only surfaced recently.

Why wasn't Emperor Hirohito prosecuted? After the war, public outcry to punish the emperor spread throughout the Allied countries; Australia and other Allied governments demanded that the Emperor be prosecuted. However, General MacArthur, commander of the U.S. Occupation Army, wanted to use Japan to confront the communist USSR. He therefore removed the emperor from the list of indicted war criminals, and sent a secret telegram to General Dwight Eisenhower, chief of staff of the U.S. Army, to the effect that there was no evidence showing the emperor's involvement in any political decisions concerning the war. He also said that if the emperor were prosecuted, mass rioting would occur on a scale that might require the mobilization of as many as one million U.S. troops. This, apparently, was MacArthur's political decision, based on inaccuracies, unfounded rumors, and the distortion of historical facts; as a result, U.S. national interests ended up denying justice for all people victimized by the war.

Breaking the Taboo against Prosecuting War Criminals

The impunity given to the emperor at the start of the postwar period has had a serious impact on postwar Japan. It has allowed both former military officials and politicians to excuse themselves by claiming that during war they were merely acting on the emperor's orders, and if he was not guilty, how could his subordinates be punished? Thus, the prosecution of war criminals in Japan has been a taboo until this day. In sharp contrast to Germany and other Western governments, who continue to prosecute war criminals even today, the Japanese government has not prosecuted one single war criminal since the Tokyo Trial. On the contrary, it has enshrined all its dead military men, including those executed as Class A war criminals, in Yasukuni Shrine, which is the former military state Shinto shrine. Despite severe criticism that they are violating the postwar Constitution, which strictly separates state and religion, government ministers continue to pay official visits to Yasukuni Shrine, where they offer tribute. In this situation, a right wing revisionist force, the so-called "liberal historical view" group, has recently started a vigorous campaign to accuse anyone willing to face Japan's past, and the issue of war responsibility, as someone with a "masochistic historical view," bent on disgracing his/her own country. They persistently condemn the Tokyo Trial as a mere revenge trial conducted by the Western colonial powers, the victors condemning the losers. These revisionists openly question, "What right do the Western powers have to accuse only Japan of war and colonial rule? They themselves caused much more damage and harm to non-Western peoples during a period of colonization that dates back to Columbus, so why have the Western imperial powers never been prosecuted?" Such nationalistic agitation by the growing right-wing force has had a substantial impact on the younger generation in Japan.

State Responsibility

In their Summary, the Tribunal judges also established state responsibility of the Japanese government, clearly stating that the Japanese government not only violated treaty obligations during the war, but has also failed to fulfill its obligation to prosecute the perpetrators and to pay reparation to victimized women after the war. Nearly ten years have passed since the issue of comfort women surfaced and became an international concern; although the demands of comfort women for apology, reparation, and prosecution have been endorsed by the international community, the Japanese government has failed to meet these demands. Even after officially acknowledging its moral responsibility in 1993, the government still continues to deny legal responsibility on the grounds that all war compensation issues were settled by the San Francisco Peace Treaty and bilateral agreements between Japan and victimized countries.

The movement to support comfort women in Japan has concentrated on the issues of apology and compensation. Eight lawsuits have been filed in Japanese courts by comfort women (three from Korea, including one Korean resident of Japan, two from China, one from the Philippines, one from Taiwan, and one from the Netherlands), demanding that the Japanese government pay state reparation. Judgments have been handed down in four of these cases. In all four decisions, the courts totally dismissed the plaintiffs' claims, mainly on three grounds: 1) During the war, international customary law did not recognize an individual victim's right to claim compensation from the State; 2) The cases were filed more than twenty years after the end of WWII, and statutory limitation had run out; 3) Until the end of WWII, under Japanese law, the State had no liability for compensation, according to the principle of no liability for the State.

Therefore, survivors have little hope of winning in Japanese courts and getting compensation from the Japanese government.

That's why Japanese lawyers and NGOs are promoting a "war compensation legislature campaign." However, there is little hope for the passage of such a bill in the Diet, because the majority of its members belong to conservative parties that oppose the very idea of war compensation. Furthermore, the campaign organized by the rising right-wing force is getting stronger, and is influencing public opinion in Japan.

However, the Japanese government realized it could no longer simply ignore public opinion, and the outcry of victimized women in Asian countries. In 1995, the fiftieth anniversary of the end of WWII, it therefore decided to establish the Asian Women's Fund as a means of fulfilling its moral responsibility. The Fund was to be raised from the private sector to give "atonement money" to each survivor.

The Fund has caused resentment among survivors, most of whom have rejected it, because they consider it a sort of "charity money" to "poor survivors," and a means of avoiding payment of State reparation. The Tribunal makes it clear that the State has a responsibility to provide reparation to cover all injuries suffered by the victims, and that the Asian Women's Fund does not satisfy the criteria. Thus, the Japanese government's obligation to provide reparation has been reaffirmed.

To End the Impunity of Wartime Sexual Violence

The Impunity of Wartime Sexual Violence as a Universal Issue

In that it is a crime against women only, military sexual slavery is different from other kinds of war crimes. It is gender-based, a sexual crime. The impunity given to sexual violence is a universal problem, not limited to Japan, because victims of sexual violence are forced to keep silent out of fear of disgrace and stigmatization. The silence of the victims makes it easy for the perpetrators to escape prosecution.

One of the serious defects of the Tokyo Trial was its failure to prosecute sexual violence, especially sexual slavery. However, only in recent years have female scholars of international law and history begun to question why the systematic wartime violence, such as sexual slavery, committed by the Japanese Imperial Army on such a large scale was not prosecuted at the Tokyo Trial, even though some individual cases of rape were charged as war crimes under the rubric of "inhuman treatment."

In 1997, when the International Conference on Violence Against Women in War and Situations of Armed Conflict was held in Tokyo, Ms. Dolgopol, who later served as one of chief prosecutors of the Tribunal, wrote in the paper she presented there: "The Tokyo Trials left another legacy of omission. Despite the extensive evidence held by the Allies of the manner in which Korean women were forcibly placed in military brothels, this aspect of enforced prostitution was not addressed during the Tokyo trial. There are quite a number of records of interrogation of Japanese war prisoners who answered questions about comfort stations."

The U.S. military knew about comfort stations, because it captured comfort women on various battlefields, including Burma and Okinawa. Park Yun-Shim, who came to the Tribunal, was pregnant when she was captured by the U.S. Army at the Burmese border, and the photograph which shows four Korean comfort women, including Park, being interrogated by the U.S. military is well known. However, in those days, American and other Allied military did not consider the comfort women system as a serious war crime violating international law.

Professor Yuki Tanaka, a Japanese scholar, mentions several reasons for this in his paper, "Why Did the US Military Neglect 'Comfort Women'?" One reason he gives is racism: most victimized women were Asians, not citizens of Western countries. The Dutch military tribunal in Indonesia was the only postwar military trial that prosecuted the Japanese military for sexual slavery, but it dealt only with the cases of Dutch women; no Indonesian women's cases were prosecuted. Another reason he mentions is the philosophy of militarism, which considers women to have a moral obligation to comfort military men.

The Summary of Findings of the Tribunal states: "Initial responsibility for this failure lies with the WW II Allies who did not prosecute Japanese officials for these crimes before the IMTFE (Tokyo Trial), despite the fact that they possessed evidence of the sexual slavery" and criticizes this failure as "unconscionable."

In addition to racism and militarism, the composition of military trials immediately after the war was gender biased: judges, prosecutors, and defense lawyers were almost all men. They had no gender awareness and didn't understand the seriousness of war crimes against women. Finally, international law itself didn't consider wartime rape and other sexual violence as violations of the human rights of women themselves. Such cases tended to be treated rather as an issue of the honor of the victim's family or community.

Contributions to the Progress of International Law

The Tribunal has made important contributions toward changing international law in various ways. International law has been criticized as being of Western origin, state-centered, and gender-blind; the Tribunal has responded positively to all of these negative aspects.

Firstly, the Tribunal has made it more gender sensitive. Through the application of a number of international conventions and treaties, it has established the criminal character of military sexual slavery. The Summary points out that "such gender blindness in international peace processes contributes to the continuing culture of impunity for crimes perpetrated against women in armed conflict," and that the Tribunal will "assist in changing the worldwide pattern of sexual stereotyping that continues to be pervasive today."

It should be pointed out that both Presiding Judge McDonald and Chief Prosecutor Viseur-Sellers are linked to the International War Crimes Tribunal for the former Yugoslavia which prosecuted sexual violence as a crime against humanity for the first time; their gender sensitivity played a vital role in the Tribunal. The results of the Tribunal will be fully utilized to punish not only sexual violence and crimes against women under armed conflict anywhere in the world, but also any kind of violence against women in day-to-day life.

Secondly, the Tribunal used international law to prosecute crimes committed against women of Asian countries under Western and Japanese colonial rule and military occupation. International law, which has hardly ever been applied to people of colonized and occupied countries, is now being used positively to prosecute the perpetrators at this Tribunal.

Thirdly, the Tribunal is not held under the state sovereignty, nor is it a mere mock trial. It is, rather, a people's tribunal based on the people's sovereignty. The judges define it as "a People's Tribunal set up by the voices of global society. The authority for this Tribunal comes not from a state or intergovernmental organization but from the peoples of the Asia Pacific region and, indeed, the peoples of the world to whom Japan owes a duty under international law to render account." They further state, "The power of the Tribunal, like so many human rights initiatives, lies in its capacity to examine the evidence and develop an enduring historical record."

It is vitally important to realize that a people's tribunal does not merely play a supplementary role in filling the gaps in the order of states. Rather, it can participate in the formation of a new order of states. Thus, the Tribunal showed that international law is not an order created and implemented only by states; the people can and do play an increasingly important role in forcing states to abide by international law.

The Vital Role of the Global Women's Movement to End Impunity

It should be noted that the history of the Tribunal actually begins with the global women's movement to highlight the issue of violence against women. Women launched a worldwide campaign with the slogan "Women's Rights are Human Rights," focusing on violence against women, working toward the UN World Human Rights Conference in Vienna in 1993. At the Vienna conference, both Asian comfort women and rape survivors from the former Yugoslavia met for the first time; both testified together to inform the whole world about the inexpressible atrocities of wartime sexual violence.

The global women's campaign succeeded in including a provision for women's human rights and violence against women in the Vienna Declaration and Plan of Action, making the Vienna Conference an epoch making event in the history of human rights. At the end of the same year, the Declaration on the elimination of all forms of violence against women was adopted by the UN General Assembly, requiring every government to take measures to support survivors and punish perpetrators of violence against women in three categories: in the family, in the community, and by the state.

Then, in 1995, the 4th UN World Women's Conference in Beijing adopted a Platform for Action which clearly states, in the section on Armed Conflict and Women, that systematic rape, sexual slavery, and other forms of violence against women in armed conflicts are war crimes and crimes against humanity, and that governments and the international community should take three measures to deal with such crimes: conducting investigations, prosecuting the perpetrators, and giving full redress to victims.

In 1994, the comfort women issue was highlighted by the international community when the International Commission of Jurists publicized the first comprehensive report on comfort women, in which it was recommended that the Japanese government pay reparation and prosecute the perpetrators.

In 1996, Ms. Radhika Coomaraswamy, the UN Special Rapporteur on Violence against Women also recommended that the Japanese government take legal responsibility for the comfort women system.

In 1998, Ms. Gay McDougall, Special Rapporteur on Systematic Rape and Sexual Slavery submitted her final report, in which she emphasized the importance of ending the cycle of impunity for wartime sexual violence. In an appendix to this report, McDougall analyzes the legal liability of the Japanese government for "rape centers," which is her term for "comfort stations," and makes recommendations for setting up mechanisms to ensure criminal prosecution and to provide legal compensation.

The UN and the international community as a whole is moving on the issue of impunity, and promoting the prosecution of human rights violators, especially heads of states. The Report of Mr. Theo van Boven, the Special Rapporteur on the Rights to Compensation for Victims of Gross Violations of Human Rights, submitted to the UN Sub-Commission of the Human Rights Commission states that victims of slavery have the right to demand that the offending state take direct responsibility not only for providing reparation and compensation for the crime of slavery, but also for the failure of that state to meet its obligation to punish perpetrators after the war.

The Principles to Combat Impunity, submitted by Mr. Louis Joinet, the UN Special Rapporteur on Impunity, suggests that the victims of serious crimes have the right under international law to know the truth, the right to justice, and the right to reparation.

This growing world movement to end impunity has promoted the establishment of the International Criminal Court (ICC), the Statute of which was finally adopted at the Rome Conference in July 1998. The global women's movement organized a campaign to create the

ICC, a court that can prosecute wartime sexual violence. The Women's Caucus for Gender Justice for the ICC was formed and its vigorous lobbying activities succeeded in integrating gender perspective into every article of the Statute. As a result, the ICC Statute clearly defines rape, sexual slavery, enforced prostitution, enforced pregnancy, and enforced sterilization as war crimes against women and crimes against humanity.

Backed by such an international trend, women who shared the same goal of putting an end to impunity for wartime sexual violence worked together toward the Tokyo Women's Tribunal, overcoming differences among countries, cultures, and individual backgrounds.

As an integral part of the Tribunal, a Public Hearing on Crimes against Women during Recent Wars and Conflicts was held on the fourth day, December 11. This hearing was organized by the Women's Caucus for Gender Justice for the ICC, and survivors from twelve conflict areas throughout the world gave testimony about their painful experiences. The aim was to link Japan's military sexual slavery in the past to current wartime sexual violence in order to prevent such violence from happening again in the future.

The Challenge to Japan, the International Community, and the Women's Movement

The Challenge to the Japanese Movement to Recognize Postwar Responsibility

The Tribunal attached nine recommendations to the Summary of Findings; seven of them are directed toward the Japanese government. They reflect the consensus of the international community concerning the need to address the issues of war and postwar responsibility. In other words, they state that three measures, namely, truth finding, compensation to the victims, and prosecution of the perpetrators are required.

Among these three measures, as I mentioned before, the movement has been concentrating its efforts on getting compensation.

As for finding the truth, enormous efforts have been made by the movement in Japan—collecting survivors' testimonies, tracing the locations of former comfort stations all over the Asia-Pacific region, searching for military documents, compiling video documentation and other supporting evidence for court cases. However, the Japanese government still refuses to publicize the related military documents, using the excuse of protection of privacy. Nevertheless, in the process of preparing for the Tribunal, scholars and activists have uncovered a considerable number of documents in order to prove the truth about Japan's military sexual slavery.

The third measure, prosecution, has been a taboo even within the movement. Actually, in 1994, twenty-seven Korean comfort women and their lawyers brought a letter of complaint to the Tokyo Prosecutor's Office to demand that the Japanese government punish the perpetrators. The Prosecutor's Office, however, refused even to accept it. Furthermore, even those actively involved in the comfort women movement opposed criminal prosecution, on the grounds that such action might antagonize the Japanese public and cause a split within the movement. Accordingly, neither the government nor the movement took any action for prosecution.

Since 1995, the growing right-wing force in Japan has been systematically attacking comfort women as prostitutes who volunteered to work for the Japanese army for money, claiming that the comfort women system was not a crime but merely a "prostitution system." This campaign to insult the victims once again has penetrated the younger generation as well. Furthermore, the right-wing campaign has succeeded in removing descriptions of comfort women from history textbooks for junior high school students.

When VAWW-NET Japan members conducted a survey among former soldiers around Yasukuni Shrine, more than two-thirds of those who responded to the questionnaire answered that the comfort women system was necessary, and that there is no need for apology or compensation because comfort women were prostitutes.

We therefore need to make use of the judgement of the Tribunal, that the comfort women system is a war crime and a crime against humanity, and that the Japanese government has legal responsibility both for monetary compensation and criminal prosecution.

The prosecution of individuals is especially important, because in Japanese society, individuals tend to hide behind the state, the company, or any other organization. This is often referred to as "the system of irresponsibility," because single members of any organization avoid taking responsibility for their actions, claiming, "I did it on the orders of my superiors or because of my position." Thus there is always the possibility of repeating the same mistakes or crimes.

An International Campaign Required

The Tribunal demonstrated that the issue of military sexual slavery cannot be solved only bilaterally between the perpetrating country and victimized countries. Instead, the issue must be dealt with globally. Some recommendations by the judges of the Tribunal are directed to the former Allied Powers and the United Nations.

It is vitally important that the UN be approached in order to put pressure on the Japanese government to respond to the Tribunal and take responsibility for paying reparation to the survivors. Specifically, the Human Rights Commission, the High Commissioner on Human Rights, the Commission of the Status of Women, and other relevant UN organizations should accept the results of the Tribunal and make recommendations to the Japanese government. It is imperative that all UN organizations recognize the judgement of the Tribunal as an official document.

The Preamble of the Charter of the Tribunal emphasizes the role of the international community in implementing the results of the Tribunal. It reads as follows:

> Convinced that the Tribunal is competent to render its judgements respecting responsibility for the commission of crimes against women in light of the principles of law, human conscience, humanity, and gender justice that were an integral part of international law at the time of, and that should have been applied by the International Military Tribunal for the Far East, as well as taking into account the subsequent developments in international law, particularly in relation to women's human rights, which have come to be recognized by the international community as a priority matter as the result of the brave struggles of many people including women survivors themselves, and insofar as these developments illuminate the proper application of international law to crimes against women, and embody evolving principles of state responsibility for past violations, mindful that while the Tribunal, as a people's and women's initiative, has no real power to enforce its judgements, it nonetheless carries the moral authority demanding their wide acceptance and enforcement by the international community and national governments.

One of the recommendations of the Tribunal demands that the Allied countries explain the reasons why the emperor was not prosecuted at the Tokyo Trial, and that all relevant documents be disclosed. Among the Allied countries, as I mentioned before, it was the U.S. that made the decision not to punish the emperor. Therefore, the United States has a major responsibility to respond to this recommendation.

It should also be noted that the Tribunal has made contributions toward the reconciliation of countries as well: South and North Korea presented a joint indictment, including even comfort women now living in Japan or China. As delegates from both Koreas pointed out, when young women were taken by the Japanese military, Korea was one nation, even if it was ruled by Japan. This was appreciated as a small step in the direction of reunification. In preparing for the Tribunal, China cooperated with Taiwan. Such unexpected, friendly, people-to-people relationships should be further promoted to form the basis for a shared future for Asia, especially East Asia, where the cold war is not yet over.

The Women's Movement to Create a New Century of Non-Violence

A sense of responsibility as women of the perpetrating country led many Japanese women to devote themselves to the task of preparing for the Tribunal. The long path toward the Tribunal can be traced back to the women's campaign against Japanese men's sex tours to Korea in the 1970s. Japanese women were shocked to hear about the demonstrations Korean women held at the airport in Seoul, holding up placards with such slogans as: "Down with prostitution tourism! Don't turn our land into a brothel for Japanese men!" Responding to Korean women's action, Japanese women formed a group against sex tours and went to the airport to distribute flyers to Japanese tourists with slogans of their own, such as "Shame on sextourists!" and "Stop prostitution tourism!"

This was the first time that Korean and Japanese women had taken joint action against a "common enemy," Japanese male sex tourists. Korean women then sent us a shocking message that Japanese men's contemporary sex tourism was a repetition of military sexual slavery in the past: just as Korean women were exploited and humiliated by Japanese soldiers during the war, today Korean women are again being sexually abused by Japanese men.

Thus, concerned Japanese feminists began to face the responsibility that Japanese women bore for supporting a war of aggression and colonial rule in the past, and for failing to take postwar responsibility for such past crimes. These Japanese women were a tiny minority, but they formed an Asian Women's Association with "Our Declaration," a statement to the effect that we Japanese women are determined never to repeat past crimes, and will make every effort to stop Japan's contemporary economic and sexual aggression toward neighboring Asian countries. Members of this organization have promoted solidarity action for women's rights and for democracy, working together not only with Korean women but also with women from many other Asian countries.

This network of trust among women of a perpetrating country and victimized countries in Asia has resulted in various solidarity actions against Japan's aggressive and dominating behavior from the past to the present.

Several decades of sisterhood and solidarity between Japanese and other Asian women have culminated in the Women's International War Crimes Tribunal, which has stimulated women from other parts of the world to join in the process. The Tribunal demonstrated to the whole world that women with a firm perspective on women's human rights and gender justice can overcome the boundaries of nation-states and take joint action.

Within Japan, however, this women's movement to challenge their own country has gotten a rather cold response; we have even been severely attacked as traitors. In sharp contrast to the flood of coverage all over the world, the Japanese media barely took notice of the Tribunal.

It is true that facing the past of your own country is not easy. At the Tokyo Conference in 1997, I declared in my speech, "History Cannot be Erased, Women Can No Longer be Silenced," that, "It is our hope that our friends from the West will not only deal with violence happening in other countries in the South or the East, but will also confront war responsibility issues in their own countries." Since then, I have yet to hear of any women's movement in the United States that has taken any action to, for example, redress the victims of chemical warfare or mass rape during the Vietnam War.

However, Professor Mark Selden, an American scholar of Asian studies who attended the Tribunal, has published a report in the Newsletter of Association of Asian Studies in which he writes, "The United States has faced no comparable demands for apology and restitution for major atrocities committed during its wars in Asia or elsewhere: despite widespread if episodic firebombing of German and Japanese cities and the atomic bombing of Hiroshima and Nagasaki, and for wide ranging atrocities including most famously the killing of noncombatants at No Gun Ri in Korea and My Lai in Vietnam, its use of Agent Orange and other life-threatening defoliants, no significant international movement presently targets the U.S. for its war crimes or demands apology and restitution for the victims. A powerful anti-war movement in the U.S. and worldwide contributed to withdrawal from Vietnam in the 1970s but not before two to three million Vietnamese had died. With the end of the war, however, that movement virtually disappeared." Now, the global women's movement must continue to support voiceless survivors, encouraging them to speak openly of crimes committed against them by the U.S. in Japan, Korea, Vietnam, or any other parts of the world. It is our hope that women in the U.S. will respond to the cries of these victims, and face their own country's past.

The globalization of sisterhood can overcome the economic globalization that aggravates the violence of the market, the violence of states, and violence against women. The globalization of women's solidarity can create a twenty-first century free of all kinds of violence. The Women's International War Crimes Tribunal is one part of this process, facing past crimes and calling for a non-violent future.

References

Arendt, Hanna. 1963. *Eichmann in Jerusalem: A Report on the Banality of Evil*. New York: The Viking Press.

Askin, Kelly Dawn. 1997. *War Crimes Against Women: Prosecution in International War Crimes Tribunals*. The Hague: Martinus Nijhoff Publishers.

Bix, Herbert P. 2000. *Hirohito and the Making of Modern Japan*. New York: HarperCollins.

Brackman, Arnold C. 1987. *The Other Nuremberg The Untold Story of Tokyo War Crimes Trials*. New York: William Morrow & Co.

Buruma, Ian. 1994. *The Wages of Guilt: Memories of War in Germany and Japan*. New York: Farrar, Straus & Giroux.

"Charter for the International Military Tribunal for the Far East." 1946.

"Charter of Women's International War Crimes Tribunal 2000," *The Summary of the. Findings of Women's International War Crimes Tribunal 2000*.

Coomaraswamy, Radhika. 1997. "Report of the Special Rapporteur on violence against women."

Coomaraswamy, Radhika. 1998. "Report of the Special Rapporteur on violence against women, its causes and consequences."

Joinet, Louis. 1996. "Final report on question of the impunity of perpetrators of human rights violations (civil and political)."

McDougall, Gay. 1998. "Final report on systematic rape, sexual slavery and slavery-like practices during armed conflict."

McDougall, Gay. 2000. "Update to the Final Report on systematic rape, sexual slavery and slavery-like practices during armed conflict."

"The Outcome Documents of Beijing Plus 5." 2000.

"The Platform for Action adopted at the 4th UN World Conference on Women." 1995.

"The Report on 'comfort women,'" International Commission of Jurists. 1994.

Sajor, Indai Lourdes (editor). 1998. *Common Grounds: Violence Against Women in War and Armed Conflict Situations*. Asain Center for Women's Human Rights (ASCENT).

Selden, Mark. 2001. "On Asian Wars, Reparations, Reconciliation."

Statute of the International Criminal Court. 1998.

Statute of the International Tribunal for former Yugoslavia. 1993
Statute of the International Tribunal for Rwanda. 1994.
van Boven, Theo. 1993. "The Final Report: Study concerning the right to restitution, compensation and rehabilitation for victims of gross violations of human rights and fundamental freedoms."
van Boven, Theo. 1993. "Study concerning the right to restitution, compensation and rehabilitation for victims of gross violations of human rights and fundamental freedoms."
A number of books and papers in Japanese for reference are not listed.

16

The Looting of Books in Nanjing

Zhao Jianmin (translated and edited by Peter Li)

Whereas scholars and the general public in China, Japan, the United States, and most of the Western world are familiar with Japan's war crimes such as the Nanjing Massacre, the bio-terrorist activities of Unit 731, the sexual enslavement of the comfort women, and the maltreatment of POWs, few know about the plunder and looting of books and cultural treasures by the Imperial Japanese Army. In fact, the systematic looting of books and cultural relics were an important part of Japan's expansionist policy of cultural domination of the enemy nations. According to the statistics of 1936 compiled by the Chinese Libraries Association, on the eve of the Japanese invasion there were 4,747 libraries in all throughout China, including independent libraries, school libraries, institutional libraries, and county and municipal libraries. But by 1943, however, following the Japanese invasion and occupation, the number of libraries declined to 940. Four-fifths of the libraries were either destroyed or looted. Before the war, there were approximately 25 million volumes housed in the various libraries, but after the war the number was reduced to 15 million volumes. Ten million volumes, or 40 percent of the books, were lost in the intervening years. This essay will discuss the looting and plundering of books that took place during the time of the Nanjing Massacre from December 13, 1937 to the middle of February 1938.

China is a country with a long history and flourishing cultural tradition, but as for the existence of public libraries, that is a relatively modern phenomenon. Although the collecting of antiquities and rare editions of old books had a long tradition in China, these objects were accessible only in private collections or government-sponsored organizations; libraries in the modern sense of the term did not exist. Only in 1905 did China begin to build a modern library system. By 1930, there were public libraries in all the major provinces and counties of China. As stated above, in 1936 there were 4,747 libraries in the country.

The Systematic Looting of the Capital City of Nanjing

A little bit of background information about Nanjing is necessary here in order for us to understand the importance of this metropolitan center. Nanjing has long been known as a famous cultural and commercial center of China, dating back to the Six Dynasties period (fifth to sixth centuries AD). The Nationalist Government moved the capital from Beijing to Nanjing after successfully quelling of the warlords during the Northern Expedition from 1926-1928. In 1927, Nanjing was designated the capital of the Republic of China. The former capital city of Beijing (Northern Capital) was changed to Beiping (Northern Peace). Beginning in 1933, the Nationalist Government founded the National Central Library in Nanjing and the University Library at Jinling University, which housed the special collection of local gazetteers. In addition, there were the Library of the National Central University and the Nanjing Municipal Library, and various specialized libraries belonging to the Nationalist Government and the Nationalist Party. According to the documents from Japan and China, during the Nanjing Massacre the Imperial Japanese Army was also engaged in the systematic looting and plundering of a total of 897,178 volumes of books from a large assortment of libraries in Nanjing.[1] 646,900 volumes were taken from various government libraries of the central government scattered in twenty-five locations. Another 197,160 volumes were taken from ten additional libraries. Finally, 53,118 volumes were taken from individual scholars' and professors' private collections. Altogether, the plundered volumes were more than the entire collection in the Japanese Imperial Library, which had only 850,000 volumes.

Even before the attack on Nanjing, the Japanese army had already set up a special committee named the Central China Committee for Taking-over of Books and Documents from the Occupied Areas. This committee was responsible for sorting, transporting, and cataloging looted materials. After the occupation of Nanjing on December 13, 1937, the fifteen-member committee sent out a directive to every army chief-of-staff to cooperate with the special committee. Beginning on January 22, 1938, after the looting of the libraries had already taken place, the committee began the task of inspecting the books taken from some seventy organizations of the Nationalist Government. The books from other outlying areas were also transported to a central location and a special "Committee for Sorting Books" was set up to handle this special task. The committee used 367 Japanese soldiers and 2,830 Chinese coolie laborers to undertake this work. 310 trucks were also requisitioned for the task.[2] The team worked on this project from March 6 to April 10, 1938. Later, from July 11 to August 31, these books were further sorted and arranged into eleven categories.

After repeated sorting, the results were published in the following three catalogues: 1) *Catalogue of Publications of the National Economic Committee*, 2) *Catalogue of Materials on Chinese Economics, Finance and Monetary Relations*, and 3) *Catalogue of Chinese Language Periodicals, Bulletins and Newspapers*, by the Nanjing Division of the Central Reconstruction Resources Bureau. The latter included the titles of 2,324 journals and periodicals, which in effect included practically all the periodical literature published in China during that time.[3]

The looting of books by the Japanese had a totally different purpose from the random destruction of property and lives that took place during the Nanjing massacre. After acquiring these precious looted volumes, the Japanese set up a number of special research organizations such as The Institute of East Asian Studies, the Institute of Oriental Culture, the Institute of East Asian Economics, the Institute of Endemic Disease in East Asia, and the Institute of Nationalities. The immediate goal of the slaughtering and looting was the destruction of Chinese nation and its cultural tradition. The ultimate objective was the establishment of the Greater East Asia Coprosperity Sphere in Asia. Japan would be its leader and chief beneficiary. It is not difficult to see that Japan regarded the looting of books to be an important part of its overall military strategy.

The History and Purpose of Cultural Looting in War

Since the time of Hideyoshi Toyotomi in the sixteenth century, who began his ambitious plan to conquer China and Korea in 1592, the looting of books and cultural artifacts have become an inherent part of the Japan's military expeditions. Hideyoshi brought along learned monks and scholars who could help in the identification of objects and books of value. In his seven-long years war, Hideyoshi had many volumes brought back to Japan from Korea, resulting in the establishment of several "literary treasuries." Even though Hideyoshi did not succeed in his mission in conquering China and Korea, he acquired many valuable volumes from Korea. These volumes on Confucianism and herbal medicine are still in Japan today.

In modern times, Japan put the looting of books into its war plans: it legitimized the looting of books in conquered lands. For example, in 1882, 1894, and 1914, rules and regulations were promulgated that gave detailed instructions on the handling of looted materials. In November 1914, after Japan invaded and occupied Port Arthur and Qingdao in China, the Japanese army looted 25,000 volumes of books from the Jiaozhou Library and the German-China University Library. These books were later listed in a *Bibliography of Confiscated Documents and Books*. After launching its full-scale invasion of China in July 1937, the Japanese Imperial Army established in its Special Task Force Section, the Central China Committee for Taking-over of Books and Documents in the Occupied Areas. This organization was later renamed the Committee for Preparation of Materials for the Reconstruction of Central China under the Central China Liaison Institute of Asian Prosperity.

From 1941 onward, as Japan expanded its war to the Pacific with the attack on Pearl Harbor, the takeover of books and cultural treasures from other parts of Asia, such as Hong Kong and Singapore, became more widespread. Private libraries of numerous individual collectors also suffered the same fate. As a Japanese scholar has pointed out, "[even though] the Japanese military's looting of books [may not appear to be] in the same order of importance as the seizing of sovereign territory and property, taking over of markets or slaughtering of people, actually the looting of books is an extension of the seizing of territory and property and an important part of Japan's policy of annihilating a nation and subjugating its people."[4]

As some scholars have pointed out, the purpose of book looting was to destroy Chinese culture in order to fulfill the Japanese long-term objective of conquering the Asian continent. Therefore, the looting of books went hand in hand with the slaughtering of the people as part of its overall military strategy. Some Japanese insisted that "Japan's war was fought as a war for cultural progress" and praised the looting of books as a strategic weapon as a unique phenomenon in world history.

The Repatriation of the Looted Books

Early in October 1945, two months after Japan's surrender, thirty-nine Chinese scholars, including Xu Guangping (wife of the famous Chinese writer Lu Xun), Zhou Jianren, Zheng Zhenduo, and others, wrote an open letter in the magazine *Zhoubao* [The Weekly News], requesting that Japan return the books that were taken from China. However, because of the impending civil war and chaos in China, it is not clear how much was actually done. After the normalization of diplomatic relations with Japan in 1972, the issue of the books surfaced again. This time twelve Japanese scholars met in October to discuss the return of the Chinese books. As a result of the meeting, a petition signed by 140 Japanese scholars was presented to the Japanese supreme academic institution, the Japanese Academic Conference, requesting the return of the looted Chinese books. However, for a variety of reasons, including Japanese rightwing resistance, these efforts came to naught. Some of the individuals who participated included Teruoka Hiroshi, director of the Chinese Institute, Koshima Shinji, professor at Yokohama Municipal University (now at Kanokawa University), Kato Yuzo, formerly at Tokyo University (now president of Yokohama Municipal University), and Fujihara Akira.

Although some 158,873 volumes have been returned to China in the intervening years, it constitutes 6 percent of the total number taken, i.e., 2,742,108 volumes. The major portion has not yet been returned. A memorandum presented to the Central Liaison Office of the Japanese Government by the General Headquarters of the Supreme Commander for the Allied Powers (SCAP), i.e., General MacArthur's office, dated March 20, 1946, listed the collections and libraries where Chinese books were kept. Some of the locations include the 1) Miyagi, 2) Imperial Household Museum of the Imperial Palace, 3) Yushu Hall of the Yasukuni Shrine, 4) Tokyo Science Museum, 5) Tokyo Arts College, 6) Tsubouchi Memorial Theater Museum, 7) Numismatic Museum, 8) Calligraphy Museum, 9) Imperial Library, 10) Tokyo Imperial University Library, 11) Tokyo Imperial University Historiography Institute, 12) Keio University Library, 13) Waseda University Library, 14) Hibiya Library, 15) Toyo Bunko, 16) Oriental Culture University, and 17) the Ohashi Library. The largest and richest collection is at the Tokyo Imperial University Library. This document amounts to a confession by the Japanese government with regard to the books taken from China and transported to Japan.

The Japanese libraries housing these books from China and other nations have now become the best libraries in the world for the study of Asian culture and history, where people can find books that cannot be found anywhere else. This is especially the case with the library at the Tokyo Imperial University, "which houses the priceless collection of the oldest and largest collection of Chinese classical texts, and the world's oldest and most extensive collection of printed texts. Only a small portion of this material is not accessible to historians inside or outside of Japan."[5] These books provided Japanese scholars with the most treasured materials for the study of China and enabled Japan to become the foremost center for Chinese studies. Even scholars from China must go to Japan to consult these precious volumes.

The return of these books would not contradict the Joint Communiqué signed by China and Japan in the 1972, namely, "China remits war reparations from China," because the return of these books is not considered to be reparations, but instead an indication of Japan's sincerity in assuming her wartime responsibilities. For China, the return of these books means recovering her sovereignty over her rightful cultural treasures. This is different from reparations and should not be confused with it. Therefore, no matter from what perspective, this act will benefit both parties in helping to build mutual understanding and confidence, and aid in removing antagonistic feelings.

The details regarding the repatriation of the Chinese books can be worked out through the Committee on Sino-Japanese Relations in the 21st Century, which could establish a semi-governmental and/or non-governmental agency to carry out the project. At the time and date of the return, a special ceremony will be held with the erection of a memorial marking the occasion. In order not to disrupt the continued access to the books by Japanese scholars, photo reduplication of the texts can be done before returning the originals to China. At the same time, testimonies of those who took part in the looting can be collected to preserve the historical facts surrounding the incident in order to educate future generations about the tragedies of war.

Notes

1.   Matsumoto, Tsuyoshi, *Ryakudatsu shita bunka—senso to tosho* [*Cultural Looting—War and Books*] (Tokyo: Iwanami shoten, 1993), pp. 75-80.
2.   Ohsa, Miyogo, "Senryo chiku ni okeru tosho bunken no sesshu to sono seiri sagyo ni tsuite [The work of receiving and organizing books and documents from occupied areas]," *The Monthly Bulletin of the Japanese Library Association*, 32.12., p. 338.

3.   See fn. 19 in Zhao Jianmin, "Lu lun 'Nanjing datusha' zhong de tushu jielue [Brief Account of the Looting of Books during the Nanjing Massacre]," *Contemporary China*, no. 122. p. 47.
4.   Matsumoto, *Cultural Looting*, p. 50.
5.   Adachi, Masataka, "Daichi, niji sekai taisenchu ni okeru nihongun sesshu tosho [Books taken by the Japanese Army during the First and Second World War]," *The Library World*, 32.2 (July 1981), p. 69.

17

Japan's Biochemical Warfare and Experimentation in China

Peter Li

Rabbi Abraham Cooper, dean of the Simon Wiesenthal Center, wrote a disturbing essay beginning with a series of "What ifs": "What if there was no Nazi hunter like Simon Wiesenthal to pursue the perpetrators of genocide? What if the U.S. bartered Auschwitz doctor Josef Mengeles' freedom in return for the results of his horrific experiments? What if postwar Germany had installed top Nazi doctors in the National Institutes of Health or as deans in leading medical schools or a surgeons general of the New German defense forces?"[1] If you think this cannot happen, then you are wrong. Substitute Japan for Germany, and Japanese military doctors of Unit 731 for Nazi doctors, and you have Japan's germ warfare program in China, which performed extensive experiments on human subjects and conducted many biochemical attacks throughout China, killing hundreds of thousands of people from 1932 to 1945. Furthermore, many of these military doctors and technical personnel who committed these gross violations of human rights have remained unrepentant and gone unpunished for over half a century. And the government of Japan has repeatedly denied the existence of the biochemical warfare program until recently.[2]

Whereas the rampant destruction and massacre in Nanking were known to the general public at the time, the Japanese experiments in biological and chemical warfare were conducted in great secrecy and not known to the general public. Known as Unit 731 and headed by Lt. General Ishii Shiro, this center of "research," consisting of more than seventy buildings occupying about six square kilometers that rivaled Auschwitz-Birkenau in size, became the ground for some of the most gruesome experiments in human history. It has gradually come to light that an estimated more than 10,000 Manchurians, Chinese, Russians, Koreans, Europeans, and Americans were killed by the Imperial Japanese Army's Unit 731.[3]

These human victims were subjected to various forms of experimentation with a variety of pathogens, including cholera, typhoid, dysentery, anthrax, and bubonic plague. Some of the other experiments involved "tying victims to stakes and bombarding them with shrapnel laced with gangrene; inserting them in pressure chambers to see how much their bodies could take before their eyes popped; and exposing them, periodically drenched in water, to subzero weather to determine their susceptibility to frostbite."[4]

Located in the newly conquered territory of Manchuria, in the village of Pingfang, twenty kilometers outside the cosmopolitan city of Harbin, the Japanese utilized the virtually unlimited supply of human subjects, selected from among the illiterate peasants in the surrounding villages, on whom they could perform their ghastly experiments. These innocent subjects were artificially infected with disease and as the infections progressed, they were dissected either with or without anesthetics to observe the state of deterioration of the internal organs. The following is a vivid description of one such operation: "After infecting him, the researchers decided to cut him open to see what the disease does to a man's inside. I cut him open from the chest to the stomach and he screamed terribly and his face was all twisted in agony. He made this unimaginable sound, he was screaming so horribly. This was all in a day's work for the surgeons, but it really left an impression on me because it was my first time."[5] The intestines and internal organs were then removed and examined. Sometime during the vivisection, the subject died, but it was of no concern to the doctors. The bodies were disposed of afterwards in the crematorium.

Sheldon H. Harris, author of *Factories of Death* (Routlege, 2002), began his study of Japan's biological warfare experimentation program in 1985 at the instigation of his Chinese colleagues at Northeast Normal University in Changchun, China, where he was giving a series of lectures. A chance visit to the ruins of an old World War II Japanese POW campsite peaked his interest in Japan's biochemical warfare program in China. Initially, he learned about the activities of Unit 100 based in Changchun. As his research expanded, Harris enlisted the help of Mr. Han Xiao of the Unit 731 Museum in Pingfang. Continuing his research in the United States, Harris scoured the National Archives in Washington, D.C. and in Suitland, Maryland for more evidence on Japanese biological warfare and the subsequent American cover-up. Part II of Harris' book is a detailed account of the United States government's part in covering up and silencing all information concerning Unit 731's activities.

Experiments of unbelievable cruelty were routinely performed. In a frostbite experiment, for example, four or five human subjects were led out into freezing weather dressed in warm clothing—only their arms were exposed to the cold to be frozen. Their arms were made to freeze more quickly with the help of large fans. "This was done until their frozen arms, when struck with a short stick, emitted a sound resembling that which a board gives out when it is struck."[6] Then the experts experimented with different kinds of treatments. The unfortunate victims, however, sometimes lost their limbs or their lives.

Ishii was the mastermind who devised all manner of insidious experiments to be inflicted on the innocent inhabitants in the surrounding region. He contaminated more than 1,000 wells in the Harbin region with typhoid bacilli in 1939 and 1940, killing or sickening many unsuspecting villagers in the area. Again, informing the local inhabitants in Changchun that a cholera epidemic was imminent, he advised the people to be vaccinated. Little did they know that the vaccine to be used was a solution containing cholera germs. Many of those inoculated died. Another scheme he used in Nanking was to provide special treats, such as *mantou* (steamed buns) to 6,000 Chinese prisoners of war and then release them to return to their homes. But the buns were laced with typhoid or paratyphoid germs. He also prepared delicacies for the local children—chocolates filled with anthrax. Japanese soldiers were also instructed to leave sweet cakes near fences and trees for the children to pick up and eat without realizing that these were also contaminated.[7]

Aside from the main center located in Pingfang, there were more than a dozen facilities located at other cities in China. There was the Beijing-based Unit 1855, which was a combined prison and experiment center for research into plague, cholera, and typhus. Unit 8604, based in Guangzhou (Canton), Guangdong province in southern China performed starvation experiments and used rats in spreading plague to the population. Unit 100 was located in Changchun, Jilin province in Manchuria; it was a bacteria factory producing large quantities of glanders, anthrax, and other pathogens. There was also the Nanking-based Unit 1644, which mixed plague germs with wheat, corn, millet, clothing scraps, and cotton, which were then dropped from the air. Another center, Unit 9420, located in Singapore, used infected fleas to transmit plague pathogens. These fleas, bred in large quantities, were shipped to Thailand to see how effective they would be in the tropical climate.

As early as 1932, an Epidemic Prevention Research Laboratory was set up in the Army hospital in Tokyo with Ishii in charge. The term "prevention" was a euphemism used for the development of bacteriological and chemical attack weapons. It was Ishii's goal to develop bacterial and chemical weapons for the Imperial Army. In China, these units were set up under the cloak of "Anti-Epidemic Water Supply and Purification Bureaus," which would not attract undue attention. The local inhabitants, including foreign visitors, all believed the Japanese were concerned about the health of the people. All told, eighteen or more of these units were ultimately established in Manchuria and in other parts of China proper. This form of murder under the guise of "medical research," many more times devastating than the experiments of the Nazi doctor Josef Mengele, became another tragic chapter in Japan's war of aggression against China.

Biological Field Tests and Attacks

General Ishii's work was not restricted to experiments in the laboratories at Pingfang. It included extensive field tests and large-scale bacteriological attacks over large areas of China. Extensive records exist documenting these attacks.[8] According to James Yin's still incomplete data, there were at least 161 bacteriological attacks affecting 190 counties in China and killing as many as 748,000 people. The figure could reach as high as 2 million when more data are gathered. Some estimate the number of attacks to be about 2,000. In addition to the biological weapons, poison gas was used by the Japanese Imperial Army. It is estimated that poison gas was used 1,131 times in fourteen provinces.[9] The following are some documented examples of "bioterrorist" attacks the Japanese inflicted on innocent Chinese people and the aftereffects of those attacks are still felt today.

The Zhejiang-Jiangxi region of central China had been a pocket of resistance stationed with Chinese guerilla fighters—a thorn in the side of the Japanese military, who had already taken the major cities of Shanghai and Nanking. The region is dotted with airfields and linked by railroads. For this reason, the Japanese resorted to germ warfare to quell the region in order to conserve their fighting forces. Germ warfare was initiated as early as August 1937 when the Japanese took Shanghai in the Wusong-Shanghai Campaign. From 1940 on, the Ningbo, Jinhua, Quzhou, Jiangshan, Yushan corridor that stretches across central Zhejiang province from east to west came under intensive biological warfare attack. The attacks became particularly intensive after August 1942, following the daring raid on Tokyo by Lt. Colonel James Doolittle and his fleet of fifteen B-25s on April 18, 1942.

Ningbo, Zhejiang

This prosperous commercial and trading port-city off the Zhejiang coast was the first of numerous targets of Japan's massive germ warfare testing. The difference between field tests and attacks has become moot at this point. Before the massive attack in July 1940, General Ishii had dispatched from Pingfang, seventy kilos of typhus bacterium, fifty kilos of cholera germs, and five kilos of plague-infested fleas. For the next five months, Ningbo was subjected to a large variety of attacks. Pathogens were dumped into water reservoirs, ponds, and wells. Flea-infested wheat and millet were disseminated by air. In November, specially equipped aircraft flew over Jinhua county dropping bombs that did not explode but cracked open on impact and gave off smoke-like objects that turned yellowish in color. It is not known exactly how many people were killed or severely affected. One source revealed that 106 people died in Ningbo and 1,617 died in Jinhua.[10]

Quzhou, Zhejiang

In the village of Quzhou there were two eyewitnesses that gave vivid accounts of the biological attacks and their devastating aftermath. In October 1940, Qiu Mingxuan, then a young boy, and now sixty-nine years of age and a bacteriologist, remembered seeing a single plane dropping rags, soybeans, and wheat instead of bombs. Then his relatives, friends, and classmates began dying mysteriously until it was discovered that the items were flea-contaminated. Another eyewitness, Wu Shigen, observed that the bombs dropped by Japanese planes did not explode. Instead, they fell harmlessly to the ground and cracked open like eggs. Then a mixture of rice and wheat covered with fleas poured from them. It wasn't until several days later that people in the village came down with sicknesses. Also, the villagers noticed that white-coated Japanese medics claiming to be from a government epidemic-prevention unit would arrive at the villages unannounced, saying that they were implementing hygiene measures, or administering vaccinations. After they left, the villagers became ill. Japanese soldiers disguised as Chinese were also spotted dropping mysterious packages into wells. The children were also warned not to eat tempting sweets left behind by Japanese soldiers, when some became ill after taking them.[11] Qiu estimates that as many as 50,000 people died in the region over a period of six years from the time of the first outbreak in 1940 to 1945.[12]

Changde, Hunan

The city of Changde in Hunan province, an important railway hub and commercial center, was another target of the Japanese BW attack. The attack began on April 11, 1941 with the dissemination of plague-infested wheat and millet by air. Again, in November of the same year, Col. Ota, one of Ishii's most trusted aids, discharged plague-infested fleas by aerial spraying and dropping contaminated mixtures of wheat and rice balls, strips of colored paper, cotton, and other fabrics. By December many residents of Changde were dead from the plague. A conservative estimate is that between 400 and 500 people died.[13] According to another account, on November 4, 1941 thirty-seven kilos of plague-carrying fleas were dropped on the people of Changde by a Unit 731 bomber. On the twelfth, the first victim, a young girl of twelve, appeared showing symptoms of the plague and died shortly thereafter. In the following year another attack was made using the same method. Altogether ten counties were affected resulting in many deaths. Even up to the present time people are still dying of the plague. It is estimated that during the intervening sixty years, up to 1998, over 10,000 people have died, as the disease would flare up periodically.[14]

The Zhejiang-Jiangxi Attack

The most massive attack on the Zhejiang-Jiangxi region came after the Doolittle raid on Tokyo on April 18, 1942. Because many of the United States airmen landed in Zhejiang and were rescued and conducted to safety by Chinese anti-Japanese guerillas in the region, the Japanese retaliated with a massive show of force followed by large-scale biological attacks. The Japanese sent fifty-three battalions on a punitive expedition against the Chinese. A hundred thousand Japanese troops rampaged across the countryside, accompanied by burning, killing, and raping equaling the savagery of the Rape of Nanking. Nearly a quarter of a million Chinese peasants were slaughtered in the next few months.[15] The BW attacks were delayed until August, after the Japanese ground troops had left the area. Cholera, typhoid, and paratyphoid bacteria were dropped into wells and reservoirs; plague-infested fleas and anthrax bacteria were spread throughout the rice fields. Contaminated sweet cakes and snacks were left for the children to pick up and eat. Twenty-two counties were affected and peopled died in the thousands.[16] According to the Imoto Diary, this bacteriological attack was the largest campaign that Lt. General Ishii carried out in the region.[17]

Baoshan-Kunming Attack

Another major attack occurred in May of 1942, which took place on the Yunnan-Burma border town of Baoshan and stretched eastward to Kunming, in Yunnan province. On May 4, 1942, fifty-four Japanese heavy bombers bombed Baoshan and the surrounding area, at the same time dropping a great number of "maggot bombs" containing cholera. According to Mr. Lin Yuyue, an eyewitness to the bombing, the bomb was about a meter long and twenty centimeters in diameter. The bomb, which did not explode but only partially shattered, contained a yellowish waxy substance with many live flies sticking to it and struggling to free themselves. According to Baoshan City records, "starting approximately on May 12, 1942, cholera spread quickly throughout the area along the highway and roads in the countryside. Especially serious were eight cities including Banciao and Jinji. The retreating soldiers, garrison troops and refugees were also infected in large numbers. Since there were no medicines to treat the sick, many dead bodies were left in the ditches by the roadside untended. Our incomplete records show that approximately 60,000 people died."[18]

According to another account, on May 4, 10,000 people were killed by the bombing itself in Baoshan. Those who survived scattered to the countryside leaving Baoshan a deserted city. When the farmers saw large numbers of the city-dwellers fleeing, as 78 percent of the houses and buildings were destroyed, they rushed into the city to gather the leftover goods and food. But this only helped to spread the cholera germs faster. There was a farmer, Ai Shan, who rushed into the city, picked up a bolt of fabric, and ate some of the food that he found. When he returned home he was vomiting and had diarrhea. He soon died and transmitted the disease to his family.[19]

The West Shandong Attack

Another major attack on the western part of Shandong, including parts of Henan and Hebei, began in the latter part of 1943. Cholera was the weapon of choice. The germs were delivered through the air and by hand. The infected area covered twelve towns in west Shandong, two counties of Henan, and nine counties of Hebei. The attack was aggravated by the Japanese soldiers' deliberate breaching of the embankment, holding back the waters of the Wei River in three separate places. The flooding of the flat plains drove the infected people into other regions, thereby spreading the disease further. The first attack took place during the latter half of September and centered about the cities of Qingping, Renping, Boping, etc. The second attack took place from September 25 to the beginning of October, centering on Henan province. The last attack was launched from the about the tenth to the twentieth of October, focusing on the same region. Altogether the estimated deaths numbered about 200,000 according to the confession of Kensan Yasaki.[20]

The Japanese bacteriological experiments and testing of the methods of delivery continued up to the end of the war. Field tests and/or attacks were conducted in all parts of China, reaching as far south as Canton, along the cities of the ancient Silk Route in northwestern China, and north into the Manchurian-Soviet frontier. As Japan was preparing for surrender, Unit 731 performed the last of its dastardly deeds. It was revealed that in April 1945 there were some 3 million force-fed rats raised to produce billions of bubonic plague-infected fleas. And 4,500 machines were running twenty-four hours a day for breeding these fleas. According to the confessions of Nobuo Kamadan, a former member of Unit 731, whose primary assignment at Pingfang was to breed plague-infested fleas: "We would inject the most powerful bacteria into the rats. On a 500 gram rat, we would attach 3,000 fleas. When the rats were released, the fleas would transmit the disease." The infected rats were also placed in porcelain bombs that were parachuted into target areas so that the rats would not be killed upon impact.[21] On the eve of Japan's surrender, the order was given to destroy the site of Unit 731 at Pingfang, whereupon thousands upon thousands of the plague-infested rats were released into the surrounding countryside causing outbreaks of the plague in twenty-two counties, killing 20,000 to 30,000 of the local inhabitants.[22]

"Sorry is Not Enough"

As more and more facts about the Japanese biological warfare program come to light, the more sinister the Japanese Imperial Army's biochemical activities appear. However, as to how this issue will be finally resolved, the answer is far from clear. The Japanese government, though awakening to the realities of Unit 731, is still in denial. As for the medical personnel involved in Unit 731, some are still in positions of leadership in Japanese society. Lt. General Masaji Kitano, who commanded Unit 731 after Ishii was assigned to Nanking, became the director of the Green Cross Corporation, a leading Japanese maker of blood products. As for other personnel, their reactions differ markedly. Yoshio Shinozuka, aged seventy-nine, a former member of Unit 731, is tormented by the vicious acts that he committed in China. Now he speaks openly about what he had done: "We did what we shouldn't have done as human beings. The Japanese government should apologize and express its sincere attitude of remorse."[23] On the other hand, there are those like Toshio Mizobuchi, aged seventy-six, who was also a member of Unit 731. His view is diametrically opposed to Shinozuka's. When Rabbi Cooper asked him if he had any regrets about what he had done in China, he almost jumped out of his chair. "No," he insisted defiantly. "The logs [a reference to Chinese human subjects used for the experiments] were not considered to be human. They were either spies or conspirators already sentenced to death. So now they died a second time. We just executed the death sentence."[24]

There are encouraging signs that grassroots efforts by Japanese citizens are bringing the knowledge about Unit 731 to the general public. From July 1993 to December 1994, after Japanese citizens discovered the existence of these biological warfare stations, an exhibition featuring the activities of Unit 731 was organized to inform the Japanese people of the atrocities committed by the Japanese military in Asia. The exhibition was organized by Japanese citizens who raised their own money, rented exhibition space, and gave their own time and energy, because they wanted to educate the public. The exhibition was shown at sixty-one locations across Japan. Medical personnel who had worked in those "factories of death" volunteered to speak about their experience at great risk to their own safety. This is evidence that the individual Japanese citizen of conscience is willing to come forward to face his past. It is quite another matter with the Japanese government.

The Japanese government's position of intransigence had been nurtured, in part, by the United States government. Lt. General Ishii was exempted from prosecution during the Tokyo War Crimes Trials in exchange for turning over the data that he collected on his numerous experiments with human subjects. The United States government connived with the Japanese in order to develop its own arsenal of biochemical weapons. The conclusion of the Committee for the Far East in Washington was: "The value to the United States of Japanese BW data is of such importance to national security as to far outweigh the value accruing from war crimes' prosecution."[25] Therefore, the matter of Unit 731 was never brought up as an issue at the Tokyo War Crimes Trial and justice was sacrificed in the name of national security.

The following example of how the American government has participated in the cover-up of the biological warfare episode at the expense of our own servicemen is instructive. Frank James, a POW captured by the Japanese in November 1942, became a subject of biological experimentation at Unit 731 when he was sent to Mukden. He was given injections upon his arrival and subjected to many extractions of blood samples. But when he was repatriated, he was forced to remain silent about his experience by our government: "We were required, when we came to the depot at Manila, on the way back from the POW camps, to sign a statement by the Army stating we would not tell about our experiences or conditions, what happed to us in the prison camps, before any audiences or the newspapers, under threat of court martial."[26] For forty years he kept silent. He finally testified before Congress in 1986 and told his story. It was indeed a grave mistake and a shameful act on the part of the United States government to have kept this secret from the world and the American people.

In the meantime, Japanese citizens have been working quietly to help the victims of the BW attacks in China. In June 1996, a small group of Japanese human rights activists, doctors, and lawyers formed an unusual alliance with the Chinese. They formed the Association to Reveal the Historical Fact of Germ Warfare by the Japanese Armed Forces and went to China to gather information on the biochemical attacks and a year later found 108 survivors of the attacks and their family members and filed a lawsuit against the Japanese government in the Tokyo District Court in 1997. Even though, to the great disappointment of the plaintiffs who had suffered in silence all these years and were looking forward to an apology and $84,000 compensation per individual, they did not win their case, the Court finally acknowledged after half a century that Unit 731 *did* engage in biochemical atrocities. It is a small victory; the larger issue, however, as one of the plaintiffs, Dr. Tan Jialin, sixty-seven, points out, still remains: "This isn't a case about money. It's about the dignity of the Chinese people."[27]

Notes

1.   Abraham Cooper, "Japan's Medical Experiments on Prisoners," April 26, 1999, http://www.geocities.com/wallstreet/floor/9597/med.htgml. Accessed 9/17/2002.
2.   On August 27, 2002 the Tokyo District Court in a written opinion finally admitted that Unit 731 did engage in biochemical warfare in China while still deciding that the plaintiffs had no rights to sue Japanese government for damages.
3.   Sheldon Harris' letter of October 1, 2001.
4.   Ibid.
5.   "Pacific War, WW2: Japanese Unit 731, Biological Warfare Unit," http://marshallnet.com/~manor/ww2/unit731.html. Accessed 9/17/2002.
6.   Sheldon H. Harris, *Factories of Death* (Routledge, 2002), p. 70.
7.   Harris, *Factories of Death*, pp. 99-100.
8.   For a series of valuable maps locating the sites of biological warfare, see James Yin, *Rape of Biological Warfare* (Northpole Light Publishing House, 2002), pp. 206-221. It should be noted that the reader should not be put off by the defective English translation in this bilingual volume. The Chinese version is well documented and includes many Chinese sources that have not appeared any English accounts of Japan's biochemical warfare in China.
9.   Tien-wei Wu, "A Preliminary Review of Studies of Japanese Biological Warfare Unit 731 in the United States," http://www.users.cs.umn.edu/~dyue/wiihist/germwar/731rev.htm. Accessed 9/17/02.
10.   Harris, *Factories of Death*, pp. 100-101; see Yin, *Rape of Biological Warfare*, p. 198 for numbers of deaths.
11.   Anita McNaught, "Sorry is not enough," *The Times*, February 1, 2002.
12.   Harris, *Factories of Death*, p. 102.
13.   Harris, *Factories of Death*, pp. 103-104.
14.   Yin, *Rape of Biological Warfare*, pp. 74-80.
15.   John Costello, *The Pacific War, 1941-1945* (Quill, 1982), p. 236.
16.   Yin, *Rape of Biological Warfare*, pp. 158-161.

17.   Recent investigative visits in March 2002 by the late Professor Sheldon Harris and Dr. Martin Furmanski accompanied by the activist Wang Xuan, to the "rotten leg" villages including Jinhua, Quzhou, in Zhejiang revealed the vestiges of glanders attacks on the villager during the war. Glanders was an extinct disease in 1942 and whose importance is only as a biological weapon. It is a disease fatal in horses but also infected humans with horrific results. See unpublished report by Martin Furmanski, "The Importance of Dr. Harris' Investigation of the Zhejiang BW Attacks" presented at the 5th Biennial Conference of the Global Alliance for Preserving the History of WWII in Asia on November 15-17, 2002 in San Diego, California.

18.   Yin, *Rape of Biological Warfare*, p. 136.

19.   Yin, *Rape of Biological Warfare*, pp. 131-132.

20.   Yin, *Rape of Biological Warfare*, p. 178.

21.   Steven Butler, "Unit 731: A Half Century of Denial," http://www.technologyartistd.com/unit_731/index.html. Accessed 9/17/02. Also see Yin, *Rape of Biological Warfare*, Preface.

22.   Wu, "A Preliminary Review."

23.   Ichiko Fuyuno and David Kruger, "Memories of Horror," *Far Eastern Economic Review*, 9/05/2002.

24.   Abraham Cooper, "Japan's Medical Experiments on Prisoners," April 26, 1999.

25.   Wu, "Preliminary Review."

26.   Harris, *Factories of Death*, p. 160.

27.   "Chinese Appeal in Germ Warfare Case," Associated Press, 9/04/02, http://asia.news.yahoo.com/020903/ap/d7lqfjd80.htmnl. Accessed 9/17/02

18

Japan's Historical Myopia

Daniel A. Metraux

Teaching in 1999 at Doshisha Women's College in Kyoto, Japan, brought to my attention two different and yet closely related facts: the vast ignorance and misinformation that Japanese college students have concerning their own history, and the attempt by various Japanese scholars to revise the whole framework of twentieth century Japanese history.

Historic revisionism is a hotly debated topic in Japan today. There are a number of scholars, journalists, and people in the government who are quite literally trying to rewrite or reframe the traditional view of Japan's involvement in World War II. They are casting Japan's war effort as a noble cause to free the rest of Asia from the clutches of Western colonial imperialism and they present Japan's war leaders, such as General Tojo Hideki, as benign heroes who gave their lives for the good of the nation.

The revisionist scholars decry the more traditional view of Japanese history during World War II: Japan's murderous aggression in China and the rest of Asia, its attack on Pearl Harbor, its dreadful torture of millions of Asians and its use of sexual slavery in the form of the comfort women. The revisionists denounce this historical view as a uniquely American image, a form of victor's justice where the winner has the prerogative to write its version of the war and to punish the loser in any way it sees fit. Japanese revisionists prefer to view the war in a more positive light; they deny the uglier truths of the war such as the "Rape of Nanjing." They proclaim that Korea and China are exploiting the system of "sex slavery" for their own benefit during negotiations with Japan.[1] The revisionists insist that Japanese children will have a "Japan as the Suffering Victim" image of their country and will be ashamed of being Japanese if they are taught the negative "lies" of the past.

The impact that the revisionists have had on what young Japanese students study about the war in school is hard to gauge, but my students at Doshisha often had a "Japan as Suffering Victim" image of the war in which the aggressive West inflicted needlessly intense bombing—including atomic bombing—on a nearly defenseless Japan. Several students expressed visible anger over what the U. S. did at Hiroshima, but were stunned and puzzled when I discussed the murder of 30-50 million Asians by the Japanese army, the sex-slaves, Unit 731, and the "Rape of Nanjing."

Every nation has its extreme nationalists and scholars who want to rewrite history, but what surprises me about Japan is the support the revisionists receive from Japan's conservative elite establishment in politics, business, the bureaucracy, and the media. To talk about conspiracies would be absurd, but it does appear that at least some establishment conservatives wish to project a more "honorable" image of Japan's past.

The conservative establishment that led Japan before 1945 was the big loser in World War II. Allied (mainly American) forces under General MacArthur wrote a very liberal and democratic constitution and sought to lay the groundwork for a progressive and democratic society ("in our image" as some Americans at the time put it) where power would actually lie in the hands of the people.

The lower classes saw the American Occupation as their "liberation" from the claws of the elite who had driven Japan to defeat and total destruction. Former Prime Minister Nakasone, a confirmed member of the conservative power structure, has expressed his own personal distaste for the American reforms, which he saw as a direct challenge to "Japanese traditions and nationhood."

The conservative establishment has been attempting to return to a dominant position in Japanese society ever since the Occupation. Its view of Japan differs sharply from that imposed by the Americans— a modified "imperial system," a carefully managed society which is much less "democratic" than today, and a "correct view" of history that whitewashes all of the ugliness of defeat.[2]

Historical revisionism in Japan thus seems to be a part of a much bigger enterprise. The tragedy is that it appears to be working. Japanese college students have a very sketchy understanding of the War Era and perceive Japan as a true victim. Younger Japanese have little interest in politics and rarely vote. It appears that the direction and social consciousness of the next generation of Japanese will play a decisive role in the future course of the nation.

A Myopic View of History and Its Dangers

Asano Kenichi, a professor at Doshisha University, recently made a comparative study of college students in Japan and Korea in which he tried to ascertain their knowledge of the history of the Pacific-War era. He found that Korean students had a much clearer understanding of Asian and world history than their Japanese counterparts and were acutely aware of their colonial history under the Japanese. Japanese students, on the other hand, were sadly unaware of their country's history of exploitation in Korea.[3]

The great danger with Japan's historical myopia is that it endangers Japan's fragile relationships with its many Asian neighbors. Koreans, Chinese, Vietnamese, Filipinos, and other Asians still have strong memories of Japan's destructive aggression in their countries. Younger Asian leaders know the economic necessity of good ties with Japan, but they are sensitive about the way Japan views World War II experiences with their countries. When Japan refuses to make amends to aging "comfort women"[4] or claims that the Nanjing Massacre never took place, Chinese and Koreans are deeply offended.

Historical revisionism, however, enjoys popular support in Japan. While contemporary Germans fully acknowledge and study the horrors of their Nazi past and continue to pay reparations, Japan has always been most reluctant to sincerely admit to the ruthless brutalities of its World War II involvement. There are, of course, many individual Japanese and numerous organizations such as the Soka Gakkai which constantly pressure the Japanese Ministry of Education [Monbusho] and other government officials and ministries to acknowledge the past. Nevertheless, my Japanese college students at Doshisha Women's College report that their high school texts and classes present only a very superficial overview of Japan's activities in the Pacific War. It appears that today the historical revisionists in Tokyo hold the upper hand.

Watanabe Takesato, Professor of Journalism at Doshisha University and a scholar of Japanese revisionist history, stresses that historical revisionism has been a common feature of Japanese government policy since the end of the Pacific War. The conservative power elite—in politics, the bureaucracy, and business—that controlled

Japan during the war, according to Watanabe, sought to retain power after the war by disguising its wartime role. Accordingly, they adopted and still continue to promote revisionist views of history to reinforce their power base.[5]

Every nation has its ultranationalists and right-wing extremists who campaign actively for a variety of nationalist causes, and Japan is certainly no exception. Generally, these individuals represent an easily defined minority fringe. By contrast, the critical problem in Japan, according to Watanabe, is the fact that the key support for historical revisionism comes from the very core of Japan's political and economic leadership. Watanabe stresses that support for historical revisionism, or "historical liberalism" as known among the conservative elite, among many of Japan's leaders comes as a result of their wish to escape public criticism for their or their families' war responsibility (Watanabe, 19).

Profiles of two survivors from the Pacific War era demonstrate the strong bias for historical revisionism among the conservative elite who remain influential in Japanese life today.

Sejima Ryuzo

Sejima Ryuzo, certainly one of Japan's more powerful postwar figures, is a graduate of the Imperial Army's military academy and distinguished himself as a staff officer in the Japanese expeditionary forces occupying China. He was captured by Soviet forces and spent eleven years as a prisoner of war in Siberia and Mongolia. After his repatriation to Japan in 1956, Sejima joined the now huge international trading company, C. Itoh Corporation, quickly rising through its ranks until he became company chairman. Sejima's corporate success has brought him considerable political clout as well. He has served on a number of high-profile national commissions, including those seeking to reform the Japanese educational, administrative, and fiscal structure. In some instances he has become the de facto leader of these state commissions. His wartime connections with fellow officers are said to have played a major though covert role in the successful conclusion of Japan's war reparation negotiations with South Korea and Indonesia. Even at his current advanced age, Sejima acts as a special advisor to C. Itoh and chairs the Inamori Foundation, founded by Inamori Kazuo, chief executive of the Kyocera Corporation. Sejima also serves as the chief lay representative of Nishi-Honganji, the base temple of one of Japan's oldest Buddhist sects, which, according to Professor Watanabe, "shows the strong relations between Japanese mainstream religion and the imperial system" (Watanabe, 23). Sejima is a strong supporter of historical revisionism.

Mizobuchi Toshimo

Another advocate of historical revisionism is Mizobuchi Toshimo, who today is an energetic 76-year-old former imperial army officer who served in Manchuria in the Japanese Army's Unit 731, which conducted Japan's not-so-secret chemical-biological warfare operations before and during World War II. Deliberately infected with plague, anthrax, cholera, and other pathogens, an estimated 10,000 Chinese civilians and Allied prisoners of war were turned into human guinea pigs by Unit 731, which also vivisected victims without anesthesia and then dispatched them by lethal injection.

In a recent interview, Mizobuchi revealed that he deliberately participated in a variety of human experiments to find out "what happened when a human being did not have water for a week. He would go insane. With water, but without food a person could last 50 to 60 days." When asked whether he had any regrets about what was done to the prisoners, he jumped out of his chair with a defiant "No! The 'logs (prisoners)' were not considered to be human. They were either spies or conspirators already sentenced to death. So now they died a second time. We just executed the death sentence."[6] Mizobuchi, who actively supports the historical revisionists, today is a chief organizer of annual reunions of the several hundred Japanese survivors of Unit 731.

The Struggle for the Heart of Japan

The battle launched by the historical revisionists is to some extent an attempt to rewrite the ideology and self-identity of Japan. The conservative elite was horrified by the social and political reforms of the Occupation and has made a concerted effort to reassert its power and to check the liberal reforms institutionalized in the current constitution. Professor David O'Brien of the University of Virginia, for example, has demonstrated how the conservative governments of the past several decades have usurped the control of the nation's judicial system to deny progressive forces the opportunity to advance their various political-cultural agendas through law suits and other legal maneuvers. Conservative control over the courts, notes O'Brien, has robbed Japan of any chance to develop an independent judiciary, which is an essential component of modern democracy. Instead, the judiciary has shown a conspicuous propensity for "deferring to the government and re-enforcing traditional cultural values and norms" (O'Brien, 23).

Sheldon Garon of Princeton University in his book *Molding Japanese Minds: The State in Everyday Life* describes how the Japanese government strives to both shape the behavior of its citizens and promote generally conservative policies for the strengthening and enrichment of the nation through widely-based moral suasion campaigns. Japan's strong commitment to social management, Garon contends, is the key factor in explaining how resource-poor Japan became Asia's first modern military and economic power. Garon suggests that the Japanese government's management of society rests in part "on its ability to modernize and Westernize everyday life with the statist objectives of extracting savings, improving the quality of the workforce, and maintaining social harmony" (Garon, 21).

This desire to manage society rests at the heart of the conservatives' desire to mold and shape the Japanese nation in their own image. They strongly oppose the Occupation/SCAP desire for a truly liberal and democratic society. Nishio Kanji, the president of The Society to Make a New Textbook of Japanese History, strongly criticized the values of a modern democratic society. He argues that democracy—giving power to the people rather than to the government and ruling power that carefully manages society on behalf of the people—is not in the best interests of the Japanese nation (Watanabe, 21).

The goal of the conservatives is to slowly erode and then remove many of the "democratic" reforms of the Occupation era. O'Brien demonstrates how the conservative control over the courts has permitted the partial return of the prewar methodology of state management of the moral spirit. Garon suggests that the government's recent revision of the Religious Corporations Law represents yet another attempt by the government to reverse the Occupation's efforts to check "Japanese propensities to manage society" (Garon, 215).

The conservative's attempts to manage society, curtail the independence of the courts, and even rewrite history textbooks have met determined opposition from a variety of progressive groups and individuals. Progressive forces thus far have retained enough political power to deny conservative attempts to amend the constitution, but the recent nearly total demise of the Socialist Party and moves by the Soka Gakkai-backed Komeito to join the ruling Liberal-Democrats in a coalition government must raise concerns over the lasting power of the progressives in Japan. O'Brien certainly demonstrates that the younger progressives who achieved a certain degree of power and stature during and immediately after the Occupation are today quickly dying off and not being effectively replaced by a younger generation of progressives.

While nobody is suggesting that Japan will return to the prewar imperial system in which government played a key role in determining the direction of society, the conservatives of Japan seem eager to return to a less fluid, less democratic system where the state plays a critical role in the management of society for the good of the people. Garon, for example, demonstrates that the Aum Shinrikyo crisis of 1995 has presented the conservative establishment with yet another opportunity to encroach on the civil liberties of Japanese in the name of public order. Garon supports this thesis by noting that the move to revise the Religious Corporations Law received broad public backing as well as the backing of a political alliance between conservatives and leftists that "bore a remarkable resemblance to the coalition of bureaucrats and secular progressives who supported the state's campaigns to manage and suppress new sects during the interwar era" (Garon, 214).

Watanabe stresses, however, that the conservative elite wishes to reestablish at least the general framework of the traditional prewar imperial system which the Occupation sought to dismantle:

There remains in Japan today an age-old social dynamic: association with the imperial system consolidates one's standing in society. As do countless other Japanese institutions in want of recognition, the Inamori Foundation, which ranks among the largest of its kind, funded by JY20 billion ($160 million) from Kazuo Inamori's private coffers, invites a member of the Imperial Family for its annual endowment ceremony. The ritual is virtually repeated at every major public event worthy of note. The dynamic is equally conspicuous and influential through the alumnae of Gakushuin University, the prestigious teaching grounds of the Imperial Family, and its affiliated schools.

This framework was kept intact even after the Japanese defeat in World War II, when the Allied Occupation under instruction of the U. S. government adopted a policy absolving Emperor Hirohito of his complicity in the war so as to facilitate its control over the country. The decision prefaced the preservation of the imperial system in postwar Japan, and with it the system's deeply rooted influence over Japanese social life including religion. That the two remain viable and inter-linked can be seen in the 1997 Ministry of Education directive mandating the singing of the national anthem, with its lyrics of adulation for the emperor, in all elementary and middle schools. And in here the linkage between Sejima's group and historical liberalists who assert that the imperial system and democracy coexist is completed. (Watanabe, 23-24)

Historical Revisionism and the Media

Historical revisionism enjoys support among some Japanese scholars and representatives of the popular media. The Society for Historical Liberalism (*Jiyushugi-shikan kenkyu-kai*) led by Tokyo University Professor Fujioka and The Society to Make New History Textbooks (*Atarashii rekishi kyokasho o tsukuru-kai*) are two major organs for the spread of revisionist ideas. Officials and members of the latter group include Hayashi Kentaro, former president of Tokyo University, Fujiwara Hirotatsu, a former professor at Meiji University, Okazaki Hisahiko, former Japanese ambassador to Thailand, and Kobayashi Yoshinori, a comic writer popular among the younger generation of the Japanese. The Society boasted a list of 6,964 members, many of them prominent members of Japanese society (Watanabe, 16-18). These scholars and writers, however, would enjoy little popularity without extensive help from elements of the mass media.

The huge publishing house of *Bungei Shunju* issues a variety of magazines that have supported the historical revisionist position. Watanabe Takesato documents how *Bungei Shunju*, along with another large publisher, *Shinchosha*, has maintained strong ties to the state security apparatus and has often engaged in the dissemination of government-inspired "disinformation" to their readership (Watanabe, 2).

The most notorious example of historical revisionism appeared in an article, "The Postwar World's Greatest Taboo: The Nazi Gas Chambers Never Existed," written by Nishioka Masanori in the February 1995 issue of *Marco Polo*, a magazine published by *Bungei Shunju*. Nishioka's article provided little reliable evidence to challenge historical facts about the Nazi Holocaust, and it quickly drew a storm of protest both in Japan and abroad. The publisher soon thereafter discontinued publication of *Marco Polo*, blaming the monthly's demise on pressure exerted by advertisers that were controlled by Jewish capital.

Later, the NHK Educational Channel 3 (Japanese Public TV) featured a commentary by Sophia University Professor Watanabe Shoichi, another prominent revisionist, on its program "Views and Opinions" (*shiten-ronten*). Watanabe's talk, entitled "A New Perspective on the Relationship Between the Japanese and the Jews," gives a highly revisionist view of Japanese history. Watanabe's main point was Japan was the one major world power that never practiced any form of discrimination against Jews, despite the fact that Japan's wartime government was very unsympathetic to the plight of any non-Japanese, particularly Jews (Watanabe, 7-9).

Kobayashi Yoshinori, a spokesman for textbook revision, gives his own view of World War II:

> The Jewish scientists from Germany who sought asylum in the United States thought that the United States should develop the atomic bomb earlier than the Nazis, but they have never referred to Germany as the target of the bomb. . . . The target was Japan from the beginning. . . . Those scientists and the U. S. government had to use the bomb on the Japanese who were just like yellow monkeys to them. . . . and the U. S. used tactics intentionally blurring the [postwar] treatment of the imperial system so as to earn time to use the A-bomb over Japan. . . . Japan saved twenty thousand Jews, but they helped the U. S. make atomic bombs and massacred so many Japanese at Hiroshima and Nagasaki. . . and so it is completely unreasonable for the U. S., which massacred Japanese as an experiment, and the U. S. and China, having such terrible weapons, to criticize Japanese war responsibility.[7]

Similar sentiments are expressed in a 1998 film produced by the large Toei Movie Company, *"Puraido: Unmei no Toki* (Pride: The Moment of Destiny)." The film depicts the postwar trial of General Tojo Hideki, who was Prime Minister of Japan during much of the war. The International Military Tribunal for the Far East (IMTFE), the allied court, convicted and executed Tojo as a war criminal. The film depicts Tojo as a hero who spearheaded Japan's war effort as an almost sacred mission to liberate Asia from the imperialist enslavement of Western powers. Japan, however, had to pay a horrible price for its unselfish attempt to liberate fellow Asians and the Japanese people suffered horrible privations including the atomic attacks on Hiroshima and Nagasaki for their heroics. [8] Such events as the "Rape of Nanjing" are said to be gross fabrications that needlessly vilify Japan. Tojo himself emerges as a martyr and selfless hero and patriot who gave his life in defense of the Japanese emperor system.

The revisionist ideas of Professor Watanabe Shoichi are deeply woven in the script and are embraced by the film's production committee chairman, Kase Hideaki. Kase, like Watanabe, asserts that the Pacific War was a noble cause that, despite Japan's bitter defeat, contributed greatly to the emancipation of Asian countries from the stranglehold of Western imperialism.

Control over the content of school textbooks is another concern of the historical revisionists. This struggle has continued for decades, but has heated up again in the late 1990s. Japanese school textbooks from elementary school through senior high school are institutionally checked by the Ministry of Education (*Monbusho*), which in effect gives the Ministry veto power over what will or will not appear in Japanese texts.

The Society to Make New History Textbooks, with the active support of its influential membership, has actively lobbied the Monbusho to delete negative description of the "Rape of Nanjing," the Japanese invasion of China, and even the massacre of Koreans in the chaos of the Kanto earthquake in the Tokyo Region in 1923.[9] The Society has stated that:

> History school textbooks at present are based on the view of class struggles and they see history only from the viewpoint of people who have resisted rulers and, especially in recent times, they tell about the so-called sex slaves. . . and the Nanjing Massacre as if they were fact. . . . The textbooks we make intend to give a self-portrait of Japan and the Japanese with a global view of decency and balance. . . to make children have confidence and responsibility and contribute to world peace and prosperity. . . . If the present history education in Japan continues, our children and grandchildren might lose their homeland and suffer hard experiences of a people without a country.[10]

The Society has written its own textbook of Japanese history. The Fusosha Press, an affiliate of the *Sankei Shinbun* Newspaper Company, which claims an immediate distribution of over 200,000 orders in 1999, published the text (Watanabe, 20).

The Comfort Women Issue

A tragic example of the contemporary problems caused by Japan's historic myopia and revisionist tendencies is a 1999 lawsuit filed by ten very elderly Chinese women who claim that they had been sex slaves under the control of the Japanese military during World War II. The suit currently being heard in Tokyo District Court alleges that the Japanese military violated international law and that the Japanese government should assume responsibility for these actions. Lawyers acting on behalf of the plaintiffs and their relatives have requested that the Japanese government pay 20 million *yen* and extend a formal apology to each of the women. According to their lawyers, the women were raped by Japanese soldiers at their homes in Shanxi Province in northeastern China or at Japanese military camps in the early 1940s. It is said that some of the women were repeatedly forced to have sex with soldiers over a period of more than a year.[11]

The lawyers read the following statement to the Court: "Considering the ages of the plaintiffs, they virtually have no time to wait. We hope the trial will proceed with all possible speed so that the plaintiffs can recover their honor while they are alive." The lawyers noted that one of the women had already died since the filing of the suit.

The question of the "Comfort Women" (women forced by the Japanese military to become sex slaves to the Japanese military from the late 1930s through 1945) has raged in Japan since the first public revelations in the early 1990s. It is alleged that the Japanese military during World War II kidnapped or otherwise dragooned tens of thousands of Korean women and smaller numbers of women from other Asian countries (as well as a few Western women) to serve as sex slaves for months or years. Hundreds of published testimonies by survivors indicate the pain and humiliation that they suffered: some women were beaten and tortured regularly and were forced to serve 30-40 men a day without a break. The Japanese often killed women who became ill or pregnant, or who tried to escape.

The Japanese government at various times has denied that this sex slavery ever existed or has claimed that these women were willing, paid "participants" in an officially approved prostitution system. More recently, some government officials have acknowledged the claims of the comfort women and have expressed *personal* regret, urging that compensation be paid through a private non-government fund. There has never been any official government apology or any government compensation.

An opposition member of the Japanese Diet speaking privately to this writer in May 1997 stated his personal belief that the government has a policy of "stall and delay" concerning this issue. Court cases in Japan can drag on for many years and the suit launched by the Chinese women is no exception. The plaintiffs, however, have led hard lives and are getting old. It is unlikely that many of them will still be alive when the current trial and the inevitable appeals process ends a decade or more from now. A verdict reached on behalf of a dead plaintiff would be moot by then and the Japanese government again will have avoided an embarrassing apology and admission of war guilt.

Conclusion

The great danger of the current crusade for historical revisionism is that it seeks to deny the citizenry the opportunity to study the nation's history in a clear and objective manner. An ignorant citizenry is unable to critically analyze information generated by the government and media conglomerates and can be easily manipulated by those in power. A historically illiterate citizenry lacks critical thinking skills and is less able to formulate individual opinions and exercise the wide variety of political options available in most modern democratic societies.

The conservative elite apparently wishes to strengthen its power by achieving some degree of power over the minds of its young citizens. My many conversations with my own Japanese students demonstrated that they have at least indirectly somewhat achieved their goal. My students' appalling lack of understanding of modern Japanese history indicates that historical revisionists have succeeded in attempts to whitewash the historical truths of Japan's misdeeds six decades ago. My students' almost total lack of interest in politics does not bode well for the future of Japanese democracy.

Furthermore, Japan's future as a respected Asian power depends at least partially on its ability to wake itself from its self-inflicted amnesia. A nation which does not sincerely admit the wrong doings of its past and correct them can lose international trust. Even deliberately neutral nations like Sweden and Switzerland have had the courage to publicly admit and atone for their misdeeds during World War II. Unless Japan adopts similar measures, it will not be able to reassure its Asian neighbors that it has learned something from the errors of its past and deserves their trust.

A young adult who believes that the "Rape of Nanjing" never occurred and that Japan's true war mission was the liberation of Asia will have great difficulty relating to and understanding Chinese, Koreans, and other Asians who have a very different perspective of history. Other Asians insist on some degree of Japanese sensitivity concerning their tragedies earlier this century. While the notion that those people who do not know history are bound to repeat mistakes of the past is an over-stated cliche, Japan's failure to come to grips with its past may harm its health in the future.

A recently published survey indicates that most Chinese university students have a negative view of Japan. When asked why, they reply that Japanese have a very false and harmful view of history.[12] Unless Japan addresses its view of World War II honestly, hostility from such important neighbors as China will continue.

Notes

1. There is unfortunately much truth to this charge. In recent years there have been times when during intense negotiations Chinese or Koreans seek to embarrass Japanese negotiators by bringing up demands for compensation for surviving "Comfort Women."
2. One finds a parallel to this tendency in the words of President Ronald Reagan who remembers the Vietnam War as a "noble cause."
3. Asano Kenichi, "'Jiyushugi-shikan' to Nihon no Wakamono: Senno kara dashite Gendaishi o Manabu Keiki O" ["Liberal Historical View" and Japanese Youth: How to Escape from "Brainwashing" of Neo-Fascist Group and Learn Modern History] in *Doshisha University Hyoron Shakaikagaku*, No. 59 (March 1999), p. 35.
4. Young women who were seized by the Japanese military during World War II and held as "sex slaves" for the duration of the war.
5. Interview with Watanabe Takesato at Doshisha University, 31 May 1999.
6. Abraham Cooper, "Time to End Tokyo's Blockade of the Truth" in *The Japan Times*, 2 May 1999, p. 8.
7. Quoted in Watanabe, p. 17.
8. *Asahi Shinbun*, 18 June 1998.
9. Asano, p. 36.
10. Quoted in Watanabe, p. 19.
11. *Asahi Shinbun*, 7 May 1999.
12. *Yomiuri Shimbun*, 26 July 1999.

Bibliography

O'Brien, David and Yasuo Ohkoshi, *To Dream of Dreams: Religious Freedom and Constitutional Politics in Postwar Japan.* Honolulu: University of Hawaii Press, 1996.

Garon, Sheldon. *Molding Japanese Minds: The State in Everyday Life.* Princeton: Princeton University Press, 1997.

Watanabe, Takesao. "The Revisionist Fallacy in the Japanese Media," *Doshisha University Social Science Review*, No. 59 (March 1999).

19

War Crimes and Redress:
A Canadian Jewish Perspective

Manuel Prutschi and Mark Weintraub

Our century brings into focus, perhaps more sharply than at any time in the past, the elastic quality of human nature: our capacity for great acts of compassion and our capacity for absolute evil. For, while extreme acts of barbarism have characterized much of human history, never before has technology reached such a sophisticated level that we can now talk of extermination or liquidation of human beings like they were insects. Technology, mass ideologies, and the revolutionary rate of change to which our world has plunged since the industrial revolution have been a fatal combination for our century.

The European Jewish community was the subject of the first hideously successful experiment by which twentieth-century systems of efficient bureaucracy and advanced technology were combined with the propaganda of dehumanization to destroy a civilization.

The Holocaust, or in Hebrew, *Shoah*, was potentially devastating to the very survival of the Jewish people. So let us refer to some of our community's practical responses to the Holocaust. Immediately after the War, when the full significance of the Holocaust was realized, elements within the world community and the Jewish community were in great shock. Some did not want to hear the survivors' stories and many of the survivors felt that their stories would not be believed or were too terrible to tell. Individually they somehow carried on with their lives; they married, had children, and tried to suppress their memories. Over time, however, the survivors started telling their stories and this courage was a major factor in enabling our community as a whole to begin to respond.

Our communal leadership started advocating for the establishment of human rights legislation in different jurisdictions. There is no question that one of the principal factors in the passage of the Universal Declaration of Human Rights was the Holocaust. As a community, our efforts in working for the establishment of the State of Israel were redoubled so that persecuted Jews in other countries would always have a refuge. And in the 1960s the cry of "Never Again" inspired the work of activists, including thousands of students, to free Soviet Jews and other dissidents. The memory of the Holocaust was also the inspiration for the world Jewish community's work in saving the tens of thousands of black Jews in Ethiopia and bringing them to safety in Israel.

In aid of these efforts on the human rights and rescue fronts were the generously funded documentation centers, memorials, museums, university Holocaust studies programs, and the reconstruction of synagogues and other Jewish infrastructures in Europe. The Jewish community funded youth trips to the concentration camps and scholarships for the study of Judaism and summer experiences in Israel. Volunteers recorded the oral histories of survivors; indeed efforts are being made to attempt to identify every Holocaust victim for the purpose of some form of memorialization—for while our people were mass murdered, we are intent on rescuing their individuality.

In summary, we think it is fair to say that in the last fifty years the response to the Holocaust has engaged Jewish communal political leadership, the artistic community, philosophers, theologians, historians, and educators, all in their different spheres of expertise.

So, as the Jewish community responded in these different ways, how did the perpetrator European states respond?

West Germany initially responded more adequately than any other jurisdiction. It replaced Nazi totalitarianism with a strong constitutional democracy. It brought and continues to bring its own Nazi war criminals to justice. It banned through legislation any manifestations of its Nazi past including making the display of the swastika illegal and criminalizing the denial of the Holocaust; not only in concern for Jewish sensibilities, but out of the recognition that Nazism brought down the entire nation of Germany. The new Germany institutionalized the Holocaust with official days of remembrance and museums. It confronted its citizens with the ugly reality of what transpired through the promotion of visits by Jewish survivors to their former homes. The new Germany established strong relations with Israel almost from their mutual beginnings, and Germans of all ages, but particularly the youth, regularly visit and do volunteer work in Israel.

Germany has also been at the forefront of an elaborate and expanding system of Holocaust redress for the Jewish State, the survivors, and the heirs of the victims. The first wave of compensation had a clearly established recipient in the State of Israel, which absorbed so many of the survivors. A subsequent initiative involved government reparations to the survivors themselves. To discuss the evolution of the payment of compensation and the successes and failures is beyond the scope of this presentation. But let us at least highlight some of the issues.

The essential question was that posed by the Canadian journalist and author Isabel Vincent, who succinctly asked: "How do you bring about justice for the expropriation and murder of a civilization?"[1] The answer of course is that we cannot bring about justice, but steps towards partial justice are possible and that in fact has occurred.

The process began immediately after the war, when Dr. Chaim Weizmann, perhaps one of the most highly regarded Jewish leaders and later to become Israel's first president, wrote to the Allies in September, 1945 calling for German redress. Six years later, Konrad Adenauer, Germany's chancellor, addressed his Legislature as follows: "... unspeakable crimes have been committed in the name of the German people, calling for moral and material indemnity... The Federal Government [is] prepared, jointly with representatives of Jewry and the State of Israel...to bring about a solution of the material indemnity problem, thus easing the way to the spiritual settlement of infinite suffering."[2]

Negotiations between Chancellor Adenauer and Nahum Goldmann, then president of the World Jewish Congress, produced a first agreement, which primarily indemnified the State of Israel. This was confirmed by the Luxembourg Treaty of September 10, 1952 between Israel and West Germany.

There were Jews in Israel and the Diaspora who, on principle, opposed accepting any damages payments from Germany. There are those who do see the logic in Israel having accepted these payments, since the State at the time was badly in need of funds to cover the costs of resettling hundreds of thousands of Holocaust survivors. There do continue to be members of the Jewish community who decry, apart from Israel, the receiving of any indemnification

as "blood money." They would agree with the views expressed by
the commentator Roger Rosenblatt who has written:

> The Holocaust not only lies beyond compensation; it also lies beyond explanation,
> reconciliation, sentiment, forgiveness, redemption or any of the mechanisms by which
> people attempt to set wrong things right. In a way, that fact is as much a sign of its
> unique enormity as the monstrosity itself. All moral thought is grounded in the possibil-
> ity of correction. Yet here is a wrong that will never be set right, and people are left
> groping for something to take the place of the irreplaceable.[3]

The majority of the Jewish community, however, agrees with the
view of Edgar Bronfman, the current president of the World Jewish
Congress:

> ...each dollar recovered represents a little piece of dignity, not just for the survivors who
> will benefit but for all mankind, who will have demonstrated that it remains morally
> unacceptable for anyone to profit from the ashes of man's greatest inhumanity to man...[4]

Financial redress, therefore, has been a central element of the post-
Holocaust world. Germany, the central perpetrator, began the process with the Federal Indemnification Law, continued it with the
Hardship Fund, and followed it with the Article 2 Fund and the Central and Eastern European Fund. Each new fund brought a new set
of Holocaust survivors into the indemnification system. Austria subsequently somewhat followed Germany's lead.[5]

Today, not only members of the former Axis are involved in restitution, included are the governments of the occupied and/or collaborator countries such as France and the various central and Eastern European states, as well as those ostensibly neutral states such
as Switzerland. It does not merely involve governments but also members of the financial and business infrastructure. Redress is for the
suffering inflicted, the forced and slave labor, the gold stolen or indeed extracted from Holocaust victims, the confiscated property and
the stolen art, as well as the bank accounts and insurance death ben-
efits not honored. More and more, the governments, industries, and
financial institutions across Europe are being called to account for
collaborating with Nazi Germany or otherwise providing the funds
and resources to wage war, perpetrate the Final Solution, and plunder two thousand years of Jewish life on the continent.

The Holocaust was directed against millions of individual Jews
but, at the same time, it was an assault on the Jewish people as a
whole and on Judaism itself. One controversy that remains within
the Jewish community concerns the distribution of redress funds.

Should the focus be on specific individuals for suffering and loss, or on the needs of the entire collectivity? It is likely that this contradiction is not resolvable. On the one hand, after all, it was individuals who were victimized, but on the other, the Jewish whole is greater than the sum of its Jewish parts.

The most recent stage is wide-ranging with responsibility shared by government and the country's entire infrastructure (all elements of which profited from the catastrophe inflicted upon the Jewish people). Redress is puny in comparison to the slave labor exploited from the victims, the robbery of their property, and even exploitation of their body parts for profit after death. But at least Germany proceeded on a course of partial justice and that must be fully and properly recognized. Some have estimated that in total over 60 billion dollars in some type of compensation have been paid by the German State or institutions but we must be careful of numbers here. We are not certain that this is a correct amount, but certainly we can say that substantial sums have been paid over fifty years though they represent a very tiny fraction of the value of that which was robbed.

Germany, after the war, also assumed with some degree of seriousness the prosecution of its Nazi war criminals. Many, nonetheless, have escaped punishment. The collaborator and/or occupied countries have been much less forthcoming on accountability for mass murder. Even the Allies have been far from vigorous in bringing to justice the criminals that fell under their jurisdiction or ended up in their midst. Between 1945 and 1948, paralleling and flowing from the two International Military Tribunals for Europe and the Far East, there were trials of some of the major transgressors. But the momentum for such prosecutions quickly dissipated after 1948.

The experience of Canada, which we know best, provides a good example. Our country's refugee policy denied safe haven to Jews fleeing Nazi Europe throughout the 1930s. Researchers have shown that after the war, it was easier for the Nazi victimizers to enter Canada than it was for those of their victims who managed to survive. Few would question that hundreds if not thousands of Nazi criminals gained refuge.

Canada, nonetheless, in 1948 unreservedly complied with a secret memorandum in which the United Kingdom directed its Commonwealth partners to cease war crime trials. The Deschênes Commission of Inquiry on War Criminals, established in February, 1985, not surprisingly thus reported that "in the third of a century which followed, Canada devoted not the slightest energy to the search and prosecution of war criminals."[6]

Today, the Canadian picture is somewhat brighter. In the last three to four years there has been a 180-degree turnaround. The government hired a former director of the U.S. Justice Department's Office of Special Investigations as a consultant. It further demonstrated its new-found determination by committing an additional 12 million dollars specifically earmarked for the prosecution of Nazi criminals. And only two months ago the minister of justice initiated steps for new legislation that will facilitate the criminal prosecution of war criminals to supplement the process of revocation of citizenship and deportation. The current War Crimes Unit has a number of active files being pursued in the courts and more new cases are promised. The Government has not been able to win all of its cases, but the will to pursue justice seems to be firmly in place and the government has allocated ample resources to get the job done.

Over half a century has elapsed since the commission of the crimes in Asia. Japan does not have another fifty years to get the process underway. The biological clock is ticking for defendants, survivors, and witnesses. It is a matter of the utmost urgency that justice be done now, otherwise justice delayed will undoubtedly mean justice denied.

For justice to be meted out fairly and swiftly there must be the confluence of three positive wills: the political, the bureaucratic, and the judicial. One can only bring about this confluence if the Japanese people realize that to move successfully from the "Era of War" to the "Era of Reconciliation, Peace and Co-Existence," it is absolutely essential that war criminals be brought to justice. This is not a matter of revenge but an issue of fundamental human rights. As the late Arnold Fradkin, a past member of Canada's War Crimes Litigation Unit in the Department of Justice put it: "Justice does not mean revenge. It means redress according to principles of law, as imposed by courts of law after a fair and impartial trial according to law."[7]

Mankind, for centuries if not millennia, has set constraints so that war, inhuman by definition, is conducted within certain delimited parameters. This was the expectation in what came to be known as the "Law of Nations" and which was enshrined in pre-World War II international agreements such as the Geneva Convention of 1864 and the Hague Conventions of 1899 and 1907. Combatants have obligations towards civilians and prisoners of war. Those who fail to uphold these obligations are termed by the community of nations to be *"hostes humani generis,"* i.e. "the enemies of mankind." The precedent setting Nuremberg Tribunal of 1945, followed by a vast corpus of briefs, undertakings, agreements, and official statements by various international bodies, certainly mandated legal action against those who carried out war crimes and crimes against humanity.[8]

Ideally the international community must function in such a way that crimes against humanity are stopped before they happen. However, when they do happen, the world must bring those responsible to account.

The Japanese Imperial Army during the Second World War (and in Asia that war can be said to have started in 1930s with the aggression against China) committed monstrous crimes that went far beyond the most callous and hard-hearted definition of normal wartime activity. It is a moral outrage that these war crimes have gone unpunished.

The message must go out, for the sake of the memory of the victims and the survivors who continue to bear witness, that no one has the legal license to engage in the persecution, torture, and slaughter of innocent civilians or defenseless prisoners. War criminals not answering for their crimes constitute a rejection of a country's commitment to the principle of the rule of law. Past war criminals are vindicated and new war criminals encouraged. This gives comfort to those possessed by chauvinism and interested in a renewed militarism.

So what can we learn from the Jewish experience? There are both differences and similarities in the historical contexts. The Jewish community's response has not been a coherent response. We staggered to our feet and slowly, bit by bit regained our dignity by drawing upon the courage of the survivors, the support of our friends in the non-Jewish community, and through seeing the establishment of Israel as a State. We ensured that members of our community funded projects and we linked our near demise as a people to the failing of a world community's response to massive human rights violations. Our artists responded and have given us hope, despite the degradation. We have tried to emphasize not only the suffering and helplessness, but the courage of Jew and non-Jew caught in horrific circumstances.

We think, in dealing with this issue with the Japanese government, the approach of the International Citizens' Forum (ICF) and the Global Alliance is a correct one. Continue to emphasize the Japanese contributions to world peace through her strong support of the United Nations while strategically countering the forces opposed to meting out justice in all its forms. Continue to reach out to your friends. Certainly we can tell you that the Jewish community stands as your good friend in solidarity with you. For your remembrance is our remembrance; your struggle for justice is our struggle for justice; and as we link ourselves together we collectively can show that the dogged, resolute, and unflinching pursuit of justice is indeed the most powerful of all human forces.

Notes

1. Isabel Vincent, *Hitler's Silent Partners* (William Morrow and Company, Inc., 1997), p. 303.
2. *Claims Conference: 1998 Annual Report, with 1999 Highlights*, p. 7.
3. Roger Rosenblatt, "Paying for Auschwitz," *Time*, April 12, 1999, p. 68.
4. Quoted in Vincent, *Hitler's Silent Partners*, p. 298.
5. *Claims Conference 1998 Annual Report*, p. 1.
6. Honourable Jules Deschênes, *Commission of Inquiry on War Criminals—Report Part I: Public* (Minister of Supply and Services Canada, 1986), pp. 26-27.
7. Arnold Fradkin, "Canada ignored war criminals for 27 years," *The Canadian Jewish News*, June 2, 1997.
8. See Debbie Raicek, "Interview with Professor Irwin Cotler—Bringing Nazi War Criminals to Justice: An Issue of Human Rights," *Quid Novi*, McGill University Faculty of Law, Vol. VI, No. 11, November 13, 1985, and Jack Silverstone, "The Deschênes Commission and Nazi War Criminals in Canada: An Issue Assessment," an undated (1985-86) Canadian Jewish Congress (CJC) paper in the CJC's NCRC Toronto files.

Selected Bibliography

Abella, Irving and Harold Troper. 1982. *None Is Too Many: Canada and the Jews of Europe 1933-1948*. Toronto: Lester & Orpen Dennys Limited.
Balabkins, Nicholas. 1971. *West German Reparations to Israel*. Piscataway, NJ: Rutgers University Press.
Barkan, Elazar. 2000. *The Guilt of Nations: Restitution and Negotiating Historical Injustices*. New York: W.W. Norton.
Bass, Gary Jonathan. 2000. *Stay the Hand of Vengeance: The Politics of War Crimes Tribunals*. Princeton: Princeton University Press.
Brooks, Roy L. (editor). 1999. *When Sorry Isn't Enough: The Controversy over Apologies and Reparations for Human Injustice*. New York: New York University Press.
Chesnoff, Richard Z. 1999. *Pack of Thieves: How Hitler and Europe Plundered the Jews and Committed the Greatest Theft in History*. New York, et al: Doubleday.
Eizenstat, Stuart E. *Imperfect Justice: Looted Assets, Slave Labor, and the Unfinished Business of World War II*. Public Affairs, forthcoming 2002.

Hogg, Peter. 1999. *Crimes of War*. Toronto: McClelland & Stewart.

Margolian, Howard. 2001. *Unauthorized Entry: The Truth about Nazi War Criminals in Canada, 1946-1956*. Toronto: University of Toronto Press.

Matas, David and Susan Charendoff. 1987. *Justice Delayed: Nazi War Criminals in Canada*. Toronto: Summerhill Press Ltd.

Paris, Erna. 2000. *Long Shadows: Truth, Lies and History*. Toronto: Knopf Canada.

Sagi, Nana. 1986. *German Reparations: A History of the Negotiations*. Palgrave Macmillan.

Salpeter, Eliahu. February 21, 2001. "IBM punchcards and the Holocaust," *Ha'aretz*.

Thompson, Janna. *Taking Responsibility for the Past: Reparation and Historical Injustices*. Polity Pr., upcoming 2002.

Troper, Harold and Morton Weinfeld. 1988. *Old Wounds: Jews, Ukrainians and the Hunt for Nazi War Criminals in Canada*. Markham, Ontario: Viking.

Vincent, Isabel. 1997. *Hitler's Silent Partners: Swiss Banks, Nazi Gold, and the Pursuit of Justice*. New York: William Morrow and Company, Inc.

Vincent, Isabel. May 6, 2000. "The fight for Nazi gold" [review of Chesnoff's *Pack of Thieves*] in the *National Post*.

Zweig, Ronald W. 2001. *German Reparations and the Jewish World: A History of the Claims Conference*. Frank Cass & Co., second edition.

Appendix: The Tokyo Appeal[1]

Translation by Yue-him Tam

As the curtain for the 20th century soon will descend, it is time for us to reflect on these past one hundred years. In the first half of this century, Japan kept expanding its war of aggression, inflicting immense suffering and woe on the people of its neighbors. Indeed, on this day sixty-two years ago, Japan's Imperial Army willfully began massive murder, rape, plunder, and arson after the fall of Nanjing.

Now fifty-four years since its unconditional surrender, Japan has not seriously reflected upon its war crimes, but instead has set off a vicious campaign whitewashing its war of aggression. Moreover, its Diet has passed new guidelines for self-defense to achieve preparedness for war, and approved a National Flag and Anthem Bill to inculcate nationalism in its people. These actions attest that Japan has been unable to make a clean break from its past, and has begun a process of regression, retracing the path of its former militarism.

Presently, we, comprising war victims in various countries, Japanese nationals who feel keenly the perpetrator's responsibility, and concerned activists, attorneys, and scholars in support of justice, have gathered in Tokyo to convene a three-day International Citizens' Forum on war crimes and redress. We have here exchanged views on a wide range of related issues.

The Forum participants examined the scope of Japan's war crimes, including the Nanjing Massacre, and the status of the post-war redress issue. The participating war victims gave painful testimonies, based on personal experience and eyewitness accounts, of massacre, rape, abuse of prisoners of war, and other atrocities committed by the Japanese Imperial army. These were further expounded by attending specialists and scholars. More than half of a century has passed and yet the wounds of the victims remain unhealed.

During the 1990s, the victims began litigation to seek apology and compensation from the Japanese government and the corporations involved. However, the government of Japan obstinately holds the position that the issue of redress has been settled. The Diet has hesitated to pass legislation regarding the redress issue. While the courts have invariably dismissed the lawsuits, they have also urged the passage of legislation to settle the litigation for redress.

The participants also explored lessons from the Jewish people's experience in seeking redress for victims of the Holocaust and the means of settlement adopted by individual countries involved in that atrocity. During the half century after the war, Germany has resolutely followed the policy of making a clean break with its past, promising to "investigate the facts of victimization and the responsibility of its perpetrators," "render support and compensation for the victims," and "prevent the replay of that historical tragedy." Even today, the government of Germany and the corporations concerned are trying to establish a reparation fund for "Memory, Responsibility and Future."

In the United States, the State of California has passed a bill to extend the date of expiration to the year 2010 for claims of compensation by the victims of Nazi Germany and its allies, including Japan. As a result, a number of lawsuits for redress have thus been filed against Japanese corporations conducting business in California. In Asia, the Human Rights Commission of the Philippine Parliament has passed a bill requiring early resolution of the "comfort women" issue. Members of the South Korean House of Representatives have introduced a bill for "victims of the conscription of forced labor."

We, the Forum participants, fully support the legitimate demands by the war victims in various countries to regain human dignity. These demands in fact ask fundamental questions about "Japan's history as a nation" and "its perception of human rights." In our view, the denial by the government of Japan of responsibility for the war crimes and its unwillingness to apologize and compensate the victims diminishes its national character.

The passage of half a century has been a heavy burden for the victims to bear. It is imperative to seek justice for the victims in a timely manner so that they may regain their human dignity. Hence, we earnestly request the government of Japan and the corporations involved to offer apology and compensation to the victims without delay.

We further request that the government of Japan make a sincere effort to disclose the true history of the war to the public and for the generations to come. In the first half of this century, Germany embarked on a similar course of aggression. Unlike Japan, however, post-war Germany has reconciled with its neighbors through continual and conscientious efforts.

We note that the pursuit for accountability of war crimes and the demand for justice and redress for the victims has reached a global dimension, and will continue to grow in depth and strength. We shall move forward in solidarity and cooperation until our request and our hopes are realized.

Hereby we solemnly declare that by boldly confronting the historical truth of the 20th century, we will seek and ensure reconciliation and peace in the 21st century.

Note

1. Unanimously adapted by the International Citizens' Forum on 12 December 1999. Tokyo, Japan.

About the Contributors

Robert P. Barker is a graduate student studying for his law degree.

Michael Berry is currently a Ph.D. candidate in modern Chinese literature at Columbia University, where he is writing his dissertation on literary and cinematic representations of violence in modern China. He is also the translator of *Nanjing 1937: A Love Story* by Ye Zhaoyan, *Wild Kids: Two Novels about Growing Up* by Chang Ta-chun, and the forthcoming novel *To Live* by Yu Hua.

Maria Hsia Chang is professor of political science at the University of Nevada, Reno and author of *The Labor of Sisyphus: Economic Development in Communist China*, *Return of the Dragon: China's Wounded Nationalism*, and most recently *The Blue Shirt Society: Fascism and Development of Nationalism*.

Werner Gruhl, previous to his book-length manuscript on *Japan's War from Manchuria to Hiroshima, 1931-1945*, worked for NASA, Washington, D.C., from 1967 to 1991 in the Cost and Economic Analysis Branch. His work involved research, collection, analysis, and organization of historic cost data to develop statistical models and techniques to forecast new program requirements. Gruhl has applied his great depth of experience in deriving meaningful information from vast amounts of historical and statistical data to the analysis of the great loss of life and human suffering resulting from Japanese aggression in the Asia Pacific region. He is a life-long student of military history and has traveled extensively to visit historic battlefields of WWI and WWII.

Linda Goetz Holmes, the author of *Unjust Enrichment* and *4,000 Bowls of Rice*, is a much sought-after speaker across the country. For more than twenty years, Ms. Holmes has interviewed over 400 military and civilian ex-POWs of the Japanese. She is the first Pacific War historian appointed to the U.S. Government Interagency Working Group. She has addressed the National Security Agency Center for Cryptologic History and numerous civic groups, veteran's organizations, and classrooms throughout the country.

Michael M. Honda was born in California, but spent his early childhood with his family in an internment camp in Colorado during World War II. His family returned to California in 1953 and later he served two years in the Peace Corps, building schools and health clinics in El Salvador. Subsequently, he earned a degree in biological sciences, a BA in Spanish, and a Masters in Education. In 1971, Honda was appointed by the then-Mayor Norm Mineta to the San Jose City Planning Commission and in 1981 was elected to the San Jose Unified School Board. Mike Honda became the first and only Asian Pacific American to serve on the Santa Clara County Board of Supervisors. He was elected to the California State Assembly in 1996, reelected in 1998, and won a seat in Congress as a representative in 2000.

Zhao Jianmin, a native of Shanghai, is professor of history at Fudan University, Shanghai, and a member of its Japanese Studies Center. His area of specialization is Japanese history and Sino-Japanese relations. He is the author of several books and nearly eighty-nine articles on Japan and its relations with other Asian nations.

Ivy Lee is currently president of the Global Alliance for Preserving the History of WW II in Asia (GA), a nonprofit, nonpartisan worldwide federation whose mission is to preserve the historical truth of the Asia Pacific War (1931-1945) so as to secure justice for victims and bring about genuine reconciliation and lasting peace among all people. A sociologist by profession, she taught for twenty-seven years at California State University, Sacramento prior to her retirement in 1997. Since her retirement she has devoted her time to the redress movement and has written and presented papers on reconciliation and various redress issues.

Peter Li received his Ph.D. from the University of Chicago and has taught Asian Studies at Rutgers University for thirty years. He is the editor of journal *East Asia: An International Quarterly*, published by Transaction Publishers. His other publications include *Anatomy of Tiananmen Square: Culture and Politics in China* and *Understanding Asian Americans*. His research on Japanese atrocities in WWII began with a seminar class on the Asia Pacific War.

Zhang Lianhong received his Ph.D. in history from Nanjing University in 1997. He has taught at Nanjing Normal University since 1992 and is director of the Research Center for Nanjing Massacre at the same university. His scholarly works include "The Major Battlefields of the Sino-Japanese War," "Report on the Investigation Concerning Japanese Troops' Comfort Station in the Xiaguan District of Nanjing," and other projects on the Nanjing Safety Zones during the Nanjing massacre and survivor testimonies.

Noda Masaaki is professor of medical psychology at Kyoto Women's University in Japan. A graduate of Hokkaido Medical School, he is the author of numerous books on psychosocial trauma, most recently *Senso to Zaiseki* (*War and Guilt*), which addressed the psychology of Japanese perpetrators of atrocities in the Pacific War. He has done extensive fieldwork on social trauma in post-Soviet Russia, and has also been widely involved in post-earthquake relief and psychology.

Yayori Matsui, an international journalist for the *Asahi Shimbun* (1961-94) for more than thirty years, was born in Kyoto, Japan. She has covered issues on human rights, environment, development, and peace from an Asian perspective. She has published more than ten books, including *Women's Asia* and *Women in the New Asia*. As director of Asia-Japan Women's Resource Center, dealing with the issue of women's human rights including international migration and other issues, and as chairperson of Violence Against Women in War Network, Japan, she organized the Women's International War Crimes Tribunal 2000 on Japan's Military Sexual Slavery in Tokyo.

Daniel A. Metraux is professor and chair of the Department of Asian Studies at Mary Baldwin College in Virginia. He has published many books and articles on Japanese and East Asian politics and religion, including *The Soka Gakkai Revolution*, *Aum Shinrikyo and Japanese Youth*, and "Japan's Search for Political Stability: the LDP-New Komeito Alliance" in *Asian Survey*. He was a visiting professor at Doshisha University, Kyoto in 1999-2000.

Manuel Prutschi is the national director of community relations for the Canadian Jewish Congress and has been on the staff of CJC since 1984. Holding undergraduate and graduate degrees in history from McGill University and the University of Western Ontario, he is the author of numerous articles on human rights, intergroup relations, equality, and multiculturalism. He has played a major role before the courts and quasi-judicial tribunals across Canada in cases dealing with discrimination, antisemitism, and racism. In addition, he served on the thirteen-person Advisory Committee to the Ontario Human Rights Code Review Task Force in 1992.

Paul Schalow teaches Japanese literature courses at Rutgers University in atomic bomb fiction and Japanese women's writing. His publications include a study and translation of Ihara Saikakau's *The Great Mirror of Male Love* and a volume of essays he co-edited, *The Woman's Hand: Gender and Theory in Japanese Women's Writing*. His current project is a study of male friendship in Japanese literature.

Lester I. Tenney is a survivor of the infamous Bataan Death March. For three and a half years he was a prisoner of the Japanese in the Philippines and then Japan. *My Hitch in Hell* was fifty-some years in the making. He spent four years researching and fifty years in the writing of the book. Dr. Tenney is a motivational speaker and lecturer on financial retirement planning and a retired professor of finance and insurance at Arizona State University.

Yoshiji Watanabe was born in 1947 in Aichi Prefecture, Japan where he attended Aichi University and was involved in anti-Vietnam War activities. For the past thirty years he has devoted himself to theatrical reform movements. In 1993 he founded a touring company called Imagine 21, devoted to the performance of his play *Reunion*. The play has been performed in 195 locations across Japan and in 1995, Imagine 21 went on a tour of China, completing performances in four locations.

Mark Weintraub is a litigation partner in the law firm of Clark, Wilson in Vancouver British Columbia. He has practiced since 1983 in the areas of commercial, estate, and immigration litigation. He received his MA in history of religions at the University of British Columbia and his law degree from the University of Toronto. Mark has been involved in promoting intergroup relations in various capacities including serving on the British Columbia Law Society's Multiculturism Committee and holding various offices with the Canadian Jewish Congress. He is currently the national chair of the Canadian Jewish Congress Community Relations Committee.

Index